# THE BEEF TABOO IN CHINA

# THE BEEF TABOO IN CHINA

*Agriculture, Ethics, Sacrifice*

Vincent Goossaert

Translated by Barbara R. Ambros

University of Hawai'i Press

HONOLULU

Printed in the United States of America

First printed, 2025

**Library of Congress Cataloging-in-Publication Data**

Names: Goossaert, Vincent, author. | Ambros, Barbara, translator.
Title: The beef taboo in China : agriculture, ethics, sacrifice / Vincent Goossaert ; translated by Barbara R. Ambros.
Other titles: Interdit du bœuf en Chine. Chinese | Agriculture, ethics, sacrifice
Description: Honolulu : University of Hawaiʻi Press, 2025. | Translation of: L'interdit du bœuf en Chine : agriculture, éthique et sacrifice. | Includes bibliographical references and index.
Identifiers: LCCN 2024021619 (print) | LCCN 2024021620 (ebook) | ISBN 9780824898472 (hardback) | ISBN 9798880700226 (trade paperback) | ISBN 9798880700202 (epub) | ISBN 9798880700219 (kindle edition) | ISBN 9798880700196 (pdf)
Subjects: LCSH: Beef—China—Religious aspects. | Taboo—China. | Beef industry—China. | Animal sacrifice—China.
Classification: LCC HD9433.C6 G66 2025 (print) | LCC HD9433.C6 (ebook) | DDC 338.1/762130951—dc23/eng/20240916
LC record available at https://lccn.loc.gov/2024021619
LC ebook record available at https://lccn.loc.gov/2024021620

Cover art: Taken from an illustrated tract of a poem lamenting the poor bovine, written in the shape of a water buffalo. Reproduced in Doré, *Recherches sur les superstitions* (Shanghai, 1911–1928), pt. 1, vol. 2, chap. 8, art. 10, plate opposite p. 308.

University of Hawaiʻi Press books are printed on acid-free paper and meet the guidelines for permanence and durability of the Council on Library Resources.

# Contents

# Preface

Having one's work not only read and commented on but translated by an eminent colleague is one of the purest joys in the life of an academic. I am deeply grateful to Barbara Ambros for her meticulous translation and in-depth engagement with my argument. She not only rendered my original French in accessible, clear English but also pushed me to engage more with the fast-growing field of animal studies in East Asia and globally. This also allowed me to revisit a text written almost twenty years ago, about which I had constantly been finding new documents. As a result, while reading the translation, I corrected several factual mistakes and added new sources, as well as some of the most salient recent scholarship. This does not amount to a comprehensive update, as we have striven to remain close to the original book. Moreover, some relevant sources and scholarship were left aside when we found they merely added to the critical apparatus without significantly affecting the argument. We also chose not to explore the comparison of the Chinese and Japanese cases, which will be the subject of a separate coauthored article.

# Translator's Preface

It has been a privilege and a pleasure to translate Vincent Goossaert's *L'interdit du bœuf en Chine.* Although much of his work has appeared in English, this important book was previously only available in French. In my translation, my goal has been to render the monograph accessible to an English-speaking audience. To this end, I aimed to make the text appealing to Anglophone readers rather than producing a literal translation of Goossaert's academic French prose. Goossaert graciously reviewed the complete translation and added important updates that had become necessary since the French edition appeared almost two decades ago. Thus, this English edition is somewhat different from the original French version.

It may be surprising to some that I, whose primary field is Japanese religions, translated a book by a colleague working on China, but this significant piece of scholarship intersects in many ways with my own work, both chronologically and topically, with its focus on human-animal (or rather, human-bovine) relationships from the Song to the early twentieth century.

I stumbled across Goossaert's *L'interdit du bœuf en Chine* while conducting research for my own book project on life releases (Ch. *fangsheng;* J. *hōjō*) in early modern Japan, which were heavily influenced by Ming-Qing morality literature. Reading this monograph was eye opening in many ways and convinced me to take on this translation project to give his book wider circulation. When I approached Goossaert with this idea, he responded enthusiastically.

Goossaert's groundbreaking research on the beef taboo should be of great interest to scholars of Chinese religions and history. However, it also sheds light on a broader context for human-animal relationships within East Asia during this period. For instance, we cannot fully understand the reluctance to consume beef in premodern Japan without knowledge of foundational and parallel discourses from the Song through the Qing. Yet scholars who have studied meat eating and the treatment of cattle and horses in premodern Japan have typically adopted approaches that only considered the Japanese perspectives rather than placing such discourses in a broader East Asian context. These cultural formations have been constructed as quintessential markers of Japanese identity—sometimes even in contradistinction to purportedly more carnivorous Chinese culinary habits—even though such rhetoric and practices were strongly influenced, if not inspired, by parallel Chinese moral discourses. Undoubtedly, Shogun Tokugawa Tsunayoshi's Laws of Compassion from the late seventeenth century, often treated as singular within an early modern context, seem far less unusual if considered in light of premodern Chinese policies toward animals—particularly bovines and equines—and the beef taboo discussed in this monograph.

I hope that this translation will expand the reach of Goossaert's innovative book, not just among China scholars but also colleagues working on Japan and other parts of East Asia, as well as animal and food studies more broadly.

# THE BEEF TABOO IN CHINA

# Introduction

THE TOPIC OF THIS BOOK is the history of a moral rule known in Chinese under several names, the most common of which is *niujie* 牛戒, which I translate as "beef taboo," with *jie* also meaning precept, injunction, or warning. The term *niujie* has two meanings in the Chinese tradition. In ancient Buddhist texts, it designates Indian conceptions of the sacred zebu (usually called sacred cow in English), generally presented as a heterodoxy of early Buddhism. This meaning does not seem to have exceeded the narrow framework of scholarly Buddhist historiography and exegesis. From the Song dynasty (960–1279), *niujie* adopted a completely different meaning—namely that of a rule of respect for cattle (oxen and water buffaloes) linking two requirements: not killing bovines and not consuming their meat. This is the rule under consideration here.[1]

Very evident until the beginning of the twentieth century, the taboo has since weakened considerably and is no longer readily mentioned in conversation today, undoubtedly because it is part of the discourses considered "superstitious." On several occasions, I had the experience of Chinese friends asking me, "What is the beef taboo in China?" before they admitted that their parents and grandparents would not have eaten beef for anything in the world. As a result, the existing scholarship on the taboo is limited. All Western and Japanese authors who, to my knowledge, have mentioned the Chinese beef taboo say it is Buddhist and/or Indian.[2] The anthropologist Eugene Anderson, who specializes in the study of food, insists on the Indian origin via Buddhism.[3] A century before him, Jan Jakob Maria de Groot (1854–1921) also spoke of the Indian influence and of a Buddhist strategy to apply nonviolence to an animal already cherished by the Chinese.[4]

The abundant extant documentation shows that this was not a Buddhist rule and even less the result of an Indian influence on Chinese society. On the contrary, it was one of the fundamental rules of Chinese religion.[5] It appeared between the ninth and the fourteenth centuries when this religion underwent a profound transformation that gave it its modern configuration. The beef taboo, therefore, emerged relatively late. Earlier, there was the notion of the need to protect bovines, the main working animals in the fields essential to agriculture: the state prohibited their slaughter since the beginning of the Common Era. However, the taboo, which defined the sin of eating beef and detailed the divine punishments inflicted on killers and beefeaters, did not appear until the ninth century. Therefore, understanding the taboo requires an understanding of the economic and political contexts in which bovines were subject to protective measures and, within this framework, an understanding of the taboo as a specific discourse that entirely belonged to the religious domain. Rather than seeing these as distinct, a full explanation of the taboo must involve agricultural ecology and economics, state ideology, sacrificial practices, and the transformation of religious worldviews and social structures.

Yet, even if it takes a multidisciplinary approach, any analysis of a topic such as the beef taboo is based on biases. A scientific study is always a personal endeavor in which the feelings and convictions of the researcher are at work. This book is eminently personal. I began my studies in sinology under the supervision of Kristofer Schipper (1934–2021), who was simultaneously an anthropologist, historian, and ordained Daoist master. As such, he could not eat beef. Therefore, I discovered the Chinese beef taboo very early in my studies by cooking for my teacher and eating with him. Intrigued by this rule, I wanted to know its origin, and a few years later, I started to look for documents on this subject as recreation between other more pressing projects. At the time, I imagined possibly writing a research note consisting of a few pages.

The documents began to accumulate, sometimes by chance, when I encountered the beef taboo while I was looking for something quite different, but also increasingly because the documents I had found referred me to even more numerous others. For about four years, I was mainly occupied with researching the history of the Daoist clergy in China, but the "beef" file grew thicker and thicker, and the issue occupied my thoughts more and more. I gave up eating beef and became more involved in this research than I was initially when it was still a mere intellectual curiosity. I also realized that the issue of the beef taboo in China was by no means a scholarly footnote but a truly fascinating topic of study that provides new perspectives on whole swaths of the social and religious history of China. The little research note gradually became a book.

Several factors, therefore, influence the specificity of the research that led to this book. There was the emotional dimension—some would say sentimental—specific to the subject, abundant in Chinese texts in which cattle complain of the fate inflicted on them. There was the pleasant feeling of stepping off the beaten track, which was reinforced by the reactions of disbelief from colleagues to whom I spoke about my work: "What beef taboo? This does not exist in China!" Finally, this subject allowed me to tackle complex themes, such as the relationship between food, religion, and the organization of Chinese society, which it would have been challenging for me to deal with directly without the change of perspective facilitated by the bovine question, a perspective that I did not initially suspect would open up such vast horizons.

The pleasure and the freedom to approach new perspectives also have their price. Given the general transformation of Chinese society over the *longue durée*, this work also presents risks, such as exaggerating or minimizing isolated facts located at various moments between antiquity and contemporary times. Casting a wide net but missing important sources constitutes another risk. Finally, there is the risk of hastily producing general conclusions from scattered data. I had to venture into areas I knew almost nothing about, such as agricultural economics or the history of food. Others would have treated the subject differently, as historians of science or economics, for example, or anthropologists. Arguably, the most significant lacuna of this book is the paucity of field data. But I believe that the method of the historian, which is mine, had something crucial to contribute to defining the subject at hand, which I hope will be taken up by others.

The importance of studying the beef taboo is twofold. On the one hand, the subject is in itself worthy of attention, as it has immediate consequences on several aspects of social life in China: diet and meat consumption; the use of cattle as working animals in the field and the relationship between the peasant and his animals; and the choice of animals in sacrifices offered in temples all over the villages and districts of the Chinese world. But beyond these concrete issues, the taboo provides perspectives on broader questions. These questions do not dictate the structure of my book and therefore are not addressed in their own right, but they are part of the context in which I attempt to analyze the literature regarding the taboo, so they are worth quickly touching on.

First, how can we understand the specificities of Chinese culture in the relationship between humans and animals, particularly in the context of agriculture? In other words, what would be the cultural aspect of an anthropozoology of China?[6] Like any historian of Chinese culture, I had to try to reconcile scholarly literature putting forward values widely shared by Western intellectuals at the start of the third millennium, such as harmony with nature and attention to living beings, and the hard facts of a less poetic, more complex social reality. Anyone who has been to China, or who will have heard of the common treatment of animals in China, not to mention the cruelties of the 1960s with campaigns to exterminate dogs and birds, may wonder about the relationship between texts describing fine ideals and actual practice. I do not attempt to deal with the concrete daily relationships of the Chinese with animals, but the texts cited here have the merit of directly raising the issue, in the case of the bovine species, of compromises between the multiple possible uses of animals and the feelings people have for them.

Second, how was a rule of conduct implemented in China in relation to political and religious institutions, moral and intellectual authorities, "customs" (if there is such a thing), and the control mechanisms peculiar to Chinese society? The beef taboo was expressed in various normative texts (penal law, local regulations, and religious precepts) while being frequently violated—otherwise, it would not have caused so much ink to flow. It therefore raises new questions about the social regulation of ethical standards in China.

Third, what is the relationship between individual moral choice and society? The beef taboo, like other moral rules, appears first of all as a choice of conscience, a purely personal matter. And yet, upon analysis, it seems indissolubly linked to the code of ritual purity, to liturgy, and to the definition of communities that subscribed to it. In other words, it is related to both individual and collective aspects of religion.

Fourth and last, by examining the taboo as an autonomous historical object (i.e., neither Confucian nor Buddhist nor Daoist) that was influenced by the Three Teachings but that also influenced them, it is possible to see at work the reciprocal adaptations—voluntary or forced—of the various actors of Chinese religion through a case study. Contemporary work on ethics tends to construct Confucianism as the moral tradition of China, which disseminated its teachings in society one way, from top to bottom. We will see to what extent the beef taboo provides a different vision.

My goal is not to answer these broad questions but the much more modest one of tracing the history of the appearance and diffusion of the beef taboo and ultimately interrogating the specific discourses and practices related to it. But in giving full meaning to this taboo, it is impossible to avoid issues of a more general nature, which are addressed directly by the sources documenting the taboo. By keeping in mind questions such as the ethical relationship with animals or social regulation and the roles of religious institutions in the production of moral standards, the study of the beef taboo can play the role of a textbook case. It then becomes an example of a discourse that one might believe to be simple (the beef taboo as a perfect example of the Buddhist love of animals), but that turns out to be something quite different and considerably more complex.

## Dietary Prohibitions

The present work is presented as a case study of a food prohibition, a classic topic in the social sciences and already explored by an abundant literature, mainly anthropological in nature. Therefore, I will first situate this topic in this scholarly context before pointing out its peculiarities. Until the middle of the twentieth century, the notions of taboo and prohibition were approached either as a form of magical thought or, on the contrary, from a positivist and functionalist perspective, which sought to identify its rational foundations—mainly hygienic or medical ones.

Thus, the prohibitions on pigs in Judaism and Islam have been interpreted as precautionary measures against pig-borne parasitic diseases or ecological measures to protect flora threatened by livestock farming. Some anthropologists continue to explore this perspective, which emphasizes the function of prohibitions rather than their reason.[7]

The work in this field was reinvigorated in the 1960s by important theoretical elaborations. The most influential author has undoubtedly been Mary Douglas, who, in her book *Purity and Danger,* published in 1967, provides a global analysis of the systems of prohibitions. She sees in them, in particular, all the taboos and prohibitions that a society gives itself as ways of isolating unusual objects and situations occurring in excessive contact with the outsider, the unknown, the other of the society, the source of both impurity and danger. For example, prohibited animals are those straddling the categories that the society in question employs to classify all living things and contravening the social and natural order. Let us note that Douglas does not say much about the prohibitions relating to certain meats, which are only one type of example among others in her argument. Other anthropologists have also considered the relationship with animals in terms of ordering the world, categories, and abnormality. Thus, Edmund Leach, in an equally famous article dating from 1964, compares language uses, in particular insults, using animals and taboos in an attempt to highlight the abnormal, atypical character of the species used in insults and avoided in the diet.[8]

Above all, the work of Leach and Douglas aimed at challenging functional interpretations of taboos taken in isolation and at giving meaning to them by placing them within the totality of the system of representations of the culture under consideration in which they serve to draw the borders of the social body. Starting from a very different topic, and while criticizing the positions of Leach and Douglas, Hocine Benkheira (2000) gave in his book on scholarly Islam and food taboos another global analysis of a complex system of dietary restrictions. Rather than focusing on the best-known prohibition against pork, Benkheira analyzes all the normative literature on the subject of permitted and prohibited meat as the implementation of a classification system at the heart of which is the human and in which all animal species are found arranged in categories that do not owe much to zoological observation but everything to relations of domestication and resemblance. In short, for Muslim jurists, the lawful animal is the humanized animal.

Such holistic models according to which the prohibitions can only be understood by their role within a much vaster system of meaning—that of

Douglas's "primitive societies" or Benkheira's scholarly Islam—have remarkable heuristic effectiveness in the cases mentioned above. However, it seems impossible to grant them a universal value. Many cases of well-known dietary prohibitions, particularly on meat, escape their capacity for interpretation. In his *Eat Not This Flesh,* Frederick Simoons offers an overview of the prohibitions against meat in use in the world throughout history. More cautious than the work of Douglas and Leach in theorizing and conceptualizing, Simoons's work, by contrast, has the great advantage of highlighting the great variety of situations and the impossibility of reducing them to a single model. It confirms that all human societies classify animal life into various categories, close or distant, and determine a limited class of edible animals among the number of species available and actually fit for consumption. But he also shows that the criteria of edibility are highly varied. In particular, Simoons extensively documents complex societies that have generated written historical documentation and in which religious and ethical rules, including dietary prohibitions, are explained, theorized, and come under a differentiated domain of social and intellectual activity. This is the case, for example, in India, where, within the same system of representation, different social groups with different religious practices consequently have to observe different prohibitions. However, such dietary prohibitions as the "sacred cow" of Hindu culture did not enter into Douglas's and Leach's analyses.

Recently, anthropologists adopting a postmodern approach and/or inspired by cognitive sciences have strongly criticized classic works on taboos for their reification of culture as the primary and coherent cause of behavior. Instead, they have sought to develop multicausal interpretations of dietary prohibitions by taking into account psychological and biological factors.[9] Even though I approve of the search for multicausal explanations—my approach to the beef taboo seeks precisely to account for various causalities that cannot be reduced to one or another—I do not subscribe to the perspective that rejects culture as a paradigm. On the contrary, I believe—like Douglas, Leach, Claude Lévi-Strauss, or Stanley Tambiah—that prohibited animals are, even before being good or not to eat, "good to think."[10] This is amply demonstrated by the cases of rare and barely edible animals that are nevertheless the subject of important developments in the normative literature, in Islam in particular.[11]

Above all, I retain from the works of Douglas and Leach the idea of a cultural categorization of the lifeworld, and in particular of animals, according to their relationship to the social body—relationships that range from the very close to the very distant. More recently, anthropological studies focusing specifically on relationships between humans and animals have contributed considerably to shedding light on our understanding of the conditions of the edibility of animals, especially those of domestic ones. I found particular inspiration in the work of Claudine Fabre-Vassas, which compares and contrasts the relationships with pigs and bovines in the European peasantry.[12] Both species are closely related to humans, but their humanization through contact and their necessary dehumanization for slaughter and consumption do not operate in the same way (e.g., women care for pigs and men for cattle) and do not present the same dangers at all, which considerably enriches Leach's linear model by placing all species on a scale of distance to humans, only the intermediate species (neither too humanized nor too strange) being edible.

It is evident from the outset that the issue of the beef taboo in China revolves around the physical, symbolic, and material proximity between humans and bovines, but it should also be noted that this proximity does not necessarily imply a prohibition a priori: as Fabre-Vassas and other anthropologists have shown, there are many ways of thinking about and controlling the distance between humans and domestic animals, and the prohibition against slaughter and consumption is but one of them. Among various ethnic groups in southern China and Southeast Asia, the water buffalo was just as close as bovines were to humans among the Han Chinese peasantry. In both cases, bovines were thought to have human traits. And yet, among these ethnic groups, the water buffalo was very frequently sacrificed and consumed: its sacrificial value was precisely linked to its humanization, even to its value as a human substitute.[13] Moreover, we will see that the contacts between the Han and these ethnic groups led to ideological confrontations relating to their divergent conceptions of the sacrifice and the edibility of bovines. According to this analysis, the Chinese beef taboo emerged from a particular way of managing relationships between humans and highly humanized animals. Therefore, it is a type of food prohibition that is distinguished from other kinds of prohibitions against animals strongly dehumanized by the culture that prohibits them, such as pork in Jewish or Muslim contexts or hunted wild species prohibited by many cultures.

It can be tempting to use a specific vocabulary to distinguish these different types of prohibitions. The term "taboo," in particular, is used by some scholars in a sense similar to that which I attribute to the Chinese beef taboo.[14] If the set of dietary rules identifying prohibited foods is referred to in the scientific literature under the name of "dietary prohibitions," the use of the notions of taboo, interdiction, and prohibition remains undetermined. In its original Polynesian and Melanesian contexts, the word "taboo" has a precise use linked to the specific rules for the exercise of political power, but in a comparative use, the term often only refers to a prohibition whose transgression involves a danger. In the article mentioned above, Leach defined "taboo" extremely broadly as any implicit or explicit prohibition. Certain anthropologists tried to restrict the semantic field of the term. For instance, Margaret

Mead saw in it "the prohibitions of participation in dangerous situations as such" to the exclusion of prohibitions whose transgression is punished by the gods.[15] This would disqualify the use of the word in the Chinese case in which the gods are employed to punish the transgressions. Nonetheless, most authors agree in linking the taboo to supernatural sanction, whatever it is, as opposed to the sanction of the social group.

The use of the word "taboo" in the case of *niujie* in China seems justified for at least four reasons. First, note that taboo and prohibition are both usually translated into modern Chinese as *jinji* 禁忌 and that several contemporary scholars use this term in dealing with the subject of beef.[16] Translating *jie* as "interdiction" may seem to work well in the case of beef. But whereas "interdiction" refers above all to a moral rule, "taboo" implies a definition of ritual purity and a delimitation between sacred and profane or between members of a group and outsiders/strangers. This latter meaning seems to constitute an essential part of the meaning of *niujie* insofar as the rules for excluding beefeaters from certain communities or sacred places are linked to a representation of the beefeater as defiled. We should also note that anthropologists have observed that taboos reinforce social hierarchies by relegating those who transgress them to marginal social status—and this is indeed the case with *niujie* in Ming (1368–1644) and Qing (1636–1911) China.

The term "taboo" also implies a high level of respect and a rarity of transgression. This is difficult to say in the case of beef in China. Beef was always available in the markets. Until the early twentieth century, those who ate it were marginalized at different levels of the social scale, which is not the same as rare consumption. Should we instead classify the slaughter and consumption of beef with other acts that were considered asocial and immoral and constantly decried in all morality books but with a relatively limited effect and widely practiced in reality—for example, gambling or female infanticide?[17] An essential difference between the beef taboo and such "offenses" lies in the social differentiation it facilitates. There were no social groups based on whether they were for or against the practice of gambling or infanticide (although, of course, some lineages may have emphasized such issues in their regulations) in the same way as many communities were defined by excluding beefeaters. For these groups, *niujie* was really a taboo, even if it was not the case for society as a whole.

Finally, the term "taboo," in its proper Polynesian meaning, refers to people and situations that are both sacred and prohibited—that is to say, with positive and negative connotations. Moreover, some anthropologists have proposed translating the term as "marked" or "set apart." Such descriptions apply well to Chinese bovines, which are loved, revered, and therefore prohibited for consumption and, under the Ming and Qing, categorically set aside (only very few top-level sacrifices included a bovine, primarily to heaven and Confucius). Also, "interdiction" seems perfectly appropriate to qualify dietary rules, such as those of Judaism or Islam, prohibiting defiled flesh unfit for humans. In contrast, "taboo" appears to me to be appropriate to describe situations in which an animal is evaluated positively while alive and, by corollary, its flesh negatively when dead, as in the case of cattle in China and zebus in India. Despite the general vagueness and sometimes the controversy surrounding the concept of taboo, and its resolutely alien character to Chinese culture, I have chosen to use it so as to insist on the particular type of rule in question here within the very disparate category of dietary prohibitions. Correlatedly, I use the term "prohibition" to refer to the state laws protecting bovines, primarily by banning their slaughter but not necessarily addressing the consumption of beef. As we will see, the articulation of these two modes (taboo and prohibition) is key to the history of the bovines in China. Finally, I use "interdiction" as a larger encompassing category, including all bans, whatever their religious or legal justification.

By using the term "taboo," I subscribe to a comparative perspective, at least in the possibility of analyzing Chinese *niujie* in conjunction with the dietary rules observed in other cultures, and I will come back to such comparisons in the conclusion. However, even though my work is inspired by the anthropological literature on dietary prohibitions, it develops a different type of analysis for several reasons. First of all, the Chinese beef taboo cannot be understood as an aspect of a total system of thought, as a constituent element of Chinese thought: it developed relatively late and was formulated in opposition to other systems of different interdictions, in particular vegetarianism. However, vegetarianism cannot be understood within the framework of a study of taboos or interdictions as developed in social anthropology by Leach, Douglas, and others. Instead, the injunctions against beef and vegetarianism are possible and divergent interpretations of the Chinese code of ritual purity (*zhaijie*), which, like the codes of ritual purity in many other cultures, is primarily concerned with food and sexuality.

Moreover, while social anthropology has explored the implicit systems of representation that underlie dietary prohibitions, I analyze the perfectly explicit discourse of the beef taboo. Many of my sources can even be called ethical, religious, and social propaganda. Third, in the case of the beef taboo, we have the relatively rare opportunity to witness, thanks to many contemporaneous documents, the formation and historical development of a new taboo. In addition, I was interested in the contexts, development, and historical contingencies of the taboo more than is customary in anthropology. If the historical anthropology of Chinese dietary prohibitions remains to be written, I hope to have provided it with milestones with the present work of history.

## Sources

The discussion of sources is common in introductions to studies in the humanities, but it would be a bit tedious here: I used everything at my disposal. My sources range from antiquity to the twenty-first century and include the sacred texts of Confucianism, Buddhism, and Daoism; official historiography; laws, jurisprudence, and administrative records; newspapers and images; novels, plays, and oral literature; collections of anecdotes and miracles; hagiographies; lineage and village rules; ritual codes; publications by observers, whether travelers or anthropologists; essays on politics and morality from Mengzi (372–289) to Mao Zedong (1893–1976); morality literature and edifying tracts; and revelations by deities and pamphlets by humans.

My materials are very varied and also surprisingly abundant. Over the course of my work, this abundance has become my best answer to the doubt induced by the perplexity of my colleagues concerning the existence of the beef taboo. These are not scraps of discourse gleaned and joined together to construct a topic at the risk of inventing it; they are themes, sentences, ideas written down by hundreds, thousands of authors. And there is much more to this topic than what is cited here. I tried to gather all possible sources on specific points, but large parts of the documentation remain open. For example, near the end of my research, I continued to search Ming and Qing anecdote collections and find more and more stories illustrating the taboo, which tended to recur as I compiled them. To finish my manuscript, I had to stop collecting this type of material at some point.

The methodology I employed to construct a coherent history out of such extraordinarily diverse materials was to constantly search for a coherent discourse regardless of the genre in which it was expressed. I paid all the more attention to various facts and ideas found in many texts belonging to different genres. I have never sought to attribute more or less importance, plausibility, or credit to an assertion according to whether it was found in administrative archives, novels, or stories told by the deities through mediums. However, I was particularly attentive when the officials, the novelists, and the deities often said the same thing, each in their own language and according to their specific constraints of expression.

Above all, the object of this book is a discourse that crosses centuries and genres of writing and (as far as we can deduce since fieldwork is almost absent here) oral genres. I wondered about the relationship of this discourse to practice and social reality, but I did not try to answer the question "Did the Chinese actually eat beef?" because the sources speak of the discourse of the taboo, of its diffusion, and of its effects more than of a concrete practice that was hardly ever exhibited independently of the debates it gave rise to. It is precisely by taking seriously the discourse of the taboo and by seeing how the adaptations and the reactions to this discourse contributed to structuring the society that one will be able to reach significant conclusions on the historical "reality" of the slaughter and consumption of cattle in China throughout history from the ninth to the twenty-first century. Therefore, the fundamental aim of this book is to construct the discourse of the taboo as an actor in history that was formed by social, economic, and religious contexts and influenced these contexts in turn.

My analysis proceeds in two main stages. The first is to sketch the context in which the beef taboo was defined. The beef taboo in China is not a part or subdiscourse of vegetarianism and the interdiction against killing animals, but it emerged in conjunction with it, against it as much as with it. Therefore, it is important to understand the history and issues of vegetarianism and the interdiction against killing before talking about beef. There are several works on this question, but few synthesize the entire historical stretch, and this is what chapter 1 attempts to sketch. The second element of context is the specific situation of bovines in China vis-à-vis other animals. Having become the primary agricultural working animals shortly before the beginning of the Common Era, bovines occupied a very special place in the Chinese economy and culture, which was reflected in particular in a policy of protection and control by the state that remained in place for two millennia. Chapter 2 provides the elements necessary to understand the situation of bovines in the Chinese economy and describes how they became animals set apart in terms of administrative and ideological aspects.

In chapter 3, we get to the taboo itself. It appears in the sources and, I believe, in reality, within a rich body of anecdotes, dated between the ninth and thirteenth centuries, illustrating the mechanisms of retribution and reward for one's actions. Killers of bovines and beefeaters are described as victims of divine curses. This chapter begins by presenting the corpus of the oldest anecdotes and detailing their themes before surveying the adaptation of this discourse in other genres, particularly in scholarly essays and revealed Daoist texts. On this basis, it is possible to sketch explanations for the causes that determined the appearance of the discourse of the taboo during this period. Chapter 4 traces how the discourse of the taboo developed in later periods, under the Ming and the Qing, by focusing on a genre that came to constitute its preeminent medium of expression and dissemination: morality books (*shanshu* 善書). The abundant *shanshu* literature devoted to the taboo shows strong continuity with the older texts while developing new themes and kinds of proselytization. In this genre, we see the whole range of justifications and multiple interpretations of the taboo by the various social actors.

The last chapter is devoted to studying how the discourse of the taboo affected Chinese society between the sixteenth and twentieth centuries. Rather than trying to quantify the observance of the taboo or slaughter and beef butchery, a task that is probably impossible, I try to specify the roles and motivations of the actors, not only beef butchers and their customers but also the protectors of cattle, from the imperial court and magistrates to militant proponents of the taboo and various religious organizations. Thus, the dividing lines between beefeaters and non-beefeaters expose well-known divisions within Chinese society: between highly structured local society and marginal groups and between defenders of "Han culture" and some outsider groups, different because of their faith or their ethnicity. These dividing lines were unraveled and recomposed over the course of the twentieth century, and the taboo then evolved to the rhythm of ideological, social, and religious revolutions.

The historical field covered is immense. The first part extends back to antiquity to understand the formation of the fundamental principles structuring the relationships of the Chinese to live animals, meat, prohibitions, and sacrifice. The second part covers the period from the ninth through the twenty-first centuries. As a historian, I tried not to essentialize my object of study but to consider it a discourse that was undoubtedly stable and coherent over the *longue durée* but was also constantly reinterpreted, understood, and used differently according to each context.

# 1 Animals, Meat, and Sacrifice in China

THE FIRST QUESTION raised by a study of the beef taboo is that of the relations with animals in Chinese culture. These relationships have indissolubly combined economic, agricultural, philosophical, symbolic, dietary, and religious dimensions. The topic of the place of animals and animality in Chinese culture is so vast and still so little explored that it is impossible to deal with it satisfactorily here. The history of science and technology (domestication, agricultural and veterinary techniques, zoology, culinary techniques) will remain peripheral to this study. What interests me is the intersection between the concrete use of animals and ethical and religious discourses and debates. In other words, what did people do, and what could they do from a moral perspective, with animals, which have always been treated in China as elsewhere as negotiable objects on the one hand and living beings on the other? This book poses such questions in the particular case of bovines, but they must be placed here in the general framework of the ethical relationships between humans and animals.

I start with a brief overview of the Chinese philosophical positions on animal life and then focus on aspects related to the beef taboo: meat consumption, vegetarianism, butchery, and animal sacrifice. Just as the beef taboo is twofold (killing and consuming meat), I outline the development of the discourse over the course of Chinese history with respect to these two points: killing animals and consuming their meat. I do so by reviewing the norms decreed by moral and religious authorities and their effects on practices.[1]

## THE STATUS OF ANIMALS IN CHINESE THOUGHT

It would be difficult to define a fundamental Chinese attitude toward animals except to freeze "Chinese thought" in a single stage of its development. It is nevertheless possible to affirm that throughout history, the relationships between humans and animals have been considered within the framework of a shared cosmology, which formed in late antiquity (fourth–third centuries BCE) and has remained valid until the twenty-first century. According to this cosmology, the universe is an organic whole, without an external creative principle or division between matter and spirit. The universe is made of a single substance that divides and recomposes itself indefinitely, a process explained by the symbols of yin and yang, the five agents (*wuxing*), and the divinatory hexagrams. This unique substance takes multiple configurations, light and heavy, spiritual and coarse, thus explaining the existence of living beings of various capacities, in all gradations and without radical breaks between them. In the universe, humans are the most spiritual (*zui youling* 最有靈) form of being because they can understand the natural moral rules that constitute the principles of the functioning of the world.[2] Animals are living beings just like humans but less spiritual and ethereal. However, since any phenomenon, including living beings, is subject to transformation, animals can also perfect themselves and reach states of wisdom or higher spiritual intelligence. They are in the same situation as the inhabitants of peripheral or barbarian regions, who can also rise to the status of being civilized.[3] For the authors of the classics, therefore, animals are distinguished from humans by lesser capacities, but this difference is simply of degree. To use Mencius's famous formulation, "What distinguishes humans from animals is next to nothing. The majority of the people lose it; the wise keep it."[4] The distinction is minor for several reasons, relating in particular to the fragility of the status of civilized humans: those who lose their moral sense are no longer human but become animals. Conversely, regardless of the period, many thinkers have held that some animals also know moral rules since they practice filial piety or loyalty. Therefore, humans and animals belong, albeit to varying degrees, to the same moral community.[5]

Since ancient times and throughout Chinese history, the feeling of closeness and compassion for animals has been a positive and widespread value. The very fact that it is a value that is promoted shows that it does not go without saying. But it is important to note that it was promoted by all those who played the role of a moral authority: Buddhists and Daoists, from the beginning of the Common Era, but before them also Confucians, and this deserves to be underlined.[6] The thinkers recommended adopting toward animals the same attitude as toward humans: benevolence (*ren* 仁). This does not necessarily imply refraining from killing and eating animals. The ultimate benevolent authorities, Confucius and Mencius, made it clear that they went hunting and fishing, albeit avoiding cruel methods, and that they loved meat, and they did not seem to have felt the slightest guilt for it.

The fundamental position of including humans and animals in the same moral community, and therefore the need to think of their relations in moral terms, can lead to quite different practical consequences. A minimum consequence is the injunction to treat domestic animals humanely and to hunt and fish using selective methods. One can also deduce the duty to treat animals with respect when they die by providing them with rituals of salvation. Danielle Eliasberg, in an article on animal burials, relates the case of a deceased bovine in the ninth century for whom its masters paid for a Buddhist ritual and composed a moving prayer—before eating its flesh.[7] According to many thinkers, the benevolence owed to animals was limited by the commitment to higher moral obligations, in particular that of filial piety, which required, for example, that one offered meat to one's parents because it was a food considered essential for the health of the elderly.

Therefore, the requirement of benevolence toward animals does not necessarily imply an interdiction against, or at least limitations on, killing and consuming meat. However, a significant segment of the moral and religious authorities started to move toward such a limitation from the beginning of the Common Era. The proponents of nonviolence toward animals, even of vegetarianism, could find in the classical tradition arguments of a philosophical nature in their favor: such positions did not constitute a heterodoxy or a marginal current of thought in China. On the other hand, the defenders of animal life offended the taste and convictions of those who reconciled benevolence and a meat diet and, above all else, certain prescribed, normative forms of animal killing. One of the major themes of the discourse on the killing of animals is the issue of sacrifice; therefore, before arriving at nonviolence and vegetarianism, we must begin by considering the role of meat and its relationship with sacrificial religion.

## Meat and Sacrifice

From antiquity through the Han, a wide variety of meats were consumed, and we do not find traces of strong interdictions against any meat. Only the horse, a prestigious animal, seems to have been excluded from consumption.[8] The descriptions of banquets in liturgical and historical texts and archaeological data clearly show that people ate beef, pork, dog, sheep, poultry, game (deer, hares), and fish.[9] After the Han, the variety of meats seems to have started to decrease gradually, and pork came to play an overwhelmingly dominant role in the meat diet until around the mid-twentieth century.[10] The decrease in variety is partly due to cultural reasons, in the case of beef or the dog (the consumption of which declined after the Han), but also ecological ones.[11] The gradual cultivation of hills and wasteland and the disappearance of forests reduced both the fauna available for hunting and the possibilities for grazing and therefore livestock farming, the latter being increasingly relegated to peripheral areas. Hunting retained a role in court life through the Tang (618–907), then again during the

Qing because of the Manchus, but it indeed ceased to play an important role in provisioning the population since the middle of the first millennium. Hunting, mainly ungulates, still exists in modern times in the hills of many parts of China but constitutes a vital food supply for only a tiny proportion of the population. Of course, this general picture needs to be qualified according to the period and region.

Changes in the species consumed have not significantly changed the dietetic status of meat. From the first medical texts, meat is presented as a secondary food compared to cereals but is nevertheless considered vital and invigorating. The medical tradition formulated prohibitions linked to specific organs of certain animals or to associations considered toxic, but these prohibitions were not very important, and they were not of an ethical nature.[12] We will not dwell on them here. In short, meat was not devalued by technical medical and dietetic discourses. Another characteristic of meat in China that remains unchanged over time is that its consumption plays, like in many other cultures, the role of a social marker. Because of its cost and, in antiquity, sumptuary laws, meat was a distinguishing feature of the court and the nobility, who qualified as "meat eaters," while peasants were said to be "vegetable eaters."[13] The diet of the Chinese peasantry is challenging to determine for the ancient period. Data from the nineteenth and twentieth centuries show that meat consumption was at a very low level.[14] Livestock farming was run by families on a very small scale, with peasant households raising one or a few pigs.

One thing seems clear: although the consumption of meat for gastronomic purposes was common at court, among the nobility, and later in affluent urban areas, it was most often linked to ritual contexts: banquets and sacrifices, which were governed by similar liturgies, the relationships between humans constituting rituals in the same way as the worship of supernatural beings. For peasants, meat and ritual were so inextricably linked that peasants often ate meat only during major collective celebrations: family (marriage, mourning) or community rituals (local cults).[15] This fundamental fact can be deduced from historical sources and can be seen clearly in ethnographic data. Undoubtedly from antiquity until today, the typical diet of peasants has consisted of cereals and pickled vegetables. On public holidays, on the other hand, cereals were excluded, and meat and alcohol were consumed.[16] The connection between meat and alcohol, which we will have to come back to, was essential. Both were linked to the banquet, a ritual and collective occasion. One neither drank nor ate richly at home with the family. By contrast, the communal banquet allowed sacred intoxication. The association of meat with collective celebrations also had a dietary dimension since it determined a regular rhythm of alternation between rich and lean food. It was also a technical and economic necessity. In the absence of satisfactory means of preserving fresh meat, it was necessary to eat quickly and share the slaughtered animal. Certainly, dried meats (raw or most often boiled, salted, and seasoned, then dried in the open air, in strips or whole) were known and appreciated since antiquity, but they constituted more of a luxury dish than an ordinary way to process meat.[17] Contrary to the European tradition, it was very uncommon in China, regardless of the period, to kill a pig (or another animal) and salt its various parts to preserve them during the winter.

From ancient texts to contemporary practice, communal consumption—the banquet—was a constituent part of any ritual: commensality was the basis of community. However, in Chinese religion, the relationship between humans and divinities was managed through the cultic community. The victim(s) was (were) purchased as a community, offered as a community, and consumed (apart from prescribed exceptions) as a community. In its foundations, the Chinese sacrificial religion presented many features in common with other religions, such as ancient Judaism, the Greco-Roman religions, or the Vedic religion.[18] Its liturgical principle was the offering of meat to the divinities, of which the latter consumed the essence or the aroma. In the case of cooked meat, which was served hot, one waited to dispose of it until the steam (*qi* 氣) had finished emanating, a sign that the divinities had finished their meal. The people offering the sacrifice then consumed the meat. The pieces of this sanctified meat were called *zuo* 胙.[19] As part of the ancestral worship practiced in the lineages that expanded quickly from the Song dynasty onward, their sharing and distribution were among the most strictly regulated and debated subjects—because when one could not physically attend the sacrifice and the banquet, one could be associated with it by receiving a *zuo*. The *zuo* corresponded to the share (*jun* 餕) of a sacrifice that the sovereign gave to his vassals during the banquet. In addition to its role in defining the cultic community, the consumption of *zuo* procured divine graces. The verbal usage of *zuo* signifying "to grant graces or favors" is attested in ancient texts.[20] *Zuo* could also be offered to someone and thus constituted the expression of a sacred alliance.

Before the rise of communal Daoism (second century CE) and Buddhism in China, all deities received meat offerings, along with other foods, notably cereals, various vegetable-based dishes, tea, alcohol, and precious inedible goods, such as silks and jades.[21] The role of meat was so crucial in sacrifices that from antiquity, the expression "bloody foods" (*xueshi* 血食) designated worship.[22] This is especially true for the worship of the ancestors of royal and noble families, the best documented among the cults of antiquity, but also the state cults to the celestial deities (heaven, the stellar deities), terrestrial deities (the main peaks and rivers, the gods of the soil), and many local cults outside the official religion, which we only see appearing in detail in sources from the Han but that existed long before.

Our sources on ancient sacrificial practices, in addition to archaeology, essentially consist of three liturgical treatises and/or ritual theories, collected and published under the Han with some earlier material: *Book of Rites* (*Liji* 禮記), *Rites of the Zhou* (*Zhouli* 周禮), and *Ceremonials and Rites* (*Yili* 儀禮). These sources, which deal mainly with ancestor worship and state ritual, show that there were, then as now, several ways of presenting meat to a deity: the whole animal, at least at the beginning of the ritual; its blood; chunks of raw meat (*xing* 腥); chunks of boiled meat; and finally pieces of meat in a dish, either alone (in slices of dried meat, *fu* 脯 or *xi* 腊) or prepared with other vegetable foods (in soup, steamed, fried, etc.).[23] Specific vessels corresponded to each of these preparations, the importance of which was fundamental because in the ancient sacrificial religion, which did not use an icon to represent the divinities or ancestors, it was the bronze vessel receiving the offering that was the body of the deity.[24] These different ways of presenting meat had ritual meaning. We notice in particular that there was a gradation from the most simple and primitive (blood, raw meat) to the most familiar/civilized (dishes of cooked and seasoned meat). This gradation corresponded to a hierarchy of divinities from the most distant to closest: heaven, distant ancestors, and deceased relatives. To the immediate ancestors that one had known, one offered food similar to that which was eaten at banquets, and the sacrificers consumed it after having offered it as a sacrifice. To heaven or distant ancestors, dishes were offered that were repugnant to humans and were not shared at the end of the sacrifice: blood and raw meat.[25] Only animal matter allowed such distinctions, and that was why, even if the sacrificial offerings were not limited to meat, the latter played a primordial role.

The great diversity and complexity of the ancient sacrificial religion, linked to a highly hierarchical social organization, partly disappeared from the Han onward. Of course, the state religion under successive dynasties continued to be the subject of heated debates concerning the procedure of sacrifices, which were supposed to conform to the ancient models, even though the details of the liturgy constantly changed. For the two millennia of the Common Era, there were two ways of presenting meat offerings: in dishes or as a whole sacrificial victim.

This second way, of course, constituted the most valued sacrifice. The offering of one or more whole animals dedicated to the recipient of the sacrifice was called "great sacrifice" (*daji* 大祭 or *dasi* 大祀).[26] The two ways are by no means exclusive: a great sacrifice included, in addition to the sacrificial victims, a certain number of dishes, some of which were meat. The prescriptions for this sacrifice were taken from the three liturgical classics.[27] They were upheld thereafter and applied essentially in the same way for the sacrifices of the state cults (in particular, the sacrifice to heaven), to the ancestors, and to Confucius.[28] The animals were chosen according to their physical qualities (the color of the coat, the shape of the horns), and some were raised expressly at the expense of the court and isolated for a variable period depending on the ritual. Their selection was validated by divination.[29] The animal was inspected shortly before the ritual (often the day before) by the principal officiant, who checked whether the animal's physical characteristics were suitable. Then the animal was slaughtered in the early morning by a servant in a room or small building reserved for this, not far from but outside the sanctuary where the animal was to be offered. The animal was then presented to the god, whole, lying on its stomach, legs apart, raw, shaved except for a band of hair on its spine, and emptied of its blood and some of its entrails and organs. A vessel containing the blood and hair was presented and then poured out as a libation (*ru maoxue* 茹毛血). After this libation, the victims were cooked, shared, presented, and finally consumed together, except during sacrifices to heaven and other state cults in which the sacrificial victims were burned in a furnace (like the burnt offerings in the Hebrew Bible).[30] This was explained by the status of the recipient divinity, heaven, which could not share a banquet with humans.

These prescriptions continued to be observed for more than two millennia. There was a strong desire to adhere strictly to ancient standards for everything relating to the technical aspects and the vocabulary of the ritual. The sacrificial procedures intended for state worship, dynasty after dynasty, which form a literature as obscure as it is abundant, essentially followed these prescriptions. The same applied to family rituals (*jiali* 家禮).[31] This did not prevent in both cases—state worship and family worship—incessant debates and modifications concerning the details of the procedures. Although sacrifices to ancestors were regulated by sumptuary laws in antiquity, they were authorized and even encouraged for the entire population since the Han. A proselytizing trend in Confucianism, particularly associated with neo-Confucianism, which emerged in the twelfth century, set itself the goal of ensuring that the practices of the whole population, and not only of the literati elites, conformed strictly to Confucian ideals. Confucian liturgical manuals were written in this context, including the famous *Family Rituals* (*Jiali*) by Zhu Xi 朱熹 (1130–1200).[32] These rituals aimed to follow, for the most part, the ancient prescriptions while considerably simplifying the procedures to make their execution possible even for a family of modest means. Since the Song dynasty, the great lineages often made at least one great sacrifice per year, at the winter solstice, sometimes several, with two sacrificial animals: pigs and sheep/goats.[33] The many other occasions, as well as the offerings that punctuated the cycle of funeral rituals, from the death until the final installation of the deceased as an ancestor, included meat offerings but not whole consecrated animals: the meats offered were generally not taken from a consecrated animal and slaughtered for the occasion but simply purchased.

Cults of local gods, which together with family rituals formed the basis of Chinese religion, were not codified like state and family rituals. Indeed, regardless of the period, the Chinese state regulated very little religion except for official cults. It enacted some principles, generally very restrictive, on authorized or prohibited cults and oscillated, in reality, between tolerance (most often) and repression (sometimes). Chinese religion itself did not have any structure of authority that could decree the correct procedures. A few historical sources, and especially field observations, show that in respect to the blood sacrifice, the practices followed the fundamental principles of the Confucian liturgy while supplementing them with others. Cults of local gods and territorial deities (*zhengshen* 正神), divinities conceived as being part of the heavenly bureaucracy, received blood sacrifices in a manner similar to what the Confucian liturgy stipulated. There were therefore the great sacrifices of consecrated animals, presented whole and raw, and then prepared, as well as the more common offerings of cooked meat dishes accompanied by glasses of alcohol. Today's offerings to deities are generally referred to as *shengli* 牲禮 (rites of offering sacrificial victims). During the great collective celebrations, in addition to the offerings made in front of the altar by the whole community, each family or group makes its own offerings, from simple dishes to whole and cooked pigs or chickens, which are placed on large tables arranged in front of the entrance to the temple. After the celebration, the families take away these offerings, which they then consume together. Such offerings have an ostentatious and competitive character, and competitions of the biggest pig are often held on this occasion.

Although the Chinese sacrificial religion particularly codified the sacrifice of one, two, or three victims (the "great sacrifice"), it nevertheless favored the multiplication of sacrificial victims, and instances of large-scale slaughter were attested in many contexts. State worship used a large number of victims due to the proliferation of secondary deities (various ancestors, stellar deities, peaks and rivers, and other gods of the earth) associated with each sacrifice and the large number of sacrifices conducted each year by the state liturgy.[34] This forced the state at all times to maintain farms for this sole purpose. In the local religion, the great annual celebrations were also occasions for competitions between the numerous groups (cultic associations, villages) participating in the celebration. Each sacrificed the greatest number of animals or the most beautiful ones possible.[35]

Anthropologists have noted that the content and form of food offerings vary according to the recipient deity.[36] Their analysis is consistent with that of specialists in the ancient liturgy.[37] This indicates the profound continuity of Chinese religion. When the recipient is close to the worshippers, especially in the case of ancestors who maintain an intimate bond with their descendants beyond death, the offerings take the form of a banquet: the dishes offered are identical to what is served among the living and surround a pot of steaming rice, provided with a spoon. On the other hand, offerings to the deities in the form of dishes filled only with large pieces of cooked but uncut and unseasoned meat without rice, condiments, or chopsticks is a further departure from ordinary cuisine. In addition to this difference in form, there is a differentiation between the offerings for the deceased and ancestors who, apart from the great sacrifices, favor cereals on the one hand and *shengli* offerings, which are essentially meat, on the other hand.[38] The type of offering made to demons—for example, soldiers of divine troops (*yinbing* 陰兵) or victims of bad death—varies according to the circumstances; in some cases, they are treated like deities and are given pieces of cooked meat. In other cases, they are treated like ancestors and are given banquet dishes but of inferior quality. However, it also happens that they are given raw foods, with the assumption that they would be unable to eat meat transformed by fire and therefore "civilized." Rather than the taste of cooked food, they like the smell of blood that characterizes raw meat. Consequently, unlike the offerings prepared for the *zhengshen* or the ancestors and shared as *zuo,* the raw meat offered to demons is discarded.

Raw meat is therefore found at both ends of the symbolic hierarchy of supernatural beings—the "great sacrifice" of animals presented whole and raw for the most sacred sacrifices (at least from a Confucian point of view) to heaven, ancestors, and Confucius and pieces of raw meat for demons. In contrast, the deceased relatives and local gods receive cooked meat. The way in which the meat is prepared (whole or cut, cooked or raw) thus makes it possible to express the entire range of relationships between humans and supernatural beings. The distinction is also expressed by the place where the offering is presented: on the ground and outside the house, which is the ritual area for the demons, or on a table and inside for an ancestor or a *zhengshen.*

Although the method of preparation of the sacrificial victim was decisive, the choice of animal species was more often left open. As much in the normative texts of the Confucian liturgy as in the descriptions from any period, the sacrificed animal was generally qualified as *sheng* 牲, which could be applied to any animal.[39] The list, however, was almost always limited to the six domestic animals (*liuchu* 六畜: horses, cattle, dogs, sheep/goats, pigs, poultry) and fish. Other animals produced by hunting (deer, rabbits) mentioned in the ancient liturgy subsequently became rarer. The dog and the horse, commonly sacrificed until under the Han, were rarely sacrificed after that. The animals most widely sacrificed since antiquity, and almost exclusively since the Han, were, in decreasing order of size, cost, and prestige, cattle, sheep/goats, and pigs, then poultry and fish.[40] However, unlike other cultures of sacrifice, Chinese deities did not have, with a few exceptions, a favorite or prohibited offering. The texts of the ancient liturgy and those of the state ritual under successive dynasties generally specify the choice of animals, mainly, it seems, to indicate the hierarchy of deities and cults. Indeed, the number of victims of each of the three species (bovine, ovine/caprine, pig) allows, with other criteria (identity and rank of the officiant: the emperor in person or his representative, duration of the ritual, quantity of other offerings) precisely placing the ritual in a symbolic hierarchy, according to the rank of the deity. On the other hand, in the worship of ancestors according to the family ritual of the neo-Confucian tradition, the authors did not give any indication in this regard. No doubt they meant that the main thing was to offer meat, according to one's means and according to the animals available, and that it would be contrary to the intention of the ritual to require a victim that some could not afford to procure. As for the cults of the *zhengshen,* much liberty existed. The same meats were offered to all the gods, and the victims were chosen according to the resources and means of the community offering the sacrifice. Concretely, it was most often a pig, but it was possible to substitute another victim.

In the great sacrifice, the sacrificial victims were usually one, two, or three. Since antiquity, the expression "three victims (of different species)" (*sansheng* 三牲) has been attested in many texts. As with many other terms of this type referring to an enumeration, various glosses were added by commentators. In the canons of the Confucian liturgy, *sansheng,* at least since the Han, was usually understood to mean bovine, sheep/goat, and pig. In this sense, it was synonymous with another term whose meaning is more apparent and more fixed: "great sacrifice" (*tailao* 太牢). The latter was opposed to the "small sacrifice" (*shaolao* 少牢), which excluded the bovine to leave only the sheep/goat and the pig. However, the term *sansheng* continued to be used through the ages with a changed meaning. Since the Song dynasty, it commonly referred to pork, chicken, and fish, pork occupying the first place among everyday culinary items. This development of the definition of the "three victims" is fundamental to understanding the beef taboo, and we will return to this in detail. It suffices to say here that the principle of sacrifice in Chinese religion considers the choice of the animal species sacrificed only as a function of a symbolic hierarchy in which the bovine has always occupied the highest rank.

This survey of the sacrificial religion helps us understand the range of meanings that meat had in the relationships between humans and divinities and, consequently, the definition of cultic communities and the resistance encountered by those who wanted to suppress animal sacrifice entirely or partially.

## *Zhaijie* and the Sanctification of Killing

Chinese religion is fundamentally a sacrificial religion grounding the alliance with the powers (celestial deities, ancestors, protective gods, demons) in a communion centered on offering and sharing meat. The slaughter of sacrificial victims is a sacred act even if a subordinate concretely carries it out without playing a role in the ritual and outside the consecrated enclosure. As such, it cannot be accomplished lightly. Killing is justified by legitimate sacrifice, whereas both the slaughter of animals and the consumption of meat are proscribed in certain other circumstances. In the first place, ancient religion held that at certain times of the natural cycle (spring, the period of reproduction and birth, as well as times of natural disasters, when life must be sustained), the fact of killing living beings (humans and animals) goes against the natural course of the world and therefore constitutes an offense against heaven; this was codified in the seasonal calendars from late antiquity onward. Hunting, fishing, butchering, and the execution of convicts were therefore prohibited during these periods. The motivations were at the same time "ecological" (linked to the management of natural resources) and religious (the fear of going against the moral order of the universe and triggering catastrophes).[41] These notions were adopted by Confucians so that from the Han until 1911, an official proclamation was issued prohibiting butchers from slaughtering any animal whatsoever during the official prayers of the emperor or local officials for rain in times of drought, the cessation of rain during floods, or in any other case of natural disaster. It was the same on numerous occasions, such as the emperors' birthdays. The interdictions against killing were sometimes expressed in Buddhist and/or Daoist terms, notably under the Tang when edicts prohibited any killing of animals during the holy days of the calendars specific to these two religions, but after that, similar prohibitions continued to be enacted in purely Confucian terms. Even at the end of the nineteenth century, some magistrates tried to enforce a systematic interdiction against slaughter on the first and fifteenth of each month with mixed success.[42]

In addition, killing and eating meat were proscribed during purifications and penances. One of the corollaries of sacrifice, and therefore one of the foundations of Chinese religion, was the preparation period of one or more days, the duration varying according to the importance of the ritual and each participant's status. This preparation (*zhai* 齋) was a purification according to a code of ritual purity (*zhaijie*) that allowed the officiant to enter into union with the recipient deities of the sacrifice.[43] The first period of light preparation (*sanzhai* 散齋) was followed by another of seclusion (*zhizhai* 致齋) immediately preceding the sacrifice and often lasting three days. For the great sacrifices of the state cult, the emperor retired to a room provided for this purpose, the *zhaigong* 齋宮. During this period, all polluting activities were prohibited: contact with death, sexual practices, and also the consumption of meat. The principle of this period of purification was ancient, but the oldest sources are not clear as to the exact obligations.[44] The prohibitions on meat were undoubtedly understood differently depending on the period, social group, or family. Regarding the dietary aspects of *zhaijie*, the locus classicus was taken from the *Analects* in which Confucius says, "In a period of purification, one must change one's diet (*bianshi* 變食)." Commentators interpreted this interdiction in various ways, depending on the custom of their time.[45]

The other circumstance in which Chinese religion required abstinence from meat was mourning. Of variable durations depending on the relationship between the deceased and the bereaved, the period of mourning continued for up to two years and several months for a child mourning a parent. The many interdictions that applied partly overlapped with those of the *zhaijie* but were motivated by different reasons: in this case, it was a question of doing penance and depriving oneself of all comforts in housing, clothing, and food. The ancient texts were precise on this last point: the prescribed diet was first limited to rice porridge and, second, included vegetables. Meat was therefore implicitly proscribed. In general, the emphasis was on eating only coarse foods, and this should most often have involved abstaining from meat. A passage from the *History of the Han* (*Hanshu* 漢書) relates an admonition made to a prince who was not satisfied with *sushi* 素食 during mourning.[46] The term *su* commonly designates vegetarian food, but its proper meaning is "simple," "unprocessed," so that a Tang-dynasty commentator on the *Hanshu* saw fit to add a note explaining that *su* implied abstinence from all meat.[47] It is possible that it originally meant food that may have been meat but was served without condiment or refinement, and this meaning remained in some later occurrences.[48]

The precise dietary interdictions of *zhaijie* and mourning were elaborated on relatively little by ancient liturgical sources, which pay more attention to the question of clothing. Perhaps dietary restrictions were considered relatively unimportant until under the Han and did not become a primary aspect of penance until later. It should also be emphasized that the practices of abstinence were not limited to the observance of liturgical rules during mourning or *zhai* and could have a social meaning, such as to mark one's emotion or, in the case of hermits, to protest silently against the powerful who ate meat, a symbol of their wealth and privileges.[49]

Nevertheless, in other sources from late antiquity, a term appears that suggests a specific interdiction that deserves to be explained a little. The *Zhuangzi*, which develops a critique of ancient sacrificial religion with its emphasis on formal procedures and social hierarchies, has a famous passage on the question of *zhaijie.* Yan Hui 顏回, one of Confucius's disciples, says he is so poor that he can go for months without drinking alcohol or eating Alliaceae (*hun* 葷). He wonders if this, therefore, counts as *zhai.* Confucius replies that this is only the *zhai* of the sacrifices, not the true inner fast, which is that of the heart (*xinzhai* 心齋).[50] The text thus implies that during the *zhaijie* preceding the sacrifices, abstinence from *hun* was prescribed, which is confirmed by a passage from *Xunzi.*[51] The commentators gloss *hun* with "plant with a strong or pungent taste (garlic, onion, shallot, etc.)." The term appears, visibly in the same sense (the glossers sometimes also mention ginger), in some passages of the classics but without allusion to an interdiction.[52] The old dictionaries are also perfectly clear on the meaning of the term. These plants are essential condiments in the preparation of meat dishes.[53] It would seem that an interdiction had developed around them, perhaps quite late, or without becoming completely orthodox since it was not explicitly formulated in the ritual classics. The commentators on the passage quoted above from the *Analects* concerning the *zhaijie* often cite this sentence from the *Zhuangzi* to say that Confucius meant by this cryptic phrase that one did not eat *hun* plants during the period of abstinence.[54]

There were undoubtedly multiple causes for this interdiction: *hun* plants caused bad breath and were thus considered impure in the context of a liturgy of the word during which one spoke to the deities.[55] As condiments of meat dishes, they could be prohibited during a period while one ate simple and lean foods. But the term *hun* had a remarkable fate because of two developments. First, the interdiction against alliaceous plants developed and was repeated among the Daoist interdictions discussed below. It was undoubtedly reinforced by immortality cults that considered these potent plants harmful. In this context, the term *hun* was defined in a list of five prohibited plants (*wuhun* 五葷 or *wuxin* 五辛, a synonymous term but of later appearance, possibly during the Han).[56] Soon after, Buddhism brought a fundamentally identical food prohibition from India and Central Asia.[57]

The *wuhun* thus became, despite religious conflicts in medieval China, a point of convergence for the three institutional religions, even if the exact list was never the same for all. At the same time, however, the term *hun* experienced a semantic shift that was both relatively logical and a source of much ambiguity. From medieval times, the primary dietary prohibition was meat, during *zhaijie* and mourning in the Confucian liturgy and in Buddhism and Daoism, so much so that *hun* came to designate meat while keeping its proper meaning of "Alliaceae." Several exegetes attempted to point out that the practice of vegetarianism during *zhaijie* and mourning was a mistake and that the classics only ask for abstinence from alliaceous plants—which was also a way of forcefully interpreting the classics, which are irremediably laconic on the subject.[58] It cannot be ruled out that the ambiguity was, if not intentional, at least measured. In any case, it is very difficult to identify with certainty the first occurrence of the word *hun* in the sense of meat. Indeed, it was often used alone or in compound expressions, such as *hunxue* 葷血, which can mean "alliaceous plants and blood (meat)" or just "meat." If the two interdictions occur together, the ambiguity is not a problem; it becomes so when specific authors (purist Confucians in particular) insist on the interdiction against only alliaceous plants. Zhu Xi himself illustrates this ambiguity. Sometimes a purist exegete, he asked for abstinence from alliaceous plants but not from meat during the *zhaijie*.[59] Yet elsewhere, he used *hun* in the sense of meat and even stipulated that the meat offered to the deceased during mourning not be consumed by the family (who observe vegetarian mourning) but given to the servants.[60] In short, the sacrificial religion and Confucianism were built on an alternation between the period of penance (the prohibition of killing animals and fasting, whether including meat or not) and the period of sacrifice (when killing and meat were sanctified). The status of meat, whether it was prohibited or not, sometimes remained uncertain, in particular because the parallel interdiction against alliaceous plants could replace it or, on the contrary, add to it. Chinese religion thus sanctified the slaughter of animals and the consumption of meat, prescribing it during rituals and prohibiting it at certain other times. However, this model, which constituted one of the foundations of Chinese religion, was directly challenged by two sacrificial revolutions at the beginning of the Common Era—one Daoist and the other Buddhist—that categorically rejected blood sacrifice and therefore the consumption of meat.

## Sacrificial Revolutions: Daoism

The emergence in China of ideas about nonviolence, condemnation of animal slaughter, and abstention from meat is generally associated with Buddhism. However, although Buddhism has indeed played a fundamental role in this regard across East and South Asia, it is probably not the first and certainly not the only one in China to have developed a discourse critical of blood sacrifice and the consumption of meat. Communitarian Daoism was founded around a sacrificial revolution that seems to have originated beyond any Buddhist influence, even if the two religions quickly found themselves in a situation of reciprocal influence.

The first communitarian Daoist organization, the Way of the Heavenly Masters (Tianshi dao 天師道), was founded in the second century CE.[61] Its founding moment was the appearance of Laozi to Zhang Daoling in 142. Zhang was appointed as the deputy of Laozi on earth and charged with reforming the misguided mores of humanity. This reform involved the abandonment of the sacrificial religion that characterized ancient China and, in its stead, the establishment of a Pact of Purity (Qingyue 清約) with the Dao. It was a question of cutting short the cults of the degenerate forces of the Six Heavens (Liutian 六天), which brought together all the cults of the ancient religion: ancestors, culture heroes, as well as many deified deceased spirits who, according to the Way of the Heavenly Masters, were nothing but demons thirsty for blood and who, far from granting graces to their devotees, in reality brought them to ruin and death.[62] The Way of the Heavenly Masters therefore rejected not only "excessive" popular cults (*yinsi* 淫祀) but also the official religion. Followers only envisioned cults to the pure breaths of the Dao, which were not deified humans: these pure forces thus did not need to eat meat, and there was no need to make the costly sacrifices requiring the services of a priest. Also, according to the Pact of Purity, "the deities do not eat, the masters do not receive a salary 神不飲食, 師不受錢."[63] Suppressing the practice of offerings was not the issue since the ceremonies of the Heavenly Masters implied the presentation of "pledges of faith" (*xinwu* 信物), which corresponded to certain offerings of precious materials also existing in the ancient religion. But they very specifically sought to remove meat and alcohol from the liturgy.

According to Kristofer Schipper, the ancient Heavenly Masters texts preserved to this day, which date from the second through the sixth centuries and form only part of the original canon, assert that the Pact of Purity was inaugurated by another, slightly earlier movement, the Taiping dao 太平道, which produced the *Classic of the Great Peace* (*Taiping jing* 太平經), a famous text that is only extant in later, incomplete versions. This pact was then said to have been institutionalized by the Way of the Heavenly Masters. Be that as it may, such a reform was radical and had to reflect the will of the entire community of the adherents to set themselves apart from the surrounding society. The cutting of ties and exclusion were indeed very pronounced themes in some texts of the Heavenly Masters. Not only could the adepts no longer participate in the sacrifices made by the unconverted, but one text even enjoined them not to use dishes that had been used for sacrifices.[64] In other words, it was a question of proscribing commensality with nonfollowers. The refusal to consume meat with others thus shaped the identity of this new religious community.

The interdictions of the Way of the Heavenly Masters concerning animals and meat were part of an ethical discourse expressed essentially in the form of precepts and rules (*jie* 戒) governing life by which the followers could maintain their purity and gain salvation. Later revelations took up and elaborated on these rules, notably those of the Highest Clarity (Shangqing 上清), which emerged at the end of the fourth century, and the Numinous Treasure (Lingbao 靈寶), which incorporated a strong Buddhist influence into Daoism at the beginning of the fifth century. The proliferation of revelations and ranks of ordination, ranging from the initiation of common adherents to the highest mystical ordinations, which crystallized in a coherent hierarchical system under the Tang, led to the composition of many varied precepts.[65] Indeed, the *jie* were rules that one vowed to uphold during an ordination, and there was a specific list for each of the ranks of ordination; there were also regulations (*lü* 律 and *ke* 科) for communities of the semimonastics (*guan* 觀 or 館), which appeared in the course of the fifth century, and for times of collective celebration.[66]

The normative texts and the interdictions relating to animals and meat formulated by Daoists from the origins of the Way of the Heavenly Masters until the Tang dynasty all relate either to the question of sacrifice or to an ethic of respect for nature and life, which, without being able to be assimilated to what we call ecology, overlaps in some respects.[67] The oldest and in many respects fundamental text is *The Hundred and Eighty Precepts of Laojun* (*Laojun yibaibashi jie* 老君一百八十戒), which seems to originate with the Taiping dao and to have been transmitted by the Way of the Heavenly Masters;[68] even if the conditions of its appearance in connection with the Taiping dao remain a matter of conjecture, it seems reasonable to date it to the second or third century.

Among the 180 precepts, there was a set of rules inspired by respect for nature and the resources available to humans, which applied to animals, plants, and minerals. Grasslands should not be burned, trees cut down, or springs polluted. Hunting and fishing, trapping animals, catching birds, and generally disturbing animals were prohibited (precepts 79, 97, 98, 132). More fundamentally, killing or injuring any living being was prohibited (precept 4); likewise, precept 176 forbade taking the lives of different animals, including the six domestic animals. In addition, a set of interdictions concerned the question of animal slaughter. The clearest was precept 24: "Drinking alcohol and eating meat are prohibited 不得飲酒食肉." This was clarified by precept 177, which says, "The ideal is to eat [only] vegetables if possible" (*ruo neng shicai zuijia* 若能食菜最佳).[69] The interdiction against meat concerned not only killing and then eating an animal but also consuming meat prepared by others. Precept 172 proscribed eating "birds, animals, or fish that people have killed themselves." Precept 173 extended the same interdiction to an animal one had seen slaughtered. In addition, breeding pigs and sheep/goats was prohibited (precept 8), undoubtedly because the only possible use of these animals was butchery.[70] The interdiction against meat was therefore evident and constituted an integral part of the dietary rules, next to the interdictions against the five alliaceous plants (*wuxin*) (precept 10), spoiled foods (precept 174), or foods of dubious origin (precept 175) and, in another register, excess, luxury, and excessively abundant banquets. Even though the interdictions in *One Hundred and Eighty Precepts of Laojun* belong to the continuity of rules for protecting natural resources and dietary observances linked to calendar paradigms (*yueling* 月令 and *rishu* 日書) dating from late antiquity, the novelty of their discourse concerning animals and sacrifices is apparent, including the fact that the interdictions are not seasonal but permanent.[71]

The numerous texts of precepts drafted subsequently involve the same types of prohibitions. In addition to the rules requiring respect and benevolence toward animals, in particular domestic animals that should not be hit or insulted, there is, on the one hand, a general interdiction against killing and, on the other hand, an interdiction against meat. The prohibition against killing is based on a conception of the Dao, which loves all kinds of life and hates death (*tiandao e sha er hao sheng* 天道惡殺而好生).[72] This justification is not explicit in the *One Hundred and Eighty Precepts* but seems to be a feature common to all ancient and medieval Daoism. According to Ge Hong 葛洪 (283–343), pity for all animals, including insects, is one of the necessary conditions for attaining immortality, and to transgress against this is a sin that involves demerits such that all hope of transcendence is ruined.[73] These conceptions were subsequently reinforced by the Buddhist influence, notably visible in the Numinous Treasure texts. There are elaborations on the fact that there is no difference in nature between humans and animals, who are also endowed with feelings and a sense of morality. The virtue of compassion (*cibei* 慈悲) is strongly developed in these texts but only reinforces a respect for life that was already present in the earlier Daoist tradition. Moreover, based on conceptions common to Daoism and Buddhism throughout Chinese history, the estates of temples and monasteries and sacred mountains were considered sanctuaries where it was forbidden to hunt and cut down trees.

As far as the interdiction against meat is concerned, things seem more complex. The *One Hundred and Eighty Precepts of Laojun,* a foundational text in all respects, seems unambiguous, yet later texts did not systematically take up the interdiction.[74] Given the context of the sacrificial revolution in which this text appeared, I would argue that one must understand that the central issue behind the interdiction against meat was the rejection of blood sacrifice. Of course, the *One Hundred and Eighty Precepts* did not explicitly refer to sacrifice; however, permanent vegetarianism was recommended "if possible" and not required as an absolute obligation. The question would then be less whether or not to eat meat than whether or not to eat it under certain circumstances. The followers of the first Daoist communities, common adherents or ordained priests, were theoretically prohibited from participating in a blood sacrifice and eating the meat offered on this occasion.

On the other hand, strict vegetarianism in ordinary times was more of an ideal than an absolute rule—even if in rural communities like those of the Way of the Heavenly Masters, the consumption of meat outside of collective celebrations was undoubtedly rare. A somewhat later and composite text of the Heavenly Masters, which specialists date variously and, depending on the sections, between the third and fifth centuries, emphasized this interdiction but seemed to apply it only to priests: "They will have to heal the sick and will not be able to drink alcohol or eat meat."[75] It seems unlikely to me, although not impossible, that the entire Heavenly Masters community has been strictly vegetarian over the centuries; such a fact would surely have been mentioned in the external literature, some of which was hostile to the Way of the Heavenly Masters, and this was not the case.[76] This interpretation is confirmed by some texts a little later, which apply the interdiction against meat specifically to the context of celebrations. In a Numinous Treasure text, the interdiction against killing was formulated as "the interdiction against killing living beings for illicit sacrifices."[77] Finally, a code from the late medieval period proscribed "eating offerings given as sacrifices to the gods." In the context of an apocalyptic text revealed in the fifth century, the *Scripture of the Divine Incantations of Abyssal Caverns* (*Dongyuan shenzhou jing* 洞淵神咒經), apparently produced by a movement issued from the Way of the Heavenly Masters, strict vegetarianism was also recommended among virtuous behaviors, but it was only required during regular collective celebrations.[78]

Even though the ordinary diet of adherents was not a significant concern of Daoist rules, the question of collective celebrations occupied the foreground. The Way of the Heavenly Masters prohibited sacrifices to "evil" gods and the banquets that accompanied them but replaced them with other forms of celebration that resembled them. The assemblies of the Heavenly Masters, particularly the days of the Three Primes (Sanyuan 三元; the 15th of the first, seventh, and tenth months), included a collective banquet called, as in the ancient religion, *chu* 廚 (kitchen).[79] The idea of commensality and communion persisted but was combined with an ideal of frugality, as opposed to the excesses of traditional celebrations (quantity, cost, and richness of food). However, in China, as we will see later, the theme of frugality was often linked to the absence of meat.[80] At the same time, the notion of *zhai,* a purifying fast preceding the sacrifice, evolved to become the main ritual in Daoism and Buddhism. Since there was no longer a bloody sacrifice in either of these two religions, abstinence, purification, and confession of transgressions constituted the primary offering and the very support for communication with the powers.[81] Although the *chu,* which disappeared under the Tang, and the different forms of *zhai,* of which there was a great variety, were distinct rituals, their principle was the same: the cultic community and the pure divinities communed in a meager meal consisting of rice and vegetables but which might include alcohol and whose merit was shared between the living and the deities.[82]

The word *zhai,* one of the most polysemous in Chinese religious vocabulary, also designates the meal of semimonastic communities (*guan*) since they permanently live in abstinence and ritual purity. The *guan* appear to have systematically practiced strict vegetarianism, unlike the laity, who only did so during celebrations. At least this permanent vegetarianism was explicitly required in various regulatory texts dating from the sixth, seventh, and eighth centuries.[83] All in all, even if both insisted on the differences, the banquets of the cultic communities of the sacrificial religion, those of Daoism, and those of Buddhism had a lot in common. Buddhists and Daoists reproached the cultic communities for their carnivorous feasts, while Buddhists reproached Daoists for the consumption of alcohol, even if some Daoist texts tried to limit it.[84] Alcohol was also prohibited in some regulatory texts, starting with the *One Hundred and Eighty Precepts of Laojun.*

Thus, the Daoist discourse on meat essentially consisted of a reflection on ritual purity. The meat issue was much less present in Daoist reflections on dietetics, which concerned another register: the techniques of immortality. To be sure, the two fields were intimately linked, and some texts dealing with dietetic techniques considered meat to be the coarsest and most impure form of food.[85]

However, Daoist reflections on diet were not concerned with the perspective of sin but with the effect of food on the body. Ordinary foods, especially cereals, rot in the body, generating excrement and nourishing the "three worms," *sanshi* 三尸, which are the body deities of death.[86] By contrast, the foods of immortality, which are simultaneously exceptional and famine foods, are dry and fully assimilable. The famous abstention from cereals (*bigu* 辟穀 or *duangu* 斷穀) constituted, in reality, a process of abandoning all ordinary food in favor of some extraordinary substances, even of the breath only.[87] Daoist dietetics rejected raw meat, which was considered repugnant, but readily adopted dried meats, which were moreover foods appreciated by the elites and frequently presented as an offering.[88] In addition, dried game meat (especially venison), procured by hunting, was valued more highly than sacrificial meat from domestic animals. Thus, there were diets of immortality that included dried meat, particularly in ancient sources, partially prior to the sacrificial reform of the Heavenly Masters.[89] It is possible that this meat included in the immortality regimes was later suppressed due to the general devaluation of meat introduced by the Heavenly Masters. In fact, the theme of vegetarianism did not appear in the oldest biographies of immortality seekers, *Hagiographies of Immortals* (*Liexian zhuan* 列仙傳) and *Hagiographies of Divine Immortals* (*Shenxian zhuan* 神仙

傳).[90] It only appeared with some regularity in the context of some ascetics in the *Hagiographies of the Adepts of the Dao* (*Daoxue zhuan* 道學傳), a collection of biographies written between 569 and 618.[91] For these figures, vegetarianism seems to have been part of a larger process of renunciation, along with celibacy and the abandonment of all material comforts. In the case of others, especially among the many who were priests of the Heavenly Masters, it is possible that vegetarianism was not mentioned because it was taken for granted.

In short, the texts of the Heavenly Masters, which established the foundations of the Daoist attitude toward animals and meat, recommended not killing animals and, if possible, not owning them.[92] They also demanded if not absolute vegetarianism, at least the banishment of all animal flesh in ritual practices and collective celebrations—and this was symbolically and concretely most important. Vegetarianism became a higher level of practice, required of priests and recommended to laypeople. The same was probably true with alcohol, which was also a fundamental part of sacrifice in Chinese religion. The latter was also strongly discouraged for laypeople. Around the fifth century, Daoists adopted a set of five precepts (*wujie* 五戒) remarkably similar to the *wujie* in Buddhism and used for the first ranks of lay initiations.[93] Killing living beings and drinking alcohol were prohibited but not eating meat. However, prescriptions for Daoist community banquets suggest that alcohol was usually consumed there. Alcohol did not constitute as controversial and identifiable a theme within the Daoist world as meat.

What were the consequences of such a profound revolution in Chinese sacrificial and dietary practices? The militant attitude of the Heavenly Masters vis-à-vis the cults of the "obsolete breaths"—that is to say, both the local gods and the deities of the state cult—resulted in a desire for forceful conversion. For several centuries, Daoists tried to destroy the temples of "excessive cults" (*yinsi*).[94] In the long run, however, the Way of the Heavenly Masters, as it deeply transformed, gave up its confrontational stance. A good number of the proscribed cults were reintroduced. While the first texts of the Heavenly Masters affirmed that the living and the dead must each go their own way, any mixture being impure, and had almost suppressed ancestor worship, this worship returned, particularly with the great Numinous Treasure liturgy for the salvation of the dead. Increasingly from the Tang, Daoism adopted some local cults originally unrelated to Daoism.

From the Song until today, there have been two main categories of Daoists who have been embedded in various local traditions in a different way in each place: the *daoshi* 道士 (masters of the Dao) who practiced the great Numinous Treasure liturgy for the living and the dead, and the officiants of vernacular rites, often but not always called *faguan* 法官 (ritual masters), especially exorcists linked to local gods. The former frequently served as managers (*zhuchi* 住持) of temples dedicated to local deities who received blood sacrifices, but the master of the Dao did not take part in the sacrifice; the vernacular priests, for their part, actively participated in the blood sacrifices.[95] However, in many places, the master of the Dao and ritual master were the same person who officiated, depending on the requested ritual, so to speak, under two different hats.

The coexistence of two seemingly contradictory attitudes toward sacrifices to local gods illustrates the complex nature of the relationship between Chinese religion and Daoism. The latter was elitist and literate, defining itself primarily in opposition to possession cults and the sacrifices. At the same time, it was indissolubly dependent on local cultic communities. Community Daoism shaped and organized local communities but failed to impose on them its sacrificial reform and its conceptions concerning the use, sacrifice, and consumption of animals in the sense that the vast majority of cults continued to practice blood sacrifices.

Nonetheless, Daoists upheld the idea that pure sacrifice, with tea, cereals, and scriptures, was an ideal: the highest Daoist deities only received a pure sacrifice, and some cults of local gods adopted this ideal to raise their status. On the other hand, when such a reform was imposed, it failed: thus, under the Daoist emperor Song Huizong (reigned 1100–1126), some deities were promoted with Daoist titles and vegetarian cults; the deities then demanded the restitution of their old diets.[96] The local gods consuming blood were integrated into the Daoist liturgy but at a lower rank: during an offering (*jiao*), the ritual area was divided into two parts, one interior (*neitan* 內壇), where the pure breaths of the Dao received pure offerings, and the other exterior (*waitan* 外壇), where the local deities received their offerings.

Undoubtedly because of this rapprochement between Daoism and the local cults, the ideal of vegetarianism appears to have receded even for the clergy. Even though it is very difficult to trace its development, it seems in any case that the consumption of meat by Daoist priests that we see today was already common under the Song. Like the laity, the priests are vegetarians during the ritual but participate in the meat banquet, which concludes it. The exceptions, common today, have been a few vegetarian priests driven by personal conviction and particularly the Complete Transcendence (Quanzhen 全真) clergy, a Daoist order formed around 1170 whose members (at least the elite part) took vows of celibacy and strict abstention from meat and alcohol.[97] Undoubtedly, the appearance of interdictions specific to certain meats must be interpreted in this context of a predominantly nonvegetarian Daoist clergy (except Complete Transcendence) that was always anxious to follow rules of ritual purity more demanding than those observed by the surrounding population. Between the Tang and the Song,

Daoist normative texts indeed introduced various innovations in terms of dietary prohibitions. Some rules expressly prohibit the six domestic animals but allow game.[98] Other interdictions concern the meat of the animal associated with the astrological sign (*benming* 本命) of one's parents' or one's own birth year according to the twelve-animal zodiac.[99] Since game, especially deer, did not figure among the twelve animals of the zodiac, Daoists concerned about the interdiction against these twelve animals also favored its consumption.[100] But the most significant phenomenon was the formation, under the Song, of the interdiction specific to several animals, notably bovines, which will be discussed at length below.

## Sacrificial Revolutions: Buddhism

Buddhism came to China gradually from the first century of the Common Era. With it, a whole set of conceptions of salvation and devotional practices involving the use of icons and the institution of monasticism with rules of renunciation (celibacy, little individual ownership of goods, and money poverty) gradually acclimatized to Chinese society. The Buddhist discourse regarding the animal condition was not the most spectacular or the most controversial element within this vast body of new conceptions, but it nevertheless represented an important part of its ethical discourse. Unlike the Daoist discourse on this question, which was constructed above all around the question of sacrifice, its Buddhist counterpart insisted on the notions of life and retribution.[101] Whatever its form, from the smallest insect to divine beings, this life was precious: removing it generated suffering for the victim and harmful consequences for the culprit because of automatic retribution for one's actions.

Because of the primacy given to the question of the act of killing, Buddhism, even more than Daoism, distinguished the two problems posed by killing and eating meat. The first was the subject of a perfectly explicit and permanent prohibition that applied to all: it is one of the five precepts (*wujie*) for lay followers and therefore appears among the longer lists of "bodhisattva vows" and monastic precepts for monks and nuns.[102] The term used to designate it, refraining from killing (*jiesha* 戒殺), punctuated all the moral and regulatory literature. The concept was particularly illustrated by the tales of retribution, which show through precisely documented examples—therefore understood as strictly true—the terrible punishments suffered by the perpetrators of various misdeeds, including those guilty of killing animals. Already rich in Indian languages, this apologetic literature would experience considerable growth in China.[103] One of its motifs was that the ways of transmigration, impenetrable to the ordinary mind, could cause parents and relatives to be reincarnated as animals. Moreover, tales describing the reincarnation of an impious human into a duly identified animal were a common trope. Therefore, killing an animal involved the risk of killing a parent.[104]

The Buddhist doctrine of refraining from killing sparked a campaign in China. Despite its somewhat different dogmatic foundations, this campaign sometimes joined forces with Daoist proselytization in that it aimed at the sacrifices of Chinese religion, among other things. Buddhists were less likely to destroy the temples of the local gods than Daoists, but they worked to reform the cults by imposing the practice of meatless offerings. For example, the monk Pu'an 普安 (530–609) redeemed the animals intended for the sacrifice to the God of the Soil and transformed the cultic communities dedicated to the God of the Soil into "associations for refraining from killing."[105] Four centuries later, Ciyun Zunshi 慈雲遵式 (964–1032), a Tiantai 天台 monk, led a campaign to replace bloody sacrifices to local gods with vegetarian Buddhist rites.[106] As with Daoism, Buddhist attempts to convert the local gods to vegetarianism only had limited and occasional success. It was such a lost cause from the start that at the same time, cults with blood sacrifices developed in chapels within Buddhist monasteries before flourishing in their own temples.[107] If monks could not convert deities, neither could they convert the devotees of deities.

The Buddhist campaign in favor of refraining from killing could not suppress the blood sacrifices, but it nevertheless had a significant impact. Its greatest success was to have the concept of refraining from killing recognized as an orthodox value within the framework of Chinese religion. Because it partly concurred with Confucian and Daoist values, refraining from killing was accepted as a noble ideal, even if it was rarely observed to the letter.

Unlike the interdiction against killing, vegetarianism did not have a clear canonical status in Chinese Buddhism of the first centuries. The meat eater was not a priori responsible for the death of the animal, a theme that widely aroused criticism from observers who criticized as hypocritical the attitude of contemporary Buddhists who employed butchers of other faiths (e.g., Muslims) and held that butchers were the only ones to suffer the retribution generated by the act of the butchery. The Buddha, in fact, had allowed monastics to eat "meat that is pure in three ways"—namely, meat from an animal that had not been slaughtered for the monastics, which the monastics ensured by three criteria: they did not see the animal being slaughtered, they did not hear it die, and they were convinced that it was not slaughtered for them.[108] The fundamental principle here was that renunciation placed monastics in total dependence on donations from the laity for their subsistence: the monk must eat what he is given, whether it is meat or not. This rule is still observed in Theravada countries, such as Thailand, where it happens that one puts pieces of a meat dish in the alms bowl of a monk begging for his food, and the monk eats it as he must. Similarly, modern Tibetan Buddhists, for reasons relating to the ecological peculiarities of their country, tend to eat meat and condemn Chinese Buddhists, who, according to them, have adopted the heterodoxy of vegetarianism.[109] In fact, in early Chinese Buddhism, the consumption of meat by monastics is documented.

Strict vegetarianism was adopted by Chinese Buddhists at the end of a complex process involving theological, social, and economic causes. A first cause was how monasticism was organized in China (and already was in Central Asia): the daily alms round was very quickly abandoned (if it was ever practiced there), and the monasteries themselves cooked the meals of the monks, which made it more difficult to obtain "meat that is pure in three ways" even when employing lay cooks, as was the case in the large monasteries, which were richly endowed by the state and the nobility. In addition, a current of thought urged not to do anything that could harm a living being, even indirectly.[110] This trend was based on the bodhisattva precepts, which aimed to inculcate an ethical practice that went well beyond the monastic vows intended only for the preservation of one's own purity. Texts initially written in Indian languages already applied this idea to vegetarianism: this was notably the case in the *Mahāparinivāna Sūtra* 涅盤經 and *Laṅkāvatāra Sūtra* 楞伽經, probably from the first centuries of the Common Era and translated into Chinese in the fifth century.[111] These two sutras constitute the canonical foundation of vegetarianism. However, Eric Greene has shown that this commonly accepted date of the early fifth century for the "conversion" of Chinese Buddhists to vegetarianism must be considered as the end of a process already begun in the third century, when they started to use the vegetarian diet as a marker of their identity and to produce apologetic texts about it.[112] In the fifth century CE, a movement in favor of the practice of vegetarianism, no doubt spurred by the dissemination of these two sutras, spread in Chinese society. Valérie Lavoix, who has authored a very well-documented article on this phenomenon, underlines the driving role played by the laity. Some monks also preached the vegetarian cause, but it was especially noted that lay Buddhists practiced it openly and went so far as to abandon any form of meat offerings to their ancestors. There are several wills extant from this period in which the authors asked their descendants to offer them only vegetables.[113] Some Buddhists—laypeople and monastics—engaged in a campaign to apply the interdiction against killing in the broadest sense and rejected any compromise regarding the act of butchery and therefore the fact of eating meat. This campaign was ultimately successful as vegetarianism became normative among the clergy.

Several circumstances facilitated the victory of the vegetarian cause. The first, more abstract factor was a general feeling, partly aesthetic in nature and specific to the period in question, of disgust with the flesh and fascination with death, implying a rejection of meat and fish as stinking and unfit for consumption. These were very often referred to by the term *xingshan* 腥羶—that is, the foul smell of meat and fish. This feeling manifested itself as neurasthenia, even as anorexia, in a number of scholars. It was not marginal in Chinese tradition as a whole because it was commonly held that before being cooked, meat must be washed to rid it of the raw smell of blood, but in those cases, this disgust was taken further.[114] Moreover, disgust with bloody flesh made certain dried meats, especially venison, acceptable in offerings and even for everyday consumption. The substitution of more or less raw flesh with dried meat merged with Daoist dietary ideas and also the fact that dried meats were an offering of choice in the sacrifices since antiquity.

A more singular event but one that forever marked the Chinese imagination was the attempt of Emperor Wudi 武帝 of the Liang 梁 (reigned 502–549) to impose vegetarianism as a law. Wudi, a staunch and zealous Buddhist, sought to establish Buddhism as the state religion and made the strict application of prohibition against killing animals and vegetarianism one of the key elements of his policy. Wudi began in 517 by promulgating a reform aimed at suppressing animal offerings in sacrifices to imperial ancestors.[115] Having thus implemented his convictions on the level of the state, he turned to the sangha and gathered, probably in 522, a large assembly of monks to plead the cause of strict vegetarianism and sobriety for the monastics and at the same time enforce it brutally under threat of harsh sanctions against the recalcitrant. The text of this imperial plea, titled "A Tract on Renouncing Meat and Alcohol" (*Duan jiurou wen* 斷酒肉文), has since remained a reference text of Chinese vegetarianism.[116] Although the change in mores represented by monastic vegetarianism cannot be attributed to an imperial decree alone, its application during the long reign of Wudi probably helped to spread it.

The growing success of the vegetarian cause was also reflected in a more discreet but no less influential way in the composition of apocryphal texts devoted to the exaltation of vegetarianism. These texts appeared around the sixth century and were widely distributed, attested by the number of copies and their influence in painted and sculpted representations.[117] According to Françoise Wang-Toutain, who has studied these apocryphal texts, they are characterized by an unprecedented association between alcohol and meat in the Buddhist tradition. Thus, as alcohol was previously, meat became an absolute interdiction because it could pollute the body and cut off one's way to salvation. No doubt it should be added that the issue of the rejection of sacrifice, with which Daoism had already associated the rejection of alcohol and meat for a long time, contributed to the dissemination of this theme in Chinese Buddhism. The most influential apocryphal text was the *Brāhma's Net Sūtra* (*Fanwang jing* 梵網經), a text of Chinese origin but very skillfully redacted and recycling elements from earlier Indian bodhisattva vows, so much so that from the Tang until today, it has been authoritative in the whole of East Asian Buddhism in which it constitutes the most common bodhisattva vows.[118] The *Brāhma's Net Sūtra* prohibits meat, quite explicitly, in the third of its forty-eight minor commandments, unlike its Indian predecessors, which have no such rule.[119]

Vegetarianism became normative among the Chinese Buddhist clergy in the fifth and sixth centuries. It was enforced by Emperor Wudi of the Liang, but since an imperial decree would certainly not have been enough, it was also spurred by a transformation of worldviews. It has been observed ever since, although the occasional exception was mocked in anticlerical literature. Moreover, the obligation of the monastics to follow a vegetarian diet was written into the penal code.[120] Along with celibacy, vegetarianism has characterized Buddhist monasticism and set monastics apart from society.[121] These two interdictions were considered forms of asceticism confirming that the clergy was defined by the mastery of techniques of renunciation and control of the body.

## Vegetarianism and Interdiction against Killing

The history of vegetarianism and interdiction against killing animals in China is that of a debate that has continued over two millennia and whose front lines and adversaries have constantly changed. Although the Daoist and Buddhist sacrificial revolutions aimed to do away with blood sacrifices, these were never abolished. While laypeople partly carried out the Buddhist campaign for vegetarianism, it became one of the constitutive features of monasticism from the fifth and sixth centuries onward. Along with celibacy, vegetarianism and abstinence from alcohol were the characteristics of Buddhist (and Daoist) monastics that defined their purity and ability to perform certain rituals effectively, which was why laypeople supported them. The two sacrificial revolutions, which made common cause on this theme, spread the idea, already ambiguously latent in the rules of purification of the ancient sacrificial religion, that abstaining from killing and consuming meat led to ritual purity.

However, the Buddhist and Daoist project to impose this rule of purity on the whole population failed. The force of resistance of the cultic communities sacrificing to the local gods and the earth gods was greater than the force of the constraint of Buddhism and Daoism. In addition, the idea that priests, whether Buddhist or Daoist, acted as intermediaries with the sacred (and therefore, they could assume the constraints of ritual purity on their own) played against the imposition of this requirement of purity on everyone, so much so that a rule of life with a universal appeal became a rule distinguishing the professionals from the laity.

From the sixth century, the vegetarianism of the clergy no longer posed a problem. Whereas Buddhists adopted it, Daoists gradually limited it only to the times of rituals. It was the vegetarianism of the laity that was debated. The continued encouragement of vegetarianism by Buddhists and Daoists toward the populations brought about two results: on the one hand, in addition to mourning and preparations for sacrifices, the regular practice of days of fasting (*zhai*) and, on the other hand, the adoption of strict vegetarianism among some groups of zealots. On fast days, the faithful observed the interdictions at home or, if possible, met in a monastery or a sanctuary, Buddhist or Daoist, took vows of abstinence for twenty-four hours under the direction of a religious specialist, celebrated a ritual together and/or listened to sermons, and shared a simple meal. This meal was often taken before noon, as stipulated by the Vinaya, although this rule became less commonly observed as history progressed.[122]

We have already seen that Daoist precepts required abstinence from meat during celebrations but generally not from alcohol, whereas Buddhist precepts demanded both. Therefore, the days of fasting continued the celebrations of the ancient religion by replacing the sacrifice with the preparatory purification. By organizing these fasts, the monks displaced the content of the traditional celebrations and the liturgical calendar. Daoists introduced the Three Primes, days of assembly (*sanyuan*), which have remained pivotal moments in the Chinese liturgical year. Buddhists, for their part, attempted to increase further the frequency of holidays, notably by instituting the monthly Six Fast Days (on the 8th, 14th, 15th, 24th, 29th, and 30th), as well as three periods of fifteen days in the year, the first two weeks of the first, fifth, and ninth months.[123] These regular fasts recommended for all laypeople who observed at least the five precepts are attested in Indian Buddhism, but they took on considerably greater importance and prestige in China.[124] Probably from the Han or even earlier, they were added to the practice of increased devotion on the first and fifteenth days of each month (*shuowang* 朔望) when people visited temples and ate a meager diet. Around the fifth century, Daoists responded to being bested by the Buddhists by proposing even denser calendars of fasts (ten days per month) that were based on the same justification: on certain days, the gods descend among humans to monitor their behavior, and it is advisable to be particularly pious and therefore to fast on these days.[125] These fasts fulfilled several functions: they were a time of reunion between the monastics and the laity and a time of true retreat. They were also a time to socialize, as in the case of the great fasts organized at court, which were also an occasion for poetic competitions.[126]

Observance of fasting days was more of a social practice than an individual spiritual endeavor. It was sometimes even a legal obligation. Various emperors of the medieval period combined the ancient tradition of prohibiting killing on certain occasions with Buddhist and Daoist obligations of fast days and decreed the prohibition of killing a living being (humans in the context of the public executions and animals in the context of hunting or butchering) at certain times of the calendar. This tradition was resumed under the Tang, when, during almost the entire three centuries of the dynasty, killing living beings was prohibited during the three Buddhist half months and the ten Daoist monthly days so that more than one hundred days per year were fast days. In other words, the interdiction appears to have been relatively widely applied and observed.[127] Note also that the interdiction against alcohol, as important as that of meat from a Buddhist point of view (and in some Daoist texts), receded into the background among the prohibitions promulgated by the state. There were temporary prohibitions on the sale and consumption of alcohol since the Tang, but they were much less important, and they were justified, at least at the explicit level, by an economic concern (not wasting cereals) rather than an ethical one.[128]

Even after the end of the legal obligation of universal fasting after the Tang, communal fasting remained one of the structuring elements of the religious organization of the population. Indeed, even if there were always people who individually observed the days of fasting out of piety or according to a vow, these practices only took on their full meaning collectively, within the framework of devotional associations. Except for the communities of ancient Heavenly Masters, and perhaps in medieval times some outlying regions that were entirely managed (including fiscally) by large Buddhist monasteries, Chinese society was never organized collectively by a clerical religion with hierarchical authority. Indeed, Daoism and Buddhism did not function as religious institutions integrating their followers into a national organization. Each temple or monastery was perfectly independent and simply subject to the tutelage, largely symbolic, of the official administration of the clergy. Likewise, the notion of the Buddhist or Daoist laity was not exclusive. Admittedly, the first Daoist movements, especially the Way of the Heavenly Masters, very clearly distinguished their adherents, the chosen people (*zhongmin* 種民), from the general population, and this notion continued to exist after that in some sectarian Daoist groups. But from the fifth century, one can already observe a situation still current today: independent cultic communities led by ordained Daoists. Likewise, Buddhism had a rite of conversion—taking refuge in the Three Jewels and the Five Precepts—but this did not imply obedience to monks or the exclusion of non-Buddhist religious practices. There were individuals who, out of conviction, conformed their entire religious lives to Buddhist norms and may be called lay Buddhists, but they were only a minority of the population even though there were quite a few examples among the literati.

Since the clergy, in the absence of any supervisory body, could in no way impose moral rules on the population, the observance of interdictions in general, and of fasts in particular, could only be implemented within the framework of voluntary associations. These associations called *yi* 邑, *she* 社, or *hui* 會 formed the basis of Buddhist dissemination in China, financing small temples and hermitages, the erection of statues and votive stelae (*zaoxiang bei* 造像碑), the organization of rituals, sutra copying, and other pious and meritorious deeds.[129] Under the Buddhist influence, similar Daoist associations were formed, undoubtedly in parallel and in addition to the structures of the Heavenly Masters, to accomplish meritorious deeds.[130] Associations probably existed from the first centuries of the introduction of Buddhism, and they developed strongly from the fifth century. A complete typology remains to be established, but especially in the early days, there were groups of a few dozen people led by monks and/or wealthy benefactors and founded for the regular organization of pious deeds. Subsequently, under the Tang, larger and more structured groups were formed. "Associations of ten thousand people" (*wanren hui* 萬人會, a symbolic rather than actual number), for example, were based on systematic mutual aid (members contributed to cover each other's wedding expenses) and intended to be permanent since each deceased member was replaced by a new recruit. These groups appear to have constituted a fusion of purely pious and charitable associations and traditional local cultic communities. Whatever their structure and primary purpose, these groups met regularly for a fast (*zhai*). Many groups, for example, specifically worshipped a sutra or bodhisattva and, on the occasion of their community *zhai*, recited a sutra or hymns to the bodhisattva in question. These *zhai* were often organized in the monastery to which the association was attached. Monastics and lay members ate together without hierarchical distinction. The *zhai* of pious associations were an essential form of commensality in medieval China.[131]

The meager Daoist banquets organized by the associations did not differ much from their Buddhist counterparts.[132] However, a liturgical difference deserves to be highlighted, which concerns the question of leftovers. Daoists, who defined themselves in relation to the Chinese sacrificial religion, constructed their banquet as an offering of pure food to the powers and the consumption of the leftovers by humans. Buddhists, on the other hand, did not feed the buddhas—at least among the clergy and in monastic contexts. The Buddhist offerings, conceived primarily in tantric terms, consisted of giving the leftover human food to the hungry ghosts in the realm of the dead. The Buddhist meal was sanctified because it was compassionate since the leftovers were distributed to the needy.

However, the duty to share with all could only be accomplished by increasing the leftovers. This was the liturgy of the *shishi* 施食, "an offering of food," which has been fundamental in the practice of Chinese Buddhism and was adopted by Daoism. *Shishi* was usually practiced at any meal and became the center of very elaborate rituals celebrated for the salvation of suffering souls. Despite this liturgical difference, Buddhism and Daoism simultaneously institutionalized and anchored regular fasting in social practice through gatherings of devotional assemblies held in monasteries on holy days that were also days of fasting.

With the formation of the early modern organization of Chinese religion between the tenth and fourteenth centuries, devotional associations underwent a transformation. By the end of this transformation, territorial cultic communities dedicated to local gods and, in some regions, lineage temples became most important.[133] At the same time, Daoist and Buddhist monasteries' role as the centers of local religious life diminished. Expressly Buddhist or Daoist *she* or *hui* associations continued to exist, but they were in the minority. Since the Song dynasty, most religious associations, the *xianghui* 香會, have been devoted to the worship of a god rather than pious Buddhist or Daoist deeds. As a consequence of this development and the relative separation from the communal life of monasteries, which fell back on their role of training the clergy, we observe much smaller, meager banquets compared to previous times. However, the practice of fast days during major Buddhist and Daoist festivals continued, and fasting was observed almost universally for Middle Prime (Zhongyuan 中元) in the seventh month and quite frequently on the first and fifteenth days of each month; various lists of six or ten fast days every month continued to be frequently observed from medieval times to the present. In addition, in late imperial times, we find extensive calendars for fast days, mostly birthdays of various gods, within which each individual would fashion their own fasting regimen based on their devotion to specific deities. The most popular of these devotional fasts were those of Guanyin 觀音齋, of the Three Officers (Sanguanzhai 三官齋), of the Thunder gods (Leizhai 雷齋), of the Dipper (Douzhai 斗齋), and of the Ten Kings of the Hell (Shiwangzhai 十王齋).[134] Families practicing such a fast hung a sign with the inscription *zhaijie* on their door.[135] In addition, *zhaijie* was strictly observed before any collective celebration.

From the Song, the most frequent type of Buddhist association was that devoted to the cult of the Pure Land, whose members gather regularly to recite the name of Buddha Amitābha, reiterate the vow to be reborn in his Pure Land, and engage in various charitable or devotional activities.[136] They apparently observed abstinence from meat during the assemblies, but members did not necessarily take a vow of vegetarianism during ordinary times.

Another type of association that experienced a significant boom during this time was concerned with the release of living beings (*fangsheng* 放生), which became the predominant way to express the interdiction against killing (*jiesha*). The two practices, the cult of the Pure Land and life releases, were also concurrently encouraged by Buddhists who at that time founded associations composed mainly of laypeople but among which the monks of the Tiantai school played an eminent role.[137] The history of life releases has been studied by Joanna Handlin Smith. She shows that its principle was known from the earliest times of Chinese Buddhism and that it was grafted onto ancient Chinese practices of the periodic interdictions against killing animals.[138] However, only under the Song did life releases become an institutionalized practice within the framework of associations that regularly dedicated themselves to it and founded and maintained animal sanctuaries, generally within the confines of Buddhist monasteries. These sanctuaries were most often called life-release ponds (*fangsheng chi* 放生池), where fish and turtles were released, because it was the simplest form of sanctuary to manage; however, there were also sanctuaries for mammals.

The real heyday of the life-release associations was between 1580 and the end of the seventeenth century when many scholars joined and developed subtle forms of charity through life releases, which allowed them to distribute money to the poor by purchasing animals without appearing to be giving alms.[139] Life releases have remained widespread to this day. Members of these associations took an oath not to kill animals. They observed fasts during their regular assemblies, during which animals were bought and then released. In addition to these regular meetings, the practitioners of life releases organized ceremonies to generate merit on all kinds of occasions: weddings, success in their official careers, funeral rituals, or even simply when the opportunity to be able to free an animal presented itself. Prayers and poems explicitly composed on the topic of life releases are extant in large numbers. In short, from the middle through the end of the first millennium, the regular observance of vegetarian fast days according to a Buddhist and Daoist calendar was a prevalent practice imposed by the state and organized by associations hosted in monasteries. From the Song, this framework became looser, but fasts continued to be widely observed in local worship associations and extended by some to specific fasts (Guanyin, the Three Officers, etc.). Thus, practices of abstaining from killing animals such as releasing animals, Confucian rules of purity (*zhaijie*), and Buddhist and Daoist fasts had become intermingled.

## The Controversial Dimensions of Lay Vegetarianism

What about the strict, permanent observance of vegetarianism by the laity? Whereas practices such as the regular observance of fast days or life releases were strongly encouraged by monastics, strict vegetarianism had a more ambiguous status. At least since the Song, and still today, vegetarianism seems to have been more common and also more socially acceptable among women than among men.[140] There were indeed Buddhist literati (*jushi* 居士) living a life of purity while devoting themselves to teaching, meditation, and pious deeds, who observed strict vegetarianism. There were many such laymen between the fifth century and the end of the Tang, and Valérie Lavoix has shown that they played an essential role in spreading the vegetarian ideal. Such practices continued but became somewhat less common in the following periods. Peng Shaosheng 彭紹升 (1740–1796), an esteemed scholar and a devout Buddhist, was an emblematic example.[141] One of Peng's works, *Jushi zhuan* 居士傳, a collection of biographies of lay Buddhists, extensively documents the spread of vegetarianism among lay intellectuals of the Ming and Qing. This seems to have been the most common toward the end of the Ming. At that time, many individual life-release practitioners were also strict vegetarians.[142] We can estimate that the period 1550–1700 corresponds, along with that from the fifth to the eighth century and the middle of the Song dynasty, to one of the surges of the Buddhist practice among the laity, but the vegetarian ideal was always present throughout Chinese history.[143] Although it was above all an ethical issue, lay vegetarianism was formalized by a vow. Throughout Chinese history, many devout scholars who became vegetarians began this practice during a period of mourning and then decided to stick to it permanently.[144] Others took a solemn vow to heaven never to eat meat again after a life-changing experience, such as a miracle they witnessed. Vegetarianism could also be formalized by taking bodhisattva vows. Many *jushi* indeed became ordained. The large monasteries that were empowered to organize ordinations welcomed both novices, who took the precepts of the Vinaya, thus becoming monks or nuns, as well as those who took the bodhisattva vows according to the *Brāhma's Net Sūtra,* but also laypeople who took the five lay precepts (*wujie*) and also, in the case of some, those of the *Brāhma's Net Sūtra.*[145] It is likely that those who did not feel ready to practice permanent vegetarianism (or other requirements of *Brāhma's Net Sūtra*) only took the Five Precepts.

The solemn, even dramatic, nature of the vow of vegetarianism is explained by the difficulties it implied. The adoption of vegetarianism posed thorny problems, especially during banquets. Some guests felt insulted if they were served vegetables. Likewise, except for occasions attended only by vegetarians, meat was served whenever one was invited, and a host could take offense at guests declining it. Of course, the popularity of refraining from killing in the seventeenth century was also driven by the rejection of extravagant banquets.[146] Vegetarianism was easily practiced in cases in which, because of a sermon or a particularly convincing miracle, a whole family or a whole village took an oath.[147] But in other cases, vegetarianism was only easy to adopt for an individual old and prestigious enough to be able to impose his demands on the circle of his social relations, his neighbors, his colleagues, and his parents. Likewise, a vegetarian could only participate in the cult of ancestors and local cults if he was the head of the family and therefore in a position to determine the type of offering and banquet. This did happen. Vegetarian scholars from the sixteenth through the nineteenth centuries turned to solutions similar to those available to their medieval counterparts since the fifth century: vegetarian sacrifices, justified on the one hand by the wishes of the deceased and on the other hand (since everything could be justified by filial piety) by the desire not to inflict a sin on one's ancestors.[148] However, this vision was hardly accepted everywhere. A few scholars of a certain age and from wealthy and respected families, who were held in esteem for their scholarship and charitable deeds, could become vegetarian, as did Peng Shaosheng, but it was challenging for a minor scholar aspiring to a career. For the latter, the pressure to participate in banquets and "normal" sacrifices that included meat was probably insurmountable.[149]

No doubt it was for all these reasons that Buddhist monastics did not make strict vegetarianism obligatory. Zhuhong 袾宏 (1535–1615), the most famous of the monks of the Ming, was also the most militant on this subject. He was particularly known for his campaigns in favor of releasing life and refraining from killing, and his *Tract on Refraining from Killing and Releasing Life* (*Jiesha fangsheng wen* 戒殺放生文) was widely used, extensively commented on, and cited as a reference text. However, Zhuhong mainly insisted on releasing animals and refraining from killing. He certainly praised vegetarianism to his lay followers but only as an ultimate ideal. He admitted that a layperson must, under certain circumstances, eat meat, and he insisted that one should buy meat rather than have the animal slaughtered oneself.[150]

Due to the constraints required by strict vegetarianism, the pious laity adopted various forms of compromise. There were undoubtedly some strict vegetarians among the devotees of releasing life and refraining from killing, but most followed a diet that included a little meat. They practiced moderation but not the total elimination of meat. These laypeople ate meat on certain occasions (family banquets or community celebrations), and the great majority practiced sacrifices in the usual way.[151] They often reserved meat for the elderly or at least adults.[152] In addition, many abstained from consuming certain animals—an issue that will be developed further below. They chose to do what was often a simple necessity for peasants: eating meat only during collective sacrifices and celebrations.

Demands by vegetarians therefore produced tension in Chinese society. One could adopt the values and practices of Buddhism as long as they did not contradict the general values of Chinese society and religion, especially the obligations of sacrifice. Monastics were allowed to be an exception, but the practice was limited only to them. From this point of view, it is possible to compare vegetarianism with cremation, another practice strongly linked to the issue of ancestor worship and sacrifice. Like vegetarianism, cremation was permitted for monastics, who were organized like a family and had their separate mortuary and ancestral rites, but not for the laity, who were subject to the common rites. Cremation had been prohibited by law for laypeople since 962 but seems, in fact, to have been quite common during the Song and continued in a residual manner in Jiangnan until the twentieth century.[153] However, it was always considered deviant by the state and criticized in texts on "the rectification of morals." Vegetarianism, meanwhile, was never prohibited by law, but it came close to it.

Indeed, from the Song and increasingly until the middle of the twentieth century, in addition to being practiced by devout *jushi,* vegetarianism came to be associated with radical groups collectively taking the vow of forever abstaining from all meat. According to the typology employed in religious sociology, these groups were of the sectarian type, insofar as membership was voluntary, individual, militant, and possibly exclusive of other forms of religious life. According to some authors, they emerged from associations dedicated to the Pure Land mentioned above, some of which seem to have embarked on a path leading them toward greater independence from monastic institutions (even, in some later cases, to a virulent rejection of institutional Buddhism and monasticism) and toward more intense and exclusive forms of religious commitment.[154] According to others, these were two types of socioreligious organizations that evolved quite independently.[155] Be that as it may, groups of lay Buddhists calling themselves "People of the Way" (Daomin 道民 or Daoren 道人) appear to have proliferated from the first half of the twelfth century, especially in southern China. Barend ter Haar, who describes them as "activists," characterizes them by the use of generic terms employed by followers to refer to themselves (such as "People of the Way") and ordination names. They often founded temples that they managed themselves without monastics and conducted liturgical services similar to those performed by monastics but free of charge.[156] The movement was primarily Buddhist in inspiration, but there are similar Daoist groups in inspiration and organization.[157]

The oldest of the known movements in this milieu of vegetarian "activists" were the White Cloud (Baiyun 白雲) and the White Lotus (Bailian 白蓮), which were formed under the influence of proselytization by the monks Qingjue 清覺 (1043–1121) and Mao Ziyuan 茅子元 (ca. 1086/8–1166), respectively. The original status of these movements is rather vague. The Song state banned "People of the Way"–type activist groups since 1198. From that date until the end of the Yuan dynasty, there were traces of sporadic, albeit modest, repression often determined by reasons of local competition between various religious groups. The teachings of Qingjue and Mao Ziyuan were criticized by some Buddhist historiographers, although they seem to have more often been considered orthodox.[158] However, the White Cloud or White Lotus groups were generally more or less accepted in Song and Yuan society. They operated quite openly, managed temples and meeting places, and participated, with other more traditional associations or institutions, in large-scale undertakings such as the publication of Buddhist canons. They were also appreciated for their zeal in performing charitable deeds. They were distinguished from nonadherents by their strong integration into support networks and did not appear to have been socially stigmatized. However, from the beginning of the Ming, this type of group was intensely persecuted by the state. Indeed, the new religious policy of the Ming state was hostile to any form of highly structured and autonomous religious organization—except for territorial cultic communities and lineages, which were considered the political base of the regime, and monastic institutions. In addition, some uprisings associated with the term "White Lotus" (but likely unrelated to the Song- and Yuan-period White Lotus teachings) during the fourteenth and fifteenth centuries aroused in the Ming administration a rejection, tinged with panic, of this type of religiosity. Their repression, in turn, helped radicalize existing groups, which went underground.

From the sixteenth century at the latest (and probably earlier), various sectarian groups, now united by the state under the generic term of "White Lotus," experienced new transformations in their theology with the emergence of a universal mother-goddess intent on saving the chosen ones from an imminent apocalypse. This soteriology was articulated in a new kind of text, the precious scrolls (*baojuan* 寶卷). From the sixteenth century to the present day, some of these groups, following their leaders, have radicalized the millenarian eschatological discourse contained in their writings and fallen into armed insurrection. More frequently, they devoted themselves to piety and meditation and blended into the religious landscape. They were discreet since they were proscribed by the state and continued to perpetuate century after century. Although it is impossible to include all sectarian groups without clergy, from the "People of the Way" of the Song to current groups such as the Yiguan dao 一貫道 (Way of Pervading Unity), in the same category, except at a very general level, we can observe that one of their most prominent common characteristics has been the strict and permanent adherence to a vegetarian diet by all members. The practice of vegetarianism by sectarian groups was so characteristic that several later nonviolent groups were considered to be part of the "vegetarian religions" (*zhaijiao* 齋教), a term that became common and officially recognized during the Japanese occupation of Taiwan. This applies especially to Longhua hui 龍華會 (Dragon

Flower Sect), Jinchuang jiao 金幢教 (Golden Pennant Teachings), and Xiantian dao 先天道 (Way of Former Heaven), which have been particularly active in southern China and which have been studied in the field in nineteenth-century Fujian and contemporary Taiwan and Southeast Asia.[159]

The adoption of vegetarianism by these groups had a noticeably controversial dimension from the start. Indeed, as early as the Song, bureaucratic sources describe their activities as "they eat vegetables and serve demons" (*chicai shimo* 喫菜事魔).[160] Initially created in 1121 to stigmatize Manichean groups established in South China, this expression would become a leitmotif systematically used over the centuries against all sectarian groups.[161] It is likely that the reproach thus addressed combined the accusation of heterodoxy and propensity to rebel with that of isolating themselves from the surrounding society by forbidding their members to participate in cults and banquets that united the local communities.

According to the analysis of Barend ter Haar, the vow of vegetarianism was a strong gesture of religious conversion with an exclusive scope. This kind of gesture was clearly distinguished from ordinary gestures of devotion, even fervent ones (pilgrimage, donations, the organization of a ritual, daily recitation, etc.), which responded to a crisis or a need and, unlike conversion, did not engage the person in a sustained search for salvation.[162] According to ter Haar, the practice of vegetarianism, outside periods of collective *zhai,* was rare among the laity during the Song and in later periods and generally corresponded to an engagement in a sectarian group. As a result, strict vegetarianism among the laity even came to be condemned by some monks, who preferred to see the laity sinning a little by occasionally eating meat rather than sinning a lot by joining sectarian groups beyond the control of the monastics.[163]

This association of vegetarianism with membership in dissident religious groups set apart from society increased over time. An episode in 1878 illustrates the suspicion surrounding the refusal to eat meat that was deeply ingrained in the worldview of China's ruling elites. That year, a sectarian group was identified and convicted by the magistrate of Yangzhou (Jiangsu Province). Sometime later, this same magistrate met former members of the dissolved group who told him that they practice recitations of the name of the Buddha (*nianfo* 念佛) and vegetarianism. He became angry, saying that it was prohibited, had pork dishes prepared, and forced them to eat these in public.[164] In doing so, the magistrate somewhat exceeded the penal code and jurisprudence, which, despite their strict prohibition of vegetarian "sects," added that it was permitted to observe vegetarianism on a strictly individual basis (without forming a congregation).[165]

One should note that all of these groups prohibited alcohol as much as meat, but meat alone became the subject of controversy. Abstinence from alcohol was taken for granted as a corollary of vegetarianism and was rarely practiced alone. Nevertheless, there was a sectarian group, the Zaili 在理 (Way of Abiding Principle), which distinguished itself by imposing strict temperance on its members and campaigning for the treatment of alcoholics and opium addicts.[166] This group, founded around the eighteenth century, mainly developed in northern China from 1850.

With the emergence of anti-superstition movements linked to the political modernization of China since the last years of the nineteenth century, the practices of vegetarianism and *zhaijie* were opposed by the state and certain social groups and deemed contrary to rationality and science. However, at the same time, they were encouraged, much more actively than before, by a Buddhism that tried to reinvent itself as an autonomous religion and therefore wanted to define practices specific to a Buddhist laity, as well as newly formed animal rights movements.[167] It is in this context that we must understand the widespread observance of vegetarianism among the middle class since the 1980s, especially in Taiwan, and the proliferation of vegetarian restaurants.[168] Similar phenomena can be observed in other Buddhist countries, where lifestyles formerly reserved for the clergy have become popular, such as a vegetarian diet or the practice of daily meditation.

Our brief historical overview of the relationship that Chinese culture had with animals and meat—through the themes of sacrifice, interdiction against killing animals, and vegetarianism—obviously does not do justice to the complexity of the subject. My goal was to outline, based on our current, certainly incomplete knowledge, the issues and the themes around which these relationships were formed. From a general perspective, we must privilege the main social actors, and this is why I focused on the moral and religious authorities that tried to shape the debate (the clergy of the three institutional religions, Confucianism, Buddhism, and Daoism) and on the groups that define communal practices (families and lineages, pious associations, and cultic communities, which all observed the interdiction against meat at certain times, and sectarian groups, which observed it permanently). Other factors were, of course, local contexts, short-term ethical-religious fashions, and individual choices.

In summary, we can observe that vegetarianism and interdiction against killing animals form an object in itself, nourishing debates and polemics, defining the identity of social groups but also that they constitute a case study, an "analytical category" as sociologists call it, that opens a new vantage point for a larger social history of religion and morality in China. Vegetarianism is illuminating because of its ambiguous status. From the twelfth century, it became associated with highly controversial lay movements, but it was not in principle discredited for this reason. As observed by a missionary writing in 1865, "The feeling that the eating of flesh is sensual and sinful, or quite incompatible with the highest degree of sincerity and purity, is a very popular one among the Chinese of all classes."[169] It was considered a noble practice among some—Buddhist monastics, the Daoist Complete Transcendence clergy, and some literati *jushi*—but not among others. It constituted a logical extension of practices (e.g., the vow of abstaining from killing animals and abstinence from meat on regular days) that were widely accepted in society until the turn of the twentieth century, when they were criticized by some intellectuals and/or revolutionaries who included them, with good reason, among the core customs of the traditional society that they wanted to destroy. Vegetarianism is both the ultimate expression of recognized values (benevolence toward all beings, frugality) and contrary to the foundations of Chinese culture, the sacrificial religion. Therefore, in every circumstance, Chinese attitudes toward sacrifice and meat result from a compromise between divergent yet orthodox religious ideals. There is a chic vegetarianism that developed a refined cuisine playfully imitating meat and another vegetarianism that is radical and militant.[170]

This tension between ideals that are partly contradictory and stem from the inclusive and noncentralized nature of Chinese religion is creative. It pushed Chinese society to find solutions that may seem like compromises but demonstrate considerable originality and inventiveness. It is from this perspective that I will analyze the emergence and durability of the beef taboo. But before entering the "bovine" part of this book, I would like to say a few more words on the question of the roles of the three institutional religions in the definition of moral discourse in the case of the relation to animals and meat.

Although it is impossible to consider any of the three institutional religions in a pure, primitive state, each has contributed a coherent overall project of its own to China. However, each was obliged to amalgamate: enmeshed in Chinese religion, which included and exceeded them, Confucians, Daoists, and Buddhists continued to set forth their project but increasingly adapted Chinese religion to their surroundings, both in terms of liturgical practices and ethical discourse. Therefore, their respective texts must be understood both within the continuity of their own tradition and within their adaptation of overarching discourses. The authors of these texts always sought to emphasize their Confucian, Buddhist, or Daoist specificity because the coexistence of the Three Teachings is not syncretism, and the three were respected as long as they maintained their identity. At the same time, they conformed to consensual values. One of the most striking aspects of the formation of Chinese religion in its early modern state between the tenth and fourteenth centuries was the emergence of a common morality and social values. Too quickly, sinologists tend to identify this common morality as

Confucian. It is in reality consensual and includes important elements of Buddhist and Daoist origins that are linked in particular to retribution and reward for one's actions and to refraining from killing animals. Likewise, all Chinese discourse during the second millennium based on retribution and reward for one's actions should not be interpreted as a Buddhist discourse. It is an orthodox discourse of Chinese religion.

The fundamentally reprehensible nature of killing an animal (except for prescribed sacrifices), slaughtering or fishing, and consuming meat is precisely one of the features of common morality in Chinese religion. Reading texts of all kinds strongly suggests that for the literate elites killing animals was widely regarded as a necessary evil (to feed essential meat to the sick or elderly or for sacrifices) but not as a natural act. The texts in which scholars defended an unyielding Confucian position and criticized Buddhist practices regarding respect for animal life were on the defensive, recognized the validity of the *jiesha* ideal, and only criticized its misinterpretation by Buddhists. One of the consequences of this attitude was that the person of the butcher became a despised character. Edifying, anecdotal, and novelistic literature was full of butcher characters, represented as detestable sinners who sometimes converted and abandoned their profession.

One of the ways to look at the ethical consensus on animals, and arguably a particularly compelling way for a Western reader, is to read the reactions from the first Western residents in China under the Ming, the Jesuit missionaries, and the Chinese feedback. One of the first, Matteo Ricci (1552–1610), opposed the Chinese conception of animals as living beings similar to humans and to whom therefore benevolence is due. He expounded to the Chinese the then-prevalent Christian position, according to which animals were created by God to serve humans and that it was lawful to kill and consume them according to one's needs. At the same time, Ricci refuted the notion of reincarnation. The Chinese exposed to the theses of Ricci and his coreligionists and successors reacted strongly. Their refutations argued that benevolence toward animals was proof of the superiority of Chinese civilization and that, conversely, Ricci's indifference showed the barbarism of Christian civilization.[171]

The Confucian discourse on animals developed, for example, in poems expressing compassion for suffering animals (beasts of burden in pain, animals destined for slaughter understanding the fate reserved for them, wild animals mistreated out of pure cruelty). More remarkably, many such poems were included in 1869 in an anthology of poetry on political and social themes that reflected an uncompromising attitude toward Buddhism and Daoism.[172] The same has been true of novels since the sixteenth century that expressed the moral positions adopted by a large part of the population. This is, for example, the case with *Passage to the East* (*Dongdu ji* 東度記), which recounted the life of the Buddhist patriarch Bodhidharma but reinterpreted him as a hero of common morality. An important part of *Passage to the East* was devoted to the defense of animal life and the promotion, though not of vegetarianism, at least of a strict limitation of the consumption of meat.[173] Finally and above all, the theme of animal life occupies a vital role in morality books (*shanshu* 善書), which expressed the common morality of Chinese religion. We will have an opportunity to return to these texts in detail. The moral discourse changed its tone depending on whether it was expressed in a more or less lofty genre or a more or less classical language, but it remained similar in its fundamental themes. While anecdotes and plays portrayed the cruelty and abjection of butchers (whose conversion was all the more edifying), the regulations of the great lineages prohibited their children from embracing despicable professions, including that of a butcher. The tone changed, but the discourse remained the same.[174]

However, while they all expounded the common morality, each religious authority wished to signal its difference. So whereas Buddhists and Daoists had no trouble emphasizing canonical justifications for the interdiction against killing animals, constructing Confucian respect for animal life was a complex task. This work was carried out in several ways, either by selecting from the classics passages that could justify the contemporary practice, sometimes even if it meant interpreting them flagrantly against the grain, or by referring not to the letter but the feeling (*qing* 情). The latter approach was particularly prevalent among the proponents of an innate, instinctive morality, a flourishing trend in the sixteenth and seventeenth centuries. According to such thinkers, animals were, like disadvantaged humans, the very object of the cardinal virtue of benevolence (*ren*), which was all the greater when it was sensitive to all forms of suffering. And since their relationship with animals was anchored in a fundamental Confucian virtue, they rejected any Buddhist or Daoist contribution to it.[175]

The singularity of the Confucian discourse, apart from its insistence on the moral superiority of the attitude based on the virtue of benevolence (as opposed to the Buddhist attitude based on the fear of retribution for one's actions), lies above all in its practical consequences. Indeed, the Confucian practice of vegetarian sacrifices, although it existed, has always been an exception. Confucianism proposed that killing and the consumption of meat be limited to cases in which a moral requirement even greater than benevolence—namely, filial piety—demanded it for sacrifices and as vital carnal nourishment necessary for elderly and sick parents.[176] Of course, this Confucian interpretation of the morality of abstaining from killing animals attracted Buddhist and Daoist criticism, which retorted that filial piety required not committing crimes in the name of parents. In response, Confucianism criticized as hypocritical the compromise proposed by Buddhists and Daoists—namely, the practice of periodic fast days. An editorial in the daily *Shenbao* 申報 published in 1879 developed this theme:[177] *zhaijie* was common to all Chinese religion and was fundamentally good and moral, but it was perverted by those who practiced it to gain merit. Moreover, although the ancient principle of *zhaijie* was to purify the mind and body, some were content to display their abstention from meat on these days while indulging in all kinds of immoral practices.

In conclusion, Chinese religion, which took shape gradually, included among the elements of its common morality respect for animal life and abstinence, as much as possible, from meat; this formed on initially separate bases—on the one hand, the times of abstinence of the ancient religion and, on the other hand, the Daoist and Buddhist sacrificial revolutions. This ideal nevertheless contradicted the practice of the sacrificial religion and thus, naturally, the taste of a good part of the privileged classes for meat. The moral authorities, the clergy of the Three Teachings, proposed compromise solutions formulated differently in the three cases but that differed only in details: general abstention from killing, the regulation of meat consumption, and periods of complete abstinence. Strict vegetarianism remained ambiguous because it ran counter to sacrifice and the obligations of commensality and had possible associations with sectarian groups. The beef taboo, which did not emanate from any of the three moral authorities, appeared against the background of this creative tension.

# 2 Chinese Cattle as Political Animals

Chinese attitudes toward animal life and flesh were determined by a complex set of prescriptions and requirements specific to various moral and religious authorities. Moreover, this variety of discourses on animals had to be accommodated to social practice, which, in China as elsewhere, has never merely considered animals as a category in the abstract but distinguished between different species. The situation of cattle in Chinese society is unique in that they were undoubtedly the species among all animals that were the object of the most significant and developed discourse.

This second chapter on the beef taboo considers the concrete situation of cattle by shifting the focus from ethics to economics and politics. After introducing the different subspecies of cattle, their domestication, and the history of their use in China, I address the issue of the state's policy concerning cattle and its effect on beef consumption, whether gastronomic or religious. I investigate the material and economic aspects of cattle in China while leaving aside the ethical and symbolic aspects for the moment.

## Bovines in China

All the texts referenced in this book refer to *niu,* a generic term for all bovines. This taxonomical category constitutes a vast subfamily belonging to the Bovidae family, including sheep, goats, antelopes, and so forth. Within the subfamily of bovines, there are seven genera of the genus *Bos,* including taurine cattle (*Bos taurus*), zebus (*Bos indicus*), yaks (*Bos grunniens*), and others; the genus *Bubalus,* including water buffaloes (*Bubalus bubalis*);[1] bison, and so forth. There are essentially three genera of cattle common in China through history, one belonging to the genus *Bubalus,* the water buffalo (*shuiniu* 水牛), and two belonging to the genus *Bos,* the "yellow ox" (*huangniu* 黃牛)[2] and the yak (*maoniu* 犛牛), which lives at high altitudes in Tibet or Mongolia, as well as crossbreeds of yaks and taurine cattle (*pianniu* 犏牛). Other species of the genus *Bos* have been attested, but they played much less important roles. The zebu, very common in

India, seems to have existed in some regions of western and southern China during the first millennium CE.[3] The domesticated banteng (*Bos javanicus*) has been present for two thousand years in the southernmost areas of present-day China, and the wild gaur (*Bos gaurus*) is found in the less populated parts of Yunnan.[4] The yak has been well known to the Chinese for a long time, but it has never been acclimatized into the agricultural regions of China. Therefore, the term "cattle" here refers to taurine cattle and water buffaloes. A 1991 census shows approximately 103 million cattle in China of which 79 million were taurine cattle and 22 million water buffaloes.[5]

Although they were well aware of the differences in anatomy, character, and even qualities of meat produced by taurine cattle and water buffaloes, the Chinese have always considered the two essentially the same category of animals. In particular, both the bovine policy and the discourse of the taboo have never made the slightest distinction between taurine cattle and water buffaloes. This attitude is different from that of Indian civilization, which sanctified the zebu but not the water buffalo.[6]

## Animal Domestication and Use

Cattle are still found in the wild in some southern border regions of mainland China, and wild cattle were common in Taiwan until the mid-nineteenth century. However, for most Chinese, contact with wild cattle became very rare by the end of the first millennium, and cattle were essentially domestic animals.

In China and elsewhere, the issue of the domestication of animals has been the object of scholarly controversies regarding dates, geographical centers, and motivations. Some specialists favor the thesis of single centers from which the technique of domestication for each species was disseminated, while a few others suggest simultaneous domestication processes in different places. Nowadays, it is commonly held that the domestication of many species occurred in the Near East (pigs, cattle, and sheep/goats), the Asian steppes (horses and perhaps dogs), and Southeast Asia (chickens). Debates about domestication centers have been intertwined with cultural issues linked to national pride and must be viewed with caution. Chinese scholars have indeed been trying to gather evidence of the early domestication in China of species, such as cattle and dogs, that other scholars believe were domesticated elsewhere. Be that as it may, the case of taurine cattle remains disputed as to whether there was a simple diffusion from the Near East to China or the domestication in China of a species that would have been somewhat different from that domesticated in the Near East; however, it seems likely that the water buffalo was domesticated in central China.

Regarding the period of domestication, we should remember that this was a long and gradual process. The data collected by archaeologists—whichever way they have been interpreted regarding the geographical origin and the spread of domestication—show that the first domestic animals in China were pigs, dogs, and chickens from the beginning of the early Neolithic (sixth to seventh millennia BCE).

Cattle can be attested shortly after that in sites from the sixth millennium.[7] Taurine cattle and water buffaloes were domesticated separately—water buffaloes probably a little later than taurine cattle. The water buffalo was present in northern China at the end of the Neolithic period, when the climate was hotter and more humid than today. Thus, the two species, both representing cattle for the Chinese, coexisted early on.

The primary reasons that led to the domestication of various animal species have been the subject of scientific debates: the consumption of meat, the need for sacrificial victims, and labor (hunting, agriculture, portage). It seems that raising animals for use as sacrificial meat was the primary motivation for the upkeep of pigs, cattle, sheep, and even dogs in Neolithic China into late antiquity. As prestige animals, only horses, first harnessed and then ridden, were an exception. Horses were sacrificed in funeral contexts (buried with their masters), but this use stemmed from their function as prestigious animals rather than as animals raised to be sacrificed. This was followed by the diversification of the uses of domesticated animals, which led to the development of a domestication system—that is, a complete and coherent range of diverse uses by humans of available animals for labor, food, and raw materials.[8]

Such a notion contradicts the widespread idea that China was a civilization without domestic animals because abundant and cheap human labor made animal labor unnecessary, that thus animals were largely absent from villages, and that instead, emphasis was placed on mythical and imaginary animals such as dragons. A list of animal uses observed for several centuries shows that such an image is false.[9] Several species were used extensively for meat, portage, and agricultural work. As elsewhere, the domestication system did not use all animals or employ all the possible uses of each animal. It was selective, partly due to ecological or socioeconomic constraints and partly due to cultural choices. In particular, in the case of cattle, some uses were favored over others.

The use of cattle in China fell into three broad categories: as working animals, as a source of food, and as a source of nonfood materials. Nonfood products mainly included dung, tallow, leather, sinews, and horns. The dung, as well as the (charred) bones, hooves, and hair, were used as fertilizer. Cattle feces were more popular than that of horses and pigs.[10] Cattle tallow was used to make soap and candles. The history of manufacturing and using leather in

China is not well known; at least, it has not, to my knowledge, been the subject of scientific studies. Cattle were never raised solely for this purpose. Instead, it was common to recover the skin from the carcass for monetary gain if one did not bury the deceased animal. The skin of cattle has been used since ancient times to make glue. The best-known uses of bovine leather, as well as that of sheep and horses, from the Han period to the twentieth century, were all military: the wet and whole hides were used to cover and protect the wooden towers against burning arrows. Hide was processed to craft armor, shields, and drums. Leather was also used to make saddles, bridles, and straps for harnessing horses.[11] The tendons of cattle and other species were used to make the strings of bows and crossbows. The horns served as the handles of certain weapons.[12] During the Tang and Song, peasants were to provide the state with the skin, tendons, and horns of their dead cattle as one form of taxation.[13] Historical sources mention that in exceptional cases, peasants had to kill cattle to be able to pay these particular taxes.[14] At the very least, trade in these strategic materials was strictly prohibited in times of war. By contrast, leather was rarely used for clothing until the twentieth century, but there were some utilitarian objects, such as boxes made of lacquered leather. Little is known about the tanning industry, which undoubtedly served the military. From the Ming period onward, this trade became the specialty of Muslims, notably the Chinese-speaking group called Hui 回. Hui furriers make sheepskin clothing, felt, and various products for civilian use, but until very recently, Hui tanners mainly sold bovine leather products to the military and businesses (e.g., leather straps for machines).[15]

The second use of cattle was their slaughter for meat in sacrificial or ordinary contexts. The consumption of beef in China is attested by archaeological evidence from the earliest times. As early as in texts from the Han dynasty, the entire Chinese medical and dietetic tradition accorded beef a high nutritional value and indicated no inconvenience to its use except for certain specific associations with other food or in some contexts. Consumption was fairly high among the social elites until the Song. It decreased sharply afterward due to the taboo but persisted to some extent as socially marginal, although not necessarily quantitatively so. We will see in detail how exactly in the following chapters.

Because of its cost and its high value in the gastronomic and medical traditions, beef was also a prestigious food considered invigorating and succulent. It was often distributed to officials (during the Han) and particularly to soldiers as an encouragement or reward. Moreover, the specific term designating these gifts (*kao* 犒) etymologically refers to cattle. In this usage, beef is always associated with alcohol, which was also an exceptional food item. Official stories and literary sources frequently mention such banquets during which beef and alcohol were distributed to the military.[16] The expression "to kill a bovine with a club" (*zhuiniu* 椎牛) was often used to designate these banquets.

The use of beef for sacrifices was more important than the distribution to the soldiers. As we have seen, bovines have always been the most valued sacrificial animal in Chinese religion. They were sacrificed in countless numbers and multiple contexts in antiquity.

Shang period documents mention a thousand bovines sacrificed at one time.[17] We must understand such figures in the context of an ancient society of breeders in which the prestige of the chiefs was linked to the possession of large herds and therefore to the possibility of offering sacrifices (and obtaining divine favors) beyond the reach of other people. The sacrificial use of cattle subsequently evolved through a dual process that occurred over the long term, particularly from the tenth to twelfth century: the state reduced the sacrificial use of cattle and attempted to exclude commoners from such a practice.

We must not forget milk and other dairy products as well as other bovine products considered as materia medica. Even though it is well known that in the contemporary period, the Chinese consume very few dairy products since so many of them lack lactase (the enzyme present in the digestive system allowing easy digestion of milk), that was not always the case. Françoise Sabban has shown that even though raw milk was rarely consumed in China, other dairy products made from bovine and also sheep milk, such as fresh or dry fermented milk since at least the Han and curds since the seventh century, have always occupied an important place in the culinary system and were valued for their health benefits.[18] It is likely that dairy consumption decreased from the Song, but it persisted at least as an ingredient in the cuisine popular among the upper classes. Less culinary than purely medical, we should also mention a product highly sought after in pharmacopeia, bovine bezoar (*niuhuang* 牛黃), a concretion of hair and plant debris formed in the stomachs of ruminants.[19]

The use of cattle as working animals comprises three aspects: the traction of vehicles, the operation of machines, and work in the fields. The use of oxcarts seems to have preceded the agricultural use of cattle. Oxcarts are already mentioned in the *Book of Odes* (*Shijing* 詩經), consisting of poems from the beginning to the middle of the first millennium BCE. These chariots had commercial and military use but were of humble status compared to those with teams of horses from around the middle of the second millennium BCE, probably later than oxcarts. Officials rode in horse-drawn carriages, while private individuals could only travel in an oxcart. Oxcarts frequently appear throughout history but have played only a minor role since the Ming. Oxen were largely replaced by teams of horses or donkeys, as well as by camels in North China.[20] Cattle were also hitched to waterwheels in hydraulic systems and to mills or presses.

Their use for work in the fields, in particular plowing, has been the primary and emblematic function of cattle in China for more than two thousand years, which is why both texts dealing with agricultural economics and morality literature mention "plow cattle" (*gengniu* 耕牛) most frequently. This did not designate a species or a category of animals but was a sort of laudatory epithet extending to all cattle. Thus, most cattle work consisted of plowing the land before sowing. They were also used for harrowing, sowing (using sowing plows), and threshing. Both taurine cattle and water buffaloes were used for plowing. The latter, which prefer to live in a humid environment, were much more suited to work in flooded rice fields, but oxen could also work in rice fields.[21] Oxen plowed either alone or in pairs, while water buffaloes always worked alone. Whereas one finds only cattle in the flooded rice fields, dry agriculture in the north also employed mules and donkeys, but the latter never challenged the supremacy of cattle in this area.[22] The use of equines (horses, mules, donkeys) for agriculture and portage developed relatively late, at the latest since the fifteenth century. They came to assist but not to supplant bovines in tasks for which the latter had the monopoly.

When cattle began to be used for agricultural labor has been the subject of debate. Cattle had been domesticated for meat long before being used for traction. The first forms of agriculture in Chinese prehistory, which were not very extensive, did not require the use of animal power. The first texts attesting to the practice of towed plowing and the use of plow cattle date from only the very end of antiquity, one or two centuries after the spread of iron tools. During the Han, there were still regions where plowing was said to be performed by human labor alone.[23] The introduction of towed plowing seems to date back to the fourth or third century BCE and became widespread during the Han, when the first figurative representations appeared.[24] During the Han, the Ritual of the Spring Ox also emerged, which was linked to the first plowing that opened the agricultural cycle of the year.[25] This important and amply documented ritual, observed both at court and in the countryside, was one of the most striking representational illustrations of the central role of cattle in Chinese agriculture. The earth was "opened" by the first plowing just after the New Year. During the Han, the bovine was then butchered and divided, but soon after that period, the live bovine was replaced by an earthen effigy. The image of the spring ox as a prop for divination that presages the coming year was found in all the almanacs.[26]

Be that as it may, the role of cattle in plowing quickly established itself and led to an increase in the size of farms as early as the Han. Subsequently, the Chinese state has always considered cattle herds essential for agriculture.

## Cattle Farming

The Chinese were thus familiar with all the possible uses of cattle, but for reasons related to ecological and economic constraints as well as cultural choices, they favored one among them: plowing. This choice dictated how livestock farming developed. As Michel Cartier has shown, one of the unique features distinguishing the Chinese agricultural economy from that of Europe is that the former separated "the farming of animals intended for human consumption and the care given to work animals."[27]

The characteristics of cattle farming in China since the advent of plow cattle a little over two thousand years ago are dictated by various factors, first and foremost, socioeconomic constraints linked to the organization of the agricultural economy. In medieval times, sizable herds of cattle existed on the large aristocratic estates with significant human and animal resources and infrastructure. However, this model of agrarian economy disappeared toward the end of the Tang and gave way to a pattern of small properties operated by peasants who owned or rented the land.[28] Even though the agricultural land market was very active throughout the second millennium, the ideal of the small family farm managed by peasant owners and inherited from father to son was constantly promoted and defended by the Chinese state from the Song until the beginning of the twentieth century. These small farms required no more than one or two work animals at most. That said, during and after the Song, there were still larger estates with a few heads of cattle that they used or rented to less fortunate peasants. These small herds could produce calves, the sale of which constituted a significant profit for their owners. Descriptions of farms with stables and appropriate feed in books on techniques and agricultural economy likely emerged from this context.[29] Most peasants with one or two bovines rarely built a cowshed but instead were content with a pen and neither grew nor bought fodder crops. At least during the Song, some areas were rich in cattle, particularly the water buffaloes of Guangdong and Guangxi, which the peasants would sell in the regions farther north in the winter.[30]

Another case of quantitatively important livestock farming was that of imperial herds. Throughout the dynasties, from antiquity until 1911, the court ensured its cattle supply for meat consumption, sacrifices, and dairy products by maintaining its own herds managed directly by an administration.[31] These herds were often divided between traditional livestock farming areas, notably in the northern steppes,[32] and imperial domains closer to the capital, where the animals could be taken quickly to the palace. During the Qing, about twenty thousand animals belonging to the court grazed in Chahar and present-day Liaoning (northeast of Beijing). However, these examples of large cattle herds were exceptions. From the tenth century, the great majority of cattle seem to have been distributed among peasants with only one or two animals together on a farm, used only for labor in the fields.

This fragmented organization of cattle farming, in which animals were scattered between multiple farms, was also partly due to ecological constraints. The Han heartland, especially as it was developed by agriculture, had only a limited number of rich pastures. The cultivation of all the hills, a gradual process that culminated between the sixteenth and eighteenth centuries, further reduced the land available for grazing. Animals, especially cattle, can graze on hills or in fields after the harvest (fallow periods practically disappeared during the first millennium), but this did not allow large herds to be maintained throughout the year. The livestock farming that subsisted in a densely populated environment was limited to enclosures where a small number of animals were kept (allowing all the excrement to be recovered as fertilizer). The animals would go out to graze only on occasion.[33] This was the case with working cattle and with sheep farmed for meat, which can still be observed today in Jiangnan.[34] Such livestock farming was particularly challenging in the case of large animals such as cattle, mainly since very few fodder plants were cultivated.[35] A text from the late Ming mentions a situation in Jiangnan where animals could not go out to graze and where "cattle are fed with rice grits, hay, and beans." By contrast, the text also describes some regions in the northwest where extensive livestock farming was possible.[36]

Indeed, throughout history, the most favorable regions for livestock farming were the borderlands, especially in the north—present-day Inner Mongolia, Manchuria, Gansu, and so forth. However, control over these regions switched back and forth: they were sometimes dominated by Chinese empires and sometimes by nomadic political entities. For a significant part of history, trade contacts between these livestock farming regions and agricultural China were limited and regulated. In addition, herding was practiced there not by the Han Chinese but by various ethnic peoples—Mongols, Tibetans, and Uyghurs from the Yuan onward. These livestock farming peoples have always engaged in the animal trade with China, but until the very recent past, they have mainly been concerned with horses. The Chinese do not appear to have many imported animals from their nomadic neighbors for meat or as working animals.[37] However, since the sixteenth century, there was a cattle trade organized by Chinese Muslims, which we will discuss later. Since the Ming, the Hui, particularly in northwestern China, were herders of sheep and cattle.[38] Moreover, they founded commercial companies that imported cattle, horses, and camels from Mongolia as work animals or for butcher shops in large cities, especially Beijing.[39] But this trade, while important locally, only involved the big cities close to the livestock farming regions and did not affect the more southern areas.

In short, since the tenth century, few large herds existed in China owned by breeders who made a living from them. The vast majority of cattle were owned individually by peasants for whom they constituted working equipment and an important asset. The family owning a bovine often had a child take the animal to graze in the hills or the wastelands between the fields. The cowherd is a character in Chinese folklore, and the romantic image of the little boy reclining on the back of his water buffalo was a reality of the Chinese countryside.[40] Often, the cowherds brought together cattle belonging to several families. On this occasion, the rare uncastrated males could impregnate the females. Families had either a male or a female; both were suitable for work in the field. Females were preferred only insofar as they could give birth to calves and thus save the cost of purchasing a new animal when the previous one died. Calves could also be sold to a neighbor or a traveling cattle dealer.[41] Cows usually were not milked. When there was a calf, it was allowed to suckle. Peasants did not typically consume dairy products, which were only of interest to an elite cuisine supplied by a few specialized producers. Often there was no cowshed, but cattle spent the night in enclosures under the awnings of the house, which made theft relatively easy. Even though livestock farming in the full sense was almost nonexistent, the peasantry nevertheless practiced veterinary science and also had evaluation techniques (*xiangniu fa* 相牛法), especially for choosing a bovine to purchase,[42] a topic about which many manuals circulated in the countryside.

The principle of one head of cattle per peasant family was an ideal that did not always correspond to reality. The density of cattle in relation to the cultivated land varied according to human and economic geography. In areas of dry agriculture in North China, farms were larger, and the density of cattle was lower. The densely populated areas, particularly the Yangzi valley from the Song onward, were characterized by small farms, high-yield agriculture (no fallow period but two or even three harvests per year), and a greater density of cattle. In addition, wet rice cultivation tended to require more cattle labor. However, population growth, especially from the sixteenth century onward, which was not accompanied by a similar expansion of the arable land, made agricultural labor cheap and did not necessitate increased reliance on animal labor. On very small farms, it was not profitable to keep working animals. Therefore, some sources describe plowing by hand and justify this practice from an economic point of view.[43]

However, even though the ratio of cattle per human population decreased between the Song and the beginning of the twentieth century, the ratio between cattle and cultivated land remained stable. That is to say that before mechanization, Chinese agriculture relied heavily on animal labor—cattle in particular. At the start of the twentieth century, there was, on average, one head of cattle for 1.4 ha. In the 1930s, for one hundred farms, there were twenty-two water buffaloes, forty oxen, seven horses, seven mules, and eighteen donkeys—in other words, a little less than one animal per farm.[44] This figure did not decrease in the twentieth century despite mechanization and collectivization from the 1950s; it has even significantly increased since the return to individual farms in the early 1980s. Taiwan is an exception since the strong mechanization of agriculture has practically eliminated working cattle.[45]

Although animal labor was generally considered essential for work in the fields, it was quantitatively quite limited and concentrated during the year, in particular during the plowing season in spring and/or autumn, depending on the number of harvests per year. It comprised ten to fifty days per year, depending on the crop type.[46] Because of the relatively few days of labor per year and the cost of purchasing cattle, various types of rental and collective ownership of animals were quite frequent. There were already instances during the Song.[47] Rental was based on a simple principle: a well-to-do farmer, who owned one or more heads of cattle, rented them by the day to poorer farmers. There were also commercial or charitable institutions that were dedicated to the rental of cattle. Buddhist and Daoist monasteries frequently played this role during the Tang and Song, when these institutions generally served not only as spiritual centers but also as centers of economic services for rural communities. The monasteries functioned as granaries, grain and money banks, pawn shops, and cattle rental services. Cattle owned by monasteries and rented out were called "eternal cattle" (*changsheng niu* 長生牛).[48] As for types of collective ownership, they resembled cooperatives that bought and maintained cattle with mutual funds. The state also rented cattle to peasants, as we will see below.

In such circumstances in which ownership of the herd was split between multiple individual owners, peasants had to regularly obtain a new animal when theirs died or when it had finished its career after ten to fifteen years of working. The exceptions were the imperial herds and sometimes the state and monastic herds or peasants' cows that gave birth to calves that their owners could keep. The presence of intermediaries who could buy and sell live animals was therefore necessary. These intermediaries had a bad reputation because they were occasionally involved in illegal practices (notably the slaughtering of animals when the carcass sold for the price of meat was worth more than the live animal) and also because they induced the undesirable effects of free trade (in particular moving livestock out of one province if the price of cattle was higher in a neighboring province). Moreover, it is rare to find a country where livestock dealers are highly esteemed. The intermediaries nevertheless played an essential role, and the dismantling of livestock farming explains why, from the Song, cattle were the object of transactions in a rural economy that was already partly integrated and monetized.

Itinerant cattle dealers and brokers, who paid the magistrates commercial taxes on the sale of animals, were therefore at the center of an interregional cattle market. They roamed the countryside, buying calves and old cattle unfit to continue working and selling young, healthy animals. Despite the proscriptions described below, numerous anecdotes show that they also participated in the butchery trade by selling sick or old animals for slaughter.[49] In some cases, they also appear to have sold dairy products.[50]

These reflections on cattle in China demonstrate a point that Michel Cartier has already highlighted. Rather than being a mere instrument of work, cattle were an asset for peasant families. Indeed, even though they were essential during the brief plowing season, they also constituted an asset during the remainder of the year that the family could liquidate more easily than the land.[51] Moreover, the cost of purchasing a bovine was relatively stable over the long term, apart from regional differences and periods of crisis or shortage. According to Cartier, "on average over the longue durée," it was around six hundred liters of grain or half of the annual harvest of a small family farm.[52]

From this overview of cattle farming in China before the twentieth century, it is clear that livestock farming for meat was virtually absent. Despite the prohibitions that already existed, the aristocracy of the medieval period and the Tang dynasty likely maintained sizable farms for meat, but this type of farming disappeared along with the aristocracy and their large estates.[53] Since the Song, some wealthy landowners were occasionally able to discreetly keep a few animals for meat or to supply dairy products[54] but only for consumption within the family. The Chinese have long been familiar with the practice of extensive cattle farming for meat, which they observed among neighboring peoples integrated into or in regular contact with the empire, such as the Mongols and Tibetans. They were also confronted with the practice when Westerners settled in large numbers in commercial ports, notably in Shanghai, from 1840 onward and introduced livestock farming to meet their beef needs. The Chinese term to designate Western cattle was "cattle to eat" (*cainiu* 菜牛). This term appears in documents from the Song dynasty[55] but was rarely used from the Song until the nineteenth century. It was occasionally used to designate animals reared in grazing areas and imported by the Hui to towns in northern China for slaughter.[56] The term most common today, "meat cattle" (*rouniu* 肉牛),[57] was not used until the twentieth century. I will return in detail to the debates provoked at the end of the nineteenth century by the intrusion of Western livestock farming. Here, I would like to mention that a few newspaper articles from that period suggest that cattle farming existed in a marginal way in some regions such as Shaanxi, Gansu, Sichuan, and Yunnan.[58] But *cainiu* was also used in these same news articles to denote a bovine that was unfit, by nature or because of age, to work in the fields.[59] This illustrates to what extent meat consumption was conceived as subordinate to labor in the fields as far as cattle farming was concerned. In theory, as we will see, the beef available in the markets could only come from culled animals or those that died of old age or disease.

## The Bovine Policy

For two thousand years, the Chinese state was constantly concerned with maintaining a sufficient cattle herd for the needs of agricultural production and justified the implementation of measures that can be described as a "bovine policy." Its importance resembles that of the equine policy (*mazheng* 馬政).[60] These two species captured almost all the Chinese state's attention in livestock farming. The parallels between the two policies are striking, and many herd protection measures were applied equally to horses and cattle. This parallel was coupled with a juxtaposition: the equine policy was "martial" since it aimed to maintain the power of the cavalry, while the bovine policy was "civil" since it came under the umbrella of agricultural policy and the protection of the peasants' farm equipment, in particular that of small-scale, independent peasants. However, although the livestock farming regions of the two species largely overlapped, the Chinese state's equine policy involved the control of breeding and a state monopoly that had no equivalent for cattle.

Since the Song, cattle herds in China increased steadily from a relatively low base.[61] Nevertheless, the bureaucracy was constantly concerned that the cattle supply was insufficient and in great danger. Indeed, various circumstances occasionally led to a local decline in the size of herds and soaring cattle prices and consequently to a shortage that spilled over into agricultural production. These shortages were caused by wars and looting by intruders in border areas, frequent epizootics, and famines during which cattle were sold or even slaughtered. These situations provoked ad hoc measures, but fear of their recurrence also motivated a long-term policy.

The bovine policy of successive dynasties was remarkably constant in its main principles. Besides the management of the imperial herds, which constituted a completely separate system, the cattle policy was divided into three primary modalities: the distribution of cattle to poor peasants or settlers, the registration of all cattle in rosters kept by the administration, and the prohibition of cattle slaughter. In addition, a set of laws and administrative practices applied specifically to famine situations. The distribution of cattle to peasants has been documented since the Han and took on different attributes according to the historical period and the specific situation. The state could distribute resources, including seeds and cattle, to ordinary peasants in a troubled region. Nevertheless, a large part of the state's efforts was focused on agricultural settlements (*tuntian* 屯田)[62] in border regions intended for cultivation or on interior areas depopulated after wars or natural disasters. Typically, settlers received cattle for one or two families.[63] However, the distribution mechanisms varied. The state could simply facilitate the peasants' acquisition of cattle by cooperating with cattle dealers[64] to organize the purchase of animals. The cattle were gathered to form herds numbering thousands of heads, transported under military escort from regions in the south and west where cattle were relatively numerous to those with a shortage, such as the Yangzi valley and the north. The state could also acquire cattle from merchants (a practice that undoubtedly had the unfortunate effect of driving up prices on the cattle market), resell the animals at moderate prices, or give them to the peasants in regions with a short supply. Sometimes the state also retained ownership of these cattle to rent them out to peasants, generally within the context of *tuntian*. These animals were considered "public bovines" (*guanniu* 官牛).[65] *Guanniu* existed since the Han, but the system peaked during the Ming when there were more than five hundred thousand heads of cattle by the fifteenth century. Bovines were regarded as one of the most critical assets of the state, which was dispersed among the peasantry. However, the system was poorly managed and prey to all kinds of malfeasance, so much so that the animals were monopolized by tenants and ended up disappearing from the public accounts.[66] The Qing did not generally use the *guanniu* system, even if magistrates distributed *guanniu* marked as prohibited for resale during some famines.[67] By contrast, the Qing regime mostly subsidized the distribution of cattle to peasant settlers.

The cattle registration in rosters (*niuji* 牛籍) kept by the administration is attested during the Han and linked to branding.[68] Branding continued in later periods—or at least it was practiced in the nineteenth and twentieth centuries[69]—but registries disappeared after the Han, except for the rosters of public cattle (*guanniu*) entrusted to peasants.[70] In any case, public-cattle rosters and branding appear to have been relatively ineffective in preventing theft and illegal slaughter.

This active aspect of the bovine policy also had a corresponding section in the penal code aimed at protecting the bovine herd. First of all, cattle theft was, of course, prohibited and severely punished. Cattle theft seems to have been a recurrent scourge among the peasantry, and sources from different periods emphasize its seriousness.[71] A seventeenth-century treatise argued that cattle were the peasants' most precious possession and the easiest to steal since they spent the night outside the house. According to this author, bands of brigands enriched themselves by stealing cattle, which they resold to accomplice butchers. This practice was so rampant that the author supported the prohibition against slaughter to reduce banditry.[72] The theft and slaughter of cattle led to the shortage of animals and inflated prices so that many peasants could no longer afford to acquire them.

The most prominent aspect of the laws relating to cattle was the prohibition against slaughter (*shaniu* 殺牛, *tuniu* 屠牛, *zainiu* 宰牛).[73] This offense was often also called "private slaughter" (*sizai* 私宰), which sometimes referred to the slaughter of any animal during a general period of prohibition against slaughter (as mentioned in the previous chapter) but more often was applied to the slaughter of cattle or horses.[74] This measure was a consistent feature of the Chinese penal apparatus from the Han until the end of the imperial era. It applied to all cattle except for state sacrifices and certain other cults—an exception that is sometimes made explicit but more often remained implicit. The first mention of the prohibition against slaughter appears, somewhat obliquely, in the *Book of the Master of Huainan* (*Huainanzi* 淮南子), a philosophical treatise compiled in the first century BCE. This text says, "Those who kill a bovine will die without exception." A commentator, writing at the end of the second century CE, explained that since cattle were essential to agriculture, the state sentenced to death anyone who killed a bovine.[75] A recently discovered bamboo strip confirms that this provision was part of the Han laws.[76] For the subsequent dynasties, the promulgation of similar laws prohibiting the slaughter of cattle and horses is found in dynastic histories from all periods: the Jin (265–420),[77] the Song (420–479),[78] the Liang (502–557),[79] the Wei (386–556),[80] and the Tang. In some cases, the prohibition was in effect for a limited period,[81] but most often, it was permanent. The slaughter prohibition constituted an article of the Tang Code, the oldest extant comprehensive code: "Whoever willfully kills a bovine or a horse belonging to the state or an individual will be sentenced to banishment with forced labor for a year and a half" and "Whoever kills his own horse or cattle will be sentenced to banishment with forced labor for one year."[82] This article, as well as a large part of the Tang Code, was incorporated into the codes of later dynasties, which would only modify the sentences somewhat and distinguish different aggravating or mitigating circumstances.[83] The presence of this article in the fundamental laws of the country did not prevent decrees reiterating the prohibition or explicitly reissuing it at the national or local level during the Song (960–1279),[84] Jin (1115–1234),[85] Yuan (1279–1368),[86] Ming (1368–1644), and Qing (1644–1911).[87] Along with the rest of the Chinese code, this article was also adopted in Korea,[88] Japan,[89] and Vietnam.

The punishments mentioned in the code clearly show that cattle slaughter surpassed the scope of theft or damage to other people's property: killing one's own animals was also prohibited. The issue of cattle was a matter of public interest. In many official texts or handbooks for officials, the slaughter of a bovine was conceived as a crime threatening the entire society on a similar scale as, for example, counterfeiting or banditry.[90] Several tenth-century decrees exclude from amnesties those who have committed serious crimes, including the killing of cattle and horses.[91] The most striking manifestation of the gravity accorded to this crime was that the punishment in some cases greatly exceeded that stipulated by the legal code and went as far as the death penalty. A text from the Han mentions the execution of the cattle killers, which is also confirmed by another text relating to events from the third century.[92] In 991, an edict was issued that imposed the death penalty on thugs in the capital who gathered to gamble, made counterfeit money, and ran butcher shops selling beef, horsemeat, and dogmeat.[93] In this case, the offense went beyond beef butchery alone, but cattle slaughter was at the center of the accusation since the legislator also intended to implicate the customers of such butcher shops.

Such laws raise the thorny question of their enforcement, especially in the context of scattered and poorly registered herds. As one might expect, there were always transgressions, but since the Han, these were nonetheless taken seriously—at least by some zealots. One of them, living at the beginning of the fourth century, intervened when the court was preparing to sell old public cattle (*guanniu*). He pointed out that the law prohibited slaughtering them for meat, that the older cattle could no longer work, and that their sale would therefore amount to exchanging unnecessary things for the people's good money.[94] Such a statement suggests a desire to enforce the slaughter prohibition strictly. During the medieval period, a few officials or commoners were punished for killing a bovine.[95] These sanctions were not systematic, but they did exist.

Our knowledge of the legal arsenal and administrative practice in this regard becomes more precise from the Song dynasty. At that time, when a bovine died, its owner had to have the body of the animal checked by a yamen employee, who certified the natural cause of death.[96] The owner could only dispose of the corpse afterward, and it then was permissible to sell it to a butcher. The omission of this formality was an offense even graver than slaughter. The obligation to have the causes of death verified remained in force until the end of the Qing. Of course, during a time when yamen employees were few in number and communication was slow, this very cumbersome procedure did not lend itself to faithful application.

In this regard, magistrates regularly complained of people's total ignorance of the law. This emerges from the section devoted to the prohibition against cattle slaughter in the *Collection of Enlightened Judgments* (*Qingming ji* 清明集), a famous thirteenth-century collection of model judgments.[97] It is likely that the law was hardly observed in the most remote villages. It nevertheless posed a risk to all cattle owners in that a denunciation—real or false—of cattle slaughter could very well lead to a conviction. This left the door open to blackmail and the extraction of bribes by neighbors and especially yamen employees[98]—a subject to which we will have to return when we discuss the situation in the nineteenth century.

Such measures were reinforced in times of famine. The Ming and Qing bureaucratic manuals on the management of subsistence crises (*jiuhuang zheng* 救荒政) highlight the fragile condition of cattle herds and the attention this issue received in such circumstances. These manuals, as well as various other extant descriptions, show that in the event of famine, peasants were forced to sell their cattle, although generally as a last resort and with great despair.[99] Often, taking advantage of the situation, unscrupulous merchants roamed the countryside and bought the animals cheaply to resell them in town to butchers who slaughtered them. The disaster ended, the peasants returned to their land but had no more animals for plowing, and they could not buy new ones because not only had they emerged financially ruined from the famine, but also there were few cattle for sale since a large part of the herd had been slaughtered. For example, when floods led to a famine in Hebei between 1920 and 1921, this caused the loss of three-quarters of the livestock among the affected population.[100]

Administrators were very concerned about this situation, both for the sake of the peasants' future and to ensure the possibility of a harvest after the disaster. To deal with this situation, they strictly prohibited the trade and slaughter of cattle during the crisis. After the crisis, they tried to make cattle and seeds available to the peasants simultaneously.[101] Perhaps the most effective policy was to free up capital to buy cattle from peasants at the height of the crisis and to shelter and keep the animals until they could be returned to their owners in the region under the best possible conditions—for example, at the initial price without interest. From the Song dynasty, such a policy was carried out occasionally,[102] but it was limited by the weak financial means of local administrations as resources were consumed by even more urgent needs, such as food distribution to starving peasants. In the nineteenth century, many charitable associations (*shantang* 善堂) took over this task, as shown in more detail in chapter 5.

All bovine policy measures were abolished with the advent of the Republic in 1912, and the slaughter of cattle and trade in beef became legal.[103] There were multiple reasons for the abolishment. First and foremost, there was a desire to make Chinese law conform to Western models, which featured nothing similar to the bovine policy of the Chinese empire, as well as a change in the spirit of the law, which was no longer inspired by the protection of the small, independent peasants' property and farm equipment but by respect for the rules of commerce, including agriculture.

## Plow Cattle and Meat

The bovine policy pursued by the Chinese state from the Han to the early twentieth century was straightforward and logical in principle but proved to be very difficult to enforce, therefore generating many debates about its usefulness and real motivations. During the Qing, in particular, some authors tried to separate a rational agricultural policy from the attitudes linked to the beef taboo, as we will see below. The source of the difficulties and debates generated by the bovine policy was the status of cattle slaughter and beef.

The bovine policy was expressed in terms of agricultural policy: the prohibition was primarily concerned with killing a bovine used for labor. But the state, reflecting a vision shared across society, especially from the Song, did not conceive of cattle beyond agricultural work. Cattle other than plow cattle (*gengniu*) did not exist in the official discourse, and livestock farming for meat was not an economic activity it recognized. Consequently, the regulations were directly related to cattle butchers, selling and serving beef, and beef consumption. There were two main options for legislators. They could hold that the prohibition of slaughter automatically implied the prohibition of all forms of trade in and consumption of beef. Or, on the contrary, they could distinguish the two issues and find arrangements allowing some forms of consumption. The attitude of the Chinese state was often ambivalent, generally leaning more toward the second option. To my knowledge, there never was an absolute prohibition against eating beef in official Chinese sources at the national level at any time. It is not impossible that such a prohibition existed, as an anecdote involving Fu Zhao 傅昭, an exemplary sixth-century official, might suggest. Fu's daughter-in-law's family once offered him beef. He summoned his son and told him to eat beef would be an offense but that he could not offend the daughter-in-law's family by refusing the gift. He therefore ordered his son to bury the meat.[104] Although the text appears to refer to a prohibition against the consumption as such, it is more likely that this case suggests either a zealous, individual interpretation of the prohibition against slaughter or a context unrelated to cattle per se. Perhaps the gift was made during a month of universal vegetarianism imposed by the Liang Emperor Wu.

A source that most directly equates the prohibition against cattle slaughter with a ban on beef consumption is an edict of the Tang dynasty that was promulgated in 723 by Emperor Xuanzong (reigned 712–756): "Edict Prohibiting the Slaughter of Horses, Cattle, and Donkeys" (Jin tusha ma niu lü zhao 禁屠殺馬牛驢詔).[105] It warrants being translated here:

> Historically, one cannot eat the meat [of an animal] that one has known alive.[106] In addition, when one has benefited from its work, one should be grateful to it. Horses, cattle, and donkeys can carry heavy loads for great distances and make themselves useful to humans. It has already been promulgated that their slaughter is prohibited, but I am told that this detestable practice has not yet been eradicated and is particularly common in the livestock farming areas in the provinces. From now on, except for what is prescribed for sacrifices, it will be forbidden to present beef, horsemeat, or donkey meat. In the homes of princes and all other people of lower rank, as well as in all civil and military districts, whether for banquets or as part of livestock farming activities, it will be forbidden to kill [these animals]. We also order all officials stationed in the various civil and military districts or placed in charge of the [imperial] herds to monitor the enforcement of this prohibition strictly, and we charge the censors to denounce officials [lax in this regard].
>
> 自古見其生不食其肉，資其力必報其功。馬牛驢皆能任重致遠，濟人使用，先有處分，不令宰殺。如聞比來尚未全斷，郡牧之內，此弊尤多。自今以後，非祠祭所須，更不得進獻牛馬驢肉。其王公以下，及天下諸州諸軍，宴設及監牧，皆不得輒有殺害。仍令州縣及監牧使諸軍長官切加禁斷，兼委御史隨事糾彈。

The edict is devoted to the prohibition against cattle slaughter, but it leaves no room for beef consumption apart from imperial sacrifices. The prohibition against "presenting" (*jin* 進) meat seems to refer mainly to the official context—namely, gifts presented to the emperor or officials and banquets held within the framework of the functioning of the administration. The allusion to herds suggests that from the imperial point of view, the main problem occurred in the herds maintained at the time by the court, the state, and the aristocracy. These herds were substantial as there were tens of thousands of animals in the imperial herds alone. Undoubtedly, some were retained to supply dairy products, and the remainder were sold as working animals. There was no mention of peasant cattle, slaughter, and everyday consumption, which would subsequently occupy the center of jurisprudence after the herds of the aristocratic estates had disappeared. In any case, one point is clear: beef was banned from official banquets, and this was seen as a model that the population should follow.

These measures prohibiting the slaughter and consumption of beef at court were to become part of Chinese imperial mores. Some texts dating from the Qing dynasty similarly emphasize abstinence from beef but without imposing it. Thus, in an edict dated 1729 in which Emperor Yongzheng vigorously reiterated the prohibition of slaughter, the emperor asserted that beef was never consumed at court apart from state sacrifices and that it was cruel to kill cattle when there were so many good things to eat in the world. However, he did not go so far as to prohibit consumption within an existing legal framework.[107]

From the Song until 1912, a legal way to obtain beef did exist. The law allowed the carcasses of animals that died of old age or disease to be sold to a butcher as long as a certificate of natural death had been obtained.[108] In addition, one could request authorization to slaughter, also after verification, sick, old, disabled animals that were unfit to work.[109] We should note that health regulations concerning the control of meat from animals dying of old age or disease do not seem to have existed before the twentieth century. Such a procedure seems to be in contradiction with the code that prohibited the slaughter of cattle without qualification. As we shall see, the ambiguity was linked to the term *gengniu,* which sometimes designated cattle in a general way and sometimes a bovine that works as opposed to a lame or useless animal. Moreover, the authorization for slaughtering animals unfit for work was only expressed in a few texts and may not have been in force universally.[110] It is obvious that this procedure stemmed from an attitude of empathy vis-à-vis a farmer who had difficulty gathering the funds necessary to buy another useful bovine and could reduce his costs by recovering some money through the sale of his old bovine.

From a theoretical point of view, all beef consumed in China for a thousand years was therefore that of working animals that had died naturally or had been culled due to old age or disease. That means beef was meat with inferior taste, poor hygiene, and barely suitable for making stews after long cooking. The reality was likely a little different. Not only was the law sometimes blatantly ignored, but unscrupulous butchers and restaurateurs also paid the bribes necessary to secure the legal documents for bovines that had allegedly died naturally or been slaughtered with permission. The animals were actually supplied by the peasants themselves, cattle dealers, or thieves,[111] especially in times of famine when peasants were ready to sell their livestock at low prices or when the relative abundance of cattle meant that the price of an animal sold for meat was higher than that of the live animal in the market for plow cattle.[112] Such maneuvers did not escape the attention of officials, who prohibited them regularly but in vain.

The first known source concerning the regulation of beef butchery dates from 927. It limits the price of meat sold legally to discourage the slaughter of animals.[113] Similar ordinances multiplied from the Song. In addition to capping the price,[114] they included the closure of illegal beef butcheries—in other words, those that slaughtered animals without authorization to sell their meat. These ordinances betrayed some ambiguity: How could one distinguish a legal beef butcher from an illegal butcher? Because even though the sale of an animal that had died naturally or following a slaughter authorization was legal, officials seemed to consider all beef slaughter as a priori criminal.[115] This suspicion was no doubt legitimate and was further reinforced when these butcher shops were located in "remote and uncrowded places."[116] Thus, all such activity was criminalized. An edict from 1014 exempted the customers of illegal butchers from legal proceedings, which implied that some customers had been convicted previously.[117] They would be again later, with the edicts of 1131 and 1134, reiterating the criminalization of the trade in meat from slaughtered cattle, even extending to the buyer.[118] In the Ming Code, the trade in beef from illegally slaughtered cattle became a crime akin to slaughter, even if the butcher or customer did not participate in slaughtering the animal.[119] The Ming Code designated butcher shops where cattle were illegally slaughtered and sold with the expression "pen shop" (*juandian* 圈店). These were considered bad places, integrated into the shady world of illegal activities along with brothels and gambling dens, which did not prevent them from being well established.

As a result, butchering and selling beef was distinct from doing the same with other meats, particularly pork. Butchers were organized in guilds, like all professions.[120] However, as mentioned in the previous chapter, pork butchery, although considered an ungodly activity, still was a recognized and perfectly legal profession whose members wanted to distinguish themselves from any illegal activity such as beef production. There was never a general butcher's guild but only guilds specializing in slaughtering and selling specific animal species. This phenomenon is reminiscent of the situation in France where, after the prohibition of horse butchery was lifted in 1866, the horse butchers formed a distinct trade, which has remained the case to some extent almost a century and a half later.

In short, the elevation of cattle as an emblem of Chinese agricultural civilization led to a rejection of beef butchery, which survived in the marginal environment of thugs and thieves from the Song. We will return to beef butchers and the stigma associated with them—which did not prevent them from prospering when they were not harshly suppressed. But the issue is even more complex because there were exceptional situations in which the slaughter of cattle, while being prohibited, was linked to a different legacy: the distribution of meat to soldiers and sacrifices. Chapter 5 will also cover situations specific to the Ming and Qing periods—namely, meat consumption within European and Muslim communities, which claimed special ethical and dietary rules. The banquets of beef and alcohol offered to soldiers were an ancient custom that continued despite the prohibition of cattle slaughter though they arguably became rare occurrences. The military likely enjoyed some immunity in this regard.[121] There is a text from the Song that defends such banquets by arguing that it was not a matter of feasting and drinking but of encouraging the fighting spirit of the military.[122] Occasionally, soldiers did not hesitate to seize the cattle of peasants to prepare their meal.[123] The state was hesitant to oppose a custom specific to the military.[124] In the case of cattle sacrifices, as in the case of military banquets, the reaction of the Chinese state was not to compromise its principle that the bovine was untouchable, but it was unable to enforce it.

## Sacrifice

For two millennia of Chinese history, the prohibition against cattle slaughter was categorical and hardly allowed for exceptions—at least in theory. Yet there was one case in which cattle slaughter was necessary from a canonical perspective: sacrifices. The state's point of view was simple. The canonical texts required the sacrifice of a bovine, the most valued sacrificial animal, in some state rituals. In these cases, the prohibition of slaughter was not applicable. Moreover, the sacrificial animals generally came from the imperial herds. In all other cases, there were no exceptions. In reality, administrative practices were more complex. Ancestor worship—especially within the great lineages that formed from the eleventh century—constituted an orthodox form of religion from the perspective of the religious doctrine of the state. This cult was not officially exempt from the prohibition against the sacrifice of cattle, but it does not seem to have ever been questioned in this regard. By contrast, many local cults practicing cattle sacrifice were attacked under the law prohibiting slaughter. It is difficult to precisely delineate to what extent these complaints were made against excessive cults (*yinsi*) in general and to what extent they were specific to the offense of cattle slaughter.[125] In some cases, the fact that cults involved massive sacrifices of cattle seems to have constituted a casus belli between local society and the administration. There were several examples of this from the early stages of the prohibition against slaughter from the Han until the Song when the emergence of the taboo changed the contours of the problem. Two cases in particular should be mentioned, one at the beginning and one at the end of this long period.

The first case ought to be highlighted if only because it was often cited in later texts and served as a reference point. In 53 CE, Diwu Lun 第五倫, an official, was posted in Kuaiji 會稽, a district in present-day Shaoxing City in Zhejiang. He observed that people were terrified by mediums and very frequently sacrificed cattle to local gods and that the extreme expenses occasioned by these cults caused the ruin of the people. In addition, if someone dared to eat beef that had not been sacrificed to the gods or did not make the requested sacrifices, they got sick and bellowed in agony before dying as divine retribution. Previous officials had never dared to intervene in this situation in which the gods demanded the first fruits of all cattle. Diwu, as a model official, opposed the mediums who propagated the cults and proclaimed that he would punish whoever killed a bovine "without good reason" (*wang tuniu* 妄屠牛). People started fearing the vengeance of the gods who had been deprived of their beef, but the interdiction held and revenge did not come, so this "bad custom," it was said, disappeared.[126] The account is typical of Confucian hagiography, as it shows that Diwu was correct in sticking to the strict Confucian canon, according to which these commoners were only allowed to sacrifice to their ancestors and domestic gods, and that the other cults were illicit (*yinsi*) and did not bring blessings. Beyond its apologetic scope, such an anecdote shows how widespread cattle sacrifices in local cults outside the state religion and the state's will to oppose them were. In Diwu Lun's actions, two grounds of opposition were explicitly invoked: the simple application of laws against the cattle slaughter[127] and the fight against excessive cults of which cattle sacrifice was only a sign. Despite laws prohibiting slaughter, cattle sacrifices continued from the Han to the Song. Various sources show that cattle sacrifice was quite common until the twelfth century.[128] The state's desire to compel cult communities to replace cattle with other animals only had a limited effect. This tension is illustrated by an anecdote from the Tang in which a god asked for a cattle sacrifice. The magistrate told him that it was illegal and proposed a sheep or a pig instead. Enraged, the god killed the official's entire family and caused a severe epidemic.[129] Likewise, in an anecdote from the tenth century, a virtuous monk, himself a former magistrate, attacked the local cult of a god that demanded cattle sacrifice. He argued that since cattle were used only for agriculture, they were an impious sacrifice. Therefore, he implemented vegetarian offerings.[130] A Song decree expressly forbade sacrificing cattle to ancestors or gods (*shen* 神) and reserved them for sacrifice to heaven. This decree attacked the popular practice of sacrificing a bovine for a simple prayer for healing, which was described as impious and sacrilegious.[131] Such a decree shows both the spread of cattle sacrifices in local cults and the state's desire to make it a political matter.[132]

These points are particularly well illustrated by the second case, which spanned from the eleventh to the thirteenth century. It concerned a local cult dedicated to King Zhang 張王.[133] The main temple of King Zhang, commonly known as Cishan miao 祠山廟, was located in Guangde 廣德, present-day Anhui Province. During the Song, he had been the recipient of many successive titles granted by the state. The cult flourished and spread, attracting many pilgrims to Cishan miao and establishing numerous branch temples throughout central China. In many respects typical of the rise of regional cults in the twelfth century,[134] this cult was nonetheless distinctive because it involved cattle. Indeed, Cishan miao owned herds of cattle donated as "eternal cattle" to the temple by devotees and rented out to peasants. However, the temple did not only rent out the cattle but also slaughtered and sacrificed them during the annual festivals. The scale of the sacrifices performed for King Zhang—some sources speak of hundreds of animals sacrificed together—spurred people's imagination. Moreover, the scale was so massive not simply out of a desire to show off one's riches by sacrificing as many victims as possible but rather as a consequence of the vast size of the cultic network. In a neighboring cult organized similarly, each of the 720 villages associated with the cult sacrificed a bovine.[135] The sacrificed animals were not eaten but buried.

Even though this cult had been officially recognized, it drew criticism from some officials, who prohibited cattle sacrifices at Cishan miao on several occasions during the dynasty to no avail, as cattle sacrifices continued there into the Qing.[136] In particular, Huang Zhen 黄震 (1213–1280), an official famous for his campaigns against popular religion,[137] wrote two memoirs calling for the prohibition of cattle sacrifices (*niuji* 牛祭) at Cishan miao.[138] In his long argument, Huang took up all the classic criticisms of the Confucian elite toward local cults and the great collective celebrations: immorality, heterodoxy, waste, disturbing public order, and so on. He did not consider the slaughter of cattle the only problem at Cishan miao, but he attached particular importance to it. One of the arguments used by Huang Zhen was that the slaughter of cattle at the temple, in addition to violating the law, contravened an imperial prerogative because only the emperor had the right to practice *tailao*.[139] In other words, the emperor had a monopoly on bovine sacrifice. This element should be underlined because it constitutes a new aspect compared to the rhetoric observed since the Han and the case of Diwu Lun in Kuaiji.

This aspect of bureaucratic opposition to cattle sacrifices—namely, the violation of imperial prerogatives—went far beyond the simple framework of sumptuary regulations. It was, in fact, a highly politically sensitive subject. Indeed, cattle use in a local cult, even in a context of complete loyalty to the dynasty, was dangerously reminiscent of imperial sacrifices. The very fact of sacrificing a bovine to heaven, an act that only the emperor could perform, constituted an act of rebellion since at least the Tang. In historical fiction, especially in the epic of the Three Kingdoms and the sworn alliance of Liu Bei, Guan Yu, and Zhang Fei, there is a well-established tradition for claimants to the empire to declare themselves by sacrificing a horse and an ox to heaven and earth, usually a white horse to heaven and a black ox to earth. Françoise Aubin has shown that it was a hybrid practice resulting from a contribution of Altaic sacrificial practices that the Kitan would have transmitted to the Chinese during the Liao dynasty.[140] Indeed, the Altaic tradition of horse sacrifice was added to the Chinese imperial monopoly on the cattle sacrifice to heaven.

Furthermore, the practice of taking an oath (*meng* 盟 or *shi* 誓) sealed by the joint consumption of alcohol and the blood of a sacrificed animal (ideally a bovine) and reinforced by curses pronounced with sacrificial blood rubbed on the lips (according to early descriptions) or drunk mixed with alcohol (in modern practice) has been very commonly attested in China since antiquity.[141] It was used in legitimate contexts, such as sworn allies for a noble cause, as well as in rebellion. Because the prohibition against cattle slaughter made it an additional offense (and therefore an act of revolt) and it also constituted a usurpation of the imperial monopoly, the act of sacrificing a bovine and swearing an oath by sharing its blood and meat became a potent symbol of rebellion. There were cases from the Tang, such as that of a magistrate who banned cattle slaughter to stop the sworn alliance banquets of bandits who "cannot take an oath without cattle and alcohol."[142] Another anecdote from the Song relates the case of a gathering of conspirators. One of the conspirators pointed out that the simple act of sacrificing a bovine together made them outlaws.[143] However, one cannot but note the double standard of such an interdiction insofar as, at the same time, soldiers in the imperial army benefited from distributions of beef and alcohol. In short, local cults that sacrificed cattle and covenant oaths, even declarations of rebellion, that were sworn by sharing the blood and meat of a bovine formed two distinct sets of practices, but the two were, though not assimilated, similarly repressed because they constituted crimes of lese majesty. Their political scope was based on the violation of the prohibition against cattle slaughter, and they acquired a symbolic dimension that transcended the simple violation of agricultural laws.

Finally, the Chinese state took measures to further increase the sacrality of cattle sacrifice by making it a rare occurrence. The bovine was already the most prestigious offering reserved for the aristocratic elite in antiquity. From the Han, the ritual codes of the empire gradually tended to establish an imperial monopoly on the sacrifice of cattle by relying on several select passages in the classics, which are actually far from unanimous on this subject.[144] However, the number of sacrifices in which the emperor participated (or was represented) and that involved cattle slaughter remained high. From the Tang and during the following dynasties, measures were taken to reduce the number of cattle sacrificed. The details in the lists of sacrificial animals for the various rituals of state worship changed very often, but there was a clear trend toward substituting sheep and pigs for cattle. There are at least two extant detailed accounts of debates between liturgists at court on this subject: one from 955 during the Zhou and another from 1170 during the Jin.[145] In each case, the emperor asked the liturgists how one could reconcile the respect due to plow cattle with the requirements of the liturgical tradition. The experts responded by proposing to keep the sacrifice of cattle to heaven, earth, the God of the Soil and Crops (Sheji 社稷, and Confucius, whose rank is aligned with that of the God of the Soil), and the imperial ancestors but to reduce the total number of victims (e.g., a single bovine for all ancestors instead of one per genealogical branch) and substituting another animal for the bovine if the emperor is not physically present. Thus, by the tenth century, the state cult "consumed" only about twenty cattle per year—compared to several hundred at the beginning of the Tang and earlier—a small number that Confucian ritualists could no longer reduce.[146] Thus scaled down to the strict "minimum," the imperial cattle sacrifice gained meaning as an exceptional act.

The glorification of plow cattle and the sustained actions of the state in its favor stemmed from the specific organization of Chinese agriculture and, more broadly, from Chinese cultural choices since the end of antiquity in favor of agriculture and in particular of cereals. This choice implies the lack of recognition of livestock farming as a form of economic activity even if the state itself practiced it with the imperial herds.

The physical, daily place of cattle in peasant life was very different from what it was or has been in other cultures such as the Christian West or India and explains why cattle played a specific and vital role in Chinese culture. Cattle are frequently represented in Chinese folklore and mythology, and several studies have been devoted to this topic.[147] However, I do not wish to explore this issue, which would obscure the precise subject that occupies me here—namely, the intersection of economic and ethical discourses about the actual animal.

For most scholars, the story of the beef taboo in China ends with the state banning cattle slaughter to protect agriculture and Buddhism encouraging vegetarianism. But in my mind, these two chapters are just an introduction, and the history of the beef taboo is yet to come because Buddhist and Daoist vegetarian discourses pertained to all living beings, and state discourse only articulated the protection of cattle as work equipment. In other words, at this point, the ethical and economic discourses had not yet intersected. However, they would merge during the Song to form an original discourse that developed independently of legal prohibitions and vegetarian discourses.

# 3 The Revelation of a New Sin

Zhou Jie, nicknamed Shengqing, was originally from Taizhou but lived in Si'an Township, Huzhou Prefecture. When Qin Chucai became prefect of Xuancheng, he appointed Zhou as head of the Nanling garrison.[1] Zhou fell victim to an epidemic and had to ask for a leave and return home. He dreamed then that he was arrested and taken to the magistrate's office and that men dressed in red like the employees of the administration ordered that he be jailed. Several dozen people dressed like officials also greeted him respectfully and sat around him to judge him together. A clerk motioned Zhou forward and asked him, "How could you indulge your cruel penchant for beef?" With that, the clerk yelled the order to whip Zhou's back, and several henchmen led him away. Zhou turned to the clerk and begged for a pardon, saying, "From this day forward, not only will I never dare to eat it again, but I swear to enforce this interdiction on all my family!" The officials participating in the judgment all pleaded for forgiveness, and the judge agreed to release him, so Zhou was able to return home. He awoke from his dream, drenched in sweat but suddenly cured of his illness. From then on, he strictly observed this interdiction (*jin* 禁), always speaking of it [to those he met]. In 1160, he was appointed inspector of the salt granaries.

周階、字升卿，泰州人。寓居湖州四安鎮。秦楚材守宣城，檄攝南陵尉。以病疫告歸。夢就逮至官府，緋袍人據桉治囚。又有緋綠者數十人，以客禮見，環坐廳事。一吏引周問曰。何得酷嗜牛肉。叱令鞭背，數卒捽曳以去。周回顧乞命，且曰。自今日以往，不唯不敢食，當與闔門共戒。坐客皆起為謝罪，主者意解，乃得歸。夢覺，汗流浹體，疾頓愈。至今恪守此禁，時時為人言之，紹興三十年，周監鹽官倉。[2]

This anecdote from Hong Mai's 洪邁 (1123–1202) *Record of the Listener* (*Yijian zhi* 夷堅志) clearly illustrates the beef taboo: eating beef is a sin that is punished by the courts of the beyond. Dating to the twelfth century, this is neither the oldest nor the most detailed anecdote concerning the taboo, but its explicitness makes it an excellent introduction to the corpus of anecdotes that I have been able to collect to document the appearance and formation of the taboo. This corpus comprises thirty-three anecdotes, dating from the ninth to the thirteenth century and covering all of China, although southern China is predominant.[3] This corpus is certainly not exhaustive, but it is sufficiently rich to constitute a coherent discourse. There were more didactic and elaborate formulations of the taboo and its justifications in a fragmentary way from the twelfth century and then abundantly thereafter and also in other literary genres, but it is through these thirty-three anecdotes that it first appeared in the sources. Therefore, the discourse on the beef taboo should be defined as precisely as possible through this anecdotal literature. Second, I assess the originality of this discourse compared to previous and contemporaneous sources relating to animals and bovines in particular. Finally, I explore the social reality of this new taboo and the possible reasons for its appearance.

## Defining the Beef Taboo

The very nature of the corpus—a set of anecdotes, each having its own logic and narrative force—means that the theme is quite fragmented: each of the anecdotes only explains a part of it. But the size of the corpus makes it possible to develop a complete picture of the subject by cross-referencing. I will successively present the themes of the revelation of sin, the vow to observe the taboo, the active role of cattle in the mechanism of retribution, and the issues of purity and defilement.

### The Revelation of a Sin

The first theme that can be traced through the various anecdotes is that of divine intervention. To a twenty-first-century reader, the beef taboo appears first and foremost as a revelation, just as it did to Zhou Jie. The author of the anecdote did not mention Zhou's reaction—whether he was surprised to have been summoned to the courts of the afterlife because of his depraved and immoderate taste for beef. We can assume that he already knew that this was a sin. But he did not seem to comprehend its seriousness. It took a hellish setting to make him aware of what was at stake: in this sense, his dream was a revelation. Other anecdotes point in the same direction. The journey—in a dream, cataleptic state, or even while alive and awake—to the judicial courts in the beyond was a fundamental motif in all Chinese didactic tales since medieval times and more than ever during the Song. The protagonists of the *Record of the Listener* anecdotes saw the yamen of the other world as frequently as they visited those of the human world. This process was therefore not original to the corpus of stories about beef, but it was employed for a reason. Retribution for one's actions could be immediate. For the unfilial son, a lightning bolt was enough since everyone understood the nature of his fault and the cause of his punishment. In contrast, during the Song, beefeaters needed a sermon to understand their sin. The dialogue in court had the advantage of clarifying and circumscribing the offense, as in an anecdote featuring Jiang Jian 蔣堅, a diviner who was taken away by infernal minions. The otherworldly judge accused Jiang of eating a lot of beef. "Sure," Jiang replied, "I like it, but I only bought some when someone sold it, and I never killed a bovine." "But," answered the judge, "it is because you bought some that the butchers killed cattle!" Jiang then accepted his guilt and was released so he could take care of his mother.[4] There is little doubt that some beefeaters shared Jiang's opinion, whether in good or bad faith. The anecdote makes it possible to dot the *i:* if the retribution meted out on cattle killers was awful, then that doled out on those who merely ate beef was hardly better. And it took a revelation, dramatic and didactic at the same time, to convince those immediately concerned.

Even though the trip to the infernal courts was the preferred mode of the revelation, it could also happen less dramatically. Sometimes there was no one who made the revelation but just a revealed text, as in the case of Sheng Zhao 盛肇. Sheng liked to eat beef. One day, he received an invitation to a banquet from a friend, which was inscribed with the following poem:

> All beings are transformed according to [the inclinations of] their mind.
> Cattle lead the hardest life.
> Look: those who fall victims to a cruel death
> Are all beefeaters!
> 萬物皆心化，唯牛最苦辛。君看橫死者，尽是食牛人。

However, this invitation was not really sent by the friend in question. Sheng realized that this was a divine warning and stopped eating beef.[5] We should note that the text appeared miraculously because short poems of this type would play a significant role in disseminating the taboo. In any case, those who received the revelation were sinners (beefeaters) who were forgiven, provided they went and preached the message of the taboo. The most remarkable example is undoubtedly that of a mendicant who told everyone he met that he was once a merchant and had been cast on the shores of an unknown island during a storm. There, henchmen welcomed him and forced him to walk on a road on which raised cattle horns wounded his feet: "You liked to eat beef," said the henchmen. "Here is your cruel retribution!" The merchant repented and was released in return for the promise that he would go and exhort the people to observe the taboo. They gave him an extraordinary object, a bleeding bamboo, which he brought back as proof of his adventure. Returning to China, the merchant abandoned his wife and children and became a mendicant promoting the taboo.[6] Another slightly later anecdote also used the theme of a distant island as a place of revelation and conversion. An official traveling by boat to his post ended up on an island where the hell of beefeaters was located.[7] His uncle, a big beefeater, was being punished there, and the official, who also ate beef, learned that he would die soon himself. Back in China, he strictly enforced the prohibition against slaughter and convinced seven hundred families to make a vow to observe the taboo. He then learned in a dream that his uncle was released from hell and that he himself had extended his life span by several years.[8]

Likewise, an anecdote recounts the downfall and salvation of an impoverished member of the imperial family. Zhao Shanyi 趙善弌 lived as an illegal distiller and occasionally slaughtered an ox to treat his friends. One day, he was taken to hell, where a judge said to him, "Cattle perform a great service toward humans. How can you kill them? I'll do the same to you," which his minions with giant claws proceeded to do. Zhao begged, was forgiven, and came back to life. He learned that his servants were going to kill an ox. He gave the animal to a monastery as "eternal cattle." Subsequently, he became a wealthy official and constantly exhorted others to observe the taboo.[9]

Does this mean that, for the twelfth-century Chinese as a collective, the existence of the beef taboo was a revelation, as it was for the individual protagonists of anecdotes? Was it a new sin that was hitherto unknown? That is difficult to say because there are older anecdotes from as early as the ninth century. But what is clear is that the taboo was not self-evident. There were actions that everyone, including those who perpetrated them, agreed were immoral: killing, stealing, and indulging in debauchery. The beef taboo, by contrast, fell into another category. Those who believed in it needed proof for themselves and to convince others, and these anecdotes provided such evidence. The taboo does not appear in the classics of any of the Three Teachings, but in China, revelation was open and was not controlled by religious authorities. This is why individual revelations were so important, especially if they were transmitted by proselytization. Those who had a revelation had to spread it just as Zhou Jie told everyone about his dream, and the merchant became a traveling preacher.

It is difficult and arguably unnecessary to speculate whether such revelations were "real." The *Record of the Listener* and other anecdotal sources mention oral histories that circulated. They were not literary inventions. For their part, the protagonists of these stories may actually have dreamed of the courts of hell or had hallucinatory visions because in many cases like Zhou Jie's, they were sick. Having acquired the conviction that eating beef was a sin, they could express it in the clear and convincing form of a visit to the hereafter because such a trope was culturally well understood and accepted. Be that as it may, there is nothing that calls into question the sincerity of these accounts. These people had life-changing experiences, after which they no longer ate beef. It is tempting to call this a "conversion."

## Vowing to Observe the Taboo

In some cases, the dramatic nature of this change was marked by making a vow to no longer eat beef and by a threat in the event of relapse. A thirteenth-century anecdote illustrates the vow particularly well. The protagonist, Zeng Feng 曾鳳, recounted that he once caught a cold and felt swallowed up by an ox in the delirium of his illness. He vowed that if he survived, he would never eat sacrificial beef (*tailao*) again. He woke up cured. He kept his vow for ten years but succumbed to gluttony at a banquet given by a friend, during which they offered slices of roasted beef. He immediately fell ill and had the same dream again, from which he only emerged by renewing his vow, this time swearing that he should die in case of a second relapse.[10] In another very similar anecdote, the glutton who ate slices of roasted beef fell ill and, in his coma, saw a man who made his options clear to him: "If you no longer eat beef, you will live, but if you continue to eat it, you will die." The man woke up, made a vow, and recovered.[11]

A somewhat atypical story within our corpus involved monks rather than the judges of hell as agents of conversion. The culprits were local tyrants for whom the consumption of beef was associated with the illegal manufacture of alcohol and participation in the world of outlaws in general. They visited a monastery one day where an artist was painting a mural; they spotted a quaint figure in the painting and made fun of it. That night, they were pursued in a dream by two monks, and they pleaded for mercy. The monks made them promise never to eat beef again and told them that if they were to do it again, the monks would cut off their limbs. The men returned to the monastery and saw the two monks in the painting. They then definitively gave up eating beef as well as their other illegal activities.[12]

The theme of the vow was linked to success in exams, a literary trope that persisted until the twentieth century. The motif of the beefeater deprived of exam success obviously represented an attempt to convince scholars of the importance of the taboo. This motif was the subject of an anecdote dated 1163. A scholar dreamed that he passed the exams but that a celestial officer crossed out his name, saying, "He is being punished for liking to eat beef!" The candidate then swore to abstain from beef forever, and his name was reinstated on the list.[13] A very similar anecdote featured a scholar who dreamed that he saw the register of destinies. His brilliant career and longevity had been crossed out in red ink with the remark "He eats beef."[14]

## Vengeful Cattle

The third theme in this corpus concerned the active role of cattle in the punishment of the guilty or in the perpetrators' adoption of the taboo. Vengeful cattle generally attacked butchers rather than mere beefeaters. The modes of intervention were varied. Sometimes the bovine was benevolent. In one anecdote, the bovine begged to be spared, but its pleas were in vain. Later, the butcher found relic beads (*śarīra*) in the meat of the animal he had just slaughtered. He placed them in a stupa and changed his profession.[15] Similarly, another protagonist served himself a piece of beef, which let out a moan. On the magistrate's advice, a cremation with a Buddhist ritual was prepared for this piece of meat, and relics were also discovered.[16] A butcher cut up a bovine, and his customers discovered relics in it. Consequently, the whole village abstained from eating beef.[17] In these cases, persuasion was painless. Very frequently, the bovine begged to be spared. In some instances, the bovine knew by prescience that it was condemned to the butcher's knife. In others, the cattle wept when they died. An official had bought a cow and her calf and had already killed the calf to make beef jerky. He was about to kill the cow when a woman appeared to him in a dream and said, "My daughter has already been killed. Spare me!" The official then had the calf's meat thrown into the river, gave the cow to a monastery, and abstained from beef for the rest of his life.[18]

In some cases, the bovine avenged itself, sometimes very violently. A cattle butcher who had just slaughtered an animal and had hung its head and legs in his storefront was cursed by the head and beaten to death by the hooves.[19] An ox about to be slaughtered by soldiers escaped with a knife stuck in its skull, killed a soldier who tried to stop it, and went straight to the yamen to bow down before the magistrate, who gave it medical treatment and placed it in a monastery.[20] Butchers who received punishment were often described as particularly cruel. Thus, in one anecdote, butchers in a region of Jiangxi poisoned cattle with a needle in such a way that the flesh remained edible, and the animals seemed to have died of natural causes, thereby thwarting the village chiefs and magistrates eager to observe the prohibition against slaughter. A butcher who was known as a master in this technique poisoned the cattle of his neighbors from whom he then bought the carcasses, which he sold legally. The butcher was found drowned, pierced with poisonous needles, and people agreed that he must have been the victim of demonic vengeance (perhaps by the spirits of his bovine victims, but this was not stated in the anecdote).[21] Another butcher manifested his cruelty by slowly bleeding the live cattle so that they suffered excruciatingly. Witnesses of such scenes recited *dharani* or invoked Jiuku tianzun 救苦天尊 for the salvation of the animals' spirits, but the butcher did not care until the day when he was brought before an infernal tribunal and condemned to be boiled in a cauldron in hell.[22] Yet another butcher had more than a thousand cattle on his conscience and boasted that he would undoubtedly become the ox-headed king, Niutou wang 牛頭王. Walking one day, he was attacked by a herd of cattle, fell ill, and saw a god who announced his death and told him that he had to pay his debt.[23]

But cattle also exacted revenge on mere beefeaters. Thus, Mr. Zhai Ji 翟楫, still childless at fifty, earnestly prayed to Guanyin to grant him a son. His wife dreamed that Guanyin gave her a son, but an ox prevented her from taking the child. She indeed gave birth to a son, but he failed to grow. A friend explained that this was due to the family's unrestrained penchant for beef. The whole family vowed to abstain from beef henceforth, and the son finally grew up normally.[24] Retribution was crueler in an anecdote set in the palace of the bovine king (Niuwang zhi gong 牛王之宮). A man was taken there in a dream and encountered his aunt, who had been very fond of eating beef during her lifetime. Her punishment was that an ox-headed man brought her a dish of needles to eat every day. After the needles pierced her everywhere, the bovine jailer scraped her flesh to the bone. The frightened nephew wanted to run away, but the vengeful bovine held him back and said, "You once ate four pounds of this meat [beef]. You must now eat two portions of needles," with which he was forced to comply.[25]

## Purity and Defilement

A final motif that cuts across the anecdotes in this corpus is that of purity and defilement. The beefeater was described as defiled and deserving of sickness and possession. By contrast, those who abstained were pure and protected against harmful influences and demons. This theme is actually the oldest one found in two early anecdotes, which indicates that the taboo already existed, or at least was in the process of emerging, in the ninth century. In passing but explicitly, the motif appears in the *Miscellaneous Pieces from Youyang* (*Youyang zazu* 酉陽雜俎) by Duan Chengshi 段成式 (?–863). The anecdote tells the story of the marriage between a human woman and a *yakṣa* 夜叉, an uncontrollable local god from Buddhist lore. The woman observed that when her *yakṣa* husband walked among humans, he sometimes amused himself by insulting and spitting on some of them. She asked him why, and he explained that he was targeting those who ate beef, whom he was allowed to treat like that.[26] The fact that this was the first known occurrence of the taboo did not escape Ji Yun 紀昀 (1724–1805), a towering scholar and enthusiast of strange tales,[27] according to whom the *Miscellaneous Pieces from Youyang* already demonstrated that the demons of epidemics targeted beefeaters.[28] However, the text cited above does not say as much, and to my knowledge, the theme of the relationship between beef and epidemics only appeared explicitly in Song anecdotes. However, as Ji Yun has also pointed out, the same theme was developed more extensively in another collection of strange tales, the *Stories from the Chamber of Dissemination* (*Xuanshi zhi* 宣室志) by Zhang Du 張讀 (834?–after 882), probably composed shortly after the *Miscellaneous Pieces from Youyang.*

Zhang's anecdote is very similar and may even have been an elaboration on Duan's or may have had a common source. A young woman was kidnapped by a *yakṣa* who placed her on top of a ramshackle pagoda. She watched the daily outings of her strange husband:

> One day the *yakṣa* had just gone out, and I watched him enter the living quarters. A commoner was coming from the opposite direction: the *yakṣa* moved back a hundred paces and did not even dare to look at him. When he came home that evening, I asked him, "How come you were so afraid of this man?" The *yakṣa* replied, "This man has refrained from eating *tailao* from childhood. That is why I cannot approach him." I asked him why, and he explained, "Cattle allow us to plow the fields. They are the source of what allows us to live. Heaven protects those who do not eat their meat. That's why I can't go near them." So I thought to myself, "Here I am, separated from my parents and united with a being of a different species [than humans]. What distress!" The next day, when the *yakṣa* was gone, I made the following vow: "I swear never again to eat the meat of the *tailao* [beef][29] until I die." As soon as I repeated the vow three times, the *yakṣa* returned to the pagoda and stared at me, saying, "Why did you want to divorce me? Now I cannot approach you anymore, and we must separate." The *yakṣa* left toward the east, and I do not know where he is now. I was delighted, and I was able to leave the pagoda and go home.
>
> 一日，夜叉方去，某下視之，見其行里中，會遇一白衣，夜叉見，辟易退遠百步，不敢竊視。及暮歸。某因詰之： 何為懼白衣者乎？夜叉曰：向者白衣，自小不食太牢。故我不得近也。某問何故，夜叉曰：牛者所以耕田疇，為生人之本。人不食其肉，則上帝祐之。故我不得而近也。某默念曰：吾人也，去父母，與異類為伍，可不悲乎？明日，夜叉去而祝曰：某願不以太牢為食。凡三祝。其夜叉忽

自郡中來，至浮屠下，望某而語曰：何為有異志而棄我乎？使我終不得近子矣。從此別去。詞畢，即東向走，而竟不知其所往。某喜甚，由浮屠中得以歸。[30]

It is not certain that the *Stories from the Chamber of Dissemination* and the *Miscellaneous Pieces from Youyang* invented the theme of the *yakṣa* who cannot approach the pure who abstain from beef, but these two collections obviously played an important role in the dissemination of this motif. This is clearly demonstrated by an anecdote from the thirteenth century, which relates events from around 1205. A demon possessed a courtesan. An official summoned to remedy this situation began by recounting an old case, taken from *Stories from the Chamber of Dissemination, Miscellaneous Pieces from Youyang,* or a very similar text—this account takes up verbatim passages from the two anecdotes from the ninth century. Enlightened by this precedent, the courtesan, in turn, took the solemn vow to no longer eat beef. Consequently, she was freed from the demon who had tormented her.[31] Such an anecdote suggests that vows to abstain from beef were used in exorcisms, which may have been one of the reasons for their widespread use. A slightly later source from the second half of the fourteenth century suggests a somewhat different link between the taboo and ritual purity. A follower of black magic explained that his curses could only work if he abstained from beef and dogmeat because these "ruined the ritual" (*pofa* 破法). His enemy defeated him by making him eat beef disguised as horsemeat.[32]

The theme of those who abstained from beef being pure was particularly developed in regard to epidemic diseases.[33] Since antiquity, such diseases were attributed to demons who were said to spread them. Epidemics were linked to beliefs in retribution as the demons of epidemics were thought to target only sinners. A survey of didactic tales and the rituals implemented to fight against epidemics shows that this theme had two variants that were not mutually exclusive: either the instigators of epidemics were *wenshen* 瘟神, members of the celestial administration sent to punish sinners, and then a Daoist priest had to petition their recall, or they were vengeful demons (*yigui* 疫鬼), in which case the appropriate response was an exorcism. The cult of the *wenshen* and Daoist rituals to keep them at a distance developed particularly from the Song.[34]

A twelfth-century anecdote fully develops the relationship between the gods of epidemics and the beef taboo. A scholar called Guan Shiren 管師仁 left his home in the early morning on New Year's Day and came across the spirits responsible for spreading epidemics. Worried, Guan asked them if they were going to his house. "No," they answered, "because you belong to one of the three categories of people that we spare: those who have accumulated merit over three generations, those who are protected by the door gods, and those who do not eat beef."[35] In a similar story, a man dreamed of a god with loose hair (we will return to him later), who went from house to house to give the inhabitants a cup to drink. As the god arrived in front of one house, he declared, "This family has not eaten beef for twenty years. Let's spare them." Subsequently, an epidemic affected all the families in the neighborhood except the one named in the dream.[36]

The author of the anecdote mentioned above, which illustrates the importance of not breaking the vow, specified that his family had observed the taboo for three generations. Yet, although several members of his family were in fragile health, none of them, not even the servants, had ever been affected by any epidemics.[37] Another, after having made a vow, was no longer a victim of epidemics.[38] A thirteenth-century compendium on calendric observances tells us that the connection between abstinence from beef and protection against epidemic diseases was widely known: an entry on 5/5, the day when pestilence was considered at its strongest, explains that the plague gods are on inspection tours on earth and people write "This household does not eat beef" on their door to repel them.[39] The conception of epidemic diseases as retribution for eating beef is even attested in a handbook for officials from the Yuan.[40]

The final three anecdotes that I would like to present here, which are among the most fascinating, explain the connection between purity and the taboo within the framework of religious organizations. In 960, a man named Zhang Shouzhen 張守真 (930–996) was possessed by a martial deity called Heisha 黑煞, the "Black Killer," and transmitted the revelations of this deity to the court. His divinations were recognized as genuine, and Zhang was responsible for overseeing the temples created at great expense for the worship of this deity, notably the Shangqing taiping gong 上清太平宮 in Shaanxi. The fervent Daoist emperor Zhenzong (reign 998–1022) recognized the divinity, canonized it in 1014 under the name of Transcendent Lord Who Assists the Saint and Protects Virtue, Yisheng baode zhenjun 翊聖保德真君, as the guardian of the dynasty, and commissioned from a high official a hagiography of the god with the record of his revelations. Historians of Daoism who have studied this text have demonstrated that this marked a crucial stage in the development of Daoist schools that formed around new, essentially exorcist rituals, notably the Tianxin zhengfa 天心正法, and their adoption by the literate elites. The adoption of these rituals led to the rise of the cults of the martial deities that play a preeminent role in them, in particular the Thunder gods and the Four Saints (Sisheng 四聖), including Yisheng baode zhenjun.[41] An anecdote states that within a radius of one hundred *li* (fifty kilometers) around the main temple of Yisheng, all those who ate beef or wore shoes made of bovine leather were struck with misfortune and even killed on the spot—that is, by the god.[42] The anecdote details the case of a man wearing leather who entered the temple. Zhang Shouzhen asked the god why he did not punish him, and the god replied that he was not an ordinary man but the immortal Liu Haichan 劉海蟾, one of the few enlightened beings who interacted with humans to save them, whom heaven therefore protected. The exceptional personality of the protagonist, Liu Haichan—one of the leading figures of inner alchemy, which, during this period, emerged as a counterpart of Chan and neo-Confucianism (still in its early stages of formation) and thus as one of the most prestigious forms of Chinese spirituality—highlights the strictness of the taboo. Only an immortal or a high god could calmly face the consequences of the ritual impurity caused by contact with the meat or hide of a bovine.

Another much shorter anecdote, which appears in an imperial historical record, takes place in a very similar setting: the Taiyi gong 太一宮, a Daoist temple built for court rituals. In 1148, shortly after the temple was built, "a beef-eater came into the temple and made slanderous remarks. He died suddenly that very evening. From then on, the capital's inhabitants all believed [in the sacrality of Taiyi gong or the importance of the taboo?]."[43]

Finally, a similar story takes place not in the capital but on Lushan 廬山, one of China's most famous sacred mountains just south of the Yangzi River. The Daoist cult of the Emissary of the Nine Heavens (Jiutian shizhe 九天使者) seems to have flourished there since the late Tang dynasty. In 1008, according to an account from a source that is no longer extant but was quoted in a gazetteer on this cult, a butcher entered the temple of the emissary with his friends. He was immediately seized, beaten, and driven from the temple by an invisible power. The butcher began to moo and died shortly afterward. The anecdote concluded, "Since then, those who eat beef do not dare to enter the temple."[44]

In these anecdotes, the physical, sensory character of the pollution caused by the consumption of beef justifies the use of the word "defilement," as opposed to the purity of those who observe the taboo. We must nevertheless be careful not to interpret this concept in terms of hygiene. As noted above, the Chinese sometimes consumed meat, whether beef or of other species, that came from animals that had died naturally or were slaughtered after becoming sick, an attitude that is sure to surprise a Westerner, heir of a strong tradition of repugnance toward "moribund" or "dead" flesh.[45] The Chinese were obviously aware of the dangers of consuming such meat, and some refrained from it, but neither the state nor collective practice banned it. It may be tempting to link the discourse on the impurity of beefeaters and their being cursed with epidemic diseases to the issue of eating animals that had died from disease. Indeed, it is possible that cases of illness caused by tainted beef helped give credence to the discourse of the taboo. However, even though some sources, one of which is discussed below, specifically mention the dangerousness of sick animals, the texts that developed the theme of defilement did not comment on the origin of the meat but clearly framed the issue on moral grounds. Beef was not unclean in and of itself but was prohibited and therefore made the person who ate it unclean. Defilement was moral, which explains why leather, as well as meat, could cause misfortune in the anecdote about Yisheng baode zhenjun.

In her classic study, Mary Douglas juxtaposed interdictions, which are related to ethics, to defilement, which is related to dirt and shame, which in turn are linked to a culturally constructed world order. She noted, however, that sin, as it is conceived in particular in monotheistic traditions, is at the crossroads of the two registers. The same is true of the beef taboo and its transgression in China. In these anecdotes, beefeaters transgress the moral order of the universe and end up being physically marked in such a way that they are rejected by humanity. Douglas further notes that defilement or pollution allows society to dispense blame, identify culprits when social structures are endangered, and arouse moral disapproval of, even retribution for, dangerous behavior that would not be possible otherwise.[46] It is possible that in Song China, the discourse of the defilement associated with beefeaters and thus about their vulnerability toward epidemics and accusations from the beyond served as a mechanism to safeguard both cattle herds and the moral order based on the proximity of bovines and humans.

## The Novelty of the Taboo

Our corpus of anecdotes highlights a coherent discourse. On the one hand, killing or eating a bovine was a severe sin, denounced by the cattle themselves and punished immediately by the infernal administration, whether directly or using the gods of epidemics as their intermediaries. On the other hand, taking and observing a vow of abstinence and exhorting others to do the same makes it possible to attract the blessings and protection bestowed by the gods. I argue that this discourse formed gradually from the ninth century and constituted a new phenomenon, distinct from other preexisting or contemporaneous discourses on animal life and meat in general and cattle in particular. The date of the formation of the taboo is the most challenging element of this hypothesis to prove. The fact of not having identified an older source does not mean that such sources did not exist, and even the absence of sources does not imply the absence of a discourse. The thesis of the novelty of the taboo from the ninth century, however, is quite convincing when one surveys anecdotes from the Tang concerning the relationship between cattle and retribution in which the theme is clearly treated differently than in the corpus dating from the Song.

In these older anecdotes, the predominant theme is that of humans reincarnating into cattle due to specific sins. This theme appeared extremely frequently during the Tang and remained prevalent until the twentieth century. The life of cattle was considered very hard, marked by much strenuous labor without any gratification. Reincarnation as a bovine was a punishment that became proverbial. In anecdotes, it was typical for someone who had not repaid a debt to be reincarnated as a bovine on his creditor's farm to pay off his debt through his labor.[47] It is important to note that this theme is distinct from the discourse of the taboo. Although some later texts about the taboo claimed that cattle were reincarnated humans, the two issues remained independent. The anecdotes about debt and reincarnation emphasized the human sin that caused reincarnation as cattle rather than what happened to bovines after their reincarnation. In some of these anecdotes, the bovine was sold to a butcher to pay off the debt.

Another theme attested during the Tang is closer to the taboo: the bovine begging for mercy (*niubai* 牛拜). The editors of the *Vast Records of the Taiping Era* (*Taiping guangji* 太平廣記, completed 981) gathered a series of three anecdotes on this theme.[48] Cattle appeared intelligent. Before being slaughtered, they understood what was going to happen and what was being said and begged to be spared. Only one of these anecdotes involved a supernatural punishment for someone who first promised the bovine that he would spare it if it begged for mercy but then reneged on his promise and slaughtered the pleading animal.[49] This theme only indicated the uniqueness of the bovine in a relative way. Other animals also begged to be spared, and the bovine was only endowed with greater sensitivity than the other animals. Moreover, it is possible to conceive of the theme of the vengeful bovine apart from the taboo. The bovine took revenge on a traitor who had not kept his promise rather than proving the cruelty of the specific act of killing a bovine.

Among the anecdotes predating the Song, except the two texts from the ninth century mentioned above, the one that dealt most directly with the issue of the morality of eating beef is a curious one—namely, an anecdote titled "The Man Who Ate Beef" (Shiniu ren 食牛人):

> Under Huan Xuan (369–404), there was a great bovine epizootic. A man ate the flesh of a bovine that had died [from the disease]. He himself fell ill and died. As soon as he died, he saw someone holding a register and rising to heaven. A nobleman asked him: "What is the fault of the deceased? The man [with the register] replied: "He must appear for having eaten the flesh of a bovine that died of disease." The nobleman retorted, "We need bovines to 'turn the wheel' [rule the world], and their flesh is also used to feed the people. Why do you still want to kill [this man]? Send him back." Indeed, the man

> returned to life and recounted what he had heard. After this, the beef-eater had no more problems.
>
> 桓玄時，牛大疫，有一人食死牛肉，因得病亡。云: 死時見人執錄，將至天上。有一貴人問云：「此人何罪？」對曰：「此坐食疫死牛肉。」貴人云：「今須牛以轉輪，肉以充百姓食，何故復殺之。」催令還。既更生，具說其事。於是食牛肉者，無復有患。[50]

In this anecdote, the nature of the sin punished by the man with a register is unclear, but it seems to relate to the pollution of meat defiled by disease rather than beef as a category. Admittedly, it is possible that the story alluded to the taboo insofar as "beefeaters" seem to be considered a separate category of people. However, the conclusion explicitly exonerated and encouraged beefeaters to continue their practices. From the Song, one no longer sees such texts that endorse the consumption of beef. Likewise, an anecdote from the ninth century recounts the punishment in hell of a monk who killed a bovine, but the one who ate the meat of the animal was exempt from all punishment.[51] In this anecdote, one can infer a worldview that preceded the formation of the taboo, the definition of which implied that killing cattle and eating beef were faults that could not be distinguished.

To my knowledge, the last text that could give credence to the existence of the taboo before the ninth century is an anecdote reported in a local gazetteer from Guangdong dated 1614, which recounts an event that took place during the Sui. A bovine entered a mountain village. The villagers killed and ate it, except for an old woman who abstained. The next day, torrential rains flooded the village and created a lake in its place. The old woman was the only survivor.[52] This anecdote seems to illustrate the divine punishment of the beefeaters, but this legend probably originated later than the date it invoked—namely, the Sui—and is perhaps even more recent than the corpus of anecdotes discussed above.

In short, dating the formation of the discourse of the taboo remains uncertain. Texts predating the ninth century may contain allusions to some of its themes. Nevertheless, even if the condemnation of killing cattle was ancient, the notion of the sin associated with eating beef seems to appear first in the anecdotes of the *yakṣa.* Thus, it seems reasonable to contend that the taboo emerged between the ninth and the twelfth centuries and was fully formed and widely attested in the twelfth century.

Leaving aside the issue of chronology, we must now situate this discourse vis-à-vis other discourses that were older and remained very prevalent from the twelfth century to the present day and that we have already discussed: the legal discourse on the prohibition against cattle slaughter and the duty to protect bovines and the moral authorities' discourses on killing animals and eating meat.

## The Taboo and Legal Discourse

Obviously, the discourse of the taboo and the legal discourse were closely related. From the twelfth century until the end of the imperial period, the discourse of the taboo frequently reiterated that the law prohibited cattle slaughter. Even the judges of the underworld occasionally repeat the legal discourse.[53] Some anecdotes mentioned officials who violated the prohibition against cattle slaughter and were punished for this offense. An anecdote from the eleventh century featuring an official and a monk provides an example of this. Each time the official passed in front of the monastery, the monk was there to welcome the "future minister." The official was surprised, and the monk explained that the mountain god alerted him in a dream before each visit. But one day, the official passed by, and the monk was not there. Later, the official reprimanded the monk, who then appeared to him in a dream and announced that having made the wrong judgment in a case of cattle slaughter, the official had been punished by heaven with the cancellation of his future appointment as minister. The official checked and reevaluated the case. During his next excursion, the monk was again there to welcome him and tell him that he would be a minister (which would later be confirmed).[54]

Some officials played a positive role by saving a bovine about to be slaughtered.[55] In the anecdotes, cattle threatened with slaughter were indeed addressing the magistrate as their best recourse. This was how three cattle appeared in a dream to a magistrate to ask for his help. The next day, the magistrate saw a man arrive at the court asking for authorization to sell a bovine that had died of disease to the butcher's shop. The magistrate ordered an investigation and discovered that the animal had in fact been slaughtered without having been ill. Then yamen employees asked permission to use a sick bovine for a sacrifice (*saishen* 賽神), which a subsequent investigation revealed to be healthy. In this latter case, it is intriguing that the community leaders considered sacrificing and offering to the gods a sick animal against all the rules that state that the sacrificial victim must be impeccable—or at least they pretended to in front of the magistrate. Thus, by ensuring that the law was strictly applied, the magistrate contributed to the popularization of the taboo.[56] Another magistrate learned in a dream that members of his family who lived as parasites in his yamen killed and sold cattle. He had them expelled and strictly enforced the taboo.[57]

Nevertheless, we can observe several differences between the discourse of the taboo and the legal discourse. The first is that the law authorized the slaughter of old or sick cattle as well as the trade and consumption of the meat resulting from such slaughter. We should recall that the law never strictly prohibited the consumption of beef as such. However, the discourse of the taboo condemned killing cattle and eating beef equally.

The second difference is that the legal discourse, which was based on an economic logic, associated the bovine with other animals that were "useful" to humans. The pairing of the ox and the horse existed from the Han onward. In the Tang Code, the prohibition applied to cattle, horses, donkeys, and camels. A Tang edict also forbade the slaughter of dogs and roosters. The dog guarded the house, and the rooster announced the daybreak. They were all useful (*youyong* 有用).[58] The prohibition against the slaughter of roosters was quite strange and was never repeated nor, undoubtedly, applied. However, the protection of the dog was serious and became, as we will see, part of the discourse on the taboo. In any case, it was included in the Song laws.[59] Even if it was punished less than the slaughter of an ox, slaughtering one's own dog was an offense. But in contrast to the legal categories of useful and useless animals, the discourse of the taboo categorically distinguished the bovine as an animal that was different from others.[60] In the Song texts, it was never associated with another animal; below, we will see how this evolved later.

In theory, the legal discourse considered cattle individually as a piece of working equipment essential to agriculture. By contrast, the discourse of the taboo took the species (and therefore all cattle regardless of whether they were capable of working, alive, sick, or dead) as sacred. Whereas the legal texts spoke of *gengniu,* the discourse of the taboo simply said *niu.* However, this distinction was blurred by two factors. First, the taboo discourse offered no other ultimate justification—why are cattle sacred?—than those present in the legal discourse. Anecdotal texts, which contained the oldest testimonies of the taboo, usually do not give an account of its causes. They merely highlighted the taboo out of respect for it. The few details of a justification they provided were the same as those that motivated the legal provisions—namely, that it was thanks to cattle that humans could eat (cereals) and that cattle therefore had considerable merit (*yougong* 有功) for humans.[61] Thus, it was intolerable (*buren* 不忍) for a human endowed with a sense of fairness to kill them.

Even though the discourse of the taboo did not offer a new justification compared to the bovine policy in place since the Han, the taboo nevertheless exceeded the policy in the magnitude of the consequences attributed to it. Most remarkably, the logic of the taboo was gradually adopted into the discourse of officials and scholars.

From the twelfth century on, Confucian scholars wrote on the issue of cattle.[62] However, these texts, even if they can also be read as a justification of the legal discourse, make little mention of the laws and the specific legal violations such as illegal slaughter and the trafficking and deception in which cattle dealers and butchers were engaged. Instead, they were essentially devoted to an elaboration on the moral duty of humans toward plow cattle. Over time, they incorporated more and more elements specific to the discourse of the taboo.

## Pity for the Poor Bovine

The discourse on cattle developed in literary genres from the twelfth century was expressed in essays and poetry. To my knowledge, the oldest of these texts was composed by the eminent philosopher Cheng Yi 程頤 (1033–1107). Cheng lamented the lack of moral sense among people who exploited cattle and slaughtered the animals when they grew old. His interlocutor pointed out that farmers needed the money to buy a new bovine. Cheng retorted that in a world where everyone acted according to a sense of fairness, there were never any shortages of natural resources, perhaps implying that "the gods will not let us starve."[63] Here, following a perfectly orthodox Confucian position, the essential point was people's sense of duty and fairness rather than the principle of retribution, which Cheng however did not deny. Other texts of similar sentiment followed. One author insisted that the prohibition against cattle slaughter had not always existed but was motivated by benevolence (*ren*).[64] Wang Xu 王旭 (fl. 1265–1297) detailed the different ways of recognizing the services rendered by animals and pointed out that cattle deserved the most consideration. This was a natural principle (*tianli* 天理) rather than the principle of retribution.[65] Other authors insisted on a sentimental register such as "The peasant loves his cattle as much as his children, so how could he kill them?"[66] A poet refused a dish of veal served to him, saying it was intolerable to eat this little animal that had not had time to pull the plow even once.[67] However, the discourse of the taboo was very prevalent among some of these authors. While Cheng Yi only talked about the slaughter of old cattle, others focused on the issue of meat. Wang Xu's essay was an admonition not to eat beef. The same was true for a text from the thirteenth century in which the author sent back a gift of beef, saying that this meat was once prized but that it was morally intolerable for him to taste it.[68] Another contemporary poem mentioned a "very strict interdiction" (*niu jin fangyan* 牛禁方嚴).[69] The motif of the divine punishment of beefeaters also appeared in poems from the twelfth and thirteenth centuries.[70] Finally, the scholar He Menggui 何夢桂 (1228–?), a high Song official, achieved the ultimate synthesis in a short text praising another author who had written on the abstinence from beef. He began by recalling that one could not eat an animal thanks to which one could practice agriculture and then affirmed that the Most High (Laozi) rewarded and protected those who would observe the taboo.[71]

Around the same time as these prose essays, a poetic theme developed: the slaughtered bovine's complaint of injustice and humanity's lack of moral sense. The most striking example was a lyrical ballad (*sanqu* 散曲) composed around 1300 by Yao Shouzhong 姚守中, who was otherwise unknown, and titled "The Bovine Lodges a Complaint against Injustice" (Niu suyuan 牛訴冤).[72] As Wilt Idema reminds us, this text and other later ones on the same theme constituted a rare case in Chinese literature in which an animal spoke in the first person, not allegorically but to defend its cause.[73] Yao Shouzhong's bovine begins its lament by describing its arduous life of working in the fields in all kinds of weather. It recalls that the emperor prohibited its slaughter, yet the peasant, its master, when the bovine was too old, sent for the butcher. The bovine describes in detail how it was butchered and how every part of its body—meat, skin, hooves, horns, bones, and tendons—was retrieved and sold. The bovine feels betrayed by humanity, files a complaint with Yama, who presides over the courts of hell, and promises to get revenge: "He who eats me will not be fat, and he who sells me will not be rich!" The guilty will meet the same fate as the animal. Like it, they will die an untimely death and will not be buried in a grave.

Yao Shouzhong's ballad was a turning point in the history of the literary theme of the pitiable bovine. Tang literati had already composed poems or prose texts on this subject, in particular Liu Yuxi 劉禹錫 (772–842), whose "Lamentation over a Bovine" described how he met a bovine taken to the butcher by his master. Liu offered to buy it, but the peasant refused.[74] From the Tang, therefore, we see the motif of the injustice toward an animal that had worked tirelessly for humans and was sold to the butcher when its strength declined. However, Liu Yuxi's text, like others from the ninth century, was essentially an allegory. The bovine symbolized a man in the service of his country, whom the sovereign ruthlessly eliminated when he had ceased to be indispensable.[75] Yao Shouzhong's point was very different. He did not treat cattle as an allegory for humans but presented the animal's misfortune as such and described the consequences of the mistreatment inflicted on it. Unlike the authors from the Tang, Yao was enmeshed in the discourse of the taboo.

Yao's poem was a convincing indictment in favor of cattle and a piece of high literary quality preserved in poetic anthologies. As we will see in the next chapter, the works of Yao's successors who would deal with this theme in the Ming and Qing were classified as morality literature rather than as elegant literature. But they all had in common that they emphasized affect, the pity for cattle, and the guilt of the peasant, the butcher, and the beefeater rather than the principle of retribution. They also insisted on the notions of debt and proximity generated by the shared labor of cattle and peasants. By contrast, Song anecdotes hardly dealt with the relationship between the peasant and his cattle. Instead, the most common relationship dramatized was that between the butcher and his client.

Between the twelfth and the fourteenth centuries, a discourse developed in the literary genres of essays and poetry that insisted on the moral duty toward cattle and on the injustice of the slaughter of an animal that worked hard and without reward for humanity all its life. These texts strictly insisted that the moral duty to return the favors one had received must not be neglected and demonstrated genuine pity for cattle. Since it developed after the discourse of the taboo and typically mentioned the divine punishment of beefeaters, the discourse of moral duty and pity should be read as a formulation that rationalized the discourse of the taboo in terms of common morality concerning relationships of reciprocity and recognition between beings.

What, then, was the relationship between the taboo in its anecdotal articulation, which insisted on retribution, and in its poetic articulation, which insisted on moral duty on the one hand and the more strictly utilitarian position of legal discourse that cattle must be protected to maintain agricultural production on the other hand? We can consider this relationship from two angles. Either they were distinct, albeit occasionally referring to each other, or one was an extension of the other. This second positivist perspective posits that to make people understand the law and to transform the simple application of official texts into moral education (*jiaohua* 教化), without which the law typically remained a dead letter, part of the ruling classes formulated the prohibition against cattle slaughter in religious terms so as to convince people. But I am not persuaded by explanations aimed at instrumentalizing religious representations. It should also be noted that the discourse of the taboo also led to changes in attitude among the ruling classes, including even the court's eating habits. Moreover, such an explanation does not consider the chronological gap between the appearance of the legal prohibition during the Han and the taboo nearly a thousand years later. Finally, as we have seen, the literati's speculative texts, which purportedly formed the foundation for this process of *jiaohua,* did not betray a concern with explaining the law in terms of "popular morality" but rather with formulating the taboo in more Confucian terms. In other words, the literati did not invent the taboo but rather allowed themselves to be persuaded by it.

In my opinion, there was no contradiction between the legal discourse and the taboo, which were both based on the exaltation of the bovine as a fulcrum and symbol of Chinese agricultural civilization. However, even if they are difficult to disentangle and isolate in some cases, these two discourses were independent in that they operated in different registers. The discourse of the taboo, which followed a logic of retribution and reward for ritual purity, developed in a direction that contributed nothing to the application of the law and even opposed its economic logic regarding the consumption of dead animals and the treatment of carcasses. For a very long time, legal texts did not concern themselves with the physical remains of cattle, except by circumscribing the authorization to have them butchered.[76] However, the discourse of the taboo was concerned with this issue, not only by prohibiting the consumption of beef but also by prescribing the care given to the carcass. The theme of cattle burial was not much developed in Song anecdotes on the beef taboo,[77] but it played an important role in later times.

## The Taboo and Vegetarianism

Anecdotes documenting the beef taboo bore a strong resemblance to an even more extensive, older, parallel set of anecdotes that promoted the discourse of vegetarianism and refraining from killing. There was much overlap between the two corpora: the theme of retribution, the dramatic arc and the summons to infernal courts, and the vows to change one's life. So far, historians have not set apart anecdotes concerning the beef taboo from all texts advocating against killing animals and for the practice of fasting or even vegetarianism. For example, Barend ter Haar includes some anecdotes from the corpus discussed above in his study of conversion to Buddhism during the Song.[78] Anecdotes illustrating the pro-vegetarian discourse involve all kinds of animals, sometimes including cattle. Thus, an account from the late sixth century relates the case of an official preparing to slaughter an ox. The animal begged for mercy, but he slaughtered it regardless before suddenly falling ill and dying.[79] In *Stories of Retribution from the Netherworld* (*Mingbao ji* 冥報記), a Buddhist didactic tale collection dating from the mid-sixth century, an official was summoned to hell and accused, among other things, of killing two bovines for a banquet.[80] In these two cases, nothing distinguished the bovine from other animals that were the subject of similar anecdotes in the same collections. Cattle were described as animals that should be saved just like the others.

The practice of the beef taboo also was closely connected with a central element of the discourse on saving animal lives: life releases (*fangsheng*), which became widespread during the Song. Anecdotes frequently describe cattle being spared and becoming "eternal cattle" in a sanctuary at a Buddhist or Daoist monastery.[81] Some men with charitable intentions were prepared to engage in the expensive act of buying a bovine on the verge of being slaughtered. This theme became very popular in the nineteenth century. There is such a case in our older corpus from the ninth through thirteenth centuries. One anecdote describes a village of brigands that engaged in various illegal activities, such as slaughtering cattle and dogs, distilling alcohol, and counterfeiting money. An official passing by saw five water buffaloes tied up in a field, one of which was crying and not grazing. He announced that this water buffalo would be slaughtered the next day, which indeed happened. When he returned the next day, the official saw one of the four remaining water buffaloes adopting the same attitude as its unfortunate companion the day before. The water buffalo approached the official to beg for mercy. The official then purchased the animal and took it to a farm where it could live out its natural life span.[82]

Anecdote collections that include stories of cattle butchers receiving divine punishment for their misdeeds also contain many anecdotes about butchers punished for having killed other animals. As we have already said, the butcher's trade was specialized by species: pigs, sheep, and cattle. Thus, cattle butchers were punished like the others, perhaps more so because of the illegal nature of their trade. A few exceptions confirm such a hypothesis. A peasant, who occasionally butchered animals, found himself before the court of the underworld, where he confessed to having killed thirteen cattle and twenty pigs. The judge advised him to change his conduct, do good deeds, and engage in a regimen of chanting Buddhist scriptures or Amitābha's name.[83]

However, reading the retribution for cattle slaughter as a particular case of the discourse on animal life is not sufficiently analytical. The major difference that distinguished the corpus of anecdotes on the beef taboo from those dealing with meat in a broader sense did not lie in the style or the dramatic arc—all featured spectacular retributions and visits to infernal courts—but in the conclusions. In the other anecdotes, the protagonists were ordered to change their profession of being a butcher or become vegetarian. They were often punished for a specific offense, such as having killed a particular animal, but the conclusion was general: they would spare all animals from then on. In some anecdotes with a darker ending, they were simply the victim of the vengeance of the animal they had killed, regardless of what kind of animal it was. In the case of cattle, however, the protagonists vowed to no longer eat beef without mentioning other meats. Those who observed the beef taboo were protected by the gods even though they continued eating pork, poultry, and so forth. In the following pages, we will dwell on this fundamental difference between saving animal lives more broadly and the interdiction against killing a particular animal.

The only exception to the difference between vegetarianism and a taboo specific to beef is found in some anecdotes relating to crabs and other crustaceans and fishes, which were also the subject of a particular interdiction.[84] This case appears to be different, however, insofar as the interdiction against crabs was linked to the cruelty of the method of cooking these animals as they were scalded alive. Moreover, crustaceans and fish were always the objects of particular attention in the discourse on animal life because of cruel fishing and preparation practices and because so many had to be killed to make a meal. This attention to seafood consumption as cruel and wasteful is found in various normative texts, including an influential Pure Land tract written in 1160, Wang Rixiu's 王日休 *Tract on the Pure Land by Master Longshu* (*Longshu jingtu wen* 龍舒淨土文), which mentions loaches, eels, softshell turtles, clams, and freshwater snails.[85] In comparison, a pork-based meal was more economical in terms of taking animal life.

Another difference should be noted between the anecdotes on the beef taboo and those on saving animal lives in general. As we have seen, refraining from killing animals quickly became a standard position across the three moral authorities—Buddhism, Daoism, and Confucianism—but was particularly emphasized by Buddhism. However, many anecdotes concerning vegetarianism have a noticeable Buddhist tone that was almost absent from the corpus concerning the beef taboo.[86] Admittedly, the two oldest anecdotes had *yakṣa,* who were of Indian and Buddhist origin, as the main protagonists, but they behaved like demons or local spirits, and the tales did not involve monks or Buddhist texts (or Daoist ones). Only a single anecdote involved a monk who appeared in a dream. In general, the taboo was enforced by an infernal bureaucracy that was not specifically Buddhist but constituted a common element in Chinese religion from the Song onward.[87]

In fact, the discourse on the beef taboo appears to have been distinct from that on vegetarianism without necessarily being opposed to it. Depending on the authors, the two could be linked, without being confused, in that they both attended to animal life, or could be more clearly separated. What can be deduced from the anecdotal sources was more clearly articulated in a revelation from the beginning of the fourteenth century, which constituted an addition to the autobiography of the god Wenchang 文昌 that was transmitted to his devotees through spirit-writing from 1194 onward.[88] A section titled "Releasing Life" began by asserting that all living beings had Buddha nature. The god then claimed that there was an official in heaven, the Star Tailao 太牢星, charged with punishing beefeaters and inflicting eternal torment on them on Tailao Mountain 太牢山, beginning with deadly epidemic diseases. Using a completely different tone, the text then moved on to other animals, which should be shown respect because, like humans, they received life from their parents. Regarding these other animals, Wenchang did not impose strict vegetarianism but demanded that his followers should not kill them themselves, according to a rule inspired by the ancient Buddhist precept of the "three pure meats."[89] This important text constituted one of the first instances in which a religious institution adopted the taboo: the worship of Wenchang and its revelations through spirit-writing occurred in a Daoist framework during the Song. The text explicitly juxtaposed the beef taboo with interdictions concerning other animals in a manner that would not change until the twentieth century. Eating pork and poultry was permitted, perhaps even commendable, as long as one did not kill them oneself. By contrast, cattle had an entirely different status, and any contact with beef was a severe sin. Written sometime after 1244 and included in a treatise on inner alchemy as part of moral rules for practitioners, a poem on the beef taboo develops a similar argument: heaven forbids humans to eat beef, while permanent vegetarianism is an ideal.[90]

## The Discourse of the Taboo and Its Social Reality

The paragraphs above have shown how the beef taboo emerged as a discourse and was articulated along with other, better-known discourses like vegetarianism and the state's protection of cattle but that it was also distinct from them. We now turn to establishing the taboo as a historical object and evaluating its social reality. The issue is a delicate one. The historical sources make it difficult to measure beef consumption before the twentieth century. Food historians generally agree that beef consumption appears to have decreased between the Tang and the Song, when it became relatively marginal.[91] If this conclusion is mainly impressionistic, it is nonetheless convincing. However, such a decline can be explained by many factors, such as the effect of the taboo, which would have reduced demand (as far as I know, a hypothesis nobody has advanced), changes in the agricultural economy, or increased efficiency in the enforcement of slaughter laws, which would have reduced supply.

The author who explored this issue most extensively is Shio Takugo, whose work is mainly based on a corpus of anecdotes concerning the taboo. His analysis is remarkably detailed but has two fundamental flaws. He ignores the taboo itself (Shio speaks simply of a "Buddhist" rule), and he relies on sources that criticize eating beef and concludes that beef consumption was widespread.[92] However, it is possible to revisit his categories of analysis and arrive at a different conclusion. Anecdotes show that in the twelfth and thirteenth centuries, beef consumption was not rare, but eating beef was not everyday ordinary consumption. It was limited to specific instances: particular situations such as times of famine, soldiers' banquets, the sharing of sacrificial meat, banquets and gifts given among the upper classes, and meat consumption among brigands and outlaws. The last two categories, though at opposing extremes of the social scale, were fundamentally similar. In the case of outlaws, killing and eating cattle was a way to challenge the authorities and a source of income, just like counterfeit money and alcohol trafficking. In the case of the wealthy elites, beef was a popular delicacy with its forbidden flavor and expensive price caused by its scarcity. In both cases, it is safe to assume that part of the appeal of beef lay in the fact that ordinary people did not eat it.

Speaking of gluttony and temptation, anecdotes frequently stress the protagonists' uncontrollable desire for this dish that was unlike any other.[93] One anecdote even recounted the punishment of an old vegetarian devotee who, while passing by a beef butcher shop, was merely tempted without even taking action.[94] Beef always remained available to those ready to look for it and pay the price. Cattle dealers always sought to take advantage of old cattle that had become unfit for work in the fields, with situations of famine constituting an exceptional circumstance in which beef became widely available. In addition to the quantity consumed, the very nature of the beef market changed during the Song. It became a trade involving an object of illicit consumption and a sign of marginality at the two extremes of the social scale—nobles and brigands who could afford what ordinary humans could not.

## The Appearance of the Taboo

To understand how and why the specific discourse of the beef taboo emerged, we must begin by questioning our sources. For several centuries, the taboo was documented only by didactic and "fantastic" anecdotes, particularly in the *Record of the Listener,* which comprise the majority of our documentation. This fact is in itself significant. The genre of anecdote collections (*biji* 筆記) is characterized by short accounts or remarks based either on the author's personal observations or his readings and devoted to remarkable facts or reflections. *Biji* are considered a minor literary genre, composed for pleasure rather than instruction. Nevertheless, official historiographies and Buddhist and Daoist hagiographies frequently drew their material from these compendia, though often without explicit attribution. The use of this kind of source material is problematic. As Vincent Durand-Dastès has shown, sinologists have employed anomaly accounts in various ways. Some scholars have presented them from the point of view of literary history as a mode of expression focused on the pleasure of narrating and based on the imagination; other scholars see them as primary sources for historical anthropology without any dimension of "fiction."[95] Indeed, the *Record of the Listener,* whose anecdotes are always brief, very factual, and cite their oral sources, has mainly been employed from the latter perspective.[96] Yet a work as complex as the *Record of the Listener* cannot be captured by a single category of analysis. Hong Mai undoubtedly believed in the vast majority of the extraordinary events he reported, some of which took place in his own circle. But he was also a great writer and did not transmit the events he reported without putting his literary mark on them. How should one interpret the anecdotes on the taboo in the *Record of the Listener?*

It seems to me that anecdote collections, particularly the *Record of the Listener,* typically reflected what people were talking about, what was in fashion, and what was under debate. Moreover, even though the anecdotes might employ traditional narrative patterns, the subjects they included quite faithfully reflected "social news." Anecdote collections were therefore the first texts to reflect changes in social practice, particularly religious ones. Many religious phenomena, such as the cult of Lü Dongbin 呂洞賓,[97] were observed first in anecdotes before influencing other kinds of sources. Admittedly, anecdotes blended literary conventions and factual events, but various works have shown a strong congruence between the descriptions in the *Record of the Listener* and liturgical manuals. Even though neither of the two (nor any text) can be considered a strict description of reality, such overlap shows that the *Record of the Listener* reflected social practices and cannot be treated as a mere fabrication.[98]

Whatever our verdict about the genre of anecdotes and fantastic tales, there is no doubt that for the Chinese, especially during the Song, these texts were a source of information about morality and the principle of retribution and reward. It is not a coincidence or the simple product of an imperfect transmission of historical sources that in extant materials, the beef taboo appears in such texts: the Song Chinese learned of its existence from these same texts and probably also through oral dissemination of these same anecdotes. In other words, it is through anecdotes that the revelation of the taboo spread from those who experienced it personally. This is clearly expressed by one of the anecdotes from the corpus mentioned above:

> Having heard this account [the story of Zeng Feng, recounted above], I marveled at it because, even though I had read many stories of people eating beef and getting sick in anecdotal accounts and tales [*chuanji xiaoshuo*], I had never witnessed such cases myself. My family has abstained from eating beef for three generations.
> 余聞其說異之，且嘗見傳記小說所載，食牛致疾事極衆，然未有耳目所接如此者。余家三世不食牛。[99]

In this author's family, who strictly observed the taboo, an act with significant social consequences, anecdotes were given considerable credit when it came to explaining and justifying the practice. For later authors, anecdotes from the ninth to the twelfth century still played a crucial role in their decision to convert to the taboo.[100] From this fact, one can draw one conclusion. The taboo did not originate in the actions of an institution (the state or the three institutional religions). It was a revelation that gradually appeared in several places within Chinese society, and because it encountered favorable circumstances, it was accepted, transmitted, and disseminated by a growing number of Chinese from the ninth and especially the eleventh century. Furthermore, rather than focusing on the immediate causes that triggered the first revelations, we should clarify the factors that contributed to its acceptance and dissemination. At this point, we stop glossing and exploring the text of anecdotes to enter a more adventurous field: reading between the lines and speculating about the motivations.

## Hypotheses Explaining the Taboo

Many food prohibitions in human history developed in ancient, poorly documented periods, and we can only examine them a posteriori to figure out their logic. The beef taboo in China allows us to observe the emergence of a taboo in a richly documented context. Therefore, before proceeding with this taboo's later history, we will explore the possible causes that contributed to its emergence.

It is most likely that a complex phenomenon such as the beef taboo did not have a single cause. Moreover, even though some causes are more plausible, they all likely played a role. The possible causes that most deserve our attention are those that best explain the spread of the taboo in the social and religious contexts specific to the period from the ninth to the twelfth century.

### Ecological and Socioeconomic Causes

The first causes that come to mind are ecological and socioeconomic factors. Such explanations have often been given for other dietary prohibitions, be it beef in India or pork in Judaism and Islam. However, they have also been strongly refuted and constitute, if considered exclusively, dead ends insofar as they often have secular and scientific motivations foreign to their object.[101] Nonetheless, it is clear that in the case of cattle in ninth- through thirteenth-century China, ecological and socioeconomic changes had an impact. As we have seen, beef cattle farming in pastoral zones existed during the Tang. It then disappeared because these pasture lands in the northern China territories came under the control of other political regimes and because demographic and agricultural expansion reduced the possibilities of residual grazing throughout China. At the same time, the end of the aristocratic estates led to the disappearance of large herds that could simultaneously yield working animals and meat or dairy. The livestock available for meat production shrank. Thus, the taboo could be interpreted as a mechanism aimed at reducing demand and adapting it to a supply in sharp decline. At the same time, more and more intensive agriculture—even some northern regions adopted two annual harvests—increased the workload and therefore the demand for working cattle while also reducing the land available for grazing, especially in spring and fall.

This explanation has the merit of providing a big picture, but it is not reflected in anecdotal sources, mainly from southern China, that were unfamiliar with the meat produced from the nomadic herds of the north and did not refer to livestock but instead described plow cattle slaughtered at the end of their lives or when the animals were worth more in the butcher's shop than in the fields. The development outlined above likely reduced consumption, but its impact on the discourse of the taboo is less obvious. We have already seen that the taboo cannot be explained solely as a simple religious iteration of a legal ordinance, the prohibition against slaughter. Another possible explanation, which we already discussed in the context of defilement, is the danger of eating the meat of animals that died of disease. Such a hypothesis based on hygiene insufficiently explains a discourse that prohibited all beef, whereas the consumption of sick animals constituted only a particular case.

Another potential, more cultural explanation is related to the arrival during the Song of a new Han ethnic culture and a new cuisine that rejected Tang customs, including the consumption of beef, mutton, and dairy products. In fact, the consumption of mutton was considerable during the Tang, at least among the ruling classes, and the state distributed mutton to officials.[102] But mutton consumption remained very high during the Song,[103] even though sheep were associated with a pastoral economy and gastronomy at least as much as cattle. In addition, we should remember that the first texts of the taboo appeared in the ninth century.

The Song Chinese did not define themselves only in relation to the northern nomadic cultures. As a result of steady and large-scale migration to the south, they also came into closer and closer contact with the various ethnic groups inhabiting the hills and mountains in the southern regions of present-day China. These contacts profoundly influenced the representations and religious practices of Han settlers and of various ethnicities, many of whom adopted Daoist rituals and organizations around that time that they still maintain today. However, a prevalent feature among the religious practices of the various ethnic groups in the south was the sacrifice of a water buffalo—their main farm animal—to the gods and ancestors.[104] Song texts composed by Chinese scholars often described the propensity of various ethnic groups in southern China to sacrifice cattle. They frequently noted that this was a trait of barbarism compared to how Chinese civilization treated its cattle.[105] We will see that such polemics gained much currency in the following centuries. Cattle were the symbol of China's agricultural civilization and were more than ever at the heart of a Chinese cultural identity during the Song. Caring for cattle was emphasized to distinguish Chinese culture from its northern and southern neighbors, who sacrificed and consumed them. However, this only serves a general context and not a real cause that sufficiently explains the emergence of the beef taboo.

## A Divine Taboo

We can search for other explanations in a completely different direction that fully considers the religious dimension of the taboo. The ninth through thirteenth centuries, the period in which the taboo emerged, correspond precisely to a major turning point in Chinese religious history. Various studies have shed light on parts of this process, but its overarching context is still poorly understood.[106] In contrast to medieval times, the religious structures that formed during this period were characterized by the rise of cults of local and regional gods, which replaced monastic institutions as religious centers, and the concomitant adoption of local gods into the Buddhist and especially Daoist liturgical pantheons; the rise of lineages and associations as economic and religious entities; the employment of Buddhist and Daoist clerics as contract managers in the temples of local gods, lineages, or associations; the democratization of salvation techniques (meditation, inner alchemy, etc.); and the extraordinary development of spirit-writing.

How did this vast process of change influence the emergence of the taboo? First of all, the monastic institutions' relative loss of control (but not of prestige or importance) triggered the proliferation of new revelations both within institutional religions (notably the very many new Daoist liturgical schools) and in society at large, either by spirit-writing or by other methods of revelation such as dreams, trances, or mediums. As noted above, the beef taboo was based precisely on such revelations, and we will see how some religious institutions tried to appropriate revelations concerning cattle. This already demonstrates that the context of this religious transformation shaped the beef taboo. But the emergence of new cults during the Song may be an even more significant factor.

To begin with, I would like to note that an a priori logical explanation that links the taboo to the cult of the god of cattle, Niuwang 牛王, is not corroborated by extant sources available to me.[107] Indeed, a few anecdotes described a bovine god punishing beefeaters, but this motif seems unrelated to cult practices. Niuwang was invoked for cattle protection, and traces of his temples can be found from the medieval period to the present day. However, the epigraphic and anecdotal data concerning the cult of Niuwang do not reflect any elements directly related to the taboo.[108] Historical and ethnographic data show that on Niuwang's birthday (which fell on different dates depending on the location), cattle received special care by letting them rest and feeding them their favorite food, but this does not suggest a permanent taboo. In addition, the two famous minions of the underworld, Ox Head (Niutou 牛頭) and Horse Face (Mamian 馬面), originated from Buddhist texts translated earlier and undoubtedly from Indian iconography. They also appear to be unrelated to the taboo.

We should instead investigate whether there were any links between the taboo and gods of much greater importance—namely, the gods associated with the new Daoist revelations of the Song. But before examining the sources that shed light on this relationship, we should explore the emergence of another Daoist food prohibition from the Song. While, through the Tang, Daoist texts referred only to the interdiction against meat, at least during celebrations, liturgical compendia from the twelfth century insisted on a new, more selective taboo: the "three revulsions" (*sanyan* 三厭) identified with wild geese (*yan* 雁),[109] dogs, and aquatic animals with pointed heads, such as eels and turtles.[110] These taboos, with the addition of beef, are still common among many Daoists today, and we must try to understand them as a unified set.

## The Taboo and Zhenwu

To my knowledge, the first text—neither anecdotal nor revealed—on the subject of the beef taboo that provides an explanation directly related to Daoism is from a collection of reflections and anecdotes by Chen Shichong 陳世崇 (1245–1308), which gave substantial attention to the taboo. Chen rejected justifications based on retribution for misdeeds in favor of "logical" reasoning:

> It is said that the character *lao* 牢 ("sacrifice") is derived from the character *niu* ("bovine"). The bovine is also said to be the domestic animal associated with earth [in the system of five agents (*wuxing*)]. [In heaven,] it resides in the [constellation of the] Heavenly Mansion. Now, Zhenwu is the divinity of the North, associated with water, and likewise resides in the Heavenly Mansion. That is why eating it is prohibited.[111]
>
> 或謂牢字從牛。或謂牛土畜也。與土宿同位。真武為北水神，亦與土同位，故不可食。

Chen Shichong offered two explanations, one etymological and the other associated with cosmological considerations, which are rather unconvincing to us as historical factors. But most important, Chen linked the beef taboo to the worship of the deity Zhenwu. This possibility is fascinating in several ways. First, it is chronologically consistent. Zhenwu has been one of the most important Daoist deities since the Song dynasty and was intimately connected to the liturgical and spiritual renewal of Daoism between the tenth and fourteenth centuries. Zhenwu (formerly known as Xuanwu 玄武),[112] a North Star deity represented by a turtle and a snake, had been known since at least the Han. However, it was an emblematic deity that was not the object of a personalized cult. In the tenth century, this name was grafted onto the identity of an ascetic character who had attained immortality and was charged by the heavenly administration to correct injustices in the universe. Subsequently, the divinity that emerged—sometimes within a group of four deities, the *sisheng,* and sometimes independently—was a martial figure, depicted barefoot, with loose hair, and wielding a sword, who responded to the summons of exorcists to slay demons. The cult spread rapidly throughout China as exorcisms presided over by Zhenwu became an indispensable element in Chinese social practice. Furthermore, in the late thirteenth century, a mountain in central China, Wudang shan 武當山, was recognized as the location where Zhenwu became immortal. Within a few decades, Wudang shan, a place of religious training and pilgrimage, became one of China's most sacred religious sites and has remained so to this day. Zhenwu even became the tutelary deity of the Ming dynasty.[113]

The beef taboo therefore emerged at the same time as the cult of Zhenwu gained importance throughout China. In addition, one of the "three revulsions," which formed around the same time, concerns the turtle and the eel. These two animals are explicitly linked to Zhenwu. We will return later to the other two "revulsions," the wild goose and the dog.[114]

The earliest mention of the taboo in the context of the Zhenwu cult is on a stele erected in 1099, which is inscribed with the text of a scripture on the Zhenwu cult followed by ritual instructions for fasting on descent days when Zhenwu is on earth inspecting humans and a list of taboo foods: wild goose, beef, dog, turtle, snakefish, and garlic 忌食雁牛犬鱉鱧蒜. The same scripture is found in the Daoist canon but without these ritual instructions.[115]

Finally, two anecdotes from the corpus on the beef taboo involved Zhenwu. One described a god with loose hair spreading an epidemic among the inhabitants of a city while sparing families that observed the beef taboo.[116] Loose hair is an iconographic characteristic of martial deities in the exorcists' pantheon, especially Zhenwu. The other, more remarkable anecdote concerned the temple of Yisheng as early as the late tenth century when the god punished all those within a hundred *li* radius who ate beef or wore leather. Yisheng is not Zhenwu, but the two deities belonging to the *sisheng* are very closely associated and even confused.

Undoubtedly, the cult of Zhenwu was thus closely related to the taboo from the eleventh century onward. It is difficult to interpret the relationship in terms of cause and effect, but the cult of Zhenwu certainly contributed to the spread of the taboo. In morality books from the sixteenth through the twentieth centuries, discussed in the next chapter, the most frequently cited text is a short admonition revealed by Zhenwu:

> Instructions on the Taboo against Cattle and Dogs by Xuantian shangdi
>
> The Dark Emperor said: in heaven, cattle are the essence of the Dark Warrior [Xuanwu], and, on this earth, they constitute the offering of the Great Sacrifice [*tailao*]. We do not dare to sacrifice them except to heaven, and only the heavenly divinity dares to accept them. In the heavens, the bovine's shape corresponds to a constellation of the stars, and here below, its strength makes the earth fruitful. It bestows blessings on humanity and does not harm people. The country has immutable laws against those who kill it, and in the next world, catastrophic punishments await those who eat it. The character *lao* [sacrifice or also prison] is derived from the character *niu* [bovine], and the character *yu* 獄 [jail] is derived from the character *quan* 犬 [dog]. Those who do not eat cattle or dogs will forever avoid being jailed. Taiyi and Laoshan both have true forms.[117] Those who eat them for three days will see demons come and seize their souls, but those who observe the taboo for three years will have their names entered in the Yuqing registers.[118] Cattle only eat plants, so what harm do they do to humans? Humans can eat all beings but must observe the taboo against cattle and dogs.
>
> 玄天上帝戒牛犬訓
>
> 玄帝曰。夫牛者，上天玄武之精，下土太牢之品。非郊祀不敢用，非天神不敢歆。其形上列天星，其力下興地利。有功於世，無害於民。殺之者，國有常法。食之者，幽有禍愆。牢字從牛，獄字從犬。不食牛犬，牢獄永免。太乙牢山俱有真形。食之三日，魔神攝精。戒之三載，名上玉清。牛食百草，與人何害。人食百物，牛犬可戒。[119]

This text comprises various elements, the most striking of which is undoubtedly the first: "Cattle are the essence of the Dark Warrior," which assimilates bovines with Zhenwu and thus makes them sacred. This is followed by the etymological explanation also cited by Chen Shichong. It is therefore possible that Chen was quoting the revelation of Zhenwu, but this text has not been transmitted independently and is only found in later anthologies. A better-known Zhenwu revelation that mentions the taboo more briefly is quite reliably dated 1302 and is titled *Golden Rules and Jade Laws by the Supreme Sovereign of Dark Heaven* (*Xuantian shangdi jinke yulu* 玄天上帝金科玉律) or *Instructions Revealed by the Supreme Sovereign of Dark Heaven* (*Xuantian shangdi chuixun* 玄天上帝垂訓).

The *Instructions Revealed by the Supreme Sovereign of Dark Heaven* deserves our attention because it confirms that from the beginning of the fourteenth century, revelations by Zhenwu helped spread the taboo. It highlighted the cosmic role of Zhenwu in the punishment of sinners and the moral rules to be observed. It emphatically affirmed the importance of the beef taboo twice: "Above all, do not kill or eat cattle or dogs" 切莫殺食牛犬 and "Those who eat beef or dog meat attract epidemic diseases" 牛犬食之招瘟.[120]

In short, it seems probable that Zhenwu's revelations, as early as 1099 and with increasing frequency during the late Song and Yuan, significantly contributed to legitimizing and popularizing the taboo. As with Chen Shichong, Zhenwu's devotees could consider this taboo specific to their deity. However, it seems much more difficult to determine whether the cult of Zhenwu created the taboo. The first texts related to the taboo appeared in the ninth century, before the rise of the cult of Zhenwu. Moreover, the taboo is absent from the vast majority of the literature related to Zhenwu, which shows that it was not a defining feature of the cult, at least until the fourteenth century. Furthermore, *Instructions Revealed by the Supreme Sovereign of Dark Heaven* was not included or even mentioned in the twenty or so texts that specifically dealt with Zhenwu and were included in the Daoist Canon compiled in 1445. The only one of these texts to mention the taboo was a commentary on the revealed autobiography of this deity. The autobiography asserted that devotees should not eat unclean things, meats, and alliaceous plants. The commentator, Chen Zhong 陳伀 (fl. 1236), specified that this especially concerned the flesh of turtles, snakes, and eels[121] and the meat of cattle, horses, and wild animals.[122] It could therefore be that the *Instructions Revealed by the Supreme Sovereign of Dark Heaven* and Chen Zhong's commentary came from some of the many cult communities devoted to Zhenwu during the late Song but that the taboo, which these texts place at the heart of the cult, was not adopted with as much enthusiasm by other groups devoted to the deity, at least until the fifteenth century, and was not generally considered as a central element of the cult of Zhenwu.

More generally, Daoism was the religious institution that most quickly and deeply integrated the beef taboo. Nevertheless, this taboo should not be considered a strictly Daoist innovation. The anecdote about the temple of Yisheng baode zhenjun could constitute a reference to a tenth-century revelation of the taboo within a Daoist framework via the Daoist priest Zhang Shouzhen, but this reference has been preserved only in a collection of anecdotes and does not appear in canonical texts about Zhang Shouzhen and Yisheng baode zhenjun.[123] The oldest firmly datable text in which Daoists recognize the taboo was another revelation: the autobiography of Marshal Wen 温元帥, dated 1274. Like Zhenwu, Wen was a martial deity invoked in exorcisms. In his hagiography, Wen is described as a soldier who had to flee because of the jealousy of his superior. He was then reduced to the most abject state, that of a bovine butcher, at the foot of Taishan. He received a visit from the god of Taishan's son, who asked him, "How can you kill cattle and violate the heavenly laws to such an extent?"[124] Wen immediately converted and set out on a religious path that would lead him to salvation. As mentioned above, the revelation of Wenchang, which clearly articulated the adoption of the beef taboo for a Daoist audience, followed a few decades later in 1316.

Remarkably, all the Daoist texts that integrated the taboo emerged from new movements around the tutelary deities of ritual exorcistic traditions (Zhenwu, Yisheng baode zhenjun, Wenchang, Marshal Wen). Modern and contemporary practice, which demands that Daoists observe taboos against beef, turtles, and eels that were formulated for the first time by Chen Zhong, did not appear in the great prescriptive and more conservative texts of the Song period, which continued to reiterate the older rule of refraining from killing animals in general. The fact remains that this almost furtive appearance of the taboo was a phenomenon of great historical importance for Daoism since these dietary rules are still observed in Daoism today.[125] The underlying reasons for such a development are obscure but certainly involved the consideration of actual practices—namely, the effective abandonment of the vegetarian ideal in medieval Daoism except during celebrations and the desire to formulate new rules of ritual purity that were both practical and significant vis-à-vis the sacrificial religion.

One of the most important texts attesting to the beef taboo being included in Daoist rules is one of the divine codes (*tianlü* 天律), detailing how gods punish humans and spirits and that flourished from the Song period onward.[126] This code, *Nüqing Heavenly Code Proclaimed by Order [of the Jade Emperor] Written in Red Ink, of the Most-High Hundong Tradition* (*Taishang hundong chiwen Nüqing zhaoshu tianlü* 太上混洞赤文女青詔書天律), was probably compiled during the Yuan period and was later reprinted in various forms. It explains that high gods inspect humans, seize whomever they see slaughtering cattle, and condemn them to hell along with their ancestors in nine generations. Those who eat beef will have their ancestors reincarnate as cattle, and they will be condemned to the Fengdu hell. If the animal has died a natural death, the eaters will have six years taken off their life span; if they did not know it was beef, there is no crime.[127] This law in the divine code has universal value; we may also note that some other Daoist ritual traditions codified the beef taboo specifically in the context of practicing the rituals.[128] We also have a mention of ritual techniques for priests to obtain the pardon of the gods on behalf of people who have been punished with illness because they had eaten beef or horsemeat.[129]

In short, the new Daoist movements of the Song, which were also possession cults, provided the framework for revelations related to the beef taboo, similar to other revelations in the surrounding society from the same period. It is unlikely that the revelations in new Daoist movements preceded and directly shaped those that occurred in other contexts. More likely, they were all part of the same larger phenomenon. But it is undeniable that these movements' adoption of the taboo, along with their pedigree within the Daoist fold, strongly contributed to the spread of the taboo, especially through texts revealed by Zhenwu.

## Sacrifice and Ritual Defilement

Another type of causality that can explain the rise of the taboo may be found in the sacrificial liturgy and its codes of purity. The transformations of sacrificial practices undoubtedly played a role in the emergence of the taboo, even if the use of beef as sacrificial meat was hardly mentioned in our corpus of anecdotes. Nonetheless, one cannot but notice that in quite a few anecdotes and didactic texts, cattle were called *tailao,* "supreme sacrificial animal."[130] We have seen that between the Tang and the Ming, the Chinese state gradually reduced the once considerable quantity of sacrificed cattle throughout the intense liturgical calendar of state cults and that according to state doctrine, sacrificial beef became an exceptional and rare meat. In the twelfth century, both during the Jin and the Southern Song, cattle were no longer sacrificed except to heaven, the imperial ancestors, and Confucius. One thirteenth-century author asserted that the beef taboo was justified by the merit of plow cattle and, above all, because it was food for heaven. An ordinary human who ate it committed a severe sin by violating the universal hierarchy, which could only provoke heavenly punishment.[131] It may be that the Confucian idea that cattle were reserved for the most sacred sacrifices had spread in society. However, it is difficult to demonstrate the influence of state rituals on Chinese religion as a whole.

At the same time, a long-term development occurred within Chinese religion: the fundamental notion of the "three sacrificial animals" (*sansheng*), attested from antiquity and still in use today, continued, but its meaning evolved. Until the end of the first millennium, the expression *sansheng* always designated cattle, sheep, and pigs; however, from the Song, apart from state sacrifices, it meant pig, chicken, and fish. The sacrificial practices of the population had changed, although it is unclear when, how, or why. We can only assume that this change was linked to the more general transformation of Chinese religion that took place between the tenth and fourteenth centuries, but evidence is still lacking. Epigraphic and anecdotal data, which are the richest for the history of local cults, almost always refer to sacrifices in terms too general for one to decipher the details of the practice.

It is almost certain that the practice of sacrificing cattle declined during the Song. However, it persisted in conjunction with cattle fights that were often organized during festivals, at the end of which the defeated animal was eaten.[132] Like the decrease in beef consumption, the reduction in sacrifices may have had ecological and economic causes: a reduction in supply and an increase in prices. However, the proscription of cattle sacrifice seems to have extended much further than a simple substitution with a victim that was easier to obtain. Conversely, the cases of persistence were very significant in their proclaimed singularity. The most famous was that of the temple of King Zhang in Cishan, mentioned in the previous chapter. The mass killing of cattle for King Zhang's festival caused a scandal among officials. However, there is a curious reference to this cult in a local gazetteer from the early thirteenth century. The text says that the devotees taking part in the sacrifice must observe the interdiction against pork.[133] This interdiction was, at the very least, strange. If one were to identify an authorized type of meat common in sacrifices and ordinary food, it would be pork. An anecdotal source explained that this interdiction was linked to King Zhang performing some of his miracles in the shape of a pig.[134] The most plausible explanation of this text is a complete reversal of the sacrificial codes in the temple of King Zhang: what was allowed elsewhere (pork) was forbidden there, and what was forbidden elsewhere (beef) was allowed there.

At any rate, the case of King Zhang demonstrates that the issue of sacrifice did not end with the simple choice of the animal offered to the god, but it brought into play notions of ritual purity and impurity. Before a sacrifice, all participants had to observe a three-day fast to participate in the ritual, but some unclean foods had to be avoided for more extended periods or permanently. I hypothesize that at the same time that many cults abandoned cattle sacrifices, they designated bovines as taboo. We will return to this issue in the context of later data showing that beefeaters were excluded from worship communities and thus from the religious life of the village. The anecdotes concerning Yisheng baode zhenjun and the Emissary of the Nine Heavens, in which the beefeaters approaching the temples of these deities were punished with death, demonstrate that the notion of exclusion linked to the impurity of the beefeaters (and not of the meat itself) already existed in the twelfth century, although it is not clear that it was already widespread. In other words, the defilement of beefeaters described in the corpus of anecdotes was institutionalized in the codes of ritual purity of some cult communities in which nonsacrificial meats were prohibited and only sacrificial animals were generally permissible. This interpretation is corroborated by comparing the beef taboo with that of the "three revulsions" (*sanyan*) with which it was closely associated. The first of the *sanyan,* the wild goose, was a Confucian sacrificial animal offered during weddings.[135] The taboo against this rare food animal cannot but be understood as a Daoist rejection of Confucian sacrifice. While this rejection was evident in the case of the wild goose, it was also likely in the case of cattle. Various groups defined themselves by prohibiting the sacrifice and consumption of sacrificial meat eaten by other groups.

A very instructive parallel can be drawn with Japan where, in addition to the abstinence from meat in certain circumstances (an idea introduced by Buddhism), the notion of more or less pollution brought about by the consumption of the meat of various animals made it formally impossible to access sanctuaries and ceremonies according to shrine codes from the ninth century. In addition, horsemeat and beef consumption disappeared quite suddenly in the eleventh century and only continued regularly among a small part of the population—namely, outcasts. This development is undoubtedly more abrupt than in China, but it occurred in the same time frame. Taira Masayuki, who has studied these interdictions, also notes that (as in China) nobles and outcasts still consumed beef, but the general population did not.[136] The parallels are striking.

However, Taira, who studied the notion of defilement, particularly regarding deer, explains the disappearance of beef consumption in Japan by another factor: the widespread concept of debtors being reincarnated as cattle. According to him, the Japanese stopped eating beef to avoid eating their reincarnated human kin. I do not know enough about the Japanese situation or the influence of Chinese religion on Japanese shrine codes to assess Taira's analysis, but I think the similarities with Japan reinforce the hypothesis of a strong link between the beef taboo and the development of ritual purity codes.

What about the explanation advanced by Taira in the Japanese case? We have noted that in Chinese texts, these two themes—the reincarnation of debtors as cattle and the beef taboo—were both well attested but independent of each other. To my knowledge, only four texts among the hundreds referring to the taboo explicitly mentioned the fact that cattle must be spared because they were reincarnated relatives. One was an anecdote from the Yuan dynasty. A cattle butcher behaved like an ox and realized that the two animals he was about to slaughter were his reincarnated father and grandfather. When he came to, he released the two animals and changed his profession.[137] A late Ming anecdote made a very similar argument.[138] The other two texts appeared in later morality books.[139] Faced with these few occurrences of this theme, I can only read them as Buddhist reinterpretations of the taboo. Moreover, the same motif of animals as reincarnated relatives appeared in connection with other animals and did not simply support the "bovine exception."[140] It is quite possible that many people understood the beef taboo in this way, but it is much more difficult to identify this as a major cause for the taboo. Rather than pointing to a common Buddhist culture in China and Japan that prohibited the consumption of an animal that was seen as a reincarnated kin, one might speculate to what extent the emerging taboo in China influenced the one that developed in Japan and whether, in both cases, the notion of a meat excluded from the sacrifices and whose consumption was therefore prohibited for participants in sacrifices played an important role.

## By Way of Synthesis

It will never be possible to pinpoint the exact roles of the various types of causality in the emergence of the taboo, from the most immediately pragmatic ones (scarcity and price of livestock) to the most profoundly cultural ones. They all played roles at different levels and in various ways, depending on the person in question. Indeed, even though an interdiction dictated by a civil or religious institution may possibly be rationalized in a uniform manner, the beef taboo emerged spontaneously and spread among actors, each of whom had their own motivations and rationalizations.

However, it is possible to outline a general picture that leaves room for the various causalities at work. In a context in which cattle were extolled—gradually from the Han and at an unprecedented level during the Song—as the precious and fragile symbol of Chinese agricultural civilization, bovines came to be regarded as an exceptional animal. This special status played out on several levels: that of sacrifices during which cattle could only be offered in exceptional circumstances and that of the relationships between humans and animals in which no other animal was described as being as close to humans in terms of familiarity, mutual dependence, feelings, and emotional expression.

The emergence of cattle as an exceptional animal made it possible to resolve an important contradiction in the ethical and religious system of medieval China: the coexistence of the ideals of refraining from killing and vegetarianism and the need for bloody sacrifices. By observing the beef taboo, the Chinese were showing their respect for life, their attention to the principle of retribution and reward, and their understanding of the teachings of the Three Teachings, which extended the moral community to all forms of life, while maintaining the need for sacrifice and commensality at banquets (with pork, which becomes the meat par excellence). It also allowed them to differentiate themselves from more radical groups that for their part obeyed similar requirements by following the radical rule of vegetarianism.

Some observers devised an explanation according to which the beef taboo in China was a compromise or a stopgap on the path to the Buddhist imposition of vegetarianism.[141] In other words, unable to save all animals, Buddhists started by saving cattle. But such an interpretation seems at odds with the evidence exposed in this chapter, which by and large does not originate from specifically Buddhist contexts. The beef taboo was not a Buddhist initiative to do with one animal what one failed to do with all animals. Instead, it was a reaction of Chinese religion as a whole intended to resolve tensions brought about by vegetarian ideals, which were promoted notably (but not solely) by Buddhists. The beef taboo legitimized and trivialized the sacrifice and consumption of pork in a way that contradicted the Buddhist ethical project. Moreover, Buddhists did not widely adopt the taboo in their doctrinal writings even though, as we will see in the next chapter, some monks did write in support of the taboo (sometimes quoting Daoist texts as they did so). By contrast, Daoists integrated the taboo gradually into their rules and, in the most remarkable way, with the revelations of Zhenwu, whereas Confucianism took a more timid stance that justified it in terms of moral duty. This does not deny that widely shared Buddhist ideals, such as the value of all life, and the notion that animals were likely to be incarnations of deceased humans significantly contributed to the cultural acceptance of the beef taboo; I propose, however, that the role of Daoist ritual and its relation to local cults was a decisive factor.

Such an adoption explains why the taboo, which appeared as an independent and fully formed discourse around the twelfth century, spread rapidly, at least from the thirteenth century, among the entire Chinese society. The apparent decline in beef consumption during the Song and Yuan (except among Mongols) corroborates such a hypothesis, as does the social condemnation attached to such consumption in the narrative sources. It is, however, difficult to assert that the taboo became a universal feature of Chinese culture since that period. The taboo attained such a status in a manifest way with the emergence of morality books.

# 4 The Beef Taboo and Late Imperial Chinese Ethics

THE METHODS OF disseminating an ethical or religious discourse are as important as its content. In the case of the beef taboo, the dissemination process was relatively slow and took several centuries. Yet it was so successful that in the sixteenth century, one scholar proclaimed, "From the court to the literati and even among the lower classes living in the alleys, there is no one who is unaware that killing a bovine is a great crime" 上自朝廷縉紳學士，下至閭巷細民，無不知殺牛之為大戾者。[1]

How did this discourse, which began as a revelation to a few individuals, become normative throughout Chinese society? From the Song dynasty, several literary genres transmitted the discourse of the taboo: first and foremost, strange and didactic anecdotes and soon afterward, revealed Daoist scriptures, bureaucratic documents, poetry, and popular ballads. These different types of texts continued to play roles in the spread of the taboo until the beginning of the twentieth century, and others joined them, such as novels and plays. But in terms of the volume of discourse transmitted and the impact on people's conscience, the genre that played the most important role was undoubtedly that of morality books (*shanshu*), especially from the sixteenth century onward. Indeed, these books not only compiled and proliferated the existing texts dealing with the taboo but also made it possible to legitimize the discourse of the taboo in its entirety. Inclusion in morality books took the beef taboo a qualitative step forward by signaling that it had become a central element of Chinese morality. I present here the discourse of the taboo from the sixteenth through the early twentieth centuries in the context of morality books. I will first introduce the morality books genre, then explore their treatment of the taboo, and finally investigate the types of moral instruction that morality literature generated around the respect for cattle.

## Morality Books

Morality books have remained understudied despite their fundamental importance in Chinese social, ethical, and religious practice since the sixteenth century.[2] They can be defined as texts devoted to exhorting their readers, by reasoning and giving examples, to behave righteously. Morality books are based on the notion—common to Chinese religion as a whole—of moral retribution and reward for one's actions. This notion is also articulated in the Confucian, Buddhist, and Daoist classics, albeit based on different theological foundations. Drawing on the Three Teachings, morality books affirm that any virtuous act sooner or later results in favorable effects, whereas evil deeds entail unfavorable consequences. This principle remains valid whether we consider the mechanism of retribution and reward as spontaneous, as resonance (*ganying* 感應), or as the work of an otherworldly moral bureaucracy. All Three Teachings are ambiguous on this point.

Moreover, the enormous profusion of morality books from the sixteenth century is indissolubly linked to spirit-writing (*fuji*, *jiangbi* 降筆, *feiluan* 飛鸞, and many other terms).[3] This had already been a common practice since at least the eleventh century. As mentioned above, an important part of the twelfth- through fourteenth-century texts concerning the beef taboo had been revealed by this means. However, most of the scriptures revealed by spirit-writing from the Song and Yuan were still more or less controlled by Daoists who supervised the mediums. From the sixteenth century, a larger, easier access to the ritual techniques for spirit-writing spawned numerous "lay" groups who disseminated their teachings by this means, thereby fueling the prodigious boom in the production of revelations, including morality books. Finally, the development of morality books was accompanied by the emergence of charitable associations (*shantang*) dedicated to implementing such moral programs and often founded by groups that practiced spirit-writing.

### Definition and History of Morality Books

Even though morality books have been a widely recognized bibliographical category since the seventeenth century, there are many continuities with other literary genres because they are defined by their purpose and not by their form. Thus, they are sometimes difficult to distinguish precisely from household rules and instructions (*jiaxun* 家訓); collections containing the maxims of the great thinkers (*geyan* 格言); Sacred Edicts (*shengyu* 聖諭) along with commentaries and adaptations; handbooks for officials (*guanzhen* 官箴), some of which have a strong moralizing dimension; encyclopedias (*leishu* 類書); popular education or pedagogical books (*mengxue* 蒙學); precious scrolls (*baojuan* 寶卷) for oral performance, many of which have a strong moralizing focus; and finally ballads and other forms of oral literature transmitted by storytellers and even some didactic novels and plays that were explicitly conceived as narrative commentaries on morality books.[4] There are many overlaps in style and objectives among these genres—namely, the concerns of common morality, such as respect for normative social relations and the virtues associated with them, particularly filial piety. Nevertheless, compared to all these other genres, morality books are distinguished by a particular emphasis on the principles of divine retribution and reward for human conduct.

Historically speaking, the morality book genre emerged gradually. During the first stage in the Song, two predominantly Daoist-inspired texts appeared that became classics. *Verses on Action and Consequence Revealed by the Lord on High* (*Taishang ganying pian* 太上感應篇), the older of the two, was revealed at the beginning of the twelfth century, and *Ledger of Merits and Demerits Revealed by the Immortal Lord of the Taiwei Star* (*Taiwei xianjun gongguo ge* 太微仙君功過格, 1171) appeared a few decades later. Other revealed texts, such as *Instructions Revealed by the Supreme Sovereign of Dark Heaven,* which likewise provided a holistic moral program drawn from multiple traditions, were composed between the twelfth and fifteenth centuries, but they never attained the status of *Verses on Action and Consequence Revealed by the Lord on High.* New texts appeared rapidly in the late sixteenth century and were widely promoted as normative guides for individual conduct in literate circles: Yuan Huang 袁黃 (1533–1606) propagated the use of ledgers of merit and demerit (*gongguo ge* 功過格), while the Wenchang cult promoted newly revealed moral tracts.

From the late sixteenth century onward, a set of three key texts emerged that was the most cited and commented on throughout the Qing. In addition to *Verses on Action and Consequence Revealed by the Lord on High,* it included the *Tract on Hidden Rewards, by the Imperial Lord Wenchang* (*Wenchang dijun yinzhi wen* 文昌帝君陰騭文, henceforth *Tract on Hidden Rewards*) from the end of the Ming, and some decades later, the *True Scripture to Awaken Humanity, by the Imperial Lord Saint Guan* (*Jueshi zhenjing* 覺世真經), revealed by Guandi during the Kangxi era.[5] The *Tract on Hidden Rewards* and *True Scripture to Awaken Humanity* are two very concise texts (about 650 characters each) that resemble *Verses on Action and Consequence Revealed by the Lord on High* in their structure (the last is about twice as long) and are very similar to each other in their inspiration. Although, as Yau Chi-on points out, the classics of the morality books genre were already present by around 1700, the last two centuries of the Qing dynasty were the golden age of the genre. During this period, the abundance of commentaries and elaborations and the extensive dissemination of an ever-increasing number of editions made morality books one of the most widespread and influential types of book across all strata of society.[6]

The content of morality books comprised three broad categories: (1) revelations, which were typically relatively short and took the form of a doctrinal scripture (*jing* 經) or a poem; (2) commentaries on these writings, which also included didactic explanations, anecdotes illustrating the retribution for various sins, and quotes from ancient classics or philosophers as well as from other revelations; and (3) ledgers facilitating the calculation of merits and demerits. These elements were usually combined because morality books were essentially cumulative and anthological. In particular, morality books systematically integrated texts revealed by the gods with other writings composed by humans.

## The Discourse of Morality Books and Chinese Religion

One of the most characteristic features of morality books was ecumenism: their tone was aggressive toward sinners, but the discourse sought to bring all good people together. Morality books did not adopt a sectarian approach. In their editing and dissemination, they transcended religious institutions, with which they, however, made a joint cause. Morality books were one of the most important expressions of Chinese religion that denied any competition between the Three Teachings. They could contain anticlerical elements, but these were expressions of an anticlericalism that criticized the Buddhist, Daoist, or Confucian clergy without questioning these religions as doctrinal and symbolic systems.[7] In other words, morality books described a world that was both very religious and very lay oriented. In this too, morality books were distinct from other literary genres with which they also had strong continuities: morality books encouraged piety in all its forms (*Tract on Hidden Rewards* and *True Scripture to Awaken Humanity* urged their readers to build temples and to pray), whereas other genres dealing with morality (Sacred Edicts, household rules, and handbooks for officials) warned against most collective religious activities. Nonetheless, these different texts were often written and disseminated by the same circles. This is not really a contradiction but rather due to differences specific to literary genres. While some texts were clearly confessional in orientation (Sacred Edicts and household rules, for example, expressed the two primary dimensions of the Confucian orthodoxy: state religion and family religion), morality books encompassed the common ground of all Chinese religion and bracketed elements that were too specific to each teaching. In other words, morality books were, in essence, consensual. They could not be otherwise since they were not supported by any institution that could enforce them and had influence only to the extent that they were widely acknowledged and accepted. However, not all morality books said the same thing. Some conveyed controversial themes and stood out from a purely conservative attitude. They also have a history, and their discourse evolved over the generations.

Despite the definition of morality books as a "consensual" genre, we should keep in mind that they were composed by scholars. Yet, although some morality books depicted mainly the world of the literati, most shared the desire to find ethical foundations common to all of society and provide the bases for a social harmony that suited everyone. Their framing was literate, but their concerns transcended social class. In other words, morality books constituted one facet of the Chinese literati's vision of society. This vision was more "religious" and more open to "popular culture" than those conveyed in other literary genres. Some scholars, notably Sakai Tadao 酒井忠夫 (1912–2010), regard morality books as a tool to popularize the moral values of the elite. One influential historiographical tradition even regards any morality book as an expression of popular Confucianism.[8] Without denying the entire validity of this approach, I would like to note that Buddhist and Daoist teachings and clerics also made crucial contributions to the common morality promoted in morality books. Designating the *Verses on Action and Consequence Revealed by the Lord on High* as Confucian is indeed absurd. In any case, morality books aimed to overcome such distinctions.[9] Rather than labeling them as popular Confucianism, I prefer to define morality books as the ethical literature of Chinese religion.

## The Discourse on Animals in Morality Books

From the genre's earliest days, respect for life was always a major injunction of morality books, along with social and familial relationships, care for the poor and the weak, honesty in business, and respect for the gods.[10] This encompasses respect for all forms of life—from tiny insects right up to humans, in a graduated way—all lives are considered precious but not to the same degree. Thus, morality books often propose vegetarianism as an ideal and not an obligation but insist on protecting those animals closest to humans, notably bovines, equines, and dogs.

I have identified six themes related to animals in the tradition of morality books over the long term that will help to contextualize the discourse on the beef taboo presented in the next section. These themes are not distinctly separated in the actual texts but overlap and combine in all sorts of ways: they follow different logics and are usually juxtaposed rather than seamlessly combined into a single unified thesis. Many elements in these arguments derive from either Confucian, Buddhist, or Daoist moral teachings, but in the context of morality books, they are recycled and presented within a universal moral discourse that encompasses the Three Teachings. The main themes, from the most general to the most specific, are as follows:

1. Respect for the natural cycles of life and the environment. This includes injunctions against killing young animals, disturbing hibernating animals, polluting rivers, and starting fires in mountainous areas. These prescriptions derive from a very ancient tradition, documented in Han texts such as the *Yueling* and in the earliest Daoist precepts.
2. Injunctions against direct involvement in killing animals for food or fun (*jiesha*). Although scholars tend to associate this precept with Buddhism, morality books consistently support it with Confucian and Daoist, as well as Buddhist, references. Permanent vegetarianism is often described as very difficult to achieve, but morality book readers are enjoined to refrain from killing animals or ordering their servants to do so. Therefore, buying a chunk of pork on the market is a lesser sin. Consuming meat and thus directly or indirectly causing an animal to be killed is tolerated for sacrifices to ancestors and deities, for nourishing aged or ill parents, and according to some texts, for treating honored guests within reasonable limits. Killing or causing others to kill animals can be tolerated in some instances, such as defending oneself against dangerous animals. The real crime is defined as killing or obtaining meat "without a proper reason" (*wu gu*).
3. Exhortations to release live animals (*fangsheng*). Once again, references are made to all Three Teachings to justify this meritorious practice that can, to some extent, offset the sin incurred by eating meat.
4. Taboos against killing or eating bovines and dogs.
5. Other specific taboos (serpents, turtles, eels, wild geese, frogs, etc.).
6. Injunctions to love and care for living animals, especially draft and other domestic animals. The question of animal welfare is also present in the morality books tradition, with numerous accounts of divine punishments being incurred by those who mistreat their animals. One of the genre's early classics, the *Ledger of Merits and Demerits Revealed by the Immortal Lord of the Taiwei Star*, lists divine punishments for those who treat their animals brutally or cruelly and rewards for those who take care of sick or wounded animals. This text also instructs people to bury dead animals just like humans. Some morality books even tell readers not to keep animals, whether as pets or for other purposes. Again, this follows rules found in early Daoist texts such as the aforementioned *Hundred and Eighty Precepts*, which discouraged animal keeping for

reasons that were not stated explicitly but were probably related to valuing austere lifestyles and condemning the practice of subordinating animals to human will.

These six themes are deployed in morality books in all sorts of ways, with more than one featuring in many of the genre's classics. A good overview of various sinners being punished in the dreary realms of the underworld is provided by the *Precious Manuscript of the Jade Calendar* (*Yuli baochao* 玉歷寶鈔, most probably compiled in the early nineteenth century). This text's extremely popular description of hells portrays the following: people who had killed animals, including children who tormented insects (and their parents who let them indulge in such cruel games); those who kept donkeys and horses without a good reason (i.e., without any genuine need for transport or work in the fields); people who had poisoned rivers and fished with nets; those who plowed their fields in winter (when insects hibernate); people who had used animal parts to make drugs; and of course, those who had eaten beef or dogmeat.

Two important developments occurred during the eighteenth and, much more markedly, the nineteenth century. The first was the appearance of books entirely devoted to the issue of animal life. Some specialized morality books that focused on a particular ethical concern began to circulate as early as the seventeenth century, particularly on the subjects of the reverence for written characters (*xizi* 惜字), filial piety, or debauchery. Books on animal life followed this trend and became numerous during the second half of the nineteenth century. The second related development was the eschatological import of respect for animals. This suggested that taking animal life not only had dire consequences for the individual concerned but that the collective behavior of humanity toward animals played a crucial role in the destiny of the world at large. The connection between killing animals and killing humans had existed for some time in Buddhist texts, morality books, and literati writings, which stated that people who choose to kill animals for no reason would be killed themselves. Yet, by applying this logic to humanity as a whole, this eschatological discourse introduced the different concept that all (or the vast majority) of humans would have to be slaughtered—not just the most flagrant sinners—as a consequence of their general disrespect for animal life.

However, a closer review of these writings reveals that this was not a sudden innovation. One idea in morality books and other related spirit-written scriptures that endured throughout history was the eschatological notion that humankind was facing annihilation due to its sins and general moral failure. In this narrative, the focus was less on individual retribution, punishment, and salvation (the habitual focus of morality books) than on the collective fate of humanity and indeed life in general, as humans and animals were ruled by the same nonnegotiable rules of moral retribution and reward. This discourse became ever more articulate and dominant by the late eighteenth century and developed further during the nineteenth century. During this same period, people's lack of respect for animal life grew into a major cause of anxiety about the end of the world. Several revealed texts from the eighteenth and nineteenth centuries explicitly express this anxiety; for instance, the *Tract on Non-killing* (*Jieshawen* 戒殺文) revealed by Patriarch Lü (Lüzu 呂祖, i.e., the immortal Lü Dongbin 呂洞賓) sometime during the eighteenth century.[11] Lü was at the center of one of the earliest and most important spirit-writing cults. In this tract, Patriarch Lü explained that killing animals was a direct cause of warfare and more general killing of humans, so if people stopped slaughtering animals, warfare would cease entirely:

> The killing *qi* 氣 and the radiance of spilled blood rise up and obscure the sun. Heaven loves lives, but humans love killing. Such misery keeps accumulating and eventually causes people to be attacked, tortured, assaulted, and killed by weapons. Humans get killed like trampled grass, collectively caught in this evil kalpa.
> 殺氣血光上昏天日。天心好生，人心好殺。積慘既久，所以災傷刑戮盜賊刀兵殺。人如草聚爲惡刦。[12]

A slightly later complete scripture entirely devoted to the topic is far more developed than this short text and others similar to it. *True Scripture on Extending Life through Non-killing [Preached by] Doumu, Mother of the Nine Emperors [of Ursa Major]* (*Jiuhuang Doumu jiesha yansheng zhenjing* 九皇斗姥戒殺延生真經) was revealed sometime between 1798 and 1804 at the Jueyuantan 覺源壇 spirit-writing altar, which was operated in Beijing by high-ranking officials led by Jiang Yupu 蔣予蒲 (*zi* Yuanting 元庭, 1755–1819)—at that time, the vice minister of war. The text was eventually included in the major collection *Essentials of the Daoist Canon* (*Daozang jiyao* 道藏輯要), published in 1806 by the Jueyuantuan group.[13] Although this is not the only eschatological text produced by this group, it articulates the discourses on animal life and the apocalypse in particularly explicit and striking ways, as well as provides a graphic description of the imminent annihilation of humanity that the accumulated butchering of animals would cause. Doumu asserts in this text that only a radical and immediate change of attitude toward life could bring humans back from the brink and even calculates the most cost-efficient way to accumulate merits in the little time available, thereby maximizing the chances of avoiding obliteration. Although this text does not seem to have been widely diffused (before the *Essentials of the*

*Daoist Canon* was reprinted in 1906) and is rarely explicitly quoted by the later texts discussed below, it is nonetheless worth providing a detailed account of its contents here, as it constitutes a particularly well-developed, early illustration of the ideas that thrived during the nineteenth century and, as we will see, reverberated in many texts.

The scripture's narrative runs as follows. Section 1 (4a–6b): A description of Doumu as she lectures to assembled deities in her heavenly palace. A stellar deity asks about her vow to save humanity and the current miserable conditions on earth. She replies by explaining that this misery is caused by human sins, chief of which is killing animals. She debunks the idea that humans and animals are different and states that taking any life has dire consequences for the whole universe. Section 2 (7a–9a): Doumu continues by detailing three reasons why humans are blind to the sin of taking life—their unrestrained appetite for meat (including exotic delicacies), tradition, and the erroneous notion that humans and animals are fundamentally different. Section 3 (10a–12a): Doumu explains that ordinary humans cannot give up eating meat in one go and offers a "gradual method" to successively reduce their sins related to meat eating. For this, she classifies animals in a complicated grading scheme, using seven categories of animals with different values and several more subcategories. At the top of this hierarchy are mammals that have "great merit"—in other words, bovines (because they plow the fields) and dogs (because they guard the home). As these two are thousands of times more valuable than ordinary animals, saving them produces enough merit to avert disasters for the time being. Section 4 (13–15a): Doumu further elaborates on the importance of protecting bovines and dogs, details their contributions to humanity, and recounts the horrors that befall those who commit the heinous crime of butchering or eating them. Section 5 (16a–18a): As the second step in her gradual method, Doumu encourages humans not only to protect bovines and dogs but also to extend this practice to other animals. She discusses the predicament of people who try but lapse because they do not see vegetarians being favored by heaven or meat eaters being punished and those who despair because they think one individual alone cannot make any difference. She then details her understanding of refraining from killing (*jiesha*) in five points. Section 6 (19a–21a): Doumu extols the practice of releasing animals (*fangsheng*) as the most efficient and powerful way of accumulating merit and averting disasters, again through the computation of merits accrued.

These six sections constitute the first round of elucidations. A second round begins with section 7 (22a–24b): After Doumu has finished her preaching, heaven fills up with auspicious omens, and the assembled deities entreat her for more instructions. Doumu begins to expound on the virtue of benevolence (*ren* 仁),

which is the root of life, explaining that humans who kill animals lose their *ren* and, as a result, bring death upon themselves and their kin. Section 8 (25a–27a): Doumu expands on her sharp distinction between acceptable and prohibited meat (beef, dog, horse, etc.) and details how everyone, rich or poor, should enforce a prohibition according to their individual circumstances. In section 9 (28a–30b), Doumu lists various types of killing that should be resisted: by cruelty or teasing, because of an appetite for unusual fare, by the wanton destruction of natural habitats, and so forth. Section 10 (31a–33a): Doumu explains how the retribution for humans who kill animals works and asserts its ineluctability even though this might not be immediately apparent to those concerned. Section 11 (34a–36a): Doumu expands on how killing animals causes disasters, using a five phases (*wuxing* 五行) scheme to explain the advent of various disasters such as fires, wars, and epidemics, then returning to the importance of each person doing their part to avert collective disasters. Section 12 (37a–38b): All the assembled deities applaud, and Doumu solemnly restates her vow to assist everyone who promises to refrain from killing and practice releasing animals.

Several dominant themes emerge from this scripture. First, the idea of impending disaster (*jieyun* 劫運) permeates the whole text. Doumu repeatedly insists that calamities—from personal misfortunes to global tragedies (wars, epidemics, droughts, etc.)—are automatically brought about by acts of killing animals. Doumu develops a naturalistic theory whereby people who kill animals cause the world's *qi* to become imbalanced, attract disasters, and are eventually reborn as animals themselves. According to this concept, black *qi* 黑氣 or killing *qi* 殺氣, which emanates from humans killing animals or doing other bad deeds, accumulates through time and eventually clogs up the universe. This theory is also found in other texts from this period, as we have seen in the Lüzu tract. Although it seems akin to Buddhist theories of karma and retribution as natural phenomena (resonance, *ganying* 感應) and of violence automatically nurturing violence, it is embedded here (and in other nineteenth-century texts) in an eschatological framework. Doumu explains that she cannot help avert disasters herself except by convincing people to repent and stop killing and supporting those who do so. Doumu presents herself as a model for her devotees, urging them "to be like her healers of the world."

The second overarching theme is the scripture's attempt to balance two contradictory positions: first, the principle that all lives are valuable and therefore all living beings must be protected and, second, the pragmatic concern for individuals to achieve maximum merit by focusing their efforts on the most valuable animals. As a result, the scripture is not entirely coherent—in fact, some passages contradict each other. Whereas the consumption of pork, poultry, and fish is at times described as a sin (less severe than the sin of butchering bovines and dogs but a sin, nonetheless), other passages imply that eating such everyday meat (*changshi zhi wu* 常食之物, 29b) is natural and unavoidable. As we have seen, the second argument directly echoes a discourse that was commonplace in Daoist texts and society at large from the thirteenth to the late nineteenth century. As a result, some meat (pork, poultry, and most species of fish) was considered entirely acceptable, while beef, dogmeat, horsemeat, and a few others were prohibited by the gods. Along the same line of thinking, the Jueyuantan scripture (18a) also accepts the consumption of meat for social banquets and sacrifices as unavoidable and acceptable since such consumption ultimately only causes the death of a few animals.

The scripture attempts to reconcile these divergent views by taking a highly quantitative approach to sin. It painstakingly counts the merits and demerits accrued by killing or saving various types of animals, exactly like the well-known ledgers of merits and demerits.[14] The text's quantification of differing lives' moral values proposes that one human life is worth ten lives of "useful" animals. In brief, the scripture attempts to weave together various divergent preexisting ethical discourses on meat eating and animal life, including Daoist prohibitions on beef and other meats; sectarian full vegetarianism (*changzhai*); Buddhist and Confucian calls to compassion and measured abstinence; and the practice of releasing animals by integrating them all in a theologically ambitious salvational scheme.

The scripture of Doumu's preaching on nonkilling was produced and edited by high-ranking officials in the Qing administration. Indeed, one of the most fascinating aspects of this text is that it was produced and printed at the same time and thus within the larger political context of the White Lotus rebellion (1796–1804), an uprising of people who were described as millenarian vegetarians. This trend would continue during the nineteenth century, with numerous Guandi revelations—many of them produced during the Taiping war (1851–1864)—both berating the millenarian vegetarian sects and admonishing nonkilling and avoidance of most meats, all of it in a strident eschatological narrative. Several tracts spirit-written by Guandi claim that when people eat beef or dogmeat and poison the rivers, the killing *qi* rises to heaven, and Shangdi 上帝, "Lord of Heaven" or "Jade Emperor," becomes so angry that he wants to destroy humanity.[15]

One of the most remarkable texts produced by spirit-writing during the war is the *Compilation of the Golden Rules, on Order of the Jade Emperor* (*Yuding jinke jiyao* 玉定金科輯要), an extensive divine law code that lists in excruciating detail the punishments (expressed in years of life and various disasters) for every imaginable sin, as well as rewards for good deeds. The thousand-odd pages of this penal code were revealed in Hunan between 1856 and 1859 by Wenchang, who was given the authorization to reveal it to humans by the Jade Emperor. Animal life is discussed as part of the chapter on justice (*yi* 義) in the rewards section of the code. Surprisingly, it is not found in the section on punishments. Articles on animals do not form an individual subchapter but are intermixed with articles on helping the poor through charity. Animals are not treated as a separate issue but are included among those weak forms of life that people should take pity on, in a continuum with infants, the sick, and the disabled. The section on rewards states that people will accrue precisely quantified merits if they financially support butchers to change their trade, along with those who pay for releasing animals.[16] Another group of quantified merits lists those who constantly keep an eye open for animals in danger, however small, and save them; people who do not cause animals to be killed by ordering meat except in circumstances when ritual prescribes it, such as at sacrifices, their parents' birthdays, weddings and funerals, formal receptions for guests, and nourishing a sick parent; individuals who observe the beef and dog taboo and convince others to do so; people who do not kill turtles and serpents; those who persuade farmers not to sell their old cattle, dogs, horses, and donkeys to butchers but keep them on the farm and bury them when they die; those who release live fish and birds; those who abstain from eating small fish and fish roe because it saves countless lives from being cut short; people who bury dead mammals; those who do not engage in and prevent others from poisoning rivers, fishing with nets, setting woods and grasslands on fire, hunting and filling up burrows; and people who feed wild animals during particularly harsh winters.[17] After an article on the beef and dog taboos, the code contains a commentary that refers to the causal connection between killing animals and war. It reads, "In the world, when wars or famines occur, this is caused by the fact that humans are unable to refrain from killing (animals). The *qi* produced by such killing naturally causes such disasters."[18]

## The Discourse of the Taboo in Morality Books

Morality books are of interest first of all because of their wide dissemination across the Chinese world, thanks to their free distribution financed by charitable associations. Therefore, they had an immense impact on society. However, these characteristics also make their study challenging: the corpus is abundant and dispersed, and so far, few comprehensive collections have been gathered in one place.[19] In addition, the texts contained in morality books were constantly reprinted, copied, abbreviated, or extended. Thus, dating each text individually necessitates extensive bibliographical studies, sometimes without much success. My analysis of the treatment of the beef taboo in morality literature is not based on an exhaustive examination of all the possible sources. Nevertheless, I was able to consult a sufficient number of the documents within my reach to build a substantial corpus.

I identified four main approaches: (1) a morality book could ignore the taboo either voluntarily or because the taboo did not relate to the focal issue of the morality book in question; (2) the morality book could include the taboo in passing within a list of precepts, sometimes with commentaries and stories appended; (3) the morality book could devote a chapter or one or more independent texts to the taboo, thus making it a well-identified moral issue; and (4) there were specialized morality books entirely devoted to the taboo. Because of the varied nature of the morality book genre and the dispersion of the corpus, it is difficult to quantify the presence of the beef taboo in morality books. Nonetheless, a large majority of "generalist" morality books from the sixteenth to the early twentieth century at least mentioned the taboo.

*Verses on Action and Consequence Revealed by the Lord on High,* the oldest extant morality book, which is still the best known and most prestigious of the genre, does not mention the taboo. There are several possible reasons for this. At the time of its compilation, in the early twelfth century, the discourse of the taboo already existed but perhaps was not yet fully recognized in the milieu in which the book was composed. However, *Verses on Action and Consequence Revealed by the Lord on High* does not oppose the taboo. It contains a sentence saying that "[it is forbidden to] kill and cook animals other than what is ritually prescribed" (*feili pengzai* 非禮烹宰), which leaves room for various interpretations.[20] The phrase is generally understood to prohibit meat except during sacrificial banquets or receptions for a guest of honor. Several later commentaries read this passage as referring to the beef taboo in particular.[21] Another early morality book classic, *Ledger of Merits and Demerits Revealed by the Immortal Lord of the Taiwei Star,* did not address the taboo either.[22]

The taboo first appeared in morality books written in the seventeenth century. Perhaps the most important inclusion is that found in the *Tract on Hidden Rewards* in which Wenchang includes the words "Do not kill plow cattle" (*wu zai gengniu* 勿宰耕牛) among his injunctions. These four characters carry much more weight than is apparent at first glance. In this formulation, the interdiction seems closer to the legal prohibition against slaughter than the fully developed taboo. However, the stream of commentaries accompanying the text from the late seventeenth century explained the sentence as prohibiting all consumption of beef. We have already discussed the revelation attributed to Wenchang, purportedly dating from 1316, that clearly articulated the beef taboo. In this case, however, the taboo was inserted into an exhaustive formulation of the moral program proposed by Wenchang and adopted by Chinese religion. With these four characters, the taboo became genuinely integrated into the fundamental values of Chinese ethics. The context of its inclusion therefore deserves some attention.

The dissemination of the *Tract on Hidden Rewards,* whose importance is only surpassed by *Verses on Action and Consequence Revealed by the Lord on High,* has only recently received due scholarly attention.[23] During the late sixteenth century, a prototype of the *Tract on Hidden Rewards* (called *Exhortations to Practice for Hidden Rewards* [*Quanxing yinzhi wen* 勸行陰騭文]) was spirit-written and circulated. Then, sometime later, the *Tract on Hidden Rewards* was composed, using material from *Exhortations to Practice for Hidden Rewards* and other Wenchang revelations. It eventually eclipsed in popularity its predecessors, becoming the most revered and widely distributed Wenchang text in the late imperial period. Around 1689, a Jiangnan scholar, Yan Zhangjing 顏章敬 (*zi* Shengyu 生愉), received dream revelations, further modified the *Tract on Hidden Rewards,* and published a lengthy commentary attributed to his father under the title *Records of the Red Cinnamon [Palace]* (*Dangui ji* 丹桂籍), which contains numerous records of spirit-writing. Among the many morality books revealed by Wenchang, the *Tract on Hidden Rewards* was a fundamental, programmatic text that was the object of a specific cult.[24]

After the Yan family's edition in *Records of the Red Cinnamon Palace,* the *Tract on Hidden Rewards* was widely distributed, and various editions, generally based on the *Records of the Red Cinnamon Palace,* appeared from around 1700. It should be noted that the taboo already appeared in *Exhortations to Practice for Hidden Rewards* in an even more explicit form: "Observing the taboo against eating dogs and bovines" (*ji shi quan niu* 忌食犬牛).[25] In short, even though the most popular edition was the work of the Yan family in the 1680s, the *Tract on Hidden Rewards* developed gradually in the late Ming, perhaps even earlier, in activist literati circles in which the Wenchang cult flourished. Thus, the beef taboo was a concern early on among those who wrote and distributed morality books.

Another piece of evidence for the presence of the taboo in the first morality books, as this genre flourished in the seventeenth century, was its inclusion in the ledgers of merit and demerit. Even though these ledgers hardly lent themselves to the theoretical and narrative elaboration that other morality books would provide, this inclusion is significant. In several classics of the genre, the fact of killing or eating a bovine is treated as a very heavy demerit. By contrast, observing the vow of the taboo is said to earn much merit.[26]

We must also mention a particular subgenre of morality books that developed around the stove god, Zaoshen 灶神 or Zaojun 灶君. This cult had existed in China since antiquity, and it acquired a moral dimension early in the Common Era: the stove god was said to report family members' good and bad deeds to heaven. However, morality books devoted to the stove god almost always contained a list of ten precepts to be observed, including one specifically concerning abstinence from beef.[27]

## Books Devoted to the Taboo

At least eight extant books (or book sections) are devoted exclusively to the beef taboo and more titles are mentioned.[28] Three lost books devoted to the beef taboo were composed during the Ming. We know of the existence of two thanks to a mention in a famous bibliography compiled toward the end of the seventeenth century: they are *Book on the Beef Taboo* (*Jieniu shu* 戒牛書) by Ding Mingdeng 丁明登 and *Collection on the Prohibition of Beef* (*Niujin ji* 牛禁集) by Guo Zizhang 郭子章 (1542–1618).[29] We know nothing about Ding Mingdeng, but Guo Zizhang had a brilliant career culminating in his appointments as provincial governor and minister. He wrote a gazetteer on a Buddhist site and various aesthetic and scholarly works. During the late Ming, Mao Qizong 冒起宗 compiled a *Newly Printed Collection of Commentaries on the Beef Taboo* (*Xinke niujie huiping* 新刻牛戒彙評) of which we have only a preface.[30] A fourth lost work devoted to the taboo was composed later by Meng Chaoran 孟超然 (1731–1797). Meng, the author of several morality books and a well-known activist, wrote a book on protecting animal lives titled *Record on Extending Love [to All Living Beings]* (*Guang'ai lu* 廣愛錄). He compiled anecdotes and more theoretical considerations devoted to refraining from killing and cited cases relating to all kinds of animals. He included several cases concerning cattle, which he introduced by saying, "In general, as for the interdiction against killing animals [*jiesha*], the case of plow cattle is the most important, and I have separately compiled the *Compendium on the Beef Taboo* [*Jieniu jilan* 戒牛集覽]."[31]

The earliest extant collection entirely devoted to the taboo is the *Collection of [Texts] Copied [from Other Books] on the Beef Taboo* (*Niujie huichao* 牛戒彙鈔, henceforth *Collection of Copies on the Beef Taboo*). This collection was compiled in the late Ming by Li Changke 李長科, a famed physician, and included in his *Treatises on Expanding Benevolence* (*Guangrenpin* 廣仁品) published in 1633. *Guangrenpin* is an anthology of morality books essentially devoted to preserving life, notably animal life. *Niujie huichao* contains one revealed text (the "Instructions on the Taboo against Cattle and Dogs by Xuantian shangdi" translated in the previous chapter), a law protecting bovines in the Ming code, six prose and poetic texts by authors active in the first decades of the seventeenth century, a series of short poems, and thirty-eight miraculous anecdotes. Most of the texts in this little anthology also appeared elsewhere in other, later morality books, but *Collection of Copies on the Beef Taboo* is, in most cases, their earliest version. These various texts are cited in the remainder of this chapter.

Very briefly hereafter, this collection was included in another anthology of morality books, the anonymous compiled *Preliminary Collection of Riqian* (*Riqian chushe* 日乾初揲), of which a late Ming copy is held in the Japanese Imperial Library, Naikaku bunko. This short six-page version includes a new preface but has deleted the name of Li Changke as editor as well as a large part of the contents, especially all the miraculous anecdotes.[32] We also have a preface by Zheng Eryang 鄭二陽 (fl. 1609–1646) for a *Collection of Copies on the Beef Taboo* that mentions three compilers, but it says that the book was illustrated, so it must be a different edition.[33] In addition, there is an early Qing edition (held at the Beijing University Library) of an imperially sanctioned edition of *Niujie huichao*, very similar to the one in *Guangrenpin* but with new prefaces, the first one dated 1656, by Emperor Shunzhi, who was then eighteen years old, and the others by three high officials: Jin Zhijun 金之俊 (1593–1670), Fu Yijian 傅以漸 (1609–1665), and Liu Zhengzong 劉正宗 (1594–1661). Several other separate prefaces and postfaces of the edition printed on Shunzhi's order are also extant, but they do not provide details on the contents.[34] The imperial preface was widely circulated independently; for instance, it is included in an important eighteenth-century morality book, *Records of Shared Virtue* (*Tongshan lu* 同善錄).[35] The *Records of Shared Virtue*'s compiler introduces this preface by asserting that the emperor had himself compiled this work, which the preface also affirms. The reality was undoubtedly different since the book already existed in the late Ming.

A well-informed nineteenth-century scholar claimed that Shunzhi indeed composed the preface to *Collection of Copies on the Beef Taboo* and asked Wei Yijie 魏裔介 (1616–1686), then one of the highest Chinese officials, who became principal vice censor in chief in 1657, to compile a sequel, the *Added Copies on the Beef Taboo* (*Niujie xuchao* 牛戒續鈔).[36] In a memoir to the throne submitted that same year, 1656, Wei recounted that the emperor had invited him to a reading of the work on the previous day and that Wei had proposed that thirty thousand copies be distributed to all schools and all officials throughout the empire, following a procedure used for several other morality books sponsored by the emperor.[37] Wei did not mention the compilation of a sequel, which was perhaps decided after the memoir was submitted. This volume was apparently distributed to all imperial officials—at least *Records of the Red Cinnamon Palace,* which appeared only a few years later, mentioned this, as did other later sources.[38]

In short, it seems plausible that we can interpret these various sources as follows. Having read Li Changke's *Collection of Copies on the Beef Taboo* from the late Ming, the emperor had Wei Yijie write a sequel and composed a preface to the two, the original and the sequel, in which he presented this compilation as his own. At Wei Yijie's formal request, he had the book printed and distributed to all levels of his administration. The copy in the Beijing University Library, however, does not contain any sequel or Wei Yijie's name. The emperor's initiative and sincerity in spreading the beef taboo were beyond doubt. Two years earlier, he had publicly declared that he did not eat beef.[39]

This book was soon reprinted as a result of local initiatives. We have a preface of an edition sponsored sometime before 1688 by a retired official, Zhou Shirong 周士瑢, who had settled in Fuzhou (Fujian Province) and was involved in life-releasing activities with the local Buddhist monasteries. He requested a preface for his edition from a prominent monk, Weilin Daopei 為霖道霈 (1615–1702). The extant preface states that both *Collection of Copies on the Beef Taboo* and the preface are from the hand of the Shunzhi emperor. It is a relatively rare case of a text about the beef taboo written by a Buddhist monk (in fact, two of the texts in the *Collection of Copies on the Beef Taboo* are authored by a monk), but Weilin, rather than drawing on Buddhist references, quotes at length from the "Instructions on the Taboo against Cattle and Dogs by Xuantian shangdi."[40]

As is often the case with morality books, different contents often circulated under the same or a very similar title. A collection of morality books first published in 1763, *Records [as Clear] as a Bell Sounding at Dawn* (*Chenzhonglu* 晨鍾錄), has a section titled "Collection of Copies on the Taboo against Beef" (Jieniu huichao 戒牛彙鈔), which includes some of the texts in *Collection of Copies on the Beef Taboo,* plus fourteen stories of retribution.[41]

The next extant collection to be published was *Compendium on the Beef Taboo* (*Niujie jilu* 牛戒輯錄), a twenty-page booklet printed in 1868 by a private print shop in Beijing. A magistrate who authored the preface explained that his own family strictly observed the taboo, and when the compiler showed him the manuscript, he not only wrote the preface but collected money from friends to have it printed in the capital. The volume consists of ten tracts or poems, either written by earlier humans or revealed by gods—some are unique to this collection, and others are well known, such as Zhenwu's "Instructions on the Taboo against Cattle and Dogs" and an extract from the Doumu scripture—as well as thirty stories of retribution or reward. A contemporary collection, *Texts on Banning Killing so as to Avoid the Apocalypse* (*Jiesha mijie bian* 戒殺弭劫編) was compiled by Xu Qian 徐謙 (1776–1864), a scholar and teacher involved in many spirit-writing groups and morality book projects throughout his life.[42] In spite of its title, the book's contents deal primarily with the beef taboo, with revealed tracts (chapter 1), anecdotes (chapters 2–3), and an added section on the dog-meat taboo (chapter 4).

The four other extant collections were compiled and printed during the Republican period, although they contain many late imperial essays, showing the continued relevance of the discourse on the taboo despite the changed political, social, economic, and religious context for the practice. *Tears of the Plow Cattle* (*Gengniu lei* 耕牛淚) is not dated but was printed by Mingshan shuju 明善書局, one of the largest presses for religious books active in Shanghai during the 1920s and 1930s. This twenty-six-page illustrated lithograph contains twelve tracts and poems, some of which were also found in the earlier collections such as *Collection of Copies on the Beef Taboo* and *Compendium on the Beef Taboo* and were mostly in the style of lamentations of the poor bovine (discussed below), as well as thirty-three stories of retribution.

*Coarse Words on the Taboo against Eating Beef* (*Jie shiniu cuyan* 戒食牛粗言) is an edition from another major religious press in Shanghai, apparently printed in 1927, and with a 1924 preface by the author, a certain Jiang Taiyi 江太易 from a place in Jiangnan, near Shaoxing. The preface explains that his pious mother had him compile and print this forty-page book and that his son added an appendix with veterinary recipes to heal sick cattle. The volume opens with the three morality books classics, then offers a short text on the taboo apparently written by Jiang himself (it is different from the passage on the beef taboo in the similarly titled late imperial sectarian scripture *Zhongxi cuyan baojuan* 眾喜粗言寶卷), which is then commented on sentence by sentence with quotations of earlier tracts or stories of retribution or reward.

*Stories I Have Heard about Cattle Trembling with Fear* (*Husu jiwen* 觳觫紀聞) consists entirely of edifying stories, without didactic tracts. Finally, *A New Collection on the Beef Taboo* (*Niujie biechao* 牛戒別鈔) was compiled and privately published in 1935 by Guo Huijun 郭慧濬, known from other publications as a lay Buddhist. Guo collected various edicts from the tenth century banning the slaughter of bovines, essays by Song and Qing scholars, and by himself; the second part of the book comprises fifty-four stories, mostly from Qing collections of anecdotes.

## The Treatment of the Taboo in Morality Books

The discourse of the taboo is relatively diffuse across morality books: sometimes there is a short sentence and sometimes a substantial chapter (especially in commentaries on the *Tract on Hidden Rewards* and *True Scripture to Awaken Humanity*) or even an entire book. This corpus contains numerous overlaps and repetitions because different books included and copied the same texts and anecdotes, but the taboo is nonetheless richly and voluminously documented. In any event, I treat it as a coherent discourse, even if the different morality books containing the various texts each have a specific orientation.

However, before delving into this corpus and organizing it, we must consider the treatment of the beef taboo in relation to the surrounding moral discourse. As was already the case in Song and Yuan texts, the beef taboo was sometimes dealt with at the same time as the issue of saving animal lives, even though it retained a special status through its specific rhetoric and justification. In various morality books conceived as anthologies, texts concerning beef were included in the same chapter as those concerning animal life in general. In such cases, the texts dealing with bovines generally formed a distinct set at the beginning or end of the chapter.[43]

One good example is *Records Clear as a Water Mirror* (*Shuijing lu* 水鏡錄), an undated anthology by an anonymous compiler. The collection comprises seven morality texts beginning with the *Verses on Action and Consequence Revealed by the Lord on High* and was included in the supplement to the Daoist canon printed in 1607. Although it is difficult to date the composition of most texts it contains, *Records Clear as a Water Mirror*, which must have been compiled between the 1580s and 1607, is one of the oldest extant morality books. It includes four general texts, two texts devoted to animal life based on Zhuhong's famous *Tract on Refraining from Killing and Releasing Life* but in reverse order and modified internal structure from Zhuhong's original and, finally, an anonymous poem titled "Song to Exhort Humans (Not) to Kill Cattle" (Quan sha niu ge 勸殺牛歌).[44] Despite its title and horrific descriptions of cattle begging to be spared from slaughtering, this poem is essentially devoted to the issue of beef and the divine blessings obtained by those who abstain from it: many things can be eaten, but only beef should be avoided. Thus, texts on animal life in general and the taboo in particular coexist within the same collection.

The seventeenth-century *Compendium of Ledgers of Merits and Demerits with a Commentary* (*Huizuan gongguo ge jian zhushi* 彙纂功過格兼注釋) contains an even more extensive articulation of the taboo.[45] This ledger devotes a chapter to refraining from killing, which, in addition to general injunctions, includes some concerning cattle: on the one hand, meritorious or demeritorious deeds specific to the taboo (exhorting others to make the vow to observe the beef and dog taboos, 8.3a) and, on the other hand, deeds regarding any animal (such as saving or burying them) for which the number of merits or demerits is increased in the case of cattle, horses, or dogs. Not killing any animal for one year brings as much merit as observing the beef and dogmeat taboo all one's life (8.5a–6a). This text thus stems from a seemingly coherent juxtaposition of the two discourses.[46]

Because of the simultaneous presence of the two discourses in the same synthetic ethical system, the authors of the morality books undoubtedly felt the need to articulate the two more clearly than previously. Different formulations emerged: some synthesized or articulated the common ground of the two rules, whereas others dissociated them radically. The first option was expressed in the double precept: not killing animals and not eating beef, which made it possible to buy and eat meat other than beef, at least when one's ritual duties (sacrifices, banquets) required it.[47] A text revealed in 1858 reminded its readers that the duty to protect animal lives was not limited to the interdiction against selling a bovine to a butcher and eating dogs but that it was also necessary to limit one's consumption of "ordinary animals" on ritual occasions.[48] In the same spirit, a new articulation of the relationship between the beef taboo and the concern for animal life was expressed in a brief sentence stating that the beef taboo was called "half fasting" (*banzhai* 半齋).[49] This term seems to support the idea that the beef taboo was a step toward vegetarianism. There was even a litany of repentance (*chanhui* 懺悔) ritual from the Qing that almost reduced the crime of killing living beings to the issue of cattle. Killing animals was one of the transgressions that the faithful had to confess and repent. However, the liturgical text only mentioned cattle and reaffirmed that the sin of eating beef was exceptionally grave.[50] Some texts went very far in their efforts to quantify the value of different animal lives. Maybe the most remarkable example is the Doumu scripture discussed above, which quantifies the value of each type of animal life.

By contrast, other texts emphasize dissociating the two rules. Even more explicitly than before, numerous texts contained in late imperial morality books affirmed that "for those who do not eat beef, all other animals are permitted" 蓋人不食牛，他物皆可.[51] One late text revealed in 1858 went even further by arguing for the beef taboo based on a distinction between useful animals (cattle and horses) and useless ones (pigs and sheep). The useless ones existed to serve as food for humans and the useful ones to assist them: it was perfectly lawful to eat the former but forbidden to eat the latter.[52] Noticeably, unlike the discourse on animal life, which tended to distinguish between the act of killing and the much less serious act of eating meat, the texts on cattle placed the two acts on the same level. Some texts emphasize the issue of slaughter but still associate consumption with sin.

In short, what I have demonstrated based on anecdotes from the Song—that the discourse of the taboo was autonomous from the legal prohibition against slaughter and the ethic of protecting animal lives—is confirmed in Ming and Qing morality literature. The articulations between the discourses became more clearly defined, and other new connections were created. Indeed, if we look closely at the most important classics among morality books, we see that the beef taboo appears in unexpected contexts other than animal life.

About halfway through the text, the *Tract on Hidden Rewards* lists several injunctions related to protecting animal lives and the environment:

> Buy animals and release them alive (*fangsheng*); observe [vegetarian] fasts and refrain from taking any life. Watch out with every step whether there are no insects or ants [so as not to crush them]; when lighting a fire, be careful not to set mountainous areas or forests on fire. Light lamps at night to illuminate the paths; establish ferries to allow travelers to cross waterways. Do not go to the mountains to catch mammals and birds; do not throw poison into rivers to catch fish and shellfish. Do not kill cattle that plow the fields; do not throw away paper with written characters.
> 或買物而放生，或持齋而戒殺。舉步常看蟲蟻，禁火莫燒山林。點夜燈以照人行，造河船以濟人渡。勿登山而網禽鳥，勿臨水而毒魚蝦。勿宰耕牛，勿棄字紙。[53]

The sequence of prescriptions is highly significant. These statements are paired in parallel prose, and the couplets thus formed are closely linked thematically. Now the beef taboo is not associated with those concerning other animal life. It is listed later, in conjunction with another well-known interdiction in Chinese morality: reverence for written characters.[54] This connection, which is not a priori obvious, deserves our attention.

Reverence for written characters (*xizi*) consisted of avoiding discarding on the ground or in the trash or in any way soiling any medium (most commonly paper) with one or more characters, whatever they may have been. For classical scholars, Chinese characters were not merely conventional symbols for writing language but the expression of transcendent truth and the very essence of the Chinese language. As such, they were the sacred soul of Chinese civilization, particularly for the literati, who made a living from professions that involved reading and writing. Stepping on characters or allowing them to be defiled was a sin that attracted terrible retribution. For zealots, showing respect for written characters went beyond simply taking care not to let paper with writing be defiled. It involved participating—physically, financially, or both—in collecting and incinerating all discarded paper with written characters. The transformation by fire was indeed the only worthy way to treat these documents. The ashes were then collected and cast into the water—a river or the sea.[55] Like many other elements of late imperial Chinese morality, reverence for written characters is of Daoist origin.[56] Indeed, more than Buddhism and Confucianism, which both originated as oral religions, Daoism, from its beginnings, was based on written communication with the sacred and on the conception of the transcendence of writing. However, the practice of revering characters spread only under the Ming in connection with the Wenchang cult and the moral activism of the literati.

How should we interpret that in the *Tract on Hidden Rewards,* Wenchang, whose cult was so closely linked to the practice of revering characters, associated the latter with the beef taboo? I can only attempt an interpretation, but it seems quite convincing. According to the logic of the *Tract on Hidden Rewards,* the interdiction against slaughtering cattle was not part of the precepts concerning animals and nature, which aimed to preserve life and the natural resources that supported it. The bovine was not mentioned as a living animal; like written characters, it symbolized Chinese civilization. The pairing of revering characters with the beef taboo consecrated two sacred values of the literati: agriculture (cereals) and writing. The transgression against the bovine that the god prohibited was not merely the act of killing animals, but like defiling written characters, it was a sacrilege that was a much more egregious act than killing animals.

A similar passage in the *True Scripture to Awaken Humanity* confirms such an interpretation though the transgression is worded differently from the *Tract on Hidden Rewards:* "Killing cattle and dogs" (*zaisha niu quan* 宰殺牛犬). I will return to the inclusion of the dog later. The *True Scripture to Awaken Humanity* is similar to the *Tract on Hidden Rewards* in that the beef taboo and the reverence for written characters are paired in both cases. In *True Scripture to Awaken Humanity,* the sacrilege is even more strongly emphasized since the previous interdictions prohibit insulting heaven and earth, rebuking the wind and rain, slandering the gods and sages, and destroying images and deceiving the gods. The classic admonition to protect lives by refraining from killing (*jiesha*) and by releasing life (*fangsheng*) is also present in *True Scripture to Awaken Humanity* but appears in a different passage.

In addition to the taboo's association with reverence for written characters, we occasionally also see an association with reverence for cereals (*xigu* 惜穀), which is also frequently associated with revering characters.[57] Revering cereals demands that not a single grain be discarded and threatens the worst retributions in the case of wealthy families who throw away the leftovers of their meals. Like the beef taboo, revering cereals makes the cultivation of grains sacred (over other forms of agriculture) as the foundation of Chinese civilization.[58] These associations—whether with the discourse on animal life or with reverence for writing and cereals—show that the beef taboo was regarded as a specific issue that could be articulated in conjunction with various other ethical issues, depending on the case.

## The Justification of the Taboo in Morality Books

Having situated the discourse of the taboo within morality books, we can proceed to examine it in depth and isolate its central themes. We must first observe a profound continuity with texts predating the surge of morality books because even though morality books formed a new genre, their content was often older, including anecdotes and revelations from the Song and Yuan. However, morality books had the great merit of reassembling and systematizing the fragmentary earlier discourse. Here, I present didactic texts (revelations, essays, and citations) and anecdotes separately before discussing new elements introduced by morality books.

### Didactic Texts

A distinguishing feature of didactic texts, as opposed to anecdotal literature, is that they tend to rationalize and justify moral interdictions. This didactic project is accomplished through two types of discourse: divine teachings revealed by spirit-writing and general introductions in which the compilers and commentators gather the main arguments before quoting revealed texts and anecdotes illustrating the retribution associated with the taboo.[59]

The most important among the revealed texts is undoubtedly the "Instructions on the Taboo against Cattle and Dogs by Xuantian shangdi," which we already discussed above and whose earliest known version dates from the late Ming. It was cited, often partially, by almost all the works that gave the issue of the taboo substantial treatment. This short text is a complex elaboration since it included theological considerations (bovines as incarnations of Zhenwu), moral reasons (the need to pay back favors that cattle bestow on humans through their work), and arguments linked to retribution and reward, and ritual purity (those who observe the taboo will not be victims of disease and misfortune). Other revealed texts appeared from the late sixteenth century, beginning with the "Exhortation Not to Eat Beef and Dog" revealed by Patriarch Lü (Lü Chunyang zushi quanshi jie shi niu quan 呂純陽祖師勸世戒食牛犬), which is undated and found in a Qing anthology.[60] This text begins by quoting Zhenwu's "Instructions on the Taboo against Cattle and Dogs" and then engages in considerations presented in a more down-to-earth tone, reminding readers that without cattle, humans would have no cereals to eat and "that is why there is no greater crime on earth than killing bovines, and this crime is shared by those who eat beef" 故天下有罪大惡極之事，殺牛者是也。天下有與罪大惡極之人分其罪者，食牛肉者是也. The text argues that people cannot depend on cattle and also eat them. This is presented as a natural principle that does not rely on the discourse on retribution. The text then refutes the hypocritical position of those who eat only a little beef without killing bovines and urges everyone to convert their family and their village by promising them divine blessings. Rich and noble families, says Lü Dongbin, have all practiced the taboo for generations, while those who are poor are all descendants of beefeaters.

Revealed texts (mostly poems), which appeared one after another between the seventeenth and twentieth centuries, similarly continued to combine moral arguments (such as the reasoning that killing bovines was a crime) with threats of retribution and promises of rewards.[61] The same is true for the essays and introductions by the literati compilers of morality books. It would be futile to contrast revealed texts advancing a religious argument and more rational essays. A book on moral philosophy written by Liu Zongzhou 劉宗周 (1578–1645), a celebrated, very orthodox Cheng-Zhu Confucian, contained a section devoted to the taboo against eating beef and dogs. Liu also used anecdotes about divine retribution and a quote from Zhenwu's "Instructions" to justify the taboo. There was no difference in inspiration from contemporary morality books.[62] Revealed texts were considered authoritative across the whole spectrum of the social scale and situated at all levels of discourse, from popular sermons to classically inspired philosophy.

Another revelation by Lü Dongbin, attested from the eighteenth century onward, is a good example of revealed texts:

> *Song to Urge People to Stop Eating Beef, by Fuyou Dijun [Lü Dongbin]*
> Look, don't you see the bovine plowing the earth,
> struggling to move forward, pulling with all its might?
> Can't you see the sun at its zenith
> drenching the bovine in bloody sweat?
> There are many domestic animals on earth,
> but none are as devoted to their masters.
> However, the loathsome and greedy peasant
> with a cruel heart like a wolf and tiger,
> when he sees the aging bovine's strength decline,
> sells it to those who will cook it!
> They cut off its head and open its stomach.
> Its blood will be used to coat the bells,[63]
> and its hide will be used to make drums.
> Its bones will be filed down to make hairpins,
> and its meat will be prepared in dried strips.
> Yesterday, in the fields, wasn't it painful?
> But today, a broken body, isn't it horrible?

Its tearful soul will seek justice from Yama.
Yama, feeling pity, does not know what to answer
but decrees that cattle killers
will receive their punishment in hell:
confined to the forests of swords
or hurled on the mountain of knives,
immersed in the boiling cauldron
or tied to the column of glowing iron.
They will never be released for all eternity.
There are also the beefeaters
who ignore the warnings of others:
people exhort them, but they get angry,
people try to dissuade them, but they laugh it off.
They are reluctant to say that cattle have merit
but claim that beef is good for them.
Thus, they commit a crime that scandalizes the whole universe.
They believe it's their own business
but ignore that when they eat beef,
the heavenly gods are immediately angered.
Even if they are honest people,
they are instantaneously entered into the register of sinners.
The misfortunes allotted to them in the hereafter are visited upon them,
and the blessings preordained for them are annulled without
recourse.
Misery and bad death fall on their descendants
until the whole lineage is wiped out.
Alas! Everyone can see that cattle plow for us
and those who kill and eat them have abandoned all humanity.
Today, possessing the spirit-writing stylus, I admonish humanity:
By observing this taboo, you will deserve to meet the buddhas and
patriarchs!

孚佑帝君戒食牛歌

君不見牛耕土，曳步前奔用力，努又不見日當，午血汗通身涎，沫吐世間畜類，多無如他報主，可憾貪財農心，狠如狼虎見他，筋力衰賣與人，烹煮割下頭剖，開肚血塗鐘皮，鞔鼓骨挫簪肉，作脯當日耕田，難不難今日粉，身苦不苦　魅，泣訴閻羅王閻，羅悲憫不能語，但說宰牛夫受，罪在地府或丟，劍樹叢或擲刀，山隖或灌滾銅，汁或烙紅鐵柱，永劫不翻身翻，身世變汝又有，食牛人不由人，勸阻勸之起爭，端阻之笑迂腐，怕說牛有功强，說牛能補一

> 任，罪通天不知何，肺腑豈知一食，牛立刻天神怒，縱有好心腸此，條登惡簿陰注，禍來侵暗折福，無數貧夭逮兒，孫甚至滅門戶，吁嗟乎牛代人，耕誰不覩殺而，食之喪心伍我，今降乩普告人，戒此方堪對佛祖。[64]

Not all revealed texts were as stirring as this song, but all shared its firm conviction. This type of revealed poem figured most prominently among the range of references collected by the compilers of morality books. Other authoritative sources cited alongside revealed texts were quotes from the classics, precedents (highlighting the fact that texts urging the observance of the taboo were produced in great numbers throughout history), and laws prohibiting cattle slaughter. The compilers especially wrote about two themes: on the one hand, the need to repay plow cattle for their service and give them recognition for their hard work and, on the other hand, the fact that without cattle, humans would be condemned to starve for lack of cereals.

The authors of morality books based their arguments on examples (such as anecdotes about divine retribution, which I will discuss below), natural moral laws, and scriptural references. These references included the Confucian classics and revelations produced by spirit-writing. Only two excerpts from the classics were cited regularly. The first is a passage from the *Book of Rites:* "Nobles do not kill cattle without reason [*zhuhou wugu busha niu* 諸侯無故不殺牛], dignitaries do not kill sheep without reason, and officials do not kill dogs or pigs without reason."[65] In the context of the *Book of Rites,* the apparent meaning of this passage was to formulate sumptuary regulations: cattle sacrifice, being the most prestigious, was reserved for the king and, under certain circumstances, for the nobility. But it was also possible, as the authors of the Ming and Qing did, to interpret the passage as meaning that the princes only killed cattle for a sacrifice and never on other occasions.

The other locus classicus was the first chapter of the *Mengzi* in which the author shows his approval of the king who, after seeing a frightened ox pass by on its way to being sacrificed, asked that it be replaced by a sheep because he "cannot bear seeing it tremble with fear [*husu* 觳觫] nor that it be put to death when it has not committed any crime." Mencius approves and comments, "When we have seen [an animal] alive, we cannot bear to witness its death. When we have heard its cries, we cannot bear to eat its meat."[66] The expression "trembling with fear" and the phrase "when we have seen [an animal] alive" were used frequently by later authors, who considered this the most convincing of the classical justifications for their observance of the taboo. However, it is clear that Mencius is not referring to a beef taboo: his point concerns the proximity between humans and animals rather than the distinctions between animal species.

It is difficult to believe that Chinese literati would think these passages directly validated the beef taboo, but the quotation played a rhetorical role in legitimizing the discourse. In their own way, these excerpts from the classics confirmed the special status of cattle in the Chinese tradition. Cheng Yi's statement that the moral duty owed to plow cattle was more important than any immediate economic consideration was closer to the discourse of the taboo. Admittedly, however, the role of these classical quotes was somewhat incidental in the reasoning presented in morality books. By contrast, revelations like those of Zhenwu and Wenchang were given much more weight. Moreover, the *Book of Rites* and the *Mengzi* were cited only by a small number of morality books, while almost all cited the revelation of Zhenwu, "Instructions on the Taboo against Cattle and Dogs." In other words, the authors of the morality books bore witness to the authority of the gods, the authenticity of revelations through spirit-writing, and the full validity of a recent moral precept with little reliance on the classics.

## Anecdotes

Anecdotes proving the reality of the retribution visited upon beefeaters or the rewards bestowed on those who observed the taboo constituted an important part of the material contained in morality books. They are appended to revealed texts and didactic essays, unlike the anecdotes included in collections of anecdotes (*biji xiaoshuo*), which are entirely independent. However, they do not differ in terms of theme or style. Some anecdotes were excerpted from our corpus from the Song and cited in morality books, although they were typically modified and listed without attribution.[67] But the great majority of anecdotes were new, undoubtedly because morality books tended to select more recent evidence to successfully convince their readers that they would be directly affected. In addition, like the collections of anecdotes from the Song, which provided us with the corpus discussed in the previous chapter, compendia from the Ming and Qing also contain anecdotes concerning the taboo. I cover them here alongside anecdotes in morality books. This body of documents is voluminous: my survey, which covered only a small segment of the extant literature, easily yielded well over one hundred anecdotes.

The themes in Ming and Qing anecdotes largely overlapped with those in the Song corpus; however, specific themes were given greater importance. This included the relationship between the taboo and passing examinations, which was hardly surprising given that the Wenchang cult was linked to the moral regulation of civil exams and official careers.[68] The details of the stories varied, but the general theme was very repetitive: the protagonists dreamed of or met deities responsible for creating the list of successful examinees. They saw their names added if their family observed the taboo, and sometimes the spot of another candidate who expected success was revoked because he had violated the taboo.[69] In some cases, they passed the examinations after a meritorious deed toward bovines.[70]

The vow to uphold the taboo was especially frequently dramatized.[71] Thus, in a dream, a god promised a man and his son success in civil exams if they observed the taboo in perpetuity (unlike other families in which everyone made the vow, they would be the only ones in their household to observe the taboo). When they woke up, they burned incense and made a vow to heaven never to eat beef again.[72] In 1872, a scholar published a testimony in a Shanghai daily in which he recounted how the gods of epidemics visited his village in 1864. These gods explained to him in a dream that the disease was inflicted by heaven because people ate too much beef and dogmeat and that he was spared because he had observed the taboo for three years. The gods enjoined him to go and preach the good cause. The scholar went to preach among the villagers, and all those who burned incense and made a vow to heaven recovered.[73] The seriousness of the vow was stretched to the limits of credibility in the account of a man who was on the verge of starvation by the side of the road. A soldier passing by offered him beef, but he refused it. Consequently, he was saved by divine intervention.[74]

One of the most interesting and most frequently cited anecdotes (it appeared in at least a dozen books) was that of a yamen employee who died and whom the judges of hell agreed to return to life for three days so that he could try to convince one thousand people to make a vow to uphold the taboo. He told his story and asked each person who listened to him to convince ten others. But they did not take him very seriously, so he fell far short of his goal of one thousand names and died suddenly after three days. However, the magistrate, his superior, realized the veracity of the man's story and asked all the people under his control to make a vow. He set up a registry for converts in the public square and invited everyone to come and register. At the end of a single day, the roster contained several thousand names, and the magistrate burned it to send it to the afterworld. His employee revived and recounted the register's arrival in the courts of the hereafter. He and the magistrate were to be blessed with divine favors.[75]

Various other anecdotes depicted an entire village making a vow after experiencing a miracle.[76] The collective dimension of the vow, by a family or a village, was constantly highlighted. In one anecdote, a man was summoned to hell and told by Yama,

> Your family has not eaten beef for several generations, and your father loved to tell stories about the retribution linked to this taboo, which is

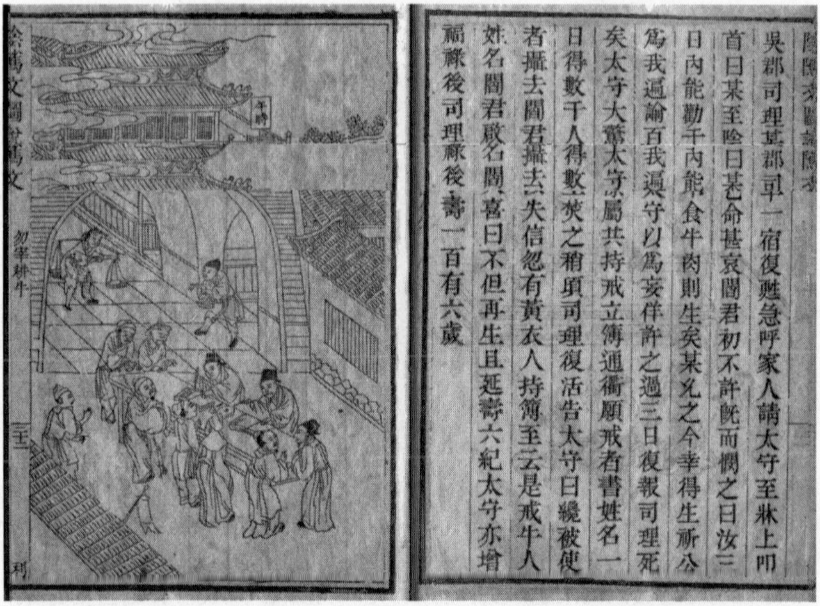


Figure 1. Illustration of the story of the yamen employee returned from hell to convince a thousand persons to observe the beef taboo: people are shown signing the registry of those who have taken the vow. In Rong Zhu 榮柱, *Yinzhiwen tushuo* 陰騭文圖說, 1801, 3.21b–22a. Original edition held in the collections of the Library of the Australian National University, available online at http://hdl.handle.net/1885/112068.

> why you were allowed to pass the civil exams at a young age. But since your success in the exams, your servants have grown more and more numerous and have started to eat beef. Even if you didn't know it, you are criminally responsible! Beef is also eaten in your village. You come from an eminent family whose advice is respected. Yet you knew it and did not make the slightest effort. You are also criminally responsible for this! The blessings intended for your offspring have been canceled.
> 汝家累世不食牛。汝父尤好演說食牛報應。故賜汝少年登第也。自汝中後，僕役日衆，率食牛。汝雖不知，罪應坐汝。且汝鄉中人，俱肯食牛。汝為一鄉之望，若輩素信汝言。汝明知不屑口勸，罪亦愿坐汝。子嗣壽祿，今損盡矣。[77]

Of course, the accused asked for a chance to redeem himself and returned to life. He forbade his servants to eat beef and went to see all the villagers whom he begged to make a vow to observe the taboo, prostrating himself before those who accepted. The villagers called him the "guardian god of bovines," and the divine blessings promised to his children had, of course, been restored. Likewise, in another anecdote, a village chief was summoned to hell and accused of killing three hundred cattle. In reality, these were bovines slaughtered in his village for which he was administratively responsible. He was sent back to the realm of the living to warn people and then died a year later.[78] In yet another anecdote, a boat carrying a habitual beefeater was attacked by demons, but the boat was spared thanks to the presence of several people who observed the taboo. In the end, all the passengers made a vow to observe the taboo.[79] In all these cases, the protagonists manage to compel communities or entire groups to make the vow.

Our corpus of morality books devoted to the taboo provides us with two distinct formularies for the vow, which are filled in with the name of the adept and burned to be sent to the gods for their records.[80] In one of them, the person vows not only to abstain from beef forever but also to convince one hundred people to take the same vow and take the gods as witnesses so that they will receive great blessings when the number is reached.[81]

More so than the Song anecdotes, the stories recounted in the morality books described a society in which the taboo had become a norm known, if not observed, by everyone, and the consumption of beef was the exception. We are witnessing a kind of one-upmanship to determine who had earned the greatest merit concerning cattle. That is what gives an otherwise classic-themed anecdote a pleasant twist: a butcher bought two bovines and slaughtered one. The other ran away and took refuge with an official before going to a shopkeeper who kept him until the animal's natural death and made a fortune thanks to the merit thus earned. The official remarked to the shopkeeper, with a certain degree of arrogance, "Our family has observed the taboo (*jieniu* 戒牛) for eight generations, yours for only a few generations (which is why the ox came to us first)!"[82] Those supporting the taboo kept a precise tally. For instance, one of them proclaimed, "Our family has observed the taboo for over two hundred years!"[83]

To complete my survey of anecdotes, I should mention other classic themes that had existed since the Song and continued to be the subject of later narrative developments: visits to hell where people witness the tortures reserved for beef-eaters[84] and epidemic diseases that strike them;[85] cattle butchers being punished by cruel death;[86] observing the taboo leading to obtaining sons;[87] and people who know they should not eat beef but cannot resist temptation.[88] One long anecdote mixed all these classic themes in telling the story of a family of beef butchers: one of them saw officials from the afterlife note their name and address in a register during an inspection tour on New Year's Day. A good man convinced him to make a vow to observe the taboo, which he did, without being able to persuade the other members of his family. Soon after, an epidemic killed them all except the one who made the vow.[89]

## New Themes

The abundant material I have surveyed shows the strong continuity between Song and Yuan sources and morality books published from the sixteenth century onward: both highlighted the importance of revealed texts and the role of the vow to observe the taboo. But alongside these classic themes, other themes emerged in morality books that were of minor importance previously or were not seen earlier.

### Lamentation of the Bovine

The lamentation of the slaughtered bovine was not a new theme per se since it had existed since the thirteenth century, notably in the lyrical ballad "The Bovine Lodges a Complaint against Injustice." This theme prevailed and became predominant during the Qing, thereby giving the discourse of the taboo a sentimental tone. Most texts of lamentation used the style established by the ballad from the Yuan: the bovine speaks in the first person and describes its painful life (back-breaking work without any rest in hot or rainy weather, insults and blows, and subsisting on a miserly diet) and its tragic end under the butcher's knife followed by promises of revenge.[90] But there are also texts in which a god laments the fate of cattle, such as one very tearful revelation from Guandi, likely from the 1840s.[91] This theme can be found in all genres of Chinese literature: from literati poetry during the Ming[92] and Qing[93] to popular ballads in vernacular languages.[94] The theme of lamentation draws attention to the relationships between peasants and their cattle and introduces new issues related to the taboo into the discourse. Even though cattle still mainly complain about slaughter, they also lament the treatment they received during their lifetime. The *Records of the Red Cinnamon Palace* enjoined its readers to adopt a caring attitude (*aihu zhi xin* 愛護之心) toward cattle under all circumstances.[95] Other texts exhorted their readers not to whip and mistreat their plow cattle.[96]

The unfortunate bovine's lamentation was a more polemical theme than it may seem at first glance. It introduced the thorny issue of the peasants being torn between their need for money and their moral duty to their cattle. Some authors did not hesitate to demonize poor, stingy peasants who had to sell their aging bovines to buy a young animal. They juxtaposed the peasant worried about money with the scholar worried about justice and the peasant insensitive to the condemned bovine's pleas to the scholar disturbed by this spectacle. This undoubtedly reflected the wealthy elites' iteration of the discourse of the taboo, which delighted in contrasting the sense of profit with the sense of justice—a leitmotif in morality literature. Thus, a scholar bought a bovine that was promised to the butcher's shop and even managed to move an old peasant—as if the literati had a monopoly on kindness.[97] To be fair, some literati poems described with compassion the despair of peasants who were forced to sell their workmates during a famine.[98] The actions of activists, discussed in the next chapter, also showed a real understanding of the peasants' situation.[99] Moreover, unlike literati poems that tended to blame peasants, anecdotes typically blamed those who profited from the crime. For example, in 1640, the Ci 磁 prefecture (south of present-day Hebei) suffered from famine. A villager owed money to a man called Kang Lin and offered to kill his bovine (to sell its meat) so that he could reimburse him. Seeing that his debtor was compelled by starvation, Kang took pity on him and accepted the offer. That same night, Kang was summoned in a dream to the court of the famous divine judge Magistrate Cui (Cui Fujun 崔府君), where his wrist was broken as punishment. Kang awoke and rushed to prevent the slaughter of the bovine, whereupon his wrist healed immediately.[100]

In poems of lamentation, bovines complain about the peasants' ingratitude and avarice; they also express their despair at being not only killed but, worse still, butchered without any respect for their bodies—which, in animals as in humans, must be kept intact to avoid a bad death and ensure a good destiny. Butchers sell the animals to profit from each part of the body: the flesh, skin, bones, horns, hooves, and tendons. As a morality text says, "It is profitable to slaughter a bovine!"[101] Enumerating the uses of the different bovine body parts already appeared in the poem revealed by Lü Dongbin, translated above. Another poem mentions still other uses: tallow to produce lamps and candles, tendons to make bowstrings, horns to craft handles for weapons, and finally, the skin and bones.[102] In addition to the crime of slaughter, the ignominy of butchering leaves no fragment of the body intact, which "runs counter to a taboo esteemed by heaven, earth, and the gods."[103]

Faced with the lack of reverence for the bovine body, supporters of the taboo urged burial. Cattle burials date back long before the taboo. The *Book of the Master of Huainan,* compiled in the second century BCE, already explains that the horse and the bovine, having rendered great services to humans, must be rewarded and receive a burial upon their deaths.[104] In fact, animal burials were practiced since antiquity.[105] Texts found in Dunhuang show that it was common to conduct funeral services for domestic animals, including bovines, during the late first millennium, but this did not preclude eating them.[106] These ancient practices betray both a sense of gratitude toward domestic animals and a careful concern for securing a good afterlife for an animal that might have grievances toward its keeper. The appearance of the beef taboo obviously reinforced the urge to treat the bodies of dead cattle with dignity. Morality texts enjoined peasants to reward their dead cattle by digging a deep grave for them, but such a meritorious act was not reserved only for peasants. Thus, a wealthy landowner paid one of the peasants who rented his land so that the peasant would bury his cattle in a pure place.[107] In another anecdote, a man rescued a bovine and welcomed it into his household. When the animal died, his family wanted to flay its skin, but he protected the bovine and buried it.[108] A zealous magistrate even had a cattle cemetery built.[109] In the seventeenth century, a temple dedicated to the bovine god, Niuwang, in Jiayi, Taiwan (which still exists today) was built on the tomb of cattle that had worked on the farms in this region.

However, even though there are cases of burials, casting the carcass into a river appears to have been just as common, at least during the Ming and Qing.[110] One of the many versions of the famous tale of the "White Serpent" (Baishe zhuan 白蛇傳), which takes place in Suzhou, has an episode in which the locals, who do not eat beef, cast the carcass of a dead bovine into the river, and the White Serpent feeds on it.[111] Discarding an animal in a river seems—at least to us moderns—much less respectful than its burial since the animal's flesh was immediately devoured by aquatic animals. Perhaps this practice existed because it was challenging to bury large animals in mountainous terrain since using arable land for this purpose was not an option. It may, however, also be seen as an echo of sacrificial practices that involved throwing offerings into waterways for the gods living therein.[112]

## Dogs and Other Tabooed Animals

A second striking feature of the texts in morality books is that dogs were frequently associated with the beef taboo. The oldest text to make such an association was a revelation by Zhenwu from 1302, the *Instructions Revealed by the Supreme Sovereign of Dark Heaven.* This association attained canonical status in *True Scripture to Awaken Humanity,* which placed the two animals on the same level. From the eighteenth century onward, most morality books linked bovines and dogs. Texts specifically on the taboo against dogs, including essays and anecdotes about retribution inspired by those dealing with bovines, appeared in morality books.[113] However, these texts were much less numerous than those concerning cattle, and some texts or revelations whose titles claimed that they were devoted to the two taboos only dealt with cattle. Moreover, the author of one morality book acknowledged in an introductory note that in the case of this double taboo, one was essential and the other ancillary.[114] The justification for the taboo against dogs reflects its subsidiary status: it was inspired by the discourse on bovines but was not as rich or forceful. Dogs were mainly upheld as guardians of the house and protectors of its inhabitants against thieves and burglars. Like bovines, dogs were faithful servants that worked day and night without reward. Humans were obligated to support them in old age and bury them when they died.[115]

What explains the emergence of the taboo against dogs in conjunction with that against beef? The two taboos share common origins, notably as Daoist rules of ritual purity. In fact, as one of the "three revulsions" (*sanyan*) along with wild geese and a group of aquatic animals, the Daoist taboo against dogs was even older (dating back at least to the early Song) and more canonical than that against beef: dogmeat was prohibited for Daoist priests and participants in Daoist rituals. Several anecdotes confirm the application of the taboo. In the early thirteenth century, a story relates the case of a woman who fell dead on entering the enclosure of a Daoist ritual after having voluntarily eaten dogmeat (as an act of provocation). Around the same time, a Daoist who conducted a ritual after eating dogmeat also fell dead.[116] However, before such anecdotes were included in morality books, only a few traces of the taboo against dogs existed compared to many anecdotes on the beef taboo, and all these examples were linked to the Daoist rule of ritual purity.[117] Dogs were commonly sacrificed and consumed in antiquity, but their consumption had already declined significantly during the Han.[118] The sacrificial use of dogs became extremely rare from the Tang onward, while their culinary use was limited to medical prescriptions, marginal social groups, times of famine, and specific cultural areas, such as the Cantonese region and Korea, where the consumption of dogmeat remained socially acceptable.[119] Therefore, the Daoist interdiction and later the association of the taboo against dogs with that against beef emerged after the consumption of dogmeat had already significantly declined and probably only had a limited impact on actual practice. This contrasts with what happened in the case of beef. The emergence of the beef taboo coincided with a decline in consumption.

Despite differences in historical development and perceived importance, the taboos against beef and dogs had much in common. By contrast, the consumption of equines (horses, donkeys, and mules) was definitely forbidden by common morality, but equines were rarely the subject of ritual purity rules. Consequently, they did not receive as much attention as bovines and dogs in morality texts. Horses have always figured alongside bovines in legal texts as a symmetrical pair of animals: one had a military significance, and the other was of agricultural importance. Both were considered necessary for the country and were therefore protected by law. However, equines only appeared very tangentially in texts on the taboo. They were often mentioned after bovines among the animals that benefit humans and should not be killed or eaten but without any specific elaborations.[120] One rare text that addressed the issue explained that the horse was loved, and no one would think of eating it; therefore, morality texts on this subject were unnecessary.[121] Such an assertion was not very accurate because, in reality, there is evidence of old horses, mules, and donkeys being slaughtered and eaten just like unfit cattle. There were even legal cases in which illegal horse butchers were convicted. This trade seems to have been particularly important in Beijing.[122]

It is certainly possible that equines and, even more so, dogs were included in a broader movement in the moral discourse to restrict the kinds of animals whose consumption was permissible. Bovines were the first to be the subject of a discourse highlighting this species' exceptional nature and excluding it from consumption. Once this discourse was widely accepted during the Qing, the moral discourse extended the exception to other species, despite the risk of weakening the argument presenting bovines as radically different animals. As mentioned above, at least since the Song, if not earlier, the discourse on animal life particularly highlighted crustaceans, fish, and turtles because the way they were killed was often cruel, and the consumption of these small animals resulted in a large number of deaths. This discourse helped to associate them with the exceptional species of bovines, equines, and dogs. The Daoist taboo proclaimed by Zhenwu against eels and turtles also played a role in including these aquatic species among prohibited animals.[123] In a text included in a very Confucian anthology, a magistrate reproached himself for having eaten eels and snails even though his constituents did not eat them. He promised to limit himself to animals reared by humans (pigs, sheep, and poultry), which were thus permissible to eat.[124] Other taboos emerged in the moral discourse in the late imperial period, particularly against frogs.[125] The latter interdiction was justified by the notion that frogs were useful since they ate parasitic insects that afflicted cereals. A book devoted to the beef taboo, the *Tears of the Plow Cattle* introduced above, ends with a whole section on frogs. A pamphlet recapitulating these various interdictions, published in a newspaper in 1874, provides a helpful overview of prohibited species: bovines, horses, dogs, two kinds of fish, turtles, eels, and frogs.[126]

Thus, while maintaining the preeminent status of the bovine, the main idea motivating these various texts was to define a short list of permissible animals: pork in particular, which emerged as the quintessential meat as early as the Song and became so even more in the late imperial period; mutton, especially as sacrificial animals; fish, except for elongated, snakelike ones; and poultry. The consumption of other animals became immoral. Thus, the relationship with meat was increasingly conceived in ethical terms, according to which only a few species could be used for meat, whereas all other animals became incompatible with food consumption. This moral discourse was combined with a decrease in animal species that were readily available and commonly consumed, a trend that also occurred in the West at the same time. In its application, this discourse partly overlapped with another that was based on the virtue of frugality, which rejected costly and extravagant dishes (swallow nests, abalone, etc.) but was clearly distinguished from the latter by its presuppositions—namely that not all animals were equal and only certain ones could be eaten.

## Confucius and the Taboo

In the entire discourse on the beef taboo in morality books, the most striking innovation compared to earlier texts was the appearance of a new theme: the justification for cattle sacrifices to Confucius. The next chapter will explore the complex social reality of such sacrifices to Confucius and the distribution of the sacrificial meat. Here, it suffices to say that bovine sacrifices to Confucius became a fraught issue during the Qing. The texts devoted to this topic seem to imply that the literate elites were being criticized from a non-Confucian perspective. On the one hand, the literati had adopted the beef taboo in their moralizing discourse toward the populace—even accusing peasants who sold their aging cattle of lacking a sense of morality. On the other hand, they continued to define themselves by sharing the sacrificial meat of cattle offered to their patron saint. To my knowledge, no text explicitly articulated this reproach. Undoubtedly, the literati were able to ensure that such an accusation was not transmitted in writing. However, morality books contain some texts that clearly responded to such accusations by justifying both the taboo and the sacrifice to Confucius.[127]

The argument for such a justification was simple: Confucius, the greatest sage in Chinese culture, had to be honored with the most precious offering—that is, a bovine. He certainly did not want to eat beef, but it was due to him. He could receive such an offering because he had been blessed with good fortune (*fufen* 福分), which allowed him to do so. The other deities were not allotted such fortune—the example systematically cited is the City god (Chenghuangshen 城隍神)—and therefore could not receive beef. They and the sacrificers would commit a crime. Even more so, humans, who had much less fortune than the City god, should not eat beef. This argument is particularly interesting in that it emphasized the rank and spiritual purity of the recipient of the offering. Beef seems to have been associated with a heavy burden that only Confucius was strong enough to bear without being polluted by it and without his spiritual power being ruined. This is quite close to the notion of a "taboo."

To my knowledge, the oldest occurrence of this argument dates to the late seventeenth century in a text revealed by Lü Dongbin that I already quoted above: "The merit of Confucius is eternal, and it is fitting that he should receive *tailao* [the great sacrifice, with beef], but how could it ever be eaten by ordinary humans?" 孔子功在萬世，宜享太牢，豈凡人所可擠口乎.[128] The fullest iteration can be found in a text titled *Precious Scroll Newly Revealed by Immortals for Making the Vow* (*Xinchu xianchuan liyuan baojuan* 新出仙傳立願寶卷). The illustrated edition that I was able to consult dates from 1897.[129] The text comprises a list of fourteen vows the faithful must take, each of which is the subject of a rather lengthy explanation in prose and then again in verse. The first few vows concern the foundations of social morality: filial piety, harmony in the family, frugality, and honesty in business—emphasizing gender issues (for the education of girls and against female infanticide). The last three vows concern showing reverence for written characters, saving animal lives, and observing the beef and dogmeat taboo. The third vow is titled "urging people not to eat bovines and dogs" 勸人勿吃牛犬.[130]

The discussion of this last vow begins by briefly recalling the duty of gratitude toward animals that work for humans. It immediately moves on to the argument: "But Confucius eats it, so why can't we?" The rest of the text also reviews more classic arguments (the demons of epidemics that attack beefeaters and the revenge of the slain bovine that pleads with Yama), but this is possibly the first text to consider the issue of the sacrifice to Confucius the most important. Subsequently, very similar formulations of the justification for the sacrifice to Confucius as the exception confirming the rule are found in other morality books or texts of very varied inspiration, notably, a play titled *The Beef Butcher's Retribution,* which will be discussed below.

The *Precious Scroll for Making the Vow* is very closely related to another similar text, the *Precious Scroll on Avoiding Disasters, Revealed by Mr. Pan* (*Pangong mianzai baojuan* 潘公免災寶卷), which was published in 1855. This *baojuan* was undoubtedly edited and partly written by Yu Zhi 余治 (1809–1874), a Jiangnan scholar discussed in more detail below.[131]

The protagonist of *Precious Scroll on Avoiding Disasters, Revealed by Mr. Pan,* Pan Zengyi 潘曾沂 (a historical figure linked to Yu Zhi, who died shortly before the Taiping invaded Nanjing in 1853), is described as a saintly man (and a vegetarian) beloved by the gods, who was promoted to general comptroller of the register of the living and the dead in the administration of the Eastern Peak immediately after his death. Pan then appears in a dream to his relatives, telling them that the Jade Emperor, furious at humanity's moral decadence, had sent down an apocalyptic disaster in the form of the Taiping and planned the death of all Nanjing's inhabitants. But thanks to Pan's negotiations, 30 percent of them would be saved on the condition that they swore a twelve-point oath of repentance. These twelve points included not killing baby girls (no. 5) and other interdictions related to human affairs, the familiar prohibition against killing animals (no. 9) and eating beef or dogmeat (no. 12). Indeed, a substantial section of the *Precious Scroll on Avoiding Disasters, Revealed by Mr. Pan* narrative recounts how the gods helped those who swore to abstain from meat and stop killing animals to escape Nanjing as it fell to the Taiping army, while those who did not were massacred by the rebels.

## Beef and Human Flesh

While the three new themes above were articulated explicitly, the final theme is of another order and relates to matters that were left unspoken or were merely implied. My remarks consist of a somewhat adventurous interpretation of several passages that stretch the comparison between bovines and humans to the limit. Some authors compare and even equate crimes against bovines with those against humans. An eighteenth-century morality book attributed to Chen Di 陳第 (1541–1617), a scholar known for his hostility to Buddhism, claims that "eating beef is worse than ignoring filial piety and benevolence (*buxiao buren* 不孝不仁); eating dog is worse than ignoring propriety and justice."[132] This was a startling statement put in the mouth of a Confucian. Similarly, Xie Zhaozhe 謝肇淛 (*jinshi* 1592) considered killing a bovine equivalent to killing a great general.[133] According to a novel of manners from the late Ming, crimes were ranked as follows: killing a sheep, killing an ox, killing a human, and killing one's loved one.[134] In an official text, bovines were described as the most spiritual living being (*zui youling*), an expression otherwise used to designate humans.[135] One author congratulated a magistrate who was zealous in his defense of bovines, saying, "You love cattle the same way you love the people!"[136] Finally, other authors emphasized feelings, saying, "For the peasant, losing his bovine is like losing his child."[137] A poem of lamentation states that "bovines especially resemble humans 牛更人相似."[138] In short, many authors did not hesitate to equate killing a bovine with murdering a human.[139] But was beef consumption comparable to cannibalism?

This is precisely what one of the most famous Chinese novels, *Water Margins* (*Shuihu zhuan* 水滸傳), suggests. The 108 rebel heroes of *Water Margins,* who are social outlaws and have their lair in the Liangshan 梁山 marshes, behave very differently from the honest subjects of the Song empire. One of the differences is their diet: they consume large amounts of beef and human flesh. The contrast is obvious: the inns run by outlaws serve slices of beef and human pâté, whereas those in the land of the Song only serve pork, sheep, and poultry.[140] This portrait is ambiguous in more than one way. The 108 rebels are demons who escaped from the Heavenly Master's prisons. It seems logical that they engage in misdeeds that violate the law and morality. But the bandits of Liangshan also represent an ideal, egalitarian society structured according to the Daoist liturgy. They are pretenders to the empire, therefore rebels, and also potentially emperors in the making. Should this be regarded as a countersociety governed by a morality specific to the world of soldiers for whom beef (and human flesh?) is permissible, in contrast to the morality of settled society? In any case, the association between beef and human flesh in *Water Margins* is pronounced and can shed light on some moral or anecdotal texts in which beef is rejected with a feeling of horror similar to that usually caused by human flesh. Eating one's workmate, an animal so human in its dedication and emotions, is almost like eating one's neighbor.[141] We may also wonder whether the Chinese may have been encouraged to make such a comparison—if only half-heartedly and more or less consciously—because cannibalism was also practiced. Documented in times of famine, cannibalism, according to some authors, would also have existed in very different contexts in which cannibalism was justified by revenge, passion, and the desire to assimilate the other. While historians have debated the reality of older descriptions,[142] such cases were attested during the Cultural Revolution.[143] Reality or fantasy, cannibalism seemed to be part of the context in which the heinous crime of eating beef was discussed.

### Cattle as Incarnated Bodhisattvas

In the 1923 *Coarse Words on the Taboo against Eating Beef* (*Jie shiniu cuyan*) appears a theme that I have not seen elsewhere in my corpus. This late text recounts that cattle are bodhisattvas incarnated as plow animals to help humans secure cereals sent to earth by the Buddha, who took pity on humans toiling in the fields. This narrative thus justifies the taboo based on the fact that the cattle are actually Buddhist sacred beings. Meir Shahar has found more popular scriptures developing this theme and argues that it reflects an early reception of the Indian beef taboo in China via Buddhism and has generously shared his insights with me.[144] As Professor Shahar's work is yet unpublished, I can only point to his forthcoming alternative understanding of the Chinese beef taboo, and for the time being, note that this theme appears late in the corpus I have at hand.

## Propagating the Taboo

In addition to the transmission of older themes, the inclusion of the beef taboo in the ethical project discussed in late imperial morality literature made possible, or at least set the stage for, the development of new facets in the discourse of the taboo, such as the respect for the integrity of the dead bovine body, the emergence of the taboos against dogs and other animals, and the relationship with sacrifices to Confucius. But the effect of morality books on the taboo was not limited to these theoretical considerations. Indeed, morality books provided fascinating justifications for the taboo, but most important, they were texts of exhortation. Their purpose was to convince and convert. It is impossible to ascertain how many Chinese made a vow never to eat beef again after reading one of these many texts, but one can only marvel at the activists' efforts to spread their message to the largest number of people possible by the most direct means.[145] In fact, the most striking efforts in terms of written moral instruction did not occur in morality books in the strict sense but in three related genres: novels, plays, and illustrations.

## Novels

Ming-Qing vernacular novels are an autonomous and well-defined literary genre. Nonetheless, the discourse in these works has noticeable continuities with that in morality books. Some novels with a militant morality that critiqued various practices and beliefs were intended to entertain and edify simultaneously. Chinese novels are not typically regarded as a genre of morality literature, perhaps partly because of the frequent campaigns against immoral folk literature. However, novels, whether in classical or vernacular language, were hardly a "popular" genre in the sense that the elites rejected them, and quite a few novels were presented as literature that was all the more edifying because it was enjoyable to read. In the case of *Passage to the East* (*Dongdu ji*), the late Ming novel discussed in chapter 1, Vincent Durand-Dastès has shown how a text adopting the format of the "literati novel" in vogue in the seventeenth century could closely adhere to the message of morality books.[146] An obvious example is Ding Yaokang's 丁耀亢 (1599–1671) *Sequel to Plums in the Golden Vase* (*Xu Jinpingmei* 續金瓶梅), which claims in the preface to be a commentary on *Verses on Action and Consequence Revealed by the Lord on High* and quotes quite a few religious texts.

Within the vast corpus of late imperial novels, several passages develop the exhortation not to eat beef in detail. I present three cases here, starting with *Sequel to Plums in the Golden Vase,* which devotes half a chapter to this topic.[147] In this novel, the story illustrating the beef taboo closely resembles anecdotes from morality books. Moreover, Ding begins by mentioning an anecdote that also appears in several morality books before embarking on a story that is really only a slightly more detailed anecdote.[148] Three scholars who once vowed to observe the taboo hide in a temple during an armed invasion. Two of them have broken their vow and are caught by enemy soldiers. Only the scholar who has been faithful in his abstinence is saved along with his family.

Predating *Sequel to Plums in the Golden Vase* by about forty years, *Passage to the East* introduced the taboo in a context rife with the discourse on animal life and vegetarianism. The taboo is mentioned three times in this novel: in chapter 83, a man, even though he was a virtuous vegetarian, falls ill and finds himself confronted in a dream by his old water buffalo that he had sold to a butcher. The bovine lodges a complaint against him (causing his illness) and gores him. The man thought that the merit of his conduct as a strict vegetarian would protect him, but the bovine disabuses him of that notion. It takes the miraculous intervention of the novel's protagonist, Bodhidharma, to save him. In chapter 88, two gangsters want to steal a bovine: one wants to resell it as a working animal, whereas the other wants it to be slaughtered. One of the novel's many animal spirits that punish sinners, a wolf charged with punishing the guilty, turns into a bovine. He explains to the two gangsters that he is their ancestor who is being punished for having killed cattle. The two thieves convert and bring the animal to a sanctuary (*fangsheng suo* 放生所). Finally, in chapter 98, a scholar who likes to eat beef dreams of a bovine denying him success in civil exams.[149] Thus, *Passage to the East* presents the taboo through classic themes but integrates them more thoroughly throughout the story than *Sequel to Plums in the Golden Vase.*

Li Ruzhen's 李汝珍 (ca. 1763–1830) *Flowers in the Mirror* (*Jinghua yuan* 鏡花緣) appeared later, but it still fits into the tradition of moralizing literati novels, although it was undoubtedly one of the last examples. In the twentieth century, this novel was sometimes regarded as an avant-garde work and even a feminist manifesto. Li indeed devotes many pages to social issues concerning women, such as their access to education, foot-binding, and concubinage. However, the morality articulated in this novel remains mainly in the tradition of the morality books.[150] The framework of the story consists of the travels of the protagonists, Tang Ao 唐敖 and Duo Jiugong 多九公. The different stages of their journey facilitate several allegorical developments and digressions. The bulk of the novelist's social criticism is concentrated in chapter 12 in which the protagonists visit a remote island called Junzi guo 君子國 (Land of Gentlemen). There they meet wise foreigners who lecture them on the barbaric mores prevalent in China. Li Ruzhen hardly intended to question China's cultural supremacy, but this rhetorical role reversal between a central, civilized China and barbarian lands strengthens his argument regarding the moral decadence of his time.

The foreign sages' harsh criticism surveys the depraved mores (*subi* 俗弊) of the Chinese: delaying burials because of faith in geomancy; slaughtering many animals for banquets for the birth of a child; the custom of giving a child to a monastery to become a cleric to obtain divine protection; the passion for trials and the influence of the yamen runners who engage in harassment of common people; the consumption of beef; extravagant and ostentatious dishes at banquets, such as swallow nests; women working for the inner quarters (such as nurses, midwives, and matchmakers) who debauch honest women; stepmothers who push men to neglect the children from a first marriage; foot-binding; the excessive use of divination for negotiating marriages; and ostentation in general.

Thus, the issue of beef is included in a list of problems that essentially concern relationships between humans. Li Ruzhen employs the fairly classic argument that beef slaughter is the act of people who are ignorant of the principle of divine retribution, are blinded by money, and do not realize that cattle make it possible for us to live and that to sell a bovine is to "repay love with hatred." He then sets out to denounce the attitude of those who disapprove of butchers but allow themselves to buy a little beef. He argues that the sin is shared between the butcher and his client. The merit of completely abstaining from beef is infinitely greater than that earned through regular vegetarian abstinence.[151]

## The Taboo in Plays: *Tuniu Bao*

Just like novels, plays conveyed the discourses derived from the morality books and strongly contributed to their dissemination. The most famous case of a play advocating for animal lives is the Mulian 目蓮 cycle, which tells the story of the pious monk who went to hell to rescue his mother being punished there. There are very many versions throughout central and southern China, many of which seem to derive from a sixteenth-century version, Zheng Zhizhen's 鄭之珍 (1518–1595) *Play of Mulian Saving His Mother and Exhorting to Goodness* (*Mulian jiumu quanshan xiwen* 目蓮救母勸善戲文). This long play reviews all the themes of common morality. Mulian's visits to hell dramatize the mechanisms of retribution in great detail. However, the specific sin of Mulian's mother was that she broke her vow of vegetarianism.[152]

One of the most spectacular works to propagate the beef taboo is a didactic play, Yu Zhi's 余治 (1809–1874) *The Beef Butcher's Retribution* (*Tuniu bao* 屠牛報). This play is inseparable from the morality book movement. Yu Zhi was one of the most famous activists of common morality in the nineteenth century. Born into a poor family of scholars in Wuxi in the heart of Jiangnan, he repeatedly failed the civil exams and devoted himself very early on to the compilation of morality books as well as to charity and moral activism. He founded many charitable associations and gained a solid reputation as a tireless preacher and organizer.[153] Yu distinguished himself in various fields, such as helping the poor during natural disasters, revering written characters, and popular education. In this context, like many other activists, he wanted to suppress what he perceived to be immoral popular literature, especially plays and novels. For intellectuals, many plays encouraged licentious behavior and undermined the foundations of their moral and educational activism. Furthermore, as early as 1847, Yu organized the collection of "licentious books" (*yinshu* 淫書) so that they could be destroyed.[154] Yu, however, did not stop there and decided to compose morality plays (*shanxi* 善戲) to replace the proscribed plays and make the theater a spearhead of his moralizing activism. He wrote about forty didactic plays and formed a troupe to enact them. Some of his friends in officialdom tried to promote this enterprise. It is unclear whether the public enjoyed Yu Zhi's morality plays very much.[155] Still, regardless of how they have been judged in the history of theater, his plays are of considerable interest in the history of moralizing activism.[156] *The Beef Butcher's Retribution* was one of these plays, composed in the style of Beijing opera, which was then very popular. It was also written in a simple language, demonstrating that Yu genuinely sought to reach a large audience rather than producing a play for intellectuals.[157] The protagonist, in a comedic clown (*chou* 丑) role, is a horrible gangster who is playful and lazy and has opened an illegal beef shop (lit. boiling cauldron, *tangguo* 湯鍋) with his brother. He makes a good living slaughtering cattle and cooking beef. At the start of the play, the brother arrives with a female water buffalo that he has bought cheaply. The water buffalo begs to be spared. A good man appears and explains that cattle should not be killed because they work for humans and lead a painful life. Moreover, it is legally prohibited. He urges them to change their profession and tells them that the sooner they change their minds, the sooner they become buddhas. Crying bitterly, the man explains that the water buffalo asked him to intercede for her. To no avail: the two brothers turn him away, saying that they have never seen the effects of the retribution and that their customers demand beef. They eventually kill the water buffalo and sing the song of the cattle killer.

The spirit of the water buffalo then appears and sings a lament that describes her hard life of uncompensated work. "I who have never wronged anyone," she cries, "was sold as beef cattle [*cainiu*], to pay for the wedding of the peasant's daughter." The water buffalo ends up announcing that it will file a complaint in front of Yama and utters a curse against those who sold, killed, and ate it. Then the magistrate's runners arrive and demand a bribe from the butchers in exchange for letting them continue their infamous trade in peace. The two brothers offer meat to the runners, who respond that they do not eat beef: their children and their village were threatened by an epidemic, but a Daoist came to convince them to stop eating beef. Thus, the whole family was spared. They still take a piece of meat for their grandmother and some beef-loving friends.

At this moment, the ghost of the water buffalo jumps into action and gores the two brothers. The moralizer returns and convinces them to vow that they will never kill cattle again. One of them dies, and his wife laments that after the runners left, there was no more money to pay for the coffin. The moralizer then offers her a coffin. The scene ends with a song explaining the principle of retribution and the need to refrain from killing and eating cattle.

The following scene takes place in hell, where Yama questions the dead culprit: "You could have chosen any trade, so why did you choose to kill plow cattle?" The gangster replies, "Confucius eats well, so why shouldn't I?" Yama then reiterates the abovementioned argument about Confucius's exceptional status. Eventually, the gangster is thrown into a cauldron and reincarnated as a bovine. In the last scene, the butcher, who has been reincarnated as a bovine, speaks to his owner, a peasant who mistreats him. He tells him the story of his previous life as a butcher and his punishment in the afterlife. Someone interjects to point out that there are many beefeaters today, so some bovines must be killed to meet this demand. The bovine responds that such slaughter is illegal and that those who eat such meat will suffer from diseases. Then the discussion about Confucius resumes. Finally, the peasant decides to treat "elder brother bovine" (*niu gege* 牛哥哥) well and promises him a peaceful old age.

This play is remarkable for how it integrates all the literary themes of the taboo: epidemics afflicting beefeaters, the song of lamentation, the ineffectiveness of the taboo against slaughter because of corruption among administrative personnel, the killer's reincarnation as a bovine,[158] the link with sacrifices to Confucius, and the need to treat one's bovine work companions well. By skillfully integrating these themes into the dramatic action, Yu Zhi demonstrates his great familiarity with all of them and his conviction that they all can contribute to moral renewal.

## Illustrations

With plays, we transition from written moral instruction specific to morality books to oral moral edification. Undoubtedly, there were also vernacular adaptations of texts excerpted from morality books that were intended to be read in public. Another form of adapting the morality books discourse for a large audience was the use of illustrations. Some commentaries on *Verses on Action and Consequence Revealed by the Lord on High* and *Tract on Hidden Rewards* were illustrated. They contain scenes of cattle begging for mercy or butchers and beefeaters who became victims of retribution.[159] Newspaper illustrations from the late nineteenth century depicted similar scenes. However, these illustrations remained intimately linked to the text and did not constitute an autonomous mode of proselytization.

The most remarkable illustration of the taboo is undoubtedly that in figure 2, which combines text and image in an original way. Far from being a curiosity, this document seems to have been widely distributed. A seventeenth-century author speaks of activists promoting the beef taboo who printed sheets devoted to the exhortation of the taboo that were meant to be posted on the walls.[160] Perhaps these were documents similar to the one in figure 2. Writing in 1865, Justus Doolittle, an American missionary living in Fuzhou, claimed to have seen a leaflet posted on walls all over the city, which was a close variant.[161] For his part, De Groot writes, "All over Fujian, we have seen these admonitions

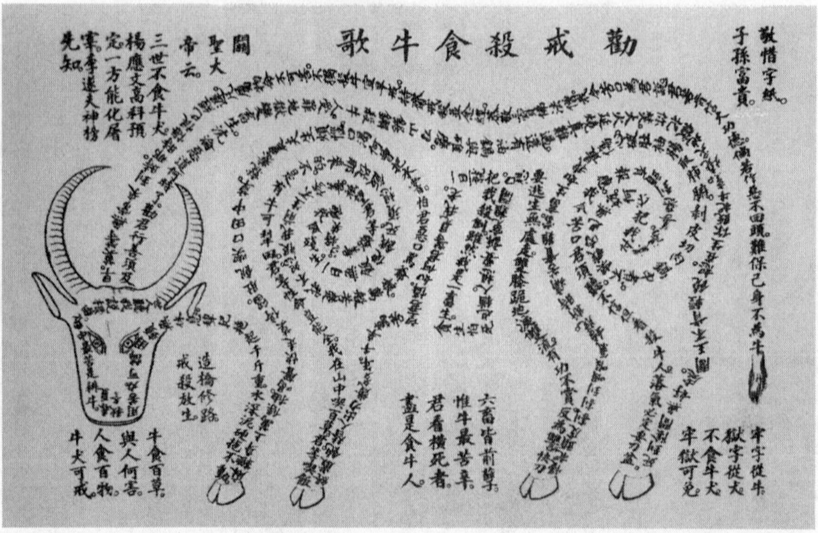


Figure 2. Illustrated tract of a poem lamenting the poor bovine, written in the shape of a water buffalo. Reproduced in Doré, *Recherches sur les superstitions* (Shanghai, 1911–1928), pt. 1, vol. 2, chap. 8, art. 10, plate opposite p. 308.

displayed in towns and villages, along roads and on bridges. In several, the characters were arranged to roughly depict a water buffalo surrounded by urgent warnings."[162] In one anecdote, a man who had come to eat beef entered a temple and saw two leaflets stuck to the wall, which caused him to repent and make a vow.[163] The document in figure 2 is therefore attested in many places. It is also extant in several reproductions and seems to have existed in several variants.[164] The central poem is also included in several collections of popular poems,[165] and a folkloric source relates that the Zhuang 壯 of southwest China sang the poem during their Cattle Festival.[166] In the center of the sheet, we see a bovine (in our illustration, a water buffalo) depicted as a calligram formed by the lines of a long poem. Only the horns, hooves, and eyes, which give the reader either an accusatory or plaintive look, depending on the version, are drawn as such. The poem is representative of the genre of "the poor bovine's lamentation." The bovine speaks in the first person, complains about its painful life, recounts the horrors of its execution, and promises revenge. The style is characteristic of popular ballads, and the text is not fixed: there were numerous variations between the different versions. Several other small poems or quotes surround this main image: in figure 2, there are two separate quotes from the revelation of Zhenwu, "Instructions on the Taboo against Cattle and Dogs" (lower left and right), one revelation from Guandi (upper left), a poem taken from an anecdote in the *Record of the*

Figure 3. "Pleading for Its Life 乞命," a cartoon by Feng Zikai 豐子愷 (1898–1975). In *Feng Zikai manhua quanji* 豐子愷漫畫全集, p. 17, reproducing a 1920s drawing.

*Listener* (bottom center), as well as two small texts that do not concern the beef taboo but other moral precepts—reverence for written characters (top right)[167] and a quote from *True Scripture to Awaken Humanity* (between the head and front legs of the ox) about protecting animal lives and the injunction to build roads and bridges.

The vibrant tradition of illustrating the beef taboo and pleading for bovine life would continue during the first half of the twentieth century, most famously under the brush of the famed cartoonist and lay Buddhist Feng Zikai 豐子愷 (1898–1975), who devoted several albums to animal life and drew several striking images of bovines pleading for their life.[168]

From the sixteenth through the nineteenth centuries, morality books became the primary platform for articulating the beef taboo. In addition to the morality books in the strict sense, the taboo also appeared in other forms of moral instruction, such as illustrated tracts, plays, novels, and textbooks.[169] With the rise of morality literature, the discourse of the taboo not only increased in quantitative terms (the number of texts produced and disseminated) but also in variety. It becomes a vibrant, multifaceted discourse, ranging from sentimental (the lamentation of the slaughtered bovine) to dramatic (divine judgment and retribution). The discourse also lent itself to various uses. It was sometimes adopted by Confucians, who criticized the immorality of the lower classes, sometimes by Buddhists, who included it in their defense of vegetarianism, and sometimes still by other voices, who criticized both the sacrifice of cattle to Confucius and the vegetarianism that did not distinguish between different animals. Like morality books as a whole, which defended a common ethic but each had a specific orientation and conviction, the discourse of the taboo remained coherent while having a particular meaning for each author.

The importance of morality books in the history of the beef taboo lies less in developing new themes or theories than in legitimizing and reinforcing the taboo through its inclusion in a comprehensive moral discourse. From a singular, isolated discourse, the taboo became a constituent part of Chinese morality. In this context, the beef taboo developed similarly to other ethical discourses, such as the reverence for written characters. Both had a nonclassical (in the Confucian sense) and even explicitly Daoist origin of which some scholars were aware, thus preventing their full adherence. With the rise of morality books and the Wenchang cult in the thirteenth century and especially from the sixteenth century, these reservations were swept away. For several centuries, it became socially untenable to actively oppose this taboo, even if not everyone practiced it zealously. As we will see, the situation on the ground was more complex than the unanimity of the prescriptive texts suggested.

# 5 The Beef Taboo in Late Imperial Chinese Society

THE BEEF TABOO did not develop until relatively late in Chinese history but gradually became a central ethical concern between the sixteenth and the early twentieth centuries. It was possible to violate the taboo but not to ignore it. Rather than being a mere point of moral casuistry, the taboo involved immediate choices in daily or, at least, frequent situations: food and meat consumption, the selection of sacrificial animals in cultic communities, and care for the primary working animal in the countryside. In addition, it was also a concern with considerable ideological weight: upholding the taboo symbolized the ideals of a civilization based on cereal agriculture and human moral conduct toward other living beings.

From its emergence until the late imperial period, the taboo grew in complexity and developed into a self-contained, rich discourse that was interpreted and appropriated in various ways by different social groups. Without counting ancient texts that were reinterpreted in light of the taboo, texts proliferated since the Song, so much so that chapters and even dedicated works were devoted to it. Consequently, from the seventeenth to the nineteenth century, the discourse was present in all kinds of writing: novels, edifying tales, morality literature, bureaucratic documents, and so on. Illustrated leaflets were pasted on the walls, and the laments of cattle appeared in plays. What effect did such propaganda have on Chinese society? The discourse was omnipresent and vibrant in its proselytism because the taboo was not self-evident, created challenges, and met with obstacles. Challenges and resistance deserve our attention in and of themselves and for what they reveal of the fissures within Chinese society. This chapter explores the concrete situation, debates, and tensions on the ground. While covering the same late imperial period as the previous chapter, this chapter pays particular attention to the late nineteenth century when the available documentation and historical context make it possible to outline the debates and the tensions with the most detail.

## The Taboo at the End of the Empire: Desires and Realities

When Westerners began to settle in the open ports after the 1842 Nanking Treaty that concluded the First Opium War, they published observations on Chinese mores. They did not fail to notice the importance the Chinese accorded to the issue of cattle. In his compendium on customs written in 1865, Justus Doolittle (1824–1880) devoted five pages to the beef taboo.[1] He mentioned the special legal status of beef butchers, the abundant morality literature on this subject, and the widespread beliefs concerning divine blessings granted to those who observed the taboo. He asserted that beef was consumed but only by a minority of people, among whom almost none were women.[2] De Groot (1854–1921), residing a few years later in Xiamen, not far from Doolittle's Fuzhou, made very similar observations: "In China, it is very rare that an ox or a water buffalo is slaughtered for its meat." He continued, "The cattle are treated with striking kindness. They never overload these working animals, beat, or mistreat them."[3] Doolittle and De Groot also recognized the existence of more or less clandestine beef butchers whose customers included Westerners.

Chinese sources confirm the findings of the early Western observers. Beef could be found in the markets, as the many anecdotes about beef butchers mentioned in the previous chapter suggest. Texts of exhortation, which naturally tend to exaggerate the problem to give urgency to their call for moral reform, claimed "there are many beefeaters 食牛肉之人愈眾."[4] However, while anecdotes from the Song period tended to portray isolated zealots trying to convince those around them to adopt the taboo, most anecdotes from the Ming and Qing periods suggest that the taboo was universally known and widely observed. Often, it was the beefeater who was isolated and in the minority. Anecdotes also outlined some geographical variations with villages and townships where people ate beef and others in which they did not. Many authors also stressed that beef butchers and consumers were concentrated in towns.[5] Of course, positioned somewhere between zealots and die-hard beefeaters, most people did not define themselves in relation to the taboo but accepted it more or less passively without having taken an oath.

Although these sources do not provide quantitative evidence on how many people ate beef and how many did not, they shed light on the social context in which beef butchers and their customers operated. As in the Song, beef was a social marker during the Qing. Beef butchers conducted their trade despite the taboo because they had a loyal clientele. Beef, as such, was not the subject of disgust in China. Medical treatises continued to claim that it was a healthy and invigorating type of meat. No one wrote that beef was a disgusting or unpleasant food. Thus, some people were ready to defy the moral taboo by consuming beef (even perhaps for the thrill of committing a transgression), while others could not bring themselves to do so. Even though morality books laid out the ethical choices of the individual, the reality of the taboo was essentially a sociological issue. Therefore, it is necessary to specify who these people were.

Undoubtedly, novels provide an excellent overview of the social realities of beef consumption in late imperial China. As Guo Jian points out, Ming and Qing novels rarely mention beef being served in meals. Descriptions of banquets refer to all kinds of meat, but beef appears in only a few instances, suggesting that this meat had been abandoned in most mainstream social contexts.[6] However, there are two exceptions: *Water Margins* and *Novel of the Three Kingdoms* (*Sanguo yanyi* 三國演義). The beef consumption in *Novel of the Three Kingdoms* is easy to explain. This historical novel is set in the second and third centuries CE and is based on ancient sources in which banquets of beef and alcohol were commonplace, especially among conspirators or for feasts offered to soldiers. How readers reacted to such descriptions is unclear, but the inclusion of beef in the novel makes sense. *Water Margins*'s case is different. The story is set in the twelfth century but reflects Ming society. As noted in the previous chapter, beef consumption in this novel is unusual: beef is associated with human flesh. It marks the diet of outlaw bandits and their exclusion from society, even if this exclusion is not portrayed as entirely negative. In short, the novel describes beefeaters as lawless bandits or rebels. Good people do not eat beef and even urge their neighbors to refrain from it. Several characters who are proponents of the taboo also appear in other novels, such as *Sequel to Plums in the Golden Vase, Passage to the East,* and *Jinghua yuan.*

It is always risky to regard fictional works as descriptions of reality, but sources that would allow a detailed study of the premodern Chinese diet—except for food served at the imperial court—are scarce. Cookbooks from the Ming and Qing sometimes contained beef recipes, such as *Recipes* (*Shidan* 食單) by Yuan Mei 袁枚 (1716–1798), but *Recipes* pointed out the rarity of this meat.[7] Others, however, excluded beef. For example, a cookbook by Li Yu 李漁 (1611–1680) criticized meat eaters and rejected beef, dogmeat, chicken, and cruel methods of slaughtering animals.[8] These two eminent authors embodied two approaches, which were sometimes combined in the same text: food was a serious matter or a pleasurable art.[9] Yuan Mei criticized Li Yu's view, while the latter denied that food could be exempt from moral rules.[10] It is tempting to presume that Yuan Mei and Li Yu were equally capable of representing an idle urban class that was relatively free from the moral constraints of the surrounding society. Would Yuan have assumed this stance more than Li, or was it simply a matter of individual conviction?

In any case, even though the social definition of beefeaters was more complex rather than being limited to marginal criminals, this last definition remained applicable to their suppliers—namely, beef butchers. We will begin our overview with beef butchers before discussing emperors and officials, local community leaders, activists promoting the taboo, and religious authorities.

## The Underworld of Beef Butchery

Since the Song, official texts systematically associated beef butchers with criminals, such as counterfeiters, salt smugglers, and illicit distillers. This reflects to what extent butchers belonged to an illegal underworld. The shops they ran were quite distinct from legal butchers that slaughtered pigs, sheep, and poultry and were designated by special terms, such as pen shop (*juandian*)—in use since the Ming and still common during the Qing[11]—and *tangguo*—which is not attested before the sixteenth century. *Juandian* refers to the enclosure where the butcher kept the animals before slaughtering them, while *tangguo* alludes to the cauldron in which the meat is cooked. The two terms were used interchangeably and were even synonymous. Like *juandian, tangguo* were essentially places that specialized in slaughtering cattle and other animals prohibited by law, such as equines (horses, donkeys, and mules).[12] The literature described *tangguo* beef butchers as amoral, dangerous, and connected to bandits who provided them with the animals if the butchers did not steal them themselves. The butcher in the play *The Beef Butcher's Retribution,* who is insensitive to pity, was a typical example.[13]

Beef butchers procured the animals and slaughtered them almost immediately. Few butchers raised cattle themselves; only one anecdotal case is attested in my documents.[14] Cattle thieves, sometimes with the complicity of soldiers, were an important source of animals for butchers. They were accomplices, if not the same people. Beef butchers also went to the countryside to buy old or sick cattle and bring them back to their shops, even if it meant deceiving peasants.[15] Peasants also brought cattle to towns to sell to butchers.[16] Such animal trade explains the public scenes of confrontation between butchers and protectors of cattle, discussed below. Peasants tended to sell their animals in winter; therefore, *tangguo* were especially busy then.[17] We must also mention the role of cattle dealers and brokers, who sold work animals to peasants but also took the opportunity to buy back old animals to resell them to butchers. Despised since the Song, their reputation did not improve in the late imperial period. One anecdote even described the divine retribution for a broker's misdeeds.[18] In the cattle markets, which were held regularly and sometimes controlled by the authorities, butchers and brokers were the main actors interested in animals for meat, even though peasants also came to engage in trade.[19] Commentators in morality books even called the beef butchers' world not only a hotbed of criminality but also a part of a sectarian milieu (*zuodao* 左道) that obeyed opposite rules as the surrounding society: there, claimed some moralists, only beef was eaten, while pork was prohibited.[20]

Beef butchers sometimes sold raw meat, as was the case with pork, but in most stories and anecdotes, they cooked it immediately after slaughter in large cauldrons (hence the name *tangguo*).[21] This is probably because this meat typically came from old and unfit animals or at least mature cattle. Thus, it was best prepared in stews or boiled for a long time. Once it was cooked, the meat was perhaps more easily concealed and stored in the event of a police raid or could be fraudulently sold as another animal's meat. The data on prices are too sparse to be meaningful but suggest that beef was cheap—cheaper than pork.[22] Unlike during the Song, beef was no longer perceived as a rare and prized type of meat but came to have a bad reputation. The price of beef was probably volatile due to the crackdowns on illegal butchery and agricultural circumstances. It plummeted in times of famine, when all peasants, under extreme duress, sold their cattle to butchers simultaneously.[23]

## The Qing State, Slaughter, and the Taboo

Chapter 2 discussed the history of the laws prohibiting cattle slaughter. Long before the taboo, the prohibition of slaughter developed during the Han. It was based on economic logic, although it quickly became a symbolic concern. But during the Qing, the enforcement of the legal prohibition became inseparable from the taboo. Even though the Qing code merely adopted the legal codes of previous dynasties, the imperial edicts allowed the state to articulate the importance of the beef taboo in a much more specific way. Even before the conquest of the Ming empire, the Manchu regime, despite its privileged relationship with a pastoral economy, spoke out very firmly against beef butchery. An edict from 1627 already strictly prohibited the use of cattle and horses for sacrifices and banquets, except for state banquets and the sacrifices to imperial ancestors.[24] Nearly three decades later, Emperor Shunzhi declared, "Deeply moved by the toil of cattle, I cannot bear to eat their meat."[25] He then sponsored the printing of the *Collection of Copies on the Beef Taboo* and its distribution throughout the empire. In his preface, Shunzhi asserted that killing a bovine went against the will of heaven, criticized peasants who lacked morals or feelings and ate beef, and claimed that if no cattle were killed, there would never be famine.[26] Subsequently, even if they did not go as far as Shunzhi in their imperial support for the taboo, other emperors promulgated edicts in which they reiterated that all animals were good to eat except cattle and that the court never used beef except for sacrifices required by state ritual.[27]

The dissemination of *Collection of Copies on the Beef Taboo* under imperial auspices presented an extreme case of fusing the administrative protection of cattle and the promotion of the taboo. During the Song, these two dimensions were linked but independent, even though they both considered bovines a sacred emblem of Chinese agricultural civilization. In the case of the imperial printing of *Collection of Copies on the Beef Taboo,* the two dimensions overlapped very closely. The prohibition of slaughter was regarded as a way of implementing the taboo, and the state proclaimed its rejection of beef consumption. In his memoir, Wei Yijie presented the dissemination of such a book as a significant element of moral indoctrination (*jiaohua*) directed at the populace. This was not a unique case of continuity between the discourse in morality books and the educational enterprise of the government. For example, compulsory public readings of the Sacred Edicts, which magistrates held twice a month in each district, were accompanied by recitations of morality books and edifying tales.[28] However, despite their overlap, the two genres remain distinct: unlike morality books, indoctrination (*jiaohua*) literature, particularly Sacred Edicts and commentaries on them, did not base its lessons on the principle of retribution. Moreover, the state's enthusiastic support for morality books such as *Collection of Copies on the Beef Taboo* evaporated as soon as Shunzhi died to make way for the distribution of works that aligned more closely with Confucianism, notably the imperial *Expanded Commentary on the Sacred Edicts* (*Shengyu guangxun* 聖諭廣訓).[29] Nevertheless, the distribution of *Collection of Copies on the Beef Taboo* during Shunzhi's reign was a special instance affirming the beef taboo as an ideology encouraged by the state.

*Collection of Copies on the Beef Taboo*'s Ming edition already envisioned a synthesis between state policy and morality grounded in divine retribution. Its introduction stated that the law prohibited cattle slaughter, that "Buddhist texts"[30] demonstrated the retribution for beefeaters, and that both complemented each other.[31] Other texts highlighted the magistrates' roles in the campaign against beef butchery. In one scholar's text, the law against slaughter and divine retribution were presented as two aspects of the same process.[32]

A particularly strong indication of the synthesis between the prohibition of cattle slaughter and the taboo in the imperial discourse is the edicts' frequent recourse to the issue of eating beef. In contrast, the legal code did not address beef consumption. A striking case was Emperor Yongzheng's conviction of a senior official, Zhao Guoying 趙國瑛, who was the military governor of Tianjin at the time, for publicly eating beef in 1728. An imperial edict stripped Zhao of his ranks and titles and accused him, as well as the prefect of Tianjin who had disregarded the slaughter prohibition, of having "eaten beef in violation of the law 犯法食牛," which gave license to the soldiers under his command and engendered open disregard for the laws.[33]

With imperial edicts constantly claiming that the court did not eat beef, did the Qing court actually set an example? As mentioned above, one edict restricted beef consumption at the Manchu court even before the conquest of China. But such decisions had limited application since part of the population ruled by those who issued the prohibition (the Mongols, in particular) kept a nomadic diet consisting of beef and mutton. Ethnic distinctions were addressed by case law. Throughout the Qing dynasty, rulings can be found that aimed at reducing this kind of consumption. In 1670, the court decreed the cessation of beef consumption during all palace banquets. The imperial cattle herds were then reduced to mainly dairy cows to meet the court's demand for milk, while the cattle in these herds were only allowed to be slaughtered to supply meat to "outside barbarians" who came to court.[34] It is undoubtedly in this context that John Bell, who was invited to a banquet along with the Russian ambassadors in 1721, ate mutton and beef.[35] In 1727, beef was replaced by mutton at the New Year's banquet for the princes and at the banquets for Mongolian nobles who came to Beijing.[36] Frequently, the Qing court's discourse differed depending on whether it was addressed to the Chinese, the Mongols, or other populations in the empire. Nevertheless, the application of the taboo at the court appears sincere even though the reality of beef consumption was more complex than the total prohibition affirmed by some edicts.

## Magistrates, Slaughter, and the Taboo

As in the case of the court, in the discourse and practice of local officials, there was a very close association between the legal code, which protected cattle as agricultural equipment, and the discourse of the taboo that considered cattle sacred. Admittedly, magistrates theoretically had no choice but to apply the legal prohibition, even though some magistrates tolerated slaughter by levying taxes from which they derived appreciable income.[37] In reality, everything depended on the magistrates' zeal in enforcing the prohibition. The plain text of the legal code remained a dead letter in the countryside if it was not supported by concrete action.[38] Morality literature highlighted the terrible punishment of lax magistrates[39] and, conversely, the divine benefits bestowed on zealots.[40] It generated pressure on magistrates by shaping expectations in public opinion. The cattle issue became one of the standards by which an official's morality was judged. Some accounts even suggest that magistrates were being subjected (by chance? by humans?) to proving themselves publicly in front of a crowd of people under their governance: a bovine escaped from imminent slaughter, came to take refuge at the yamen in front of a crowd of attentive spectators who watched the magistrate's reaction, and won its case—according to such stories.[41] These stories suggest that regarding this moral issue, the relationship between officials and the people under their administration was more complex than the enlightened magistrate simply indoctrinating (*jiaohua*) the ignorant populace with moral values through the process of disseminating the taboo, as some texts would have us believe.

As suggested by anecdotal accounts or prescriptive sources such as handbooks for officials, the attitude of magistrates ranged from a degree of detachment to a zealous commitment to the welfare of cattle.[42] In a chapter devoted to the cattle issue, a nineteenth-century handbook for officials even included fourteen miraculous anecdotes on divine punition or recompense for lax or zealous magistrates.[43] Another handbook describes the retribution in hell for beefeaters and officials who did not know how to prevent cattle slaughter.[44] What options did a magistrate have who wanted to protect cattle? Most were content to issue official rulings reminding all their constituents of the law and proclaiming that it would be enforced firmly. Such texts were issued in great abundance. Examples have been preserved in the compendia comprising the administrative documents of specific officials, such as Chen Hongmou 陳宏謀 (1696–1771), a paragon of Chinese bureaucracy.[45] Others were engraved on steles, which required a significant investment.[46] From the 1870s onward, many were published in newspapers.[47] In 1691, a prefect had his slaughter prohibition posted in all markets and public places and added it to the program during readings of the Sacred Edicts.[48]

In their texts, certain magistrates elaborated on the legal code and gave justifications for the prohibition of slaughter that appealed to the discourse of the taboo.[49] An official in charge of managing a food crisis in 1691 prohibited the sale and slaughter of cattle, proclaiming, "If you sell your old bovine for slaughter, the gods will inundate you with misfortune!"[50] Another magistrate, reporting to Emperor Yongzheng about his vigilance in the application of the slaughter prohibition, began by affirming that "since my childhood, I have upheld the celestial beef and mutton taboo 自幼天戒不食牛羊"—I have no satisfactory explanation for the addition of mutton here.[51] Several rulings by officials explicitly cited Zhenwu's revelation "Instructions on the Taboo against Cattle and Dogs."[52] Even though they did not always mention divine retribution, at least they specified that cattle slaughter violated natural laws (*tianli* 天理).[53] Thus, some magistrates were driven to act out of conviction.[54] Some, however, chose to foreground less spiritual concerns instead by pointing out that the cattle issue was linked to theft since many bovines slaughtered and sold in *tangguo* were stolen.[55] According to several authors, cattle theft was one of the most profitable activities of outlaws; therefore, banning beef butchers also reduced the number of bandits. One source even mentioned racketeering bandits who extorted money from peasants for cattle protection.[56] As a magistrate claimed, preventing beef butchery made it possible to simultaneously reduce the number of bandits, encourage agriculture, and instill the spirit of kindness toward living beings in the populace.[57]

Whatever the arguments were in the texts promulgated by the magistrates, their ordinances did not propose unprecedented administrative action[58] but relied on a procedure already in place during the Song, which had already demonstrated its weaknesses: the death of a bovine required a declaration of natural death and, in some cases, the yamen's authorization for slaughter and the dismemberment of the animal's carcass.[59] It was an offense to use a dead bovine's body without official permission. For most magistrates, butchering dead cattle remained lawful, if not laudable, even though an imperial edict ordered cattle to be cared for until their natural deaths.[60] Some magistrates banned cattle slaughter and made it compulsory for peasants to bury the animal.[61]

Thus, the procedure was in the hands of yamen employees and subject to corruption. This was an omnipresent theme in debates about the administration during the late imperial era: official texts blamed all of society's wrongs on the infamy and corruption of yamen employees, whose social status was very low. This discourse referred partly to real and proven practices and partly to a controversy: what was called corruption most often corresponded to the levying of fees for the registration of complaints and requests, allowing the yamen to function without any operational budget from the state.[62] The fact remains that Chinese and foreign observers said it very clearly: bribes given to yamen employees allowed beef butchers and their customers to conduct their business.[63] Various administrative sources affirmed that the protection of beef butchers and gambling dens was the primary source of income for yamen employees.[64] A corrupt runner (although himself very sensitive to the discourse of the taboo) is one of the characters in the play *The Beef Butcher's Retribution*, written ca. 1860–1870. An archival document dated 1745 related the case of a Beijing police officer who caught a man guilty of killing a bovine, divided the seized beef among his men, and kept a good part for himself.[65]

In an attempt to circumvent the perennial problem of corruption among yamen employees, a governor of Fujian proposed to give the peasants a choice between burying their dead cattle without any official procedure or butchering cattle with authorization provided directly by the nearest yamen in exchange for a guarantee provided by their neighbors and without inspection by yamen employees.[66] But texts that addressed employee corruption suggested that village chiefs (*dibao* 地保) were just as inclined to demand bribes and threaten denunciation.

Depending on the zeal of the magistrate and his employees, cattle butchers operated secretly or openly. The difficulty of enforcing the law and the ephemeral nature of the short-lived campaigns to eradicate illicit beef butchers, after which *tangguo* always ended up reappearing, were a cause of frustration for magistrates and, even more so, activists. Such remarks were common throughout the Ming and Qing, so much so that it is difficult to determine whether the situation worsened during the Qing or whether there were substantial regional or local differences. The situation in Jiangnan is particularly well documented in multiple newspaper articles, notably in the famous Shanghai daily, *Shenbao,* published from 1872 onward.

*Shenbao* ran many articles that recounted the efforts of magistrates and cattle activists.[67] These sources suggest that an arrest and punishment of a beef butcher was the exception rather than the rule and that there was a widespread sense of impunity.[68] It is difficult to cross-reference these sources with the judicial archives because extant archives are essentially those of the central government, which primarily concern severe crimes. Only a few local archives are extant that can shed light on the typical relationships between yamen and beef butchers.[69] Among the case law reports, there were a few cases of convictions concerning either well-organized *tangguo* that were provisioned by cattle theft or isolated instances of theft and slaughter.[70] As in many cases of misdemeanors, it is likely that the culprits convicted by a court of cattle slaughter in many cases ended up there because of a denunciation or because they were implicated in a more severe crime.[71] The issue of cattle thus served as an aggravating circumstance.

In short, concerning the cattle issue, as in the case of many others, the majority of magistrates favored a posture of intransigence expressed in various official rulings, which allowed them to take the moral high ground, but for lack of means, they contented themselves with taking actions of limited effectiveness, apart from occasional spectacular operations of repression. This is why local communities took the matter into their own hands.

## Local Enforcement of the Law

In late imperial China, it was common for local communities to take charge of law enforcement in place of the magistrate and add their own regulations. In the case at hand, communities exceeded the legal code by prohibiting not only cattle slaughter but sometimes also the consumption of beef. With one exception, the magistrates' rulings that I have seen never banned the consumption of bovine meat.[72]

The slaughter prohibition was included in several local regulations adopted by communities (villages, lineages, and economic and religious networks). Such regulations were often formalized after being recognized and approved by magistrates, but they were initiated, formulated, and applied independently of the administration. This is particularly the case with "community compacts" (*xiangyue* 鄉約), lineage, temple, and village regulations.

Community compacts, in particular, are well documented by numerous examples and have been the subject of several studies. These were regular assemblies (often the first and fifteenth days of the month) during which a whole local community, comprising several villages, met according to a very similar ritual from one place to another, paid homage to the emperor and the elders of the community, and listened to a reading of the Sacred Edicts or other official morality texts, as well as the rules specific to the community, possibly followed by a sermon and a banquet. Often, community compacts doled out rewards or public reprimands depending on individual behavior. The first community-compact projects were proposed in the writings of Confucian activists during the Song, but they became a social reality from the fifteenth century onward.[73] The roles of the authorities who sometimes required the implementation of these contracts and the local elites or dominant lineages who took the initiative, even if it meant having it ratified by the magistrate, varied according to the case and the period. The magistrates considered community compacts primarily as an instrument of social control (inculcating respect for the established order and strengthening the *baojia* 保甲 system—an organization that registered all households in groups of one hundred for mutual surveillance and accountability), while the elites and lineages also used them to establish their cultural and economic dominance. In both cases, however, such use did not preclude community compacts from expressing concerns of the whole population, and this was certainly the case with community compacts that integrated the issue of the taboo.

Perhaps the most remarkable document in this regard was an oath sworn in conjunction with a community compact drafted in 1535 by a high official, Zhu Zhe 朱浙 (1486–1552), not ex officio but as a member of the local elite from his native prefecture. Zhu remarked that the prefect had banned slaughter but that the good men of his prefecture needed to take charge of the situation: beef consumption was widespread, and cattle thieves, who openly sold the meat in the markets, were a major scourge. Zhu's justifications were classic: it was intolerable to kill and eat an animal that worked for humans, and there were so many other animals that were good to eat that it was inexcusable to harm cattle. The consequences he drew from this reasoning were more radical. He gathered the prefecture's population and had them take a solemn vow before heaven to no longer eat beef unless the animal became ill or too old to work (in which case, its owners could butcher and eat it themselves). They swore that whoever bought beef and ate it be immediately punished by heaven, that they and their descendants fall victim to epidemic diseases, and that their lineages be wiped out to avenge the bovine's death.[74] The oath was repeated a few years later in 1540 and again in 1546 because butchers from outside the prefecture continued to come and sell beef there.[75] Zhu envisioned that the list of all those who had taken the oath would be read before the Earth god twice a month. He acknowledged that while some residents might not want to take the oath, they would no doubt be marginalized and excluded from many aspects of community life.

The oath drafted by Zhu goes against a common conception of the literati official who is assumed to be agnostic and rational. In this case, it was a high official who invited his neighbors to make a curse that asked heaven to annihilate the descendants of all those who would not observe the beef taboo. His text provides a curious contrast between the authorization to eat the meat of one's own dead cattle and the condemnation expressed against those who eat beef bought from a butcher. Even though this was not a full articulation of the taboo (according to which even eating one's own animal was prohibited), it nonetheless was marked by the same fervor and involved the element of a curse.

Zhu Zhe's initiative was clearly articulated with the role of magistrates: the latter enforced the law, which prohibited slaughter but not beef consumption. But he noted that consumption encouraged slaughter and tried to stop consumption, not by coercion but by persuasion. No one was obliged to join the oath, but social pressure was undoubtedly very strong. By being an extension of the law, community compacts made it possible to exceed the legal code in formalizing the taboo. Other examples show community compacts prohibiting cattle slaughter and beef consumption.[76] In a very similar fashion, lineage regulations prohibited beef butchery.[77] A neighborhood community in Taiwan established a local regulation in 1889 banning the sale of beef in the market.[78] The slaughter prohibition was even found in the regulations of agricultural fields and rental contracts.[79] In short, the slaughter prohibition, often supplemented with a beef taboo, was not only imposed from above but was the common concern of many organized communities that were structured ritually and economically.

## The Theory and Practice of Morality: The Activists

Thus, the campaign against beef slaughter and the restriction of beef consumption was led by state agents and various local communities, but a category of people who were particularly involved in efforts to enforce and disseminate the taboo—whom I call activists—produced equally important results. They urged the authorities to act by means of petitions and various kinds of moral pressure and by taking individual and collective initiatives.[80] The forms of moral activism varied. Some had a long history but evolved from the sixteenth century in conjunction with the development of morality books. This literature tended to make everyone an activist rather than only the political or economic elites.[81] The discourse of morality books was inseparable from the social figure of the "good person" (*shanren* 善人) and the structures established by activists—charitable associations (*shantang*).[82]

Traditional forms of moral activism related to the beef taboo included oral proselytization to relatives and neighbors and the distribution of illustrated books and leaflets. An essay from the end of the seventeenth century mentioned activists who distributed booklets devoted to cattle or printed posters that were likely similar to the illustrated leaflet discussed in chapter 4 (figure 2) to post on walls.[83] An anecdote from the beginning of the seventeenth century described an official who had printed a "Chart of the Eight Virtues of the Beef Taboo" (Jinniu bashan tu 禁牛八善圖), which he distributed wherever he went.[84] Starting with the rise of newspapers between 1860 and 1870, activists sent editorials to papers. *Shenbao,* in particular, published several texts directly taken from morality books that addressed the beef taboo and other subjects. For these activists, the distribution of texts was often linked to oral moral instruction, as in the case of Wen Qixiang 聞啟祥 (fl. 1612). Wen had observed the taboo for thirty years when, in conversation with a friend, he concluded that observing the taboo within their respective families earned them only limited merit. Therefore, they decided to write a manifesto with a membership roster and take it everywhere, exhorting people and entering the names of converts in the roster. They enthusiastically concluded that they would not be like those activists who would ask people for money for a good cause but would only ask them to stop killing animals and eating beef.[85]

This case already indicates the transition to collective forms of activism. Given the importance accorded to the beef taboo in morality books, it is surprising that it did not lead to much institutionalized social practice. Most charitable associations engaged in a variety of charitable activities. Some were more specialized, particularly concerning the reverence for written characters (*xizi*). However, I have encountered only a few charitable associations that explicitly devoted all or a large part of their activities to rescuing cattle and enforcing the beef taboo. The issue of the taboo was well integrated into the practice of many charitable associations in two ways: the purchase of endangered cattle and the obligation of recipients of charity to take an oath to observe the taboo.

The practice of redeeming cattle was a predominant theme in anecdotes dating from the late imperial era. There are many cases of individual purchases. Usually, the protagonist stumbles upon a bovine that is taken to the butcher by its owner and begs for help. The protagonist asks for the purchase price offered by the butcher and offers to pay the same amount. Since this is a significant sum, he then tries to form a group to finance the purchase of the bovine collectively but does not always succeed. One such protagonist managed to convince a group holding a banquet to redeem a bovine that passed in front of their restaurant.[86] Another less persuasive protagonist could not convince his friends and had to pledge his clothes to pay.[87] As in the stories in which a bovine escaped from the butcher's shop and took refuge with the magistrate, stories of redemption often took place in the middle of a crowd. In an anecdote published in a pictorial, the bovine led to slaughter chose a generous man and begged him. The man agreed to redeem it, but in this unusual case, the butcher refused to sell it, whatever the price. He slaughtered the ox but ended up falling into the cauldron that he had prepared to cook the meat and died, which was an irrefutable sign of retribution.[88] Likely, the pressure of the crowd often obliged the beef butcher to agree to sell the animal.

The sentimental theme of the bovine that is led to the butcher shop and finds itself a savior is associated with the literary tradition of the "lamentation of the pitiful bovine." The dramatic scene centers on the pleading animal trembling with fear (*husu*), a cliché expression used systematically in this case.[89] The bovines' ability to express their fear in such a humanlike way and identify the generous person whom to address among the crowd is narrated as striking. Many other animals were described as sensitive, but cattle were regarded as the most sensitive. Or perhaps Qing Chinese had become especially sensitive to the emotions of cattle. As one journalist wrote, slaughtering a bovine was commonplace, but refusing its pleas was inhumane.[90]

Several anecdotes continue the story by relating how the bovine thanked its savior by saving him in return. Thus, in an illustrated story published in a newspaper, a water buffalo escaped from the butcher's shop and took refuge with a peasant who took pity on it and redeemed it. Later, the water buffalo protected the peasant's children from an accident. When it died, the peasant buried it.[91] A man who redeemed a bovine from a butcher hung a sign around its neck that said, "Released and [dedicated] to the gods" (*shenming fangsheng* 神明放生). The bovine then saved his life twice.[92] While the corpus of redemption anecdotes formed a literary topos, it also reflected reality: peasants took their old cattle to butchers, the animals cried with fear, and activists (of all social classes, scholars, peasants, merchants, yamen employees) intervened to redeem them.[93] It is impossible to say how common this scene was, but I believe that it was not rare.[94]

Most redemption stories dealt with isolated cases in which a benefactor unexpectedly stumbled upon and saved a bovine about to be slaughtered.[95] But some activists decided to institutionalize the practice. An anecdote, which is frequently cited and must have inspired later generations, reported the case of Dong Geting 董個亭 (early Qing?), a philanthropist from Suzhou, who saw a hungry peasant sell his bovine to the butcher in a time of scarcity. Dong decided to redeem it from him and keep it during the winter before returning it to him.[96] According to another author, Dong institutionalized this practice by founding an association dedicated to liberating cattle, Fangniu hui 放牛會, which owned the land where cattle were kept, provided fodder, paid a cowherd, and maintained a cemetery for dead cattle.[97] This famous case seems to have inspired emulators. During a flood in 1823, a magistrate was inspired by the example of Dong to institutionalize sheltering cattle in winter.[98] Various authors praised the practice of redeeming cattle without killing them.[99] In the nineteenth century, several charitable associations devoted themselves to this activity. They set up an "Office for Redeeming Cattle" (Dangniu ju 當牛局), financed by their private funds but benefiting from the support and infrastructure of the local officialdom (such as military grounds).[100] During famines or in the winter, these offices bought cattle from poor peasants, sheltered them, and kept them through the winter to resell them to their initial owner at the same price in time for the plowing season in the spring. During the great famine of 1876–1878 in northern China, an association took in the children and animals of affected peasants. A newspaper illustration in a story that reported this good deed portrayed mainly cattle and some horses.[101]

Another association, called Bureau to Welcome and Nourish Animals, Liuyang wu ju 留養物局, based in Suzhou, was dedicated to keeping old cattle that had become unfit for heavy labor. The association redeemed and fed them until their natural deaths and then buried them.[102] Another, the Society for Prohibiting the Illegal Slaughter (of Bovines), Jinzhi sizai she 禁止私宰社, seems to have focused primarily on monitoring to prevent the clandestine slaughter of cattle.[103] Thus, in the nineteenth century, several charitable associations were devoted to protecting cattle. However, most cattle rescued from slaughter and cared for by activists or charitable institutions were not entrusted to specialized shelters but to animal sanctuaries maintained at religious institutions, especially monasteries. There, cattle joined other animals that had been released (*fangsheng*) because they had been donated or redeemed by individuals, charitable groups, or even magistrates. Cattle made up a significant percentage of the animals housed in these sanctuaries.[104]

Other practices linked to charitable associations related more directly to the taboo and less to the agricultural economy. The basic expression of the taboo was the vow never to eat beef, and some charitable associations had their members or the recipients of their charity take such vows. The most extensive documentation comes from Yu Zhi, whose play was discussed above. Yu's most famous work is *Records of Reaching Unity* (*Deyi lu* 得一錄), an extensive collection of charitable association regulations predating Yu or written by Yu.

The moral obligations imposed on the poor receiving charity were among the most remarkable aspects of the various charitable associations described in *Records of Reaching Unity.* Thus, an association distributing medicines to the needy, Shiyao ju 施藥局, and placed under the aegis of immortal Lü Dongbin, required the poor to take an oath consisting of twelve points. These twelve points included general moral obligations (respecting social relations, honesty), reverence for written characters, and the taboo against eating beef, dogs, and frogs.[105] This type of vow is found in the regulations of many other charitable associations. An association dedicated to the reverence of cereals, Xigu hui, promised to revere cereals, written characters, and cattle.[106] Thus, these three themes, already associated in morality books, were connected in actual practice.

The vow to observe the beef taboo was also imposed on groups of people in a completely different context: the civil exams. Passing the exams was a spiritual ordeal for candidates, and many believed that family karma played a critical role in success or failure. We have seen many anecdotes describing the observance of the beef taboo as a means to ensure success in exams. Holding exams was also an opportunity to distribute religious or ethical propaganda.[107] Justus Doolittle mentioned activists handing out leaflets about the beef taboo to candidates entering the exam facilities.[108] According to De Groot, "while overseeing literary competitions in college [academies, *shuyuan* 書院], a zealous magistrate made each of the competitors sign a form printed on a sheet of red paper, by which they pledged never to eat beef, after which they had to solemnly burn the paper on the altar of the City god [Chenghuang]."[109] This vow was similar to those composed by Yu Zhi for his charitable associations.

How should we characterize the activists dedicated to the beef taboo? For some, like Yu Zhi, it was one moral concern among several others, whereas it was a consuming obsession for others. In some texts, we can sense a general enthusiasm for the bovine cause that borders on a frenzy.[110] The reasons for their commitment to the cause ranged from individual experience and family tradition to revelations. Many activists were members of groups practicing spirit-writing that led to morality books and more individual revelations, which reinforced their feeling of being endowed by the gods with a mission to spread morality in society. In a cultural context in which the defense of cattle was considered a noble task since even an emperor had undertaken it, many were eagerly waiting for a sign from the gods to make it their personal campaign.

There were many scholars among the activists. However, the protection of cattle was not a cause limited to the gentry. The cases reported in the sources compiled by scholars naturally tended to highlight their seminal roles, but they did not have a monopoly on charity. Just as some charitable societies dedicated to saving animal lives had a Buddhist monk as their spiritual master, so did some groups dedicated to protecting cattle gather around Daoist leaders. The well-documented case of a charitable society organized around Shi Daoyuan 施道淵 (1616–1678), an eminent Daoist figure from Suzhou, was one example. The members of this society were visited in dreams by cattle that said they were humans condemned to reincarnate as cattle for their severe sins and would be sent to slaughter. Starting with Shi himself, the association collected contributions to redeem and release the animals, and Shi Daoyuan ensured their posthumous salvation by adding them to the beneficiaries of community rituals he conducted.[111]

## The Beef Taboo and Its Integration into Chinese Religion

The prohibition of slaughter and the discourse of the taboo were disseminated by law and propaganda, and a good part of the state apparatus, from the court to the district magistrates, was committed to it. Local communities and activists supported this cause in every village and every family. This created the beautiful semblance of unanimity that separated good people—the friends of cattle—from villains—butchers, thieves, and gangsters. The reality was probably somewhat more complex. The prohibition against slaughter and beef consumption was discussed so much at all levels of society because the consumption of beef was a social marker that led to the inclusion or exclusion of certain people. We must now explore this aspect of the taboo, starting with the Three Teachings (Confucianism, Daoism, and Buddhism).

### Confucianism

The most militant figures—proselytizers and activists—were found among the gentry. Western observers from the late nineteenth century, moreover, believed that the literati were the primary observers of the taboo.[112]

Not only did they contribute abundantly to the production of morality books, but the discourse of the taboo was also found prominently in explicitly Confucian texts. In the sixteenth century, Liu Zongzhou, who criticized morality books for being too influenced by Buddhism and Daoism, nonetheless fully subscribed to the discourse on the beef taboo.[113] The same unreserved support is also apparent in *Poetry of Our Qing Dynasty, Announced by a Bell* (*Qingshi duo* 清詩鐸, compiled in 1869), an anthology of literati poetry classified by theme, especially highlighting social and moral topics. The compendium contained several poems devoted to cattle that clearly articulated the discourse of the taboo, including retribution. Representatives of the most official Confucianism, such as Ji Yun, the chief compiler of the official canon of all imperially sanctioned books, *Siku quanshu* 四庫全書, clearly spoke out in favor of banning beef.[114]

However, the beef taboo was not Confucian. We should set aside exegetical strategies of justifying the taboo by quoting the *Mengzi* or the *Book of Rites*. We should also set aside righteous battle cries saying that the discourse of the taboo based on retribution was secondary and that only morality mattered—the weapon of choice of Confucians. Magistrates affirmed in their rulings that the "Buddhist and Daoist" discourse on retribution for the cattle killers and Confucian texts limiting cattle sacrifice to heaven complemented each other perfectly.[115] Still, Confucianism was a sacrificial religion in which cattle were killed and eaten. One morality text frankly outlined the problem:

> Daoist texts forbid eating beef. For Confucians, the classics frequently mention *tailao*, and dynastic histories recount the distribution of beef and alcohol. However, among the families who prepare their children for civil exams, nine out of ten do not eat beef. As for the others, they cannot resist their appetites, and everyone knows what to think of them.
> 道經戒食牛肉。儒者每以經有太牢，史有牛酒為解，而科第人家不食牛犬肉者。往往十人而九。若區區口腹。尚不能戒。其人可知。[116]

In other words, Confucians had to make the difficult choice between the beef taboo and loyalty to Confucian scriptures and liturgy.

Whereas the taboo was an individual decision, Confucian sacrifices were prescribed by the state. Since the end of the Tang, the Chinese state reserved cattle sacrifice for the two higher categories of worship (*shangsi* 上祀 and *zhongsi* 中祀). The third category, *qunsi* 群祀, including the great majority of local cults adopted into the official sacrificial register, was not entitled to it. *Shangsi*, including cults to heaven and imperial ancestors, were all performed by the emperor himself in the capital. *Zhongsi* included rites for Confucius as well as Guandi and Wenchang, the last two of whom were canonized with this rank and given the right to *tailao* in 1727 and 1801, respectively.[117]

For the general populace, sacrifices to heaven and the imperial ancestors were too distant and had little meaning. By contrast, sacrifices for Confucius were practiced in the temple of Confucius of each district twice a year on the first *ding* 丁 day of the second and eighth months since the seventh century. All the gentry (*shenshi* 紳士), in other words, those who had passed at least the first grade of the civil exams, participated.[118] This participation, both a privilege and a duty, was strictly reserved for them. The sacrificial meat was then distributed to the officiants and some participants (officials, recent successful examinees). Unlike the cults of local gods, the meat from sacrifices to Confucius was not eaten together at a banquet but taken away by the participants who could eat it at home, keep it, offer it, or choose not to eat it. During the Ming, the sacrifice of a bovine to Confucius was reserved for the temple in the capital, where the emperor led the sacrifice. The other Confucian temples had to be content with offering a sheep and a pig.[119] This distinction was abolished under the Qing: a bovine was sacrificed to Confucius twice a year in each district.[120] A newspaper article from 1880 stated that butchers in a district of Jiangsu used the pretext of sacrifices to Confucius to sell beef on this occasion.[121] In 1909, the director of an impoverished school sold sacrificial beef.[122] During the Qing, the gentry as a class was therefore defined ritually as those who regularly ate beef (as well as mutton and pork) that had been sacrificed to Confucius, their patron saint (lit. patriarch, *zushi* 祖師). In contrast, professional associations sacrificed only a pig to their *zushi*.

We have discussed the importance accorded in Qing morality books to the justification that Confucius ate beef. It should also be noted that this discourse does not mention that Guandi or Wenchang received a bovine sacrifice every year. The cases of Guandi and Wenchang were particularly embarrassing for Confucians as these deities were closely associated with revelations that formed the basis of the taboo. Moreover, morality texts that excused Confucius also sidestepped the issue of sacrificers who then ate this meat. One can understand the motivations behind such avoidance strategies since this was a thorny issue. If some enjoyed the sacrificial beef too much, they became guilty of impiety in the eyes of the public.[123] Yet if someone refused to participate, he insulted Confucius.[124]

The scholar Liang Gongchen 梁恭辰 (1814–1887) recounted that his family observed the beef taboo for more than two centuries. However, returning empty-handed from the civil exams, his father fell victim to a malaria attack. To cure him, his grandfather gifted his father beef left over from the sacrifice to Confucius. This sacred meat was intended to bring the blessing of healing; moreover, a doctor consulted affirmed that beef was a superb remedy for malaria. Despite these arguments, Liang's father was reluctant to violate the taboo. Pressed by his father, Liang's father took a small piece of it, which he spat out immediately before sinking into a terrible outbreak of fever. Yet, Liang added, the meat had not even gone down his throat.[125]

Thus, a bifurcation emerged among the literati: those who sacrificed and consumed beef and those who, while participating in the cult of Confucius, never ate sacrificial beef because they either did not receive it or did not eat the portion that was given to them. This divide was not erased by the fact that activists invested in cattle protection were likely to come from both groups. To the advantage of the literati, the emphasis the most explicitly Confucian texts placed on moral duty and the suffering of the unjustly slaughtered cattle shifted the discourse toward the guilt of the peasant and avoided mentioning the physical defilement caused by contact with beef, an essential issue for much of the populace, as we shall see.

It is almost impossible to delineate precisely the two categories of scholars, those who ate sacrificial beef and those who did not. Hypothetically, it seems that the first category was closer to fundamentalists—that is to say, following the classic definition of fundamentalism in religious studies, Confucians who adhered strictly only to Confucian canonical writings and categorically rejected all the ideas and rituals that had been added to social practice over time.

Fundamentalists tried to cut all ties with the religious structures of the surrounding society to practice only a "pure" religion.[126] They did not hesitate to eat the beef sacrificed to Confucius but also sacrificed cattle to their ancestors or Confucian sages. As noted above, around the twelfth century, cattle disappeared from the vast majority of sacrifices to local gods and thus became a Confucian sacrifice in the strictest sense.[127] The protagonists of the novel *The Scholars* (*Rulin waishi* 儒林外史), written in the mid-eighteenth century, devote all their energy to building a temple to a Confucian sage whose inaugural ritual, the focal point of chapter 37, involves the sacrifice of a bovine and distribution of beef. This is the ideal vision of fundamentalist Confucianism. Moreover, directors of academies (*shuyuan*) organized cattle sacrifices for Confucius and Wenchang. They also sacrificed cattle to their ancestors, especially in the Cantonese region.[128] Other lineages more integrated into local cults categorically refused to do so.

I would like to add another hypothetical point about fundamentalist Confucians. Many became literati doctors (*ruyi* 儒醫) whose discourse was known for demanding rationality and being intolerant of ritual healing practices (such as exorcism and symbolic therapies).[129] These doctors adhered to the medical theories of balancing the breaths and the five agents and did not accept etiologies such as demonic forces or supernatural punishments commonly accepted in society. We have already seen that the medical tradition was never associated with the discourse of the taboo. However, various anecdotes described cases in which a man who usually observed the taboo violated it because he was sick and was given beef to reinvigorate him.[130] Or a doctor wanted to prescribe beef to a patient, but the patient firmly refused and got better.[131] Liang Gongchen, who observed the taboo very devoutly, recounted how his father nearly died when, on the advice of a doctor, he was made to eat sacrificial beef. Liang related other cases in which a man, a member of a family that observed the taboo, was fed beef during an illness and was summoned to hell for his deed.[132] It is possible that literati doctors and Confucian fundamentalists were united in passive resistance against the taboo accepted by the majority of Chinese society.[133]

## Buddhism

Like Confucians, Buddhists sometimes found it challenging to adapt to the discourse of the taboo prevalent in the surrounding society. However, these challenges were less pressing compared to those affecting Confucians since Buddhists were entirely on the side of those who never consumed beef. Contrary to the widespread idea that the beef taboo was merely one of the ways in which Buddhists tried to promote the protection of animals in Chinese society, the taboo was extremely rarely incorporated into texts issued by Buddhist institutions—in other words, written by a monk or considered authoritative in monasteries (we have seen in chapter 4 a few Ming and Qing cases of monks and prominent lay Buddhists writing to support the taboo). From the Song, the discourse of the taboo was distinct—both in its objective and in its argument—from the discourse of protecting animal life propagated by Buddhists, and this distinction became even more apparent during the Ming and Qing. Buddhist institutions and their leaders consistently upheld the fundamental principle that life was precious in all its forms and did not promote radical distinctions between living species—humans, cattle, and others. The two types of discourse were not generally perceived as opposed, however, and many Buddhists indeed approved of both; some may not have written at length about the taboo because they saw it as part of the larger ideal of nonkilling and vegetarianism. Some people reconciled the two discourses by observing a double precept: do not kill animals and do not eat beef (and dogs).

Indeed, Buddhists could hardly denounce a practice that aimed to save animal lives, and some authors, beginning with Zhuhong, recognized the exceptional merit of cattle.[134] In their texts devoted to refraining from killing and releasing life, Buddhist writers mentioned the cases of saving bovines or, conversely, described the retribution of killing and eating cattle, but they did not set cattle radically apart and instead treated them as animals like all the others. There was one late exception dated 1922, a compilation of anecdotes related to the retribution for acts concerning animal life that was partially devoted to the beef taboo.[135] Moreover, Buddhist anecdotes dealing with cattle, unlike those found in morality books, were not accompanied by the discourse of the taboo, such as divine revelations and the threat of epidemics targeting beefeaters.

A good example of this Buddhist treatment of the taboo was found in a fascinating treatise written by a lay Buddhist that has enjoyed great authority since the eighteenth century: "Forty-Eight Questions on the Interdiction against Killing" (*Jiesha sishiba wen* 戒殺四十八問) by Zhou Mengyan 周夢顏 (1656–1739).

> Someone objected that cattle plowed the fields and the dogs protected us [from thieves] at night, so we should take pity on them, but since the pigs and sheep are of no service, what good was [maintaining them] if we didn't eat them?
>
> I answer: the interdiction against killing and releasing life simply means to fully embrace compassion. How could anyone stop at the distinctions between useful and useless? Whoever is content with not eating useful animals gives free rein to their selfishness. Alas! Moral nature thus degenerates into a simple custom, and gestures of love [toward animals] come only from desire.
>
> 客曰。牛可耕田。犬可守夜。固當憐之。豬羊一無所能。不食何用。答曰。戒殺放生。不過自全其惻隱耳。豈因物之有用無用哉。因有用而不食。仍然自私之念矣。甚矣性蔽於習。愛起於貪也。[136]

Without directly refuting the beef taboo, this text denied it special moral status, at least within the framework of the discourse on animal life. However, the same author who rejected the discourse of the taboo in this context also included it in another work, a morality book, *Canon of Master Anshi* (*Anshi quanshu* 安士全書).[137] It was, therefore, not a question of opinion but of textual genre: beef can be proscribed at the same time as pork is allowed but not in a strictly Buddhist framework.[138]

What implications did the reserved Buddhist attitude have for the social practice of taboo? We should not be misled by the occasional anecdotal mention of a killer monk or beef-eating monk.[139] Most monks were undoubtedly sympathetic to the cause of cattle even if they tried to draw the faithful's attention toward other animals as well. Some monks were even able to participate fully in the implementation of the taboo.

One anecdote from the Ming period recounted that on the advice of a medium, a bovine was about to be sacrificed to ensure the success of the construction of a dike. The bovine escaped and took refuge with a monk who saved it and then buried it when it died.[140] Holmes Welch relates the case of a famous monk who experienced the classic episode of the bovine begging to be saved from a butcher and that of another who administered the Three Refuges (taking refuge in the Buddha, his teachings, and the clergy) to all cattle he saw.[141] Ultimately, the Buddhist monasteries played a significant role in cattle protection networks by welcoming the redeemed animals into their sanctuaries (*fangsheng suo*). However, Buddhist communities did not define themselves in relation to the taboo and therefore did not give it as much importance as many other cultic communities.

## Daoism

In contrast to Confucianism and Buddhism, the Daoist adoption of the taboo was frank and unreserved from the late Song onward. Along with the "three revulsions," the beef taboo became a fundamental precept for much of the Daoist clergy. It was observed by an elite practicing the great classical communal and funeral liturgy called Qingwei Lingbao 清微靈寶 (Pure Tenuity Numinous Treasure) from the Ming. In contrast, Daoists in the local vernacular traditions (such as Lüshan 閭山 or Meishan 梅山), who, unlike Qingwei Lingbao priests, actively participated in the bloody sacrifices of local cults, did not always observe the taboo.[142]

The beef taboo was explicitly associated with Daoism in several sources, although it was even more commonly associated with Chinese religious values in general or with both Buddhism and Daoism. Daoist priests and preachers figured quite frequently in anecdotes.[143] Despite this association, there were relatively few Daoist canonical texts devoted to the taboo. The most profound consequence of the Daoist adoption of the beef taboo was not doctrinal—through textual production—but liturgical. It was implemented through the notion of ritual impurity associated with beef in cults framed by Daoist liturgy, which was the case for most Chinese cultic communities, as field studies have shown. We have seen how the rejection of (Confucian) bovine sacrifice played a crucial role in the emergence of the taboo between the ninth and thirteenth centuries. More specifically, the ritual defilement associated with beef already appeared in anecdotes from the twelfth century. The exorcistic deity Yisheng baode zhenjun struck down with misfortune those who approached within a hundred *li* from his temple after eating beef or while wearing leather. Another Daoist deity also prohibited beefeaters from entering his temple during the Song period.[144] In other words, beefeaters were excluded from the cultic community and treated as outcasts. As noted above, this was reminiscent of the situation in Japan.

The theme of the physical defilement caused by eating beef was particularly developed in Daoist contexts starting from the Ming. Thus, a late version of the legend of Zhenwu added an episode in which the Earth god put him to the test by taking the form of a water buffalo that blocked his passage. Zhenwu became angry and threatened to eat him. Guanyin intervened and announced that this single thought had ruined his merit and that he must undergo "surgery" involving opening his belly and washing his bowels defiled by the mere idea of eating beef.[145] The defilement caused by beef was also linked to the oldest theme attested in anecdotes concerning the taboo: *yakṣa* and other demons could not approach those who had taken the vow to abstain from beef. This theme appeared in a later anecdote: a ghost boarded a boat, but when the passengers swore not to eat beef anymore, he had to leave the ship because he could no longer approach them.[146]

From the Ming, the institutionalization of ritual purity became a more frequent topic, even if such mentions remained somewhat scattered. I am inclined to think that such a rule was widely practiced until the twentieth century, even if the sources do not prove it explicitly. At the very least, extant sources document the practice of the taboo in a wide variety of cultic communities. During the Ming, those who ate beef or dogmeat did not dare approach, for fear of guaranteed misfortune, two temples within the imperial palace—the Daoist Qin'an dian 欽安殿 and another, Longde dian 隆德殿, where Daoist and Tibetan Buddhist rituals, respectively, were performed. Qin'an dian, one of the most sacred places of the Forbidden City, was a temple dedicated to Zhenwu.[147] In a completely different context, though also linked to Zhenwu, who played a role in the dissemination of the taboo since the thirteenth century, pilgrims to Wudang shan had to abstain from beef, dog, snake, eel, turtle, and wild goose.[148] Even in contemporary Bangkok, during the festival of the Nine Emperors (Jiuhuang 九皇, the stars of the Big Dipper), which is very important among the Chinese diaspora in Southeast Asia, temples display a sign marked "Prohibited to beefeaters."[149] One anecdote insisted on the sectarian character of the purity rules: two brothers, one Buddhist and the other a self-declared Confucian, who was ignorant of Buddhism and Daoism, were at a temple. A merchant selling dogmeat passed by. The first brother forbade him to enter the temple. The second, by provocation, invited the merchant in and bought some meat from him but immediately fell dead.[150]

The purity regulations in the cultic communities were even more strictly observed within the ritual arena. A remarkable anecdote included in a nineteenth-century morality book reported the case of a traveling merchant who died far from home. His family sponsored the performance of the rites for the salvation of his soul, but the deceased appeared to his traveling companion to say that because he loved to eat beef, the gods who came to fetch him from hell and lead his soul to salvation could not approach him because "the stench of the foul smell of meat is still in my house." As a result, the companion made a vow to observe the taboo, and the demons no longer approached him.[151] Ritual purity required during rites for the salvation of the soul was not limited to cases in which Daoist clerics officiated. A similar anecdote described a Buddhist ritual in which Guanyin forbade a ghost to approach the altar during the distribution of food for hungry ghosts because he had eaten beef during his lifetime.[152]

Other sources mentioned the obligation of the taboo for certain specialists rather than for general members of the religious community. This was the case for a significant percentage of the Daoist clergy and others who had received religious initiations. Thus, in contemporary Fujian, some men or women who have reached the age of sixty join a group of laypeople who regularly recite the names of the buddhas and sectarian texts in collective celebrations. Those who join such troops are initiated by "receiving a rosary" (*jiezhu* 接珠) and vowing not to eat wild goose, dog, and beef, while women are encouraged but not compelled to become vegetarians.[153]

In a third scenario, spiritual masters or charismatic leaders forced their followers or clients to observe the taboo. One example is found in the biography, written no later than the early eighteenth century, of an orphan from Guangxi Province who became a well-known rural exorcist: he pressured those who used his services to refrain from eating beef.[154] As late as the 1990s, a qigong master required his followers to observe the beef taboo.[155] The Daoist emphasis on the issue of ritual purity primarily concerned beef, but it also extended to products derived from slaughtering cattle. Thus, the clerical precepts and those of cultic communities included taboos almost entirely absent in Confucian texts, particularly those against bovine leather and candles made of ox tallow.[156] These candles are quite common,[157] but their use has traditionally been prohibited in Daoist temples.[158] An anecdote from 1695 recounted how a scholar witnessed humans who made and used candles produced from beef tallow sentenced in the hereafter to being condemned to blindness for eternity.[159] In 1873, a group of activists received their strict interdiction from a magistrate in northern China, who argued that the use of such candles was sacrilegious.[160]

## The Taboo and Chinese Religion

Can we say, in short, that the beef taboo was specifically Daoist? Yes and no. Because even though contemporary Daoist Qingwei Lingbao priests remain the primary observers of the taboo, this is only a remnant of an observance that was much more widespread until the late nineteenth century. The taboo was an element of the common morality of Chinese religion reflected in morality books, which transcended each of the Three Teachings. And this concern delimited one of the boundaries separating Chinese religion from the other religions present in China, notably Islam and Christianity.

In short, who ate beef? This overview has covered various groups that did not adhere to a taboo otherwise widely recognized in society. In the first place, soldiers, whose specific tradition of banquets of beef and alcohol had a long history that persisted until the Qing, when cattle slaughter was strictly prohibited.[161] We also discussed the milieu of gangsters and outlaws, who had their own rituals and dietary rules. Next came fundamentalist Confucians, who were not integrated into local cultic communities and observed only their own religious rules. Finally, there were the wealthy, idle urban classes, itinerant merchants, and all those who were not integrated into tightly structured social groups. These different environments collectively represented a large number of people, but all were, in their own way, marginal or constituted closed groups with distinct social organization and rules of purity, just like vegetarian sectarian groups. By contrast, many structured cult communities, notably territorial cults, did adopt the rule of ritual purity that prohibited the consumption of beef. Throughout the corpus of anecdotes, the great importance of collective oaths in which an entire village or lineage vowed to abstain from beef demonstrates the crucial link between the taboo and the religious organization of society. It is possible that some individuals within these cultic communities violated the beef taboo with a frequency that we cannot determine; however, this does not detract from the significance of the taboo in delimitating and shaping the identity of these communities.

At the level of the regulations, the cultic communities that subscribed to the taboo were defined in opposition to recalcitrant groups (Confucian fundamentalists and outlaws) and the marginalized. At the level of practice, activists worked to ensure that the taboo was upheld both within the communities that promoted it and in the groups that ignored it.

## The Emergence of the Taboo as a Nationalist Theme

The fissures within Chinese society revealed by the beef taboo were only part of the tensions highlighted by this discourse and related practices. Another dimension was the discourse directed at the non-Han or groups not fully assimilated into Han culture, particularly Hui Muslims, colonized ethnic groups in the south, and Westerners. In these three cases, the majority discourse represented caring for bovines, the prohibition of slaughter, and abstinence from beef as characteristics of Chinese culture—in other words, civilization. The barbarians' or foreigners' failure to observe these rules was evidence of their moral inferiority. Still, this inferiority was not thought to be innate—at least, not until the acculturation of Western notions of race at the end of the nineteenth century.[162] Barbarians could be educated and brought to civilization, for example, by convincing them of the need to protect cattle; but as with the Han themselves, observing the taboo was a mark of civilization that was never acquired definitively but had to be constantly learned and reaffirmed.

## The Case of Islam

Conflicts around the interdiction against cattle slaughter arose between the Han and some subjects of the Chinese empire who followed distinct moral and dietary rules while being subject to the same common laws. This issue was not raised in the case of Tibetans, Mongols, and Uyghurs, who were all significant consumers of beef,[163] but it became a subject of conflict in the case of Chinese Muslims, the Hui. Muslims claim to have lived on Chinese soil since the first decades of the Hegira, but from the Yuan, a sizable community of Muslims emerged who, whether sinicized non-Han or converted Han, were linguistically and culturally Chinese and lived integrated within the general population. They were called the Hui. They obviously observed the interdiction against pork. Therefore, the Hui had distinct dietary practices as they built their social identity around Muslim food and hygiene.[164] Muslim prohibitions also implied the need for the Hui to obtain other meats within a society where pork was the primordial meat. The Hui have always been renowned for their consumption of mutton and beef. This also led to their professional specialization: many Hui were cattle and sheep/goat breeders; tanners who produced sheep or bovine leather; horse merchants; cattle, goat, and sheep butchers;[165] or restaurateurs.[166] The specialization of Muslims in butchery and catering has been a widespread phenomenon throughout the world.

However, while the slaughter and consumption of sheep did not pose a problem, when it came to cattle, this was directly at odds with the law and common values, which created an ongoing tension between the Hui community on the one hand and the surrounding society and the state on the other hand. Not much is known about society's judgment, but there is evidence that it was unfavorable. Thus, an eighteenth-century anecdote portrayed the Hui as cattle butchers and thieves: two of them manage to escape the runners who have come to arrest them, but they are caught thanks to two bovines that block their escape.[167] For its part, the state at its highest level adopted a radical position and systematically refused to make an exception for the Hui in consideration of the fact that cattle slaughter constituted a habitual crime of this community. The argument was used by some officials hostile to Muslims. In a 1729 edict, Emperor Yongzheng responded to anti-Muslim attacks by defending the Hui as being fundamentally honest subjects of the empire like others, who could not a priori be the object of discrimination. He nevertheless stressed that his defense did not exempt the Hui from observing the common law, particularly regarding the prohibition against cattle slaughter.[168] The emperor thereby demonstrated that the bovine issue remained a major dispute even from a perspective favorable to the Hui. Two months later, in response to rumors circulating among Beijing's Hui community that the prohibition against slaughter had been lifted, the emperor issued a scathing edict, proclaiming that the prohibition remained strictly and definitively in effect and that one should not jeopardize people's lives for a few Muslim ruffians.[169] The issue arose again in 1806. That year, Emperor Jiaqing received the report of a censor who supported the Hui community that imported Mongolian beef cattle. As it did not involve plow cattle, the censor asked the emperor to lift the slaughter prohibition in this specific case. The emperor reacted violently by dismissing and punishing the censor and refusing to distinguish between plow and beef cattle. He reiterated the duty of humans toward cattle and the universal and absolute scope of the law against cattle slaughter.[170] The case of Beijing, which was under the direct purview of the emperor and had a large Hui community since the Ming, is particularly well documented, but it was not unique. Thus, an edict from 1878 by the governor of Jiangxi reiterated the prohibition against cattle slaughtering specifically for the Hui.[171]

In this context, as in many others, concrete administrative practices deviated somewhat from the letter of the law. There were cases portrayed in narrative sources in which the law was applied strictly to the Hui. Thus, an episode in the famous novel *Rulin waishi* described a conscientious Muslim official, Magistrate Tang 湯. The town's Muslim butchers offered him fifty pounds of beef, hoping he would be sympathetic to their illegal trade. Advised by a colleague and hoping to build a reputation for perfect integrity, Tang refused the bribe and put the chief of the butchers in a cangue with the enormous package of meat placed on top of it during a heat wave in the summer. The butcher died from the treatment, causing the city's Hui to riot.[172] In this fictitious case, the Hui did not get their way. But traditionally, the Hui have been masters in the art of collective mobilization in the face of injustice with much more effective results.[173] An anecdote from the late sixteenth century described a similar conflict in Beijing. An official issued a ruling prohibiting cattle slaughter in the capital's Muslim quarter, but the Hui protested so vigorously that the official had the order withdrawn.[174] The scholar who authored this story emphasized that even if the law was good, it was wise not to insist on its application in the case of the Hui. He compared this situation to the difficulty of applying Chinese law to the Indigenous tribes of the south, discussed below. An official in Beijing in the early Qing stated that he had banned the slaughter of donkeys but that regarding cattle, whose butchers were all Hui, the imperial edicts and interdictions had never been observed.[175] Archival data from local administrations in Sichuan

Province further confirm that during the eighteenth and nineteenth centuries, Hui butchers benefited from local magistrates' tolerance to run a semilegal beef trade and even provided the latter with sacrificial meat for rituals in honor of Confucius.[176]

In addition, historical sources openly mention Hui beef butchers in various places during the Ming and Qing, for example, particularly in a district still known nowadays as "Cattle Street" (Niujie 牛街).[177] The data confirm the impression left by the repetition of the imperial edicts: Hui beef butchers flourished despite repeated prohibitions.[178] They were also remarkably well organized for clandestine trade. Hui commercial firms imported Mongolian cattle into Beijing as well as horses and camels, either as work animals or for slaughter.[179] This evidence suggests that although the prohibition against slaughter was largely ignored in the case of Hui communities, this transgression had not become so trivial that it was taken for granted because it continued to generate tensions.

After 1912 with the disappearance of the laws against cattle slaughter, the Hui practiced this trade freely and openly. In Beijing, a guild of cattle butchers was founded in 1940 and a guild of beef dealers in 1941, both consisting entirely of Hui.[180] Over one thousand families were affiliated with them. In the 1940s, around thirty-five thousand cattle were slaughtered annually in Beijing. This trade employed only Hui and constituted the profession of about one-third of the city's Hui community.[181]

Thus, the Hui have defined themselves partly in relation to the Chinese beef taboo. Nowadays, many say they are proud to eat cattle because these are pure and good animals that may be consumed.[182] In this way, they inverted the Han perspective regarding which meats are defiled. Nevertheless, the tension caused by the beef trade and the discourse of the taboo in the surrounding society affected the Hui. A nineteenth-century observer noted that cattle killers were prohibited from accessing the mosque on Fridays.[183]

## The Miao

The slaughter and consumption of beef among the ethnic groups of southern China differed from the case of the Hui in that it was not a well-organized trade in the very center of large Chinese cities but rather village practices with which the Han settlers came into contact only gradually. As noted above, beginning in the Song, texts written by Chinese scholars criticized cattle sacrifices practiced by the various ethnic groups in southern China, noting that this was a barbaric trait compared to Chinese civilization, which was concerned with cattle.

Such comments became much more frequent from the fifteenth century when the demographic expansion of the Chinese in the south accelerated, and the state became increasingly concerned with integrating the various ethnic communities culturally and politically. This expansion became more rapid in the seventeenth century when provinces such as Guizhou, Yunnan, and Guangxi were effectively colonized. At that time, Qing authorities tried to control and assimilate the local populations and become familiar with the ethnic groups through various descriptions such as "Miao albums," which illustrated and described the mores and customs of the different groups. In doing so, the Chinese state intervened in the collective identity of local populations by manipulating both ethnic religious groups and social formations—a process that is still ongoing today.[184]

The efforts of the Chinese state during the Ming and Qing to assimilate and "civilize" took various forms (the founding of schools, prohibitions against ethnic clothing, prohibitions against Indigenous weapons, etc.) and quite frequently included the issue of cattle. There were many accounts of "good officials" forcing the stalwart natives to abandon cattle sacrifices by various means ranging from persuasion to coercion. A magistrate by the name of Xu Jian 徐鑑 (1390–1450) was said to have convinced the Li 黎 of the Meizhou peninsula to abandon cattle sacrifices even if it meant converting them to Buddhism and Daoism because at least these religions did not practice sacrifice.[185] The most frequently targeted population was the Miao 苗 (also called Hmong in Southeast Asia), particularly in Guizhou, Hunan, and Guangxi. The Miao were indeed known for raising water buffaloes that they used in sacrifices. The magistrates stationed in these regions employed classic methods such as promulgating edicts to prevent the Miao from sacrificing cattle,[186] but some lamented that they could not put an end to the practice.[187] A magistrate claimed to have achieved this by making the Chinese settlers swear to respect the Miao people and their land and the Miao to no longer sacrifice cattle.[188]

One anecdote demonstrating the colonial bovine policy is particularly compelling not only because it was illustrated but also because it was an autobiographical rather than a hagiographic account. Linqing 麟慶 (1791–1846) was a Manchu dignitary and heir to a noble and ancient family.[189] On November 4, 1832, Linqing was resting in the official residence of the administrative head (Buzhengsi) of Guizhou Province, when a water buffalo galloped into the courtyard and bowed down in front of the main building with the attitude of a plaintiff coming to seek justice.[190] The warden alerted Linqing, who let the buffalo in. The water buffalo had escaped from a Miao butcher, whom Linqing summoned and reprimanded while redeeming the animal.[191] This is a typical anecdote of morality literature adapted to the colonial context.

Moreover, the Chinese tried to disseminate the morality books among the colonized peoples. Thus, one such book written in the Naxi language expressed the message of the taboo in clear terms: you may breed sheep, goats, pigs, and chickens for meat but not cattle, horses, and dogs. Working plow cattle are like your father and mother. You must adapt to the Han rites, according to which you can sacrifice pigs and sheep, not cattle. "Among the Han, virtuous families have not eaten beef or horsemeat for thirty generations." Cattle killers are reincarnated into cattle.[192]

## The Arrival of the "Beefeaters"

Europeans had been present in China since the sixteenth century, but it was not until the opening of five treaty ports to foreign trade and the emergence of concessions in 1842 that this presence became sufficiently important to have significant consequences on Chinese customs. One of these consequences was the relationship to beef. Europeans brought to China the habit of and preference for eating beef. This preference varied by nation and was particularly pronounced among the English, the "beefeaters."[193] Westerners imported canned meat[194] but quickly turned to local markets. They received their supplies from illegal butchers and simultaneously developed small farms for their exclusive consumption. In 1873, the Chinese authorities in Shanghai refused to recognize the special status of Western cattle bred for slaughter or to exempt them from the slaughter prohibition.[195] A few years later, however, they adopted an attitude of tacit tolerance.[196] The scandal caused by Westerners in Shanghai and the strained tolerance toward them is reminiscent of the situation of the Hui in Beijing.

The impact of the arrival of these beefeaters in Chinese society was twofold. It provoked reactions of rejection, which radicalized the ideological commitment to the beef taboo. At the same time, it opened a way to avoid the taboo in the name of Western modernity. In this confrontation, the notion of cultural differences between China and the West dominated, whereas Christianity did not play such an important role. However, one might wonder whether missionaries, who waged a cultural war against Chinese religion, were not also seeking to convince the converts to break the beef taboo.[197]

The first reaction of Chinese observers was to be horrified by the Western treatment of cattle. The presence of cattle slaughterhouses in the concessions was seen by many Chinese as an extreme source of defilement and an insult to the gods, which could only result in disasters. Thus, during a drought in 1873, a Chinese crowd set fire to the slaughterhouses of the French concession in Shanghai, claiming that the drought was heaven's punishment for the sins Westerners had committed toward cattle.[198]

The Chinese who observed the cattle trade in the concessions considered such activity proof of barbarism and the lack of moral sense in foreigners, but this trade also laid bare what many knew already: for a profit, many Chinese were ready to betray the values of their culture by selling their cattle to Westerners. The genie was out of the bottle.

The charged climate is best represented in *Pictorial from the Lithography Studio* (*Dianshizhai huabao* 點石齋畫報), an illustrated magazine accompanying the Shanghai daily *Shenbao* from 1884 to 1898. The image (figure 4) was accompanied by the following caption:

> Westerners eat beef as if it were pork or mutton; they do not feel the slightest remorse when they think of the hard work of cattle that plow the fields. Who knows how many millions of cattle have been slaughtered [for them] since the ports opened to foreigners? It really is a calamity [*haojie* 浩劫]. Recently, calves have been slaughtered, which people find even more distressing. A few days ago, a farmer tied up a bovine near a teahouse in the Baxian Bridge area and tried to sell it. In this area, there are several shops where cattle are slaughtered. There, one can witness all the cruelty of the peasants. A police officer named Deng was passing by. [Seeing him,] the bovine knelt and wept profusely while begging for mercy. Deng was deeply moved. He redeemed the bovine for ten Mexican silver dollars, leading it to a place where it could graze. The bovine died two days later. Knowing that it was promised to the butcher's shop, the animal had chosen a passerby and begged him, and he had saved it. This bovine was both inspired [*ling*] and fortunate because dying of illness and being slaughtered are two radically different things. If only all humans could be as devoted as Mr. Deng.
>
> 洋人食牛如豬羊，曾不以其力能耕作而少惜之。設埠以來，不知宰割了億千百萬頭，亦浩劫也。近更有宰及乳牛者，言之更慘。日前八仙橋左近某茶寮，有鄉人繫一耕牛於旁以求售。該處多殺牛作，鄉人之意，可知矣。巡防局員鄧君，散步經此，牛即屈膝跪地，涕泗交流，若求救然。鄧君見而心惻，出鷹餅十枚，取之而歸。閱兩日而牛死。噫！牛知人之殺己也，擇人而求之；而果能救之，牛之靈，牛之幸也。病死與刃死，相去天壤矣，安得天下人盡如鄧君之存心乎！[199]

The illustration did not show a Westerner, thus avoiding a frontal attack—the publishing house that published *Pictorial from the Lithography Studio* was run by an Englishman, Ernest Major (1841–1908), after all. The cause of the tragedy, however, was clearly identified as the eating habits of Europeans. Another

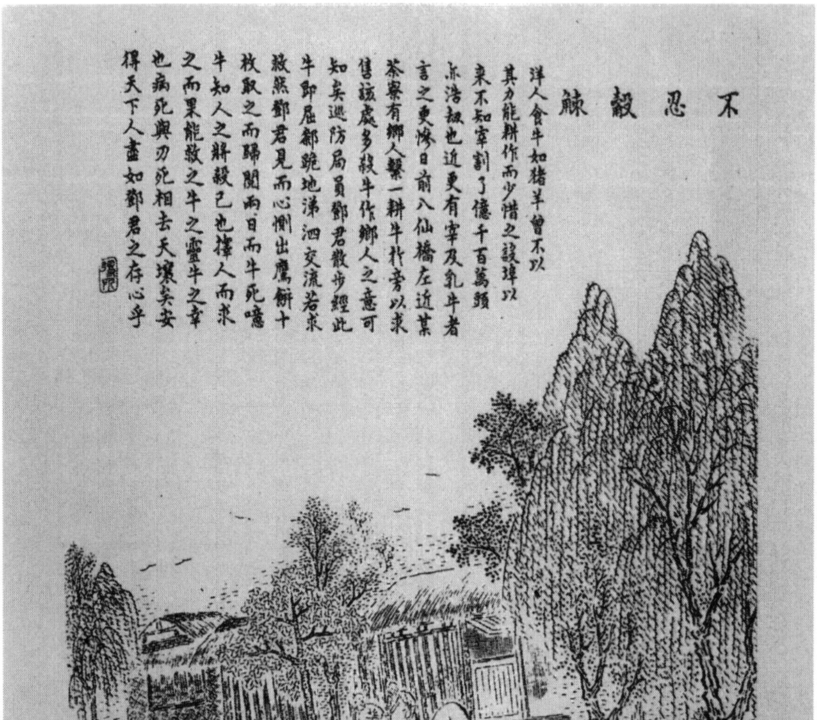


Figure 4. "Not being able to bear seeing it tremble with fear. In "Buren husu 不忍觳觫," *Dianshizhai huabao* 點石齋畫報, vol. Geng, p. 73 (published in 1886).

illustrated anecdote depicted a very similar situation: a peasant took a bovine to the concessions to sell it to a butcher, but a guard prevented him from doing so, taking pity on the animal that pleaded with him.[200] The proliferation of such anecdotes shows the perceived importance accorded to the problem of increased cattle slaughter due to the Western presence.

For the members of the gentry who were already mobilized for the protection of cattle, the confrontation with Westerners added another dimension to their activism. Beef became a national and even a nationalist cause in ways that may recall the Indian Rebellion of 1857. Although it strengthened the conviction of some, however, the Western attitude undermined the faith of others. The confrontation between "beefeaters" and zealots of the taboo led to a profound modification in the discourse and the religious attitudes of the Chinese elites.

## The Taboo under Debate

Besides turning the taboo into a nationalist cause, the presence of the "beefeaters" provoked debate and allowed some Chinese to question the taboo. Criticism of the taboo, the prohibition against slaughter, and its associated practices began to appear in the Ming but remained limited and tentative. Fundamentalist circles that practiced cattle sacrifice did not make public claims about it. The authors of critical texts were obviously aware that they were going against public opinion. All parties proceeded carefully and took precautions as to what they said publicly. The debate in the newspapers beginning in the 1870s was the first time that the moral consensus around the protection of cattle was questioned frankly. Two distinct approaches were at work in this questioning. On an ethical level, the beef taboo was criticized for giving too much importance to an animal and too little to humans. On a practical level, observing the taboo was thought to cause more problems than it solved. The first type of argument had already been made in the early Qing by Zhang Erqi 張爾岐 (1612–1678) in his "Essay to Broaden the Interdiction against Killing Cattle" (Guang jiesha niu wen 廣戒殺牛文).[201] Zhang took a cautious approach that left much unspoken and ambiguous. He did not fundamentally refute the position of the activists invested in cattle protection but reproached them for articulations and arguments that expressed excessive compassion toward these animals; he was undoubtedly alluding to highly sentimental texts about the lamentation of pitiful cattle. His classic argument, still used today by critics of animal welfare movements, was to establish a hierarchy between the concern for humans and for animals.[202] Activists, he wrote, mourned the deaths of bovines but did not seem as moved by that of humans who perished due to poverty and living conditions that were left insufficiently attended to. Zhang therefore called for extending the spirit of compassion, which was abundantly displayed toward cattle, to humanity.

In a similar vein, some writers who published their opinions in newspapers two centuries later held that although the activists' concern for cattle was laudable in several ways, their obsessive fixation and zeal dedicated to this issue were excessive because they overstated its importance and consequently ignored many more pressing social problems.[203] One author thought it scandalous that people cared about cattle so much while humans were starving or had to sell their children. "I understand the love of cattle," he stated, "but I hate the love that is only directed toward cattle."[204] Without so radically opposing the concern for cattle with that for humans, some instances illustrate the delicate balance between the two. In a district where the members of the well-organized gentry managed to track down all cattle butchers, the magistrate decided, against the activists' will, to release an imprisoned butcher so that the man's family would not be forced into poverty.[205] From the Song, there were many lenient rulings against beef butchers despite the heavy punishments stipulated by the legal code because the magistrates considered humans more important than cattle.[206] This attitude can be interpreted as a reaction to the many essays, anecdotes, and poems in which cattle were treated as equal to humans.

One late Qing text also based its argument on the relative importance of humans and animals, emphasizing an economic logic. The author began by recalling that beef had not always been banned in China. He then insisted that keeping old cattle was a luxury that was laudable and attainable by the rich but certainly not ordinary peasants. Peasants probably regretted selling their old cattle to the butchers but were forced to do so. Burying cattle would waste otherwise valuable land, and dumping them in the river was unhealthy and might cause epidemics. In short, the law undoubtedly started with good intentions, but it was unenforceable.[207]

The second category of arguments was more concrete. The corruption of yamen employees so tainted law enforcement that its results were totally against the law's intention. Authors writing in this vein criticized the legal prohibition against slaughter much more than the beliefs related to the taboo. This argument was especially developed in a series of articles published by the daily *Shenbao,* an invaluable source because it was the site of a real debate. The newspaper published tracts either urging readers to observe the taboo or criticizing it, sometimes in response to the former.[208] Critical essays claimed that beef butchery was in fact widespread. One author quoted the real-life case of a peasant whose old bovine died naturally. The village chief (*dibao*) came to demand all the beef and, when offered only half, denounced the peasant to the yamen for slaughter. The peasant's family had to pay large sums to have him released, and they were ruined.[209] This pragmatic author wanted the interdiction against slaughter to be maintained (in an attempt to control cattle thieves, soldiers, and clandestine butchers) but thought that it would be much better observed if its enforcement were entrusted to the gentry, who were "honest and knowledgeable about the situation on the ground," and not to yamen employees. This observation that the magistrates' runners were too corrupt to be able to enforce the interdiction was even shared by the author of a handbook for officials, who also recommended entrusting the enforcement of the bovine policy to the local elites.[210]

Most other authors went further. They frequently recalled that peasants needed their cattle to work and were not stupid enough to slaughter them voluntarily, especially since the price of a butchered animal was much lower than that of a living animal. However, these authors did not mention theft or food shortages. They insisted that a law routinely broken was worse than the absence of a law. It fostered corruption among yamen employees and undermined the respect for public authority. Moreover, this argument was also used to demand the lifting of general prohibitions against slaughter on the first and fifteenth days of the month and during periods of drought.[211] Thus, they called purely and simply for the abolition of the slaughter prohibition.

One author, giving as an example the laws among Westerners, affirmed that what mattered was the health of humans and that the sale of sick animals should be prohibited while allowing that of healthy animals.[212] This author was undoubtedly correct to write that illegal, and therefore uncontrolled, cattle slaughter was dangerous because another author demonstrated how, during epizootics, the meat of sick animals found its way into markets.[213] But whereas one author deduced the need to legalize beef butchery, another saw it as an additional reason to prohibit slaughter strictly and proposed that charitable associations redeem sick animals to compensate the owners and eliminate the temptation to sell them to butchers.

Another argument used to call for the abolition of the slaughter prohibition was to promote the distinction observed by Westerners between animals raised for slaughter, *cainiu,* and cattle used for work in the fields, *gengniu.* We have already seen that the term *cainiu* existed in China before the arrival of Westerners, although it was rarely used. Its exact meaning does not seem fixed. For some, it was a different species. For others, animals unfit for work by innate weakness, disease, or old age were sent to slaughter and were therefore called *cainiu.*[214] Some others simply called cattle bred for meat *cainiu.*[215] A stele from 1807 prohibiting slaughter employed this last meaning since it stated that there were very few *cainiu* in Suzhou and that the animals killed in beef butcheries were stolen or sold by the peasants.[216] Some authors, however, opposed the very use of the word *cainiu* and considered all cattle fit for work.[217]

For another author, respect for plow cattle was essential, but Westerners, who, he wrote, do not use cattle for work in the fields, were correct to think that livestock (*cainiu*) were animals like any other that do not deserve the respect due to plow cattle or sacrificial animals. While acknowledging the generosity of activists and the respect due to plow cattle, this author did not want to extend this feeling to the species but only to those animals that deserved it.[218] The rebuttal to this article, published shortly afterward, criticized the distinction between livestock and working animals as hypocritical and invented by butchers to justify the illicit appetites of some people. According to the author of this rebuttal, the distinction was not based on a difference between animals but only on the fate that was arbitrarily reserved for them. To admit the notion of *cainiu* is to leave the door open to killing all cattle. The customs of Westerners were different, and the author did not want to blame them for what they did in their home countries. But in China, cattle were used either for sacrifice or plowing, and there was no such thing as *cainiu.*[219] Another equally aggressive article, on the other hand, held that cattle only deserved respect according to the service they provided. An animal raised for meat had no reason to be treated differently from pigs. Sanctifying the entire bovine species was arbitrary and constituted an injustice to equines, which often worked harder than cattle.[220]

This very lively debate did not only concern the definition of the term *cainiu* and the differences between Western and Chinese agriculture. If one accepted the term *cainiu* and, by implication, the notion that certain cattle may be intended for slaughter, the whole edifice of the beef taboo collapsed. The stakes were clearly expressed in an article in which the author, who had already published an editorial pleading for a distinction between *cainiu* and *gengniu,* justified himself. "Aren't you afraid of going to hell?" a friend had asked him. The author responded by distinguishing between the legal prohibition of slaughter and the unfounded discourse of the taboo promoted "by Buddhists and Daoists."[221] This was a rare case from before the 1900s of an author who distinguished the law from the taboo. He showed that there was an economic logic behind the slaughter prohibition, but this logic would be best served by letting the farmer do what he wanted with his animal, based on the maximum profit: make it work or kill and butcher it. He recalls the example of Westerners and the Hui, who made a living from beef butchery. Another similar case of denouncing the taboo was a text taken from a handbook for officials. It was an isolated voice in this genre, which, until the second half of the nineteenth century, much more often frankly adopted the discourse of the taboo. The author asserted, moreover, that most magistrates were mistaken in confusing the sacred law of the dynasty, which aimed to protect agriculture, and the "Buddhist and Daoist" discourse on the merit of cattle that prohibited eating them and granted them the same protection as frogs, snails, and other animals, which he considered the pinnacle of ridiculousness.[222]

## The End of the Taboo

The editorials published in newspapers during the 1870s to 1890s were the harbinger of the end of a long period starting in the Song and culminating between the sixteenth and nineteenth centuries, during which cattle were regarded as emblems of Chinese agricultural civilization and became off-limits. The voices speaking out against the slaughter prohibition and advocating for a practical distinction between working animals and animals raised for slaughter were likely still very much in the minority around 1880, but they proliferated throughout the following decades during the last years of the Qing and through the revolutions of the twentieth century. The repeal of laws prohibiting slaughter during the Republican era was only the official recognition.[223]

Influenced by the dietary practices of Westerners and Chinese converts to Christianity and spurred by the very fact that literati were eager to associate cattle protection with traditional Chinese culture, those Chinese who were keen on adopting Western modernity to save China were motivated to reject the beef taboo as a logical consequence. A similar situation had arisen in Japan, where a radical change occurred: the young Meiji emperor announced in 1872 that he had tasted and loved beef as the prohibition against slaughtering cattle was lifted there.[224] Although such a dramatic turning point did not occur in China, it is likely that for many individuals, the adoption of beef as a "modern" food was a symbolic rejection of mainstream culture.

Such an attitude was clearly illustrated by a fictitious discussion in *Short History of Civilization* (*Wenming xiaoshi* 文明小史), serialized between 1903 and 1905 and among the most influential social protest novels of the early twentieth century.[225] A Shanghainese intellectual finds it ridiculous that a friend observes the beef taboo even though he presents himself as a supporter of "Western studies." A third explains that beef cattle raised by Westerners can be eaten.[226] An editorial in *Shenbao* from 1890 on the issue of food was one of the most striking articulations of rejecting the taboo in the name of Western modernity. The author virulently criticized Chinese food culture as a whole, from the preparation of dishes to the organization of banquets, and proposed a strict adoption of the Western model. And nothing seemed to him more ridiculous and hateful in the Chinese diet than the refusal to eat beef.[227]

In addition to westernization, other factors also played a role. Most political elites abandoned their adherence to Chinese religion and its moral discourse.

Although this religious culture did not disappear and was transmitted by various groups, notably the redemptive societies, its social base changed and shrank. Another related and equally fundamental phenomenon was the dismantling of the religious structures of society through "anti-superstition" policies from 1898 onward.[228] The cultic communities for whom the beef taboo was a rule of purity and who constituted the collective foundation of observing the taboo faced expropriation and political hostility.

Likewise, the coherent body of beliefs undergirding the taboo was falling apart. Thus, a booklet for children, published in 1923 and titled *Big Bovine Brother to Whom We Owe So Much* (*Yougong de niu dage* 有功的牛大哥), adopted the traditional discourse on bovines as work companions that lived a life of arduous labor in service to humanity, suffered an excruciating death at the hands of heartless butchers, and ended up on the dinner plate. However, religious elements had disappeared from the narrative; consequently, beef consumption was no longer condemned. The little boy protagonist of the book, who once was best friends with "Big Bovine Brother," eats the meat unknowingly in a restaurant (Western or Muslim, the author notes), then sees the bovine in a dream and understands that he has eaten his friend. This resembles an anecdote from the morality books but lacks the same conclusion. The little boy is not punished but marvels at the various ways that humans are indebted to cattle, including their meat. The little boy will continue to eat beef. There is reason to believe that the author of this children's book, produced by a large publishing house in Shanghai, quite consciously intended to appropriate and completely divert the discourse from the traditional didactic message of morality books.

If we put the action of radical intellectuals in perspective, however, the abandonment of the taboo appears much more gradual. The taboo offered resistance against modernity in some ways, as suggested by a story recounted by Japanese observers during the occupation of Taiwan. A Chinese man sold beef to the Japanese, but he was looked down on by his relatives and became ill. The cattle accused him in a dream. He repented, went to pray to the Cattle god (Niuwang) at Eastern Peak temple (Dongyue miao), and was cured.[229] In fact, the Japanese colonial regime in Taiwan tried to promote the beef industry,[230] but surveys conducted in the 1940s showed that beef consumption remained very low among the Chinese.[231]

During the Republican era, several local gazetteers in northern China still noted that the Hui were the only people to eat beef.[232] Urban surveys conducted by foreign observers confirmed this.[233] In the countryside, categorical rejection of beef butchery persisted. Mao Zedong himself noted in his famous report from March 1927 about the peasant movement in Hunan,

> [Peasants say,] "The killers of cattle will be reincarnated into cattle," and this has become a religion for them, so it is prohibited to kill a bovine. When peasants had no power, they could only use religious views to oppose cattle slaughter since they could not effectively prohibit it. Since the advent of the peasant movement, their power has extended to cattle, and they have effectively banned cattle slaughter in the cities. In the town of Xiangtan 湘潭,[234] there used to be six beef butchers, and now five have disappeared. A single one remains who slaughters sick or unfit plow cattle. In the whole of Hengshan 衡山 District, cattle slaughter has been banned.
> "殺牛的來生變牛"，簡直成了宗教，故牛是殺不得的。農民沒有權力時，只能用宗教觀念反對殺牛，沒有實力去禁止。農會起來後，權力管到牛身上去了，禁止城裡殺牛。湘潭城內從前有六家牛肉店，現在倒了五家，剩下一家是殺病牛和廢牛的。衡山全縣禁絕了殺牛。[235]

Communist enthusiasm for the beef taboo would be short-lived, but this astonishing text by Mao shows how the beef taboo was a key value for the peasants that they defended against more westernized urban culture. Another humbler observer, who published a gazetteer on a village in Shandong in 1945, noted quite the same phenomenon: peasants all condemned beef butchery, which they considered a cursed profession, and would never sell a bovine to a butcher. Beef was excluded from sacrifices and meals, even though the little that was available was very cheap.[236]

The consumption of beef became significant from the 1960s onward. The increase in beef supply due to technical developments and agricultural policy played a role, but demand responded slowly. In Taiwan, the mechanization of agriculture reduced the number of water buffaloes, while the breeding of taurine beef cattle (*huangniu*) emerged, although in the early twenty-first century imports covered more than 90 percent of consumption. Those who break the taboo, especially in cities, allow themselves to make a distinction between working animals (generally water buffaloes) and animals raised for slaughter (beef cattle). Beef noodles, popularized by the Hui, have become a popular street food.[237] In the People's Republic of China, consumption is also spurred by urbanization and by the encouragement of the state, which tries to develop the beef industry.[238] But beef consumption has remained low in China during the first decades of the third millennium, and a large part of the population has little taste for this meat.

In Taiwan, as in the People's Republic of China, the taboo constitutes one of the many issues at stake in the tension between modernized urban culture and residual traditional culture in the countryside. The breakdown of family structures makes it easier for children to abandon the taboo still observed by their parents, but I know Taiwanese friends whose parents made them swear on their deathbed never to eat beef. Others eat it with a feeling of diffuse guilt and explain when asked (because they do not readily talk about it spontaneously) that they only eat beef cattle (*cainiu*) and never plow cattle (*gengniu*). One may wonder to what extent the reappropriation of traditional culture within the framework of nationalist projects and also the renewal of the cultic communities, both territorial and lineage ones, might make the beef taboo appealing again.

# Conclusion

The many diverse documents and testimonies cited in this book have firmly demonstrated that since the Song dynasty, the beef taboo existed as a coherent discourse known across all social classes and in relation to which the Chinese had to position themselves. This taboo is far less prevalent nowadays but has not disappeared entirely. It has been a highly complex phenomenon with multiple causes and implications. The agricultural economy, which protected cattle as essential working animals, contributed to its development, while cattle farming was complicated by the disappearance of pastures and large estates after the ninth century. Another factor was the political ideology glorifying cattle as an emblem of Chinese agricultural civilization focused on cereals. This was an important notion since the Han but took on a new dimension during the Song. Religion also played a crucial role. The beef taboo was closely linked to the emergence of a common morality of Chinese religion between the Song and the Ming that was grounded in the liturgical and sacrificial organization of society cutting across Confucian, Daoist, and Buddhist institutions, vegetarian sects, and local cults that each had different codes of ritual purity. The phenomenon of the taboo cannot be comprehended by exclusively focusing on a single dimension, such as bovines as work companions and peasants' gratitude or its relationship to reincarnation. In their perception or their own rationalization of the taboo, some actors were able to emphasize one dimension or another, but this should not limit our analysis.

In presenting this argument, I particularly emphasized one dimension of the taboo, the ritual purity codes connected to the liturgical organization of Chinese society. This does not mean that I am placing undue stress on this aspect of the issue; in fact, the development and widespread observance of the taboo remain incomprehensible if one also does not take into account agricultural policy and ethical discourse. However, this liturgical dimension should be particularly illuminating since it has received less scholarly attention than the economic and ethical aspects, and it best explains the idiosyncrasies of the Chinese beef taboo. In several Southeast Asian countries that have also been influenced by Buddhism and where cattle serve as work companions, similarly to China, we observe reverence for cattle and low levels of beef consumption (only older animals are sold to butchers, who are socially stigmatized). Yet there was no discourse contrasting beefeaters with those who observed the beef taboo.[1] The latter, specific to China, must be understood as an ethical precept in the particular context of sacrificial cultic communities. A rule of purity and a social marker, the taboo displaced and complemented the older precept that separated Confucian blood sacrifices and "pure" Buddhist and Daoist sacrifices.

The beef taboo existed, then, both in textual representations and in practice, and it reveals its full range of meanings if contextualized within the economic, moral, and religious organization of Chinese society. But how important was it? Was it a fundamental trait of Chinese civilization? It was not included in the values expressed in classical texts, in other words, according to a very influential historiographical tradition, in the "civilizational choices" made during the "axial age" of late antiquity, during which Chinese culture was essentially formulated. The civilizational change that took place in the beginning of the second millennium is just as deep running and crucial to the *longue durée* cultural and social history of the Chinese world, however. In my opinion, the taboo that developed between the ninth and the fourteenth centuries is a major element of a social, ethical, and religious system that is still in place today, even after a century of revolutions. Thus, it must be understood as a reaction to vegetarianism that was the dominant model of ethical eating in medieval times, as well as an identity marker among local cult communities that became the building blocks of Chinese society during that period.

## The Beef Taboo and Chinese Culture

Beyond its role in the functioning of the codes of ritual purity, the beef taboo provided one of the moral standards—alongside other concerns such as sexual morality, reverence for written characters (*xizi*), commercial ethics, the condemnation of gambling and undeserved gain debated in moral lives and anecdotal and vernacular literature—by which Chinese culture was defined throughout the second millennium and in the encounter with foreigners. It also allowed different social groups to define themselves in relation to one another. However, in the twentieth century, Chinese intellectuals radically redefined Chinese cultural identity and abandoned several moral standards that were previously considered central, including the beef taboo. We have seen how the taboo symbolized the confrontation between traditional culture and westernization in Shanghai at the end of the nineteenth century. In addition, the disappearance of a large part of the cultic communities during the twentieth century also lessened the relevance of the taboo as a marker for differentiating various communities. These two developments have made it difficult to think about the taboo in contemporary Chinese culture. Moreover, the taboo contradicts well-established Chinese cultural notions toward animals and food.

The beef taboo allows us to question some stereotypical images of China that many Chinese intellectuals have frequently invoked in the twentieth century. One of them is the idea that the Chinese eat everything. We know the proverbs circulating, especially about the Cantonese, who eat everything that has four legs except chairs and everything that has wings except airplanes. Non-Chinese, including Europeans and North Americans as well as Japanese and other Asians, who reiterate such a discourse tend to forget that very similar ideas circulate about assorted Westerners, such as the French, who eat things such as frogs and snails.[2] Such discourses emphasize difference and reinforce the idea that the Chinese have a rational relationship to food that maximizes the use of resources and pleasure in ways that are radically different from those that are deeply marked by the notion of the sin of gluttony specific to the Judeo-Christian tradition. Moreover, the moral judgment underlying such assertions is highly ambiguous, blending admiration and disapproval. As the remarkable rise of vegetarianism in Europe and North America since the 1960s, which revived an ancient tradition that traces back to Pythagoras, demonstrates, ethical and religious debates regarding the consumption of animals are universal.

Views about the Chinese or a segment of Chinese—such as the Cantonese "who eat everything"—are not limited to racial or regional prejudices or popular culture. They also inform scholarly conceptions of Chinese culture. For this reason, it is interesting to reexamine what researchers have said about the beef taboo. By investigating the academic discourse about the taboo, we can lay bare the incongruities that arise when trying to reconcile the beef taboo with the dominant paradigms about Chinese cultural identity.

First, defining religion as a separate domain from society during the twentieth century and reducing politically and intellectually legitimate religion to a few recognized religious institutions, notably modernist Buddhism, have led to the taboo being interpreted as a Buddhist rule. Such a view stems, I believe, from the importation by Chinese intellectuals of outdated Western categories regarding Chinese religion and society, according to which Buddhism is the only "religion" among the indigenous traditions, an image often shared by Japanese scholars. Even though nineteenth-century authors already prefigured this view (Confucianism is not a religion, and Daoism is only a superstition), the notion that the Chinese are either atheists (and therefore without dietary prohibitions) or Buddhists (and therefore vegetarians) has gained widespread ground in the contemporary period.

The reasons for such a perspective lie in the tumultuous history of Chinese religion in the twentieth century when owing to the acculturation of modern notions of "religion" (*zongjiao* 宗教) and "superstition" (*mixin* 迷信), translated from Western languages into Japanese, Chinese, and other languages and then appropriated by and hybridized between these languages, the major world religions were protected. This included Buddhism, which, especially through its fundamentalist iterations, succeeded in China and other Asian countries in reinventing itself as a religion based on the Christian model that is congruent with science and modern values—such as democracy and social justice—and differentiated from superstition and sectarian movements, whereas Daoism was largely rejected as superstition.[3]

This situation, which faced intellectuals in China and contemporary China scholars, explains why the religious dimensions of Confucianism have long been ignored by intellectuals (even as these dimensions lived on in various religious groups such as the redemptive societies) to be rediscovered in the past few decades and Daoist studies only emerged in the 1960s.[4] For a long time, Confucian rationality was too readily contrasted with Buddhist religion and the superstitions of "popular religion" and Daoism. Yet, in the case of the beef taboo, Confucians were just as "religious" based on their own religious teachings. In short, the idea that a Chinese religious precept, such as the beef taboo, was necessarily Buddhist is nothing more than the result of twentieth-century history.

In addition, some scholars working on Chinese food culture insist on emphasizing its difference from culinary systems marked by religious dietary rules and prohibitions. They have praised the rationality of Chinese cuisine. As Eugene Anderson states, "Relatively free from taboos and avoidances, the Chinese have achieved a unique balance with their world, a unique success at supporting maximum populations over maximum time."[5] It is not my intention to criticize such an interpretation. On the contrary, as a great admirer of the Chinese culinary system and sensitive to issues of natural resource management, I readily support such an analysis. I am simply suggesting that the opposition between interdictions on the one hand and rationality on the other hand is a misconception. Anderson points this out himself by noting that it makes sense, in terms of agricultural economics, to reject the most "inefficient and wasteful" of all farm animals raised for meat—namely, cattle—an issue that has become hotly debated in the 2020s. But the Chinese beef taboo was mainly driven by another kind of reasoning.

Food in China was (and to a significant extent still is) sacred, or rather, in a society that historically had no conception of the dichotomy between sacred and secular, food has never been relegated to a category of secondary or trivial activities. Eating and drinking were acts laden with meaning and consequences. The gods ate, communion with the gods made life possible, and commensality among humans was the basis of social life. However, the world's order was moral in nature, and it was therefore unfathomable not to consider the moral character of food. Despite this general agreement on the ethical import of food, there has been, unsurprisingly, no consensus about specific food rules. To moralize food, some have proposed permanent or calendric vegetarianism, others frugality and moderation, and still others have distinguished between permissible and prohibited animals. Each of these solutions has had its own rationality, while they were often combined in practice.

Ultimately, religious dietary rules in China have had as much social significance as Christian prohibitions (e.g., Lent) in Europe and, after the sixteenth century, globally. In both regions, these rules are varied: Orthodox, Catholic, and Protestant traditions have differing relationships to fasting, meat, and alcohol, and all three have both high internal diversity and have changed historically. The decline of Catholic fasting practices in the twentieth century, for instance, is remarkable. The Chinese situation, if anything, is even more complex and diverse because different types of religious communities have vastly different types of communal rules (regular fasts, permanent vegetarianism, the beef taboo, other interdictions of Daoist origin, such as those against dogs, turtles, or eels) in addition to individual commitments (fasts specific to certain cults, such as the fast of Guanyin or the Three Officers). Chinese scholars who have addressed the issue of cattle have had difficulties reconciling texts reflecting the beef taboo with dominant paradigms about Chinese religion and culture, but other strategies have also been at work. Some scholars have attributed food prohibitions to superstition or, at least, to religious attitudes that scholarly work should not support. This attitude is shared by the scholar who authored the main history of Chinese cattle farming and by various historians and folklorists who took advantage of the cultural heritage boom in the 1990s and published works on *niu wenhua* 牛文化, "the culture of cattle."[6] One such scholar has dedicated his book to all those like him who enjoy eating beef.[7] All these works are compendiums of folklore relating to cattle in Chinese history. Their few remarks that refer to the taboo are embedded in a very richly documented whole and highlight the importance of cattle in Chinese culture, but the taboo is not constructed as an autonomous epistemic object.

Thus, these works generally devote a few lines to saying that some Chinese sometimes refrained from eating beef. The most frequent explanatory principle is totemism (one does not eat beef if one has a bovine ancestor). Examples invariably come from ethnic minorities.[8] However, we have seen how the Han Chinese imposed the beef taboo on colonized peoples living in what is now southern China. The idea that ethnic minorities retained primitive notions and customs (because what could be more primitive than totemism?) that have long since disappeared among the Han seems like common sense, but it is not true.

Authors working on "the culture of cattle" also cite anecdotes concerning the taboo among the Han Chinese (especially anecdotes from the Song, such as those mentioned in chapter 3). These anecdotes are then explained as reflections of a local custom: if an anecdote was set in such and such a region, then people of such and such a region avoided eating beef—implying that the same is not true elsewhere.[9] Describing the beef taboo as a "custom" and a "local" phenomenon denies that it had meaning for the collective culture of the Chinese.[10] But my research has demonstrated that it was a structuring element of Han society, from Manchuria to Hainan and even from China to Chinatowns worldwide. Finally, one scholar quotes an illustrated tract on the lamentation of the pitiful bovine and concludes that this was the peasants' cry protecting their work equipment. All right, but how can this be reconciled with a chapter on beef cuisine in the same book?[11]

This survey of the secondary literature demonstrates how the beef taboo is difficult to reconcile with some of the prevalent conceptions of Chinese culture. The titles of recent Chinese publications on "the culture of cattle" nevertheless raise a crucial issue: Has Chinese civilization, so steeped in humanism, not also placed an animal at the center of its value system?

## One Food Prohibition among Others?

Designating *niujie,* the beef taboo, as a food prohibition—a term used in anthropology and religious studies and intended to convey a universality—allows us to better understand its role in a cultural system such as Chinese culture by making it an object comparable to others. What should the beef taboo in China be compared to? The most immediate comparison is with Korea and Japan. We have already seen that a beef taboo developed in Japan around the same time as in China in the eleventh century.[12] The two are indeed linked, but I lack the expertise to specify their relationship of influence. Whatever the connections were when the interdiction emerged in these countries, they have been intertwined since the late nineteenth century in pan-Asian discourses of modernity: beef became a modern, healthy, commendable meat in Japan (and Japan-run Manchukuo) shortly before it became so in China, and in both cases, this was linked to the East Asian elaborations of the global notions of "religion," "superstition," "science," and "hygiene."

We should also compare the Chinese taboo with the Hindu taboo against the "sacred cow" (actually, the zebu), which, as I have argued, does not imply an Indian influence on China via Buddhism. The Hindu taboo has noticeable differences from the Chinese one. It distinguishes zebus and water buffaloes—the latter are excluded, while the Chinese discourse includes all species of cattle. The Hindu discourse is also partly built around milk as a pure and nourishing product that is the bovines' gift to humanity. By contrast, though dairy products are not entirely absent from China, they do not play a role in the taboo.

Other comparisons are possible as well. I am not thinking of the interdiction against pork in Judaism and Islam, which is very different. Indeed, even though its origins are the subject of debate, in both cases, the interdiction against pork is a prescriptive rule imposed by religious and political authorities beginning with the oldest written sources. This prohibition is widely observed (although not universally, especially in the context of secularization). Unlike China (and like contemporary India), it is the focal point in the strife between zealots and a significant number of "infidels" within that society. It is also a different kind of prohibition grounded in the animal's abnormal, improper, and amoral character. The pig is prohibited because nothing is good about it. Thus, people do not want to look at, approach, or eat it. I do not know of any such prohibition in China. In Hinduism, the zebu is sacred and too human. In Islam and Judaism, pork is disgusting and too inhuman. The case of Chinese cattle is situated between these two poles of prohibition. They are loved, familiar, and the object of attention, but they are also to be pitied since being reincarnated as a bovine is a punishment. Nonetheless, the Chinese case is closer to the Hindu taboo because of the sanctity of the animal concerned. This is a particular type of prohibition, which, as I suggested above, can be described as a "taboo." Beef was prohibited in China without ever being described as unhealthy. That its consumption caused epidemic diseases implies some ambiguity, but it would be wrong to read a logic of hygiene into it (even though there was the additional problem of sick animals being slaughtered and butchered). In this case, the defilement was exclusively moral in nature.

While the Jewish and Muslim prohibitions against pork do not offer many points of comparison, other examples may be more revealing, such as debates around whaling, especially in Japan, where the gigantic mammal is both respected as a high-order sentient being, and its meat is emblematic of national identity.[13] Two taboos in China—namely, against horses and dogs—also existed in Europe and offer fascinating comparative perspectives.

The interdiction against horses was, according to some scholars, decreed by the Christian Church, partly because of the Greco-Roman heritage and partly in reaction to the sacrificial practices of the Germanic peoples. Secular authorities reinforced this prohibition.[14] Horse slaughter and butchery were legally prohibited in predominantly Christian countries. European countries only gradually lifted this prohibition starting in 1841. Horse butchery was authorized in France in 1866 following a scientific campaign promoting the consumption of horsemeat and stressing its dietary value.[15] However, the old notion that the horse, as a working companion and friend of humans, should not be eaten persisted, even after the interdiction was lifted in the nineteenth century, severely limiting the consumption of this meat.[16] This therefore resembles the case of beef in China in the confluence of law and religion and the status of an animal elevated as the closest companion of humans. The interdiction against the dog has been much less formalized but is even more significant at the level of collective worldviews.[17] The campaigns of animal lovers against dog consumption in various other countries (e.g., Korea), as well as kill shelters, animal experimentation, and dog fighting among other issues in North America and Europe, offer analogies with those of the Chinese campaigning for the beef and indeed dogmeat taboo—a topic that remains understudied. The most striking difference may lie in the relative marginality of the discourse on horses or dogs in the West, which historically never occupied a role of primary importance in public debates and the collective conscience, unlike the Chinese discourse on the issue of cattle, which was long presented as a civilizational linchpin.

However, despite its highly varied social importance from one culture to another, the issue of delimiting edible animals and prohibiting other animals arises everywhere because animal life is never perceived as a closed and homogeneous whole but as a continuum that ranges from species so close to humans that they occupy an ambiguous position to others dangerously impure or harmful. Between these two poles, a small group of species is reserved for meat and represents "meat" par excellence. The motivations behind the ever-changing, ever-debated delimitation between edible and prohibited animals are complex and involve elements found in various cultures: the idea that such and such an animal resembles humans in their feelings, its proximity through work or cohabitation, differentiation, and sometimes its mutual exclusion of uses (e.g., work, livestock farming, and sacrifice).

China is far from the only civilization to single out cattle as a special case. As Marcel Detienne (1935–2019) asserts, "the rights of humans to eat beef, especially when the bovine acts as plow cattle, are less than obvious."[18] In Greece and Rome, as in imperial China, the slaughter of plow cattle was a severely punishable crime,[19] whereas the sacrifice of a bovine was also the most prestigious, rarest sacrifice, which was the foundation of the Greek city-state. But this common basis led to different choices. The Chinese permitted cattle sacrifice in particular circumstances (for heaven and Confucius), but unlike the case of other sacrificed animals, they restricted or even prevented the consumption of sacrificial beef. By contrast, Greeks and Romans used the need for sacrifice to legitimize beef consumption. During the Buphonia in Athens—the annual sacrifice of a bovine to

Zeus Polieus—the animal's skin was filled with straw and put back to work plowing as if it had never died, and a trial was held to find the culprit for the killing. Ultimately, the sacrificial knife was judged to be the only guilty party and cast into the sea. After that, the citizens could eat the animal "without remorse."[20]

The problems raised by the dietary use of working animals are articulated in many agricultural cultures. We should remember that the use of beef as the meat par excellence in Europe and the Americas is a recent phenomenon, dating from the middle of the nineteenth century.[21] The Chinese case was highly idiosyncratic but more in terms of its responses than the actual formulation of the issue. It is not incommensurable with other cases involving cattle or other species that have played the role of the "most human animal," such as horses or dogs. Compared to the European context, the most distinct element of the Chinese taboo is not rationality (or the absence of rationality) in determining the use of animals, but the importance of sacrificial practices and the resulting rules of ritual purity because such practices and rules disappeared in Europe with Christianization (except perhaps on a subconscious level).

In anthropological terms, China can contribute much to understanding the evolving intricate relationship between an animal that is too close and humans who nevertheless use, sacrifice, and eat it. This situation is much more similar to the European and North American contexts than it might appear at first glance. Is not the motif of the sinner's reincarnation into a bovine a way of thinking about this proximity and managing it—a proximity that other cultures have represented by other means, as shown by Claudine Fabre-Vassas in the case of the pig?[22] Is not the pig-ox couple, both familiar and part of the family but opposites in their relationships to humans, found in Europe just like in China? And the role of animals in identifying in-group and out-group individuals, which we have seen at work in late imperial China, where beefeaters were identified with marginals and bandits, Muslims, southern "barbarians," or Westerners, certainly also existed in premodern Europe, which was always religiously diverse and became increasingly so in modern times, with various groups practicing vegetarianism, avoiding pork, or keeping a variety of pre-Christian practices.

These issues can be studied both historically and ethnographically. We can only hope that anthropologists working on China will expand their interest beyond the topics of killing animals into day-to-day human-animal relationships and will examine relationships with animals that are so dangerously close and human. As concerns about the consequences of beef eating—for humans (in the wake of mad cow disease and due to growing awareness of the health impact of red meat), the environment, and the animals themselves—and movements for animal welfare are spreading across the globe, the Chinese case of the taboo may become less exotic and curious. This book is decidedly historical and does not engage with the contemporary period but may begin a conversation.

More generally, I hope this book will contribute to the fast-growing field of animal studies by showing the rich resources afforded by a *longue durée* religious-historical approach to understanding the factors that cause the human classifications of animals to change, especially when, such as in the Chinese world, the abundant and continuous sources invite such an approach. In particular, I have insisted on the persistent importance of rules of ritual purity and sacrifice, which are central in studies of ancient cultures and religion but rarely so in modern historical, sociological, and anthropological approaches to animals and meat. Yet in the Chinese world, as in the Indian world and others, these issues remain decisive in modern and contemporary times. Raising animals and living with them seem to contribute to keeping our world enchanted.

# NOTES

## INTRODUCTION

1. In this study, I use "cattle" and "bovine" as synonyms to translate the Chinese *niu* 牛. See chapter 2 for an explanation of the genera included in this encompassing category.
2. Xu Hualong, "Baishe zhuan yu yinshi wenhua," 273–274; Eberhard, *Local Cultures,* 183–184, which also mentions the question of sacrifices; Freeman, "Sung," 164; Mote, "Yüan and Ming," 201; Shio Takugo, "Sōdai gyūniku."
3. Anderson, *The Food of China,* 66, 82, 119–120, 177.
4. De Groot, "Miséricorde envers les animaux," 479.
5. Chinese religion as defined here includes all forms of individual religious practices (meditation, salvation techniques, body techniques, access to knowledge and revelation through trance and spirit writing), and collective religious practices (cults to local gods, ancestors, funeral rites), which fall within the framework of Chinese cosmology. It integrates the ancient sacrificial religion, Confucianism, which continued it, Daoism and Buddhism, as well as sectarian movements of later formation.
6. On the emergence of this field of study, see Elisseeff, "L'anthropozoologie." For major recent advances, see Kowner et al., *Animals and Human Society in Asia;* Sterckx, Siebert, and Schäfer, *Animals through Chinese History.*
7. See, in particular, Harris, *Culture, People, Nature,* which develops the case of prohibitions of pork and beef (in India).
8. Leach, "Anthropological Aspects." Halverson, "Animal Categories," has provided a close critique of Leach's method, including his use of the notion of taboo.
9. Whitehead, *Food Rules,* and the critical review around this work in the *Journal of Ritual Studies* 17, no. 2 (2003): 97–126.
10. Tambiah, "Animals Are Good to Think."
11. Benkheira, *Islam et interdits alimentaires,* and Douglas, *Purity and Danger,* suggest that some prohibitions developed in normative literature relate to animals that have never been eaten.
12. Fabre-Vassas, *The Singular Beast.*
13. Holm, *Killing a Buffalo,* 205–215.
14. For example, Taira Masayuki, "Tabous et alimentation carnée." Taira's translator, Pierre F. Souyri, freely uses the word "taboo." I have used the English term "taboo" in another publication: Goossaert, "The Beef Taboo."

15. Keesing, "Tabou."
16. Ren Cheng, *Zhongguo minjian jinji,* 320–321; Zhu Yueli, *Dangdai Zhongguo zongjiao jinji,* 90.
17. On the frequency of female infanticide in China up to the twentieth century, see Lee and Wang, *One Quarter of Humanity,* 47–53. Lee and Wang assert on p. 61 that infanticide was not considered immoral. A careful reading of morality books would put such a statement in perspective. See also Fuma Susumu, *Chūgoku zenkai,* 335–375.

## CHAPTER 1: ANIMALS, MEAT, AND SACRIFICE IN CHINA

1. The term "killing" translates *sha* 殺 or *shasheng* 殺生, which designates the act of killing a living being—whether a human (murder) or an animal (killing)—and implies an awareness of the continuity of living beings.
2. The oldest formulation is found in *Shangshu,* "Taishe 泰誓," *shang.*
3. These considerations are developed by Sterckx, *The Animal and the Daemon.*
4. *Mengzi,* "Lilou, xia 離婁下." However, Gernet, "Ce qui distingue l'homme de l'animal," shows how some later thinkers insisted on the importance of this difference. As is usual in Chinese studies, Chinese classics, such as *Mengzi,* are just quoted by chapter, without a reference and page in a specific edition.
5. This notion of a moral community, and the debates it engenders, has been developed by Campany, *Strange Writings,* 384–394, pertaining to anomaly tales from the first centuries of the Common Era.
6. Gernet, " Pitié pour les animaux," draws attention to the important role of animal discourse in Confucian ethics.
7. Eliasberg, "Pratiques funéraires animales."
8. Needham and Huang, *Fermentations and Food Sciences,* 56.
9. Ibid., 55–61, and numerous passages in Chang, *Food in Chinese Culture.*
10. In the early 1980s, 94 percent of the mammalian meat consumed in China was pork (Needham and Huang, *Fermentations and Food Sciences,* 59). This proportion is currently declining in particular due to the development of the beef industry: DuBois and Gao, "Big Meat."
11. Needham and Huang, *Fermentations and Food Sciences,* 59–60.
12. Engelhardt, "Dietetics in Tang China," 181–184.
13. Sabban, "La viande en Chine."
14. DuBois, "Counting the Carnivores."
15. Kleeman, "Licentious Cults," 189, notes that China can be compared to other sacrificial cultures (such as ancient Judaism and ancient Greece), which tend to limit the consumption of meat to sacrificial offerings. Moreover, consumed in such a context, the meat is distributed among all members of the community, rich or poor, rather than monopolized by the rich. For classic studies on meat sacrifice and consumption, see Détienne and Vernant, *La cuisine du sacrifice,* and Malamoud, *Cuire le monde.*
16. Fermented cereal drinks that could be called "beer" from antiquity to the present day, grape wine at certain times (under the Han, the Tang, and since the nineteenth century), and distilled spirits from the Song. The technique of distilling alcohol has been known since the Han, but the consumption of

distilled alcohol did not become common until the Song. Needham and Huang, *Fermentations and Food Sciences,* 149–282. On the importance of alcohol in the formation of the bonds between humans and with the divinities, see ter Haar, *Ritual and Mythology,* 160–161.

17. Needham and Huang, *Fermentations and Food Sciences,* 419–424. Dried fish seems to have been much more common.
18. Kleeman, "Licentious Cults."
19. Ibid., 189n15.
20. For example, *Guoyu*, "Zhouyu, xia 周語下."
21. For a general discussion of sacrificial foods, see also Qu Ming'an, "Jisi yinshi."
22. For example, *Zuozhuan,* Zhuanggong 6.
23. Some theorists distinguish the sacrifice (an animal) from the offering (a piece of meat), but this distinction does not seem relevant in the Chinese context; Kleeman, "Licentious Cults," 185n1.
24. More so than the study of texts, archaeology allows us to follow the historical transformation of sacrificial practices through the vessels used; we can thus detect a change at the beginning of the first millennium BCE when the role of alcoholic beverages decreases sharply in sacrifice: Rawson, "Western Zhou Archaeology," and Cook, "Moonshine and Millet."
25. Boileau, "Some Ritual Elaborations," and Li Fengmao, "Jieqing jidian," provide anthropological perspectives on the texts of sacrificial rituals and offer comparable analyses, notably by oppositions between whole/cut and raw/cooked.
26. *Daji* has a more restricted technical meaning in the classics of the ancient liturgy.
27. Including *Yili,* "Tesheng kuishi li 特牲饋食禮" (the sacrifice of a pig for an ancestor) and "Shaolao kuishi li 少牢饋食禮" (the sacrifice of a pig and a sheep for an ancestor).
28. One of the best Western observers of Chinese religion in the early twentieth century notes that this "great sacrifice," which he describes, is "the essence of Confucian religion." Shryock, *Temples of Anking,* 39.
29. Qu Ming'an, "Jisi yinshi," 155–157; Bujard, *Le sacrifice au ciel,* 54–56, 92–95. In general, an animal that was fat but not large and had a uniform coat was preferred.
30. From antiquity, the victims consecrated to heaven were burned, and those for earth were buried. In ancestor worship (from the *Yili* to Zhu Xi's *Jiali*), the raw animal was divided into several parts: the head and some organs were set aside, and the carcass was divided into nine pieces. All these pieces were cooked before the ritual and offered separately. In contemporary practice, people continue to present whole and raw animals at the start of sacrifice.
31. The four family rituals are the capping ceremony for men (in adolescence), marriage, burial, and ancestor worship. The first has hardly been practiced since antiquity.
32. Translated and studied in Ebrey, *Chu Hsi's Family Rituals.*
33. The term *yang* 羊 includes sheep and goats; in fact, both food and sacrificial use include sheep, lambs, and goats, although the goats appear to be a second choice. On sheep farming and consumption, see Xie Chengxia, *Yang niu yang shi.*
34. Lavoix, "La contribution," 133, quotes a text of 472 mentioning 75,500 animals sacrificed in one year for the state worship.

35. Kleeman, "Licentious Cults," 188, quotes a Song text that mentions mountains of sheep in connection with a local cult.
36. For example, Wolf, "Gods, Ghosts, and Ancestors," 176–179.
37. Boileau, "Some Ritual Elaborations"; Li Fengmao, "Jieqing jidian."
38. Thompson, "Death, Food, and Fertility."
39. The technical vocabulary of sacrifice in antiquity is rich, and *sheng* is only one of the terms used to designate the sacrificial victim. There are others, notably *xi* 犧. It was nevertheless *sheng* that subsequently became a generic term.
40. In state rituals, from antiquity to the present, a calf has been preferred to an adult bovine or even required. All three species of mammals can be sacrificed intact, while poultry and fish can only be offered as meat dishes. Poultry, very commonly offered nowadays, is seldom mentioned in ancient texts. However, fish are frequently mentioned and occupy the least prestigious rank of all animal offerings. For example, *Guoyu,* quoted by Kleeman, "Licentious Cults," 193.
41. Zhao Kesheng, "Tudiao zhi jin." Rols, "Les interdits," details the historical development of these rules and critically examines the contemporary claims of their being a form of proto-ecological discourse.
42. Late Qing newspapers, such as the *Shenbao,* provide extensive documentation on this subject. There are many temporary decrees prohibiting butchery, as well as articles describing the difficulty of their application and debates on the subject. See, for example, "Quan beizai riqi jinzhi tuzai wen 勸被災日期禁止屠宰文," *Shenbao,* August 19, 1879, saying that the disasters of civil wars (Taiping, etc.) were punishments inflicted by heaven as a result of Chinese cruelty to animals and proposing one day per month of abstinence and repentance; "Guang shuowang jin tuzai shuo 廣朔望禁屠宰說," *Shenbao,* July 19, 1878, denouncing the hypocritical application of the fast days. See also Doolittle, *Social Life of the Chinese,* 183–184.
43. *Zhai* is often written *qi* 齊 in ancient texts. On Confucian *zhaijie,* see Wilson, "Sacrifice and the Imperial Cult," 271–277.
44. *Liji,* "Jitong 祭統," gives only an abstract, spiritual interpretation of the period of purification.
45. *Lunyu jishi,* "Xiangdang 鄉黨," 686–689.
46. *Hanshu,* 68:2940.
47. The exact definition of vegetarianism in China depends on the context; it would be in some instances (Buddhist ones in particular) more precise to speak of veganism since the substances secreted by animals (eggs, honey, dairy products) are also prohibited; Lavoix, "Croisades et polémiques," 121. In contemporary practice, eggs and dairy products are consumed by some and rejected by others.
48. Sabban, "La viande en Chine," 84–85; Lavoix, "Croisades et polémiques," 107.
49. Sabban, "La viande en Chine," 86; Lavoix, "Croisades et polémiques," 105.
50. *Zhuangzi jishi,* "Renjian shi 人間世," 146–147.
51. *Xunzi jijie,* "Aigong pian 哀公篇," 538.
52. *Yili,* "Shi xiangjian li 士相見禮"; *Liji,* "Yuzao 玉藻."
53. Much later, in 1865, a missionary observed that these plants were considered meat: Doolittle, *Social Life of the Chinese,* 183.

54. It is not the least enjoyable paradox of Chinese exegesis that a passage from *Lunyu* is explained by a text that develops a radical critique of Confucius's ideas. Some purist commentators give another explanation for the passage, which may be of philological interest but probably never corresponded to practice.
55. Van der Toorn, "La pureté rituelle," 351, notes that the consumption of these same plants, because of their smell, was prohibited for people visiting the temples of ancient Mesopotamia and that this prohibition was transmitted to Islam.
56. *Xin* is one of the five taste categories and covers all intense flavors (acrid, pungent, etc.), especially those provided by alliaceous plants, hot pepper, and ginger. The list of *wuhun/wuxin* fluctuates according to the sources. Buddhist, Daoist, and Confucian lists are different but generally include garlic, chives, shallots, leeks, and onions.
57. Wang-Toutain, "Pas de boissons alcoolisées," 93–94; Heirman, "The Consumption of Garlic."
58. *Lunyu jishi,* "Xiangdang," 686–689.
59. Ebrey, *Chu Hsi's Family Rituals,* 157.
60. *Zhuzi yulei,* 89:2281.
61. Kleeman, *Celestial Masters;* Goossaert, *Heavenly Masters.*
62. On the theological basis of this rejection of cults, see Lai Chi-tim, "Opposition of Celestial-Master Taoism."
63. Schipper, "Le pacte de pureté."
64. Another ancient text, Xiang'er's 相爾 commentary on *Laozi,* also prohibited eating the leftovers of a sacrifice: Bokenkamp with Nickerson, *Early Daoist Scriptures,* 119–120.
65. On this hierarchy and the precepts accompanying it, see Schipper, "Taoist Ordination Ranks."
66. *Guan* can only be called "monasteries" in a broad sense since they were centers of training and retreat around ascetics and eminent masters, who gathered celibate anchorites and families of followers around them. *Guan* developed during the fifth century, particularly in conjunction with the holy places and the Highest Clarity masters. They were recognized and sometimes financed by the state, which gave them a status similar to that of the Buddhist monasteries that were already fully developed by then. Subsequently, the state tried to impose on *guan* rules of Buddhist inspiration, in particular absolute celibacy, but only with limited success.
67. Schipper, "Daoist Ecology."
68. The text of the 180 precepts has been preserved in four different copies in the *Daozang,* notably in *Yunji qiqian,* 39.la–14b. Since the precepts are numbered there, it is preferable to refer to the precept number rather than the pagination.
69. This precept is followed by a directional prohibition that seems unrelated to the question of food consumption.
70. In later precept texts, the prohibition against farming pigs and sheep extends to the six domestic animals. See, for example, *Shangqing dongzhen zhihui guanshen dajie wen,* 3a. We can undoubtedly imagine farming sheep for wool and pigs for leather, but these two activities are little attested in China even at the beginning of the Common Era.

71. Rols, "Les interdits."
72. This quotation, which became a ubiquitous phrase in religious writings of all faiths, is not found in the classics. The oldest occurrence seems to be in the *Taiping jing*—if this passage is indeed from an early (Han period) textual layer of the received version, which is far from certain. *Taiping jing hejiao,* 174.
73. *Baopu zi neipian jiaoshi,* 6:126. Subsequently, a famous anecdote developed about the very eminent Daoist scholar and pharmacologist Tao Hongjing 陶弘景 (456–536), for whom everything promised the apotheosis of immortality but who was punished by the gods for having included insects in his pharmacopeia, thus inciting their killing. Strickmann, "Saintly Fools," 43.
74. See, however, *Dongxuan Lingbao Daoxue keyi,* 2.4b–6b, which maintains a strict interdiction against meat, alcohol, and *wuxin.*
75. *Santian neijie jing,* 6a.
76. Note that Mouzi 牟子 (second or fourth century) reproaches Daoists for banquets of meat and alcohol: Pelliot, "Meou-tseu," 318–319.
77. *Wushang neibi zhenzang jing,* 6.6b.
78. *Xuandu lüwen,* 5b; Mollier, *Apocalypse,* 73, 150, 177.
79. Stein, "Les fêtes de cuisine"; Stein, "Spéculations mystiques"; Mollier, "Cuisines," 45–47; Mollier, *Buddhism and Taoism Face to Face,* chap. 1; Kleeman, "Feasting without the Victuals."
80. Lavoix, "Croisades et polémiques," 131, discusses the largely rhetorical nature of the frugality of the vegetarian diet among scholars of medieval times. Likewise, for the seventeenth century, see J. Smith, "Liberating Animals," 63–65.
81. On the notion of *zhai,* see among others Malek, "Ieiunium and Zhai."
82. Several texts very explicitly prohibit any meat during a *zhai* or a *chu;* for example, *Taiji zhenren shuo ershisi men jiejing,* 23, and Chen Guofu, *Daozang yuanliu kao,* 325–326, which cites, in particular, *Laojun yinsong jiejing,* 13a–b, and *Yaoxiu keyi jielü chao,* 12.1a–2b. However, a text from the turn of the fifth to sixth century contains an allusion to the fact that the *chu* and offertory rituals (*jiao* 醮) were not necessarily vegetarian since a Daoist, Dongxiang Zongchao 東鄉宗超, required that they be so when he was present. *Daoxue zhuan* cited in *Sandong zhunang,* 5.7b–8a; Bumbacher, *Daoxue zhuan,* 242. It is difficult to determine whether such a deviation was frequent or justified. This same anecdote specifies that the reforms of Emperor Liang Wudi, which will be discussed below, played an important role in forcing vegetarianism on Daoists.
83. Kohn, "Daoist Monastic Discipline," 165–174.
84. Stein, "Les fêtes de cuisine," 434–435.
85. An undated text (Northern and Southern Dynasties?) found in Dunhuang and devoted exclusively to food in the perspective of salvation, the *Laozi shuo fashi jinjie jing,* recommends first the abandonment of meat, then vegetables, then mushrooms, and finally breaths.
86. Huang, *Picturing the True Form,* 52–65.
87. Lévi, "L'abstinence des céréales"; Eskildsen, *Asceticism,* chap. 4.
88. Stein, "Spéculations mystiques," 495–496; Stein, "Conceptions," 460.
89. In particular, the *Taishang Lingbao wufu xu* 太上靈寶五符序; Eskildsen, *Asceticism,* 115.

90. I found one single reference in Campany's translation of *Shenxian zhuan, to Live as Long,* 314 (biography of Kong Yuanfang 孔元方).
91. On this work, see Bumbacher, *Daoxue zhuan.* Vegetarians include Dongxian Zongchao, already cited, Yan Jizhi 嚴寄之 (246), Yu Chengxian 庾承仙 (259), and Xin Xuanzi 辛玄子 (175), who ate only one vegetarian meal a day. Xin Xuanzi was already mentioned in the *Zhen'gao,* 16.6b–7a. See also Eskildsen, *Asceticism,* 35–39.
92. *Dongxuan Lingbao Qianzhen ke,* 10b, 14a, prohibits giving cattle and horses to a *guan.*
93. Kohn, "Five Precepts."
94. Stein, "Religious Taoism."
95. On ritual masters, see Schipper, "Vernacular and Classical," and Davis, *Society and the Supernatural.* Even when the ritual masters and masters of the Dao are different people, their collaboration is symbiotic.
96. Kleeman, "Licentious Cults," 202 and 190, citing a text in which the Sichuan god Li Bing complains about the vegetarian diet imposed on him (by the Daoist clergy of his temple, it seems).
97. The literature on the Complete Transcendance is abundant. See, among others, Goossaert, "The Invention of an Order." However, the issue of dietary restrictions is not explicitly addressed anywhere in the historiography, except to say that it would be a simple adoption of the Buddhist rules.
98. For example, *Daodian lun,* 3.13b, which dates from the Tang, and *Taiwei lingshu ziwen xianji zhenji shangjing,* 2b.
99. This system was formed at the end of antiquity. Versions of this zodiac already appear in manuscripts from the end of the Warring States found in Shuihudi and Fangmatan. For Daoist rules, see, for example, *Taiwei lingshu ziwen xianji zhenji shangjing,* 2a, and "Xiandao ji shibai 仙道忌十敗," *Yunji qiqian,* 33.6a. "Chengshilang Gu jun muzhiming 承事郎顧君墓誌銘," *Rongchun tang ji, xuji,* 15.10b, relates the case of a Ming literatus who never ate beef because it was the animal associated with his mother's year of birth.
100. Strickmann, *Chinese Magical Medicine,* 54–55.
101. This does not negate the very important role of the rejection of the Vedic sacrifice in the formation of the Indian Buddhist discourse on animal life.
102. Bodhisattva vows articulate the highest moral ideals of Mahāyāna Buddhism and are taken by both laity and monastics during ordinations. On the Indian Buddhist origins of vegetarianism, see Schmithausen, *Fleischverzehr und Vegetarismus.*
103. Campany, *Strange Writings,* 389–394, which also demonstrates the role of Buddhist karmic tales in the formation of the Chinese anomaly tale (*zhiguai* 志怪).
104. The *Mahāparinirvāṇa Sūtra* explains that to eat meat is to eat your children: Lavoix, "Croisades et polémiques," 123; Wang-Toutain, "Pas de boissons alcoolisées," 103.
105. Gernet, *Buddhism in Chinese Society.*
106. Stevenson, "Protocols of Power," 350–357.
107. A well-known example is that of Wutong 五通. Von Glahn, *Sinister Way,* chaps. 6 and 7; see also Kleeman, "Licentious Cults," 208. An explicit case of

blood sacrifice inside a monastery is discussed in a Song period inscription, "Song Nanhai dashi Zhaojun taming 宋南海大士趙君塔銘," *Lequan ji,* 40.27b–31a. On Buddhism's failure to convert local gods, see ter Haar, "Buddhist-Inspired Options," 130–132, which gives some counterexamples. Kleeman and ter Haar perhaps underestimate Buddhism's accommodation to local cults by considering only monasteries, which were (in theory at least) the sites of pure Buddhist practice, and by neglecting the presence of Buddhist clerics serving as managers (*zhuchi*) of the temples dedicated to local gods.

108. Lavoix, "Croisades et polémiques," 104; Wang-Toutain, "Pas de boissons alcoolisées," 92; Kieschnick, *Eminent Monk,* 22–28; Kieschnick, "Buddhist Vegetarianism"; Lin Boqian, "Sushi yu Fofa xingchi," cite a rich bibliography. The Buddhist disciplinary codes, however, mention specific meats that are prohibited under all circumstances, the list of which varies from one code to another.
109. Schmithausen, *Fleischverzehr und Vegetarismus;* Barstow, *Food of Sinful Demons;* Welch, *Buddhist Revival,* 176–177.
110. As several medieval texts note, it remains theoretically possible, while abstaining from being associated with the killing of an animal, to eat the flesh of a naturally dead animal. Lavoix, "Croisades et polémiques," 124.
111. Wang-Toutain, "Pas de boissons alcoolisées," 92–93. The *Mahāparinirvāṇa Sūtra* was translated in its long version in the north in 421 and distributed in the south in 430. Lavoix, "Croisades et polémiques," 116.
112. Greene, "A Reassessment."
113. Lavoix, "Croisades et polémiques," 113.
114. Sabban, "La viande en Chine," 87.
115. Lavoix, "Croisades et polémiques," 118–120. This reform met with multiple oppositions and only suppressed specific offerings so that a good number of animal sacrifices continued in the state worship under the reign of Wudi.
116. The *Duanjiurou wen* has been preserved in *Guang Hongming ji,* 26:294b–303c.
117. Wang-Toutain, "Pas de boissons alcoolisées."
118. The classic study on *Fanwang jing* is De Groot, *Le code du Mâhayâna.* For up-to-date scholarship, see Funayama, "The *Fanwang jing,*" and Greene, "A Reassessment." The text was used in ordination ceremonies throughout the second millennium.
119. De Groot, *Le code du Mâhayâna,* 42; the following article is devoted to the interdiction against the five alliaceous plants.
120. Wang-Toutain, "Pas de boissons alcoolisées," 126. In the codes of the Song, Yuan, Ming, and Qing dynasties, the failure of monastics to respect their vows (*bushou qinggui* 不守清規), including vegetarianism, is an offense that can lead to forced laicization, but cases of monastics punished by the state for eating meat were very rare.
121. Kieschnick, *Eminent Monk,* 22–28.
122. This rule was also adopted in certain Daoist circles; for example, Mollier, *Apocalypse,* 150.
123. Forte and May, "Chōsai."
124. The six days per month are clearly attested, but the Indian origin of the three half months is much more uncertain.

125. Soymié, "Dix jours de jeûne." There were still other, older practices related to this belief of periodic divine inspections, such as *gengshen* 庚申 days of the sexagesimal calendars, during which people held a vigil and recited sacred texts.
126. Martin, "Les quatre portes," 87–94.
127. Liu Shufen, "Niansan yueshi"; Hulsewé, *Periodieke executie en slacht-verboden.*
128. Liu Shufen, "Niansan yueshi," 20; *Shenbao,* December 6, 1899.
129. These associations are known from the votive stelae they erected everywhere. The secondary literature on associations is quite abundant. I would like to mention Gernet, *Buddhism in Chinese Society;* Liu Shufen, "Art, Ritual, and Society"; and Hao Chunwen, "She Association Manuscripts."
130. These Daoist associations justify their meritorious deeds in terms directly derived from Numinous Treasure texts. Bokenkamp, "Yao Boduo Stele."
131. Numerous and detailed descriptions have been left to us by the Japanese pilgrim Ennin 圓仁, who was in China between 838 and 847.
132. See references to *zhai* and *chu* above; see also the descriptions provided by the *Dongxuan Lingbao Qianzhen ke,* and Kohn, "Daoist Monastic Discipline," 165–174.
133. Lagerwey, "Introduction."
134. A detailed presentation of these different fasts, together with a liturgical calendar, can be found in *Tongshan lu,* 10.67a–81a, compiled in the eighteenth century. The same book also offers a calendar of days of sexual abstinence; see Goossaert, "Late Imperial Chinese Piety Books." See also Doolittle, *Social Life of the Chinese,* 185–186. In addition to strict vegetarianism during certain periods, the fasts specific to some deities could also imply a permanent interdiction against specific meats. For example, during the Ming, a person who observed the Fast of the Three Officers claimed to never eat turtles. "Shi bie biming 食鱉斃命," *Shuyi ji,* 3.12a–b.
135. "Zhaijie bian 齋戒辨," *Shenbao,* September 11, 1879.
136. Getz, "Pure Land Societies."
137. Ibid., 483.
138. J. Smith, *The Art of Doing Good,* chap. 1.
139. Ibid., 76–78.
140. Lu Huitzu, "Women's Ascetic Practices."
141. On Peng, see in particular Goldfuss, *Vers un bouddhisme,* 132–142.
142. J. Smith, "Liberating Animals," 57.
143. It even appears in the utopia presented by Kang Youwei 康有為 (1858–1927) in his posthumously published *Datong shu* 大同書 in which the whole world becomes vegetarian.
144. Lavoix, "Croisades et polémiques," 110.
145. Welch, *Practice of Chinese Buddhism,* 361–365. Unlike the ordination of monks according to the Vinaya, which must be performed in a monastery, laypeople can take the Five Precepts and the bodhisattva vows under any circumstances. Nevertheless, participation in a monastic ordination and the preceding period of training and preparation confer on it solemnity, spiritual experience, and a network of fellow disciples that were much appreciated by the *jushi.* On this

occasion, they also make crucial donations to the monastery that make possible the organization of an ordination, a costly undertaking.

146. J. Smith, "Liberating Animals," 65–67.
147. Ibid., 66.
148. Ibid., 58, even cites the case of a magistrate who wants to prohibit any blood sacrifice in his jurisdiction.
149. In the famous eighteenth-century novel *Rulin waishi,* a scholar relates how he had to interrupt his vegetarian practice to eat the sacrificial meat of Confucius offered by the superior of the school. *Rulin waishi,* chap. 2, 25.
150. Yü, *Renewal of Buddhism,* 27, 76, 85–87; J. Smith, "Liberating Animals," 57–62; Eichman, *A Late Sixteenth-Century Chinese Buddhist Fellowship.* The difference between practicing the interdiction against killing and adopting vegetarianism is generally implicit in the texts and should be emphasized. J. Smith, "Liberating Animals," n21, quotes an anecdote in which a man who "hypocritically" practiced releasing living beings while eating meat is punished, suggesting that this was a common attitude. On Zhuhong's impact in Japan, see Ambros, "Tracing the Influence."
151. J. Smith, "Liberating Animals," 61. A very similar discourse, which seems to me to correspond to a consensus bringing together a large part of the literate elites of the sixteenth century, appears in *Dongdu ji* 東度記, a novel published in 1635. See Durand-Dastès, *La conversion de l'Orient.*
152. A fourteenth-century lineage rule prohibited meat for children and adolescents. Fei Chengkang et al., *Zhongguo jiafa zugui,* 260. In the same way, the rules of a school allow for (optional) meat only three times a month. "Yuedong yishe yishu 粵東議設義塾," *Deyi lu,* 10:624.
153. Ebrey, *Confucianism and Family Rituals,* 94–95; Ebrey, "Cremation in Sung China"; Rowe, *Saving the World,* 435.
154. Getz, "Pure Land Societies."
155. Ter Haar, *White Lotus,* 31.
156. This characteristic of sectarian movements continues to this day and is one of the reasons for their success.
157. The Zhen dadao 真大道, which was founded in North China in the twelfth century and aimed to form communities living in autarky, also required its followers to be vegetarian.
158. The literature on the White Lotus is abundant. I draw on the classic work of ter Haar, *White Lotus.* On the White Cloud, see also Overmyer, "The White Cloud Sect."
159. De Groot, *Sectarianism,* 176–241; ter Haar, *Practicing Scripture;* Jones, *Buddhism in Taiwan,* 14–30; Broy, "Moral Integration or Social Segregation?"
160. Ter Haar, *White Lotus,* 48–55; Chikusa Masaaki, "Kissai jima."
161. Manicheans from Central Asia settled in China since the Tang. Communities of Chinese converts are documented in China from the ninth century and at least until the end of the Yuan. The Manichaeans were indeed vegetarians, but it does not seem that their vegetarianism could have significantly influenced that of the Buddhist groups.
162. Ter Haar, "Buddhist-Inspired Options," 129–137. The conversion stories discussed by ter Haar often involve people particularly concerned with the

sin of killing and eating meat, including butchers. Giving up one's profession further reinforced the separation involved in becoming a vegetarian and joining a sectarian group.

163. Ibid., 137, suggests that some Buddhist monks criticized lay vegetarianism but gives no other example than the use of the *chicai shimo* stereotype by some historiographers.

164. "Le ling kaihun 勒令開葷," *Shenbao,* June 18, 1878.

165. De Groot, *Sectarianism,* 137ff., 151, 158. The Christian missionaries also required converted followers who were previously members of vegetarian sectarian groups to eat meat publicly. Malek, "Ieiunium and Zhai."

166. On Zaili, see Li Shiyu, "Tianjin Zaili jiao," and Goossaert, *The Taoists of Peking,* chap. 9.

167. Poon, "Buddhist Activism and Animal Protection"; Schumann, "For the Sake of Morality and Civilization"; Leung, "To Build or to Transform"; Lu Lianghao, "The Confluence of Karma and Hygiene."

168. Goossaert, "Les sens multiples du végétarisme en Chine."

169. Doolittle, *Social Life of the Chinese,* 183.

170. Sabban, "La viande en Chine," 84–86, analyzes the fake meat cuisine but, in my opinion, underestimates its ethical dimension.

171. J. Smith, "Liberating Animals," 62–63. A Buddhist scholar, Yu Chunxi 虞淳熙 (1553–1621, *jinshi* in 1583), wrote a detailed refutation of Ricci's views on the relationship between humans and animals. "Tianzhu shiyi shasheng bian 天主實義殺生辨," *Shengchao poxie ji,* 5.12a–15a. Malek, "Ieiunium and Zhai," has developed a very detailed analysis of the relationship between Chinese and Christian notions of fasting, based in particular on an abundant Christian literature in which missionaries aimed to distinguish themselves as clearly as possible from vegetarian sectarian groups (for fear of being assimilated to them). The fact that fish were allowed on Christian fast days, in particular, was very poorly understood by the Chinese. Reinders, *Borrowed Gods,* chap. 10, gives a detailed analysis of the anti-vegetarian missionary discourse in the late nineteenth century.

172. *Qingshi duo,* "Jiesha," 906–917, "Aiwu 愛物," 917–921, and other poems elsewhere in this collection.

173. Durand-Dastès, *La conversion de l'Orient.*

174. For examples of lineage regulation, see *Wuzhong yigui,* "Xunsu yigui," 2.25b–26a, and Fei Chengkang et al., *Zhongguo jiafa zugui,* 263.

175. J. Smith, "Liberating Animals," 60–62. One of the most remarkable texts of this Confucian thought of releasing life that claims to be non-Buddhist is the *Guang'ai lu* (eighteenth century).

176. J. Smith, "Liberating Animals," 59, citing a text by Jiao Hong 焦竑 (1541–1620).

177. "Zhaijie bian," *Shenbao,* September 11, 1879. There is also a criticism of periodic *zhaijie* as inferior to Confucian permanent moderation in *Yuewei caotang biji,* 4:75–76.

## CHAPTER 2: CHINESE CATTLE AS POLITICAL ANIMALS

1. *Bubalus bubalis,* found throughout Asia, is commonly called a "water buffalo" to distinguish it from the African buffalo, which is not domesticated and belongs to another genus, the *Syncerus.*
2. *Huangniu* actually designated several breeds of taurine cattle. In this book, "ox" refers to *huangniu* and other Western taurine cattle breeds. Unlike species, which are distinguished by taxonomy, breeds within each species are considered cultural as well as genetic. Likewise, the Chinese generally recognize two breeds of water buffalo.
3. Zhang Zhongge, "Gudai de niuzhong," 279–280; Guo Fu and Cheng Qingtai, *Dongwuxue shi,* 393–395.
4. Guo Fu and Cheng Qingtai, *Dongwuxue shi,* 386–399.
5. *Zhongguo nongye nianjian 1991,* 338. According to this census, there were also 10 million horses, 11 million donkeys, 5 million mules, 460,000 camels, 97 million goats, and 113 million sheep.
6. The literature on the sacred cow is extremely abundant. Here, I would like to mention Korom, "Holy Cow!"
7. Cartier, "L'homme et l'animal," 180; Guo Fu and Cheng Qingtai, *Dongwuxue shi,* 396–397. An archaeologist recently proposed much later dates for cattle. See Yuan Jing, "Zhongguo xinshiqi shidai jiachu."
8. Elisseeff, "Des animaux sous une chape de plomb."
9. See in particular the table in ibid., 26.
10. Cartier, "L'homme et l'animal," 194. The importance of cattle dung as a fertilizer seems to explain the absence of its use as fuel in China.
11. A memoir from the eighteenth century details the problems posed by the supply of leather to the military. See *Shizong Xian huangdi zhupi yuzhi,* 174–5.38a–b (memoir from 1727).
12. Needham and Yates, *Military Technology,* 180, 200, 272 passim.
13. Sogabe Shizuo, "Godai Sō no gyūhizei"; Xie Chengxia, *Yangniu yangshi,* 58–60. These forms of taxation date back to the third century BCE since they are mentioned in the Longgang manuscripts. I am indebted to Roel Sterckx for this information.
14. *Jinshi,* 5:110, 82:1846. "Shang Fu sicheng lun minjian libing liutiao" 上傅寺丞論民間利病六條, *Beixi daquan ji,* 47.4b–5a, affirms that the purchase of leather for the military encouraged illegal slaughter by cattle thieves because of the corruption of the authorities concerned.
15. Qiu Shusen, *Huizu shi,* 480–481, 646–648. Allès, *Musulmans de Chine,* is an ethnography of Hui tanners from northern Henan.
16. *Shiji,* 102:2758; *Hanshu,* 50:2314; *Hou Han shu,* 43:1482 and *zhi* 5:3129; *Nan Qi shu,* 40:705; *Beishi,* 23:853; *Jiu Tangshu,* 142:3866; *Xin Tangshu,* 86:3716; *Jiu Wudai shi,* 25:335, 54:727; *Songshi,* 334:10738, 466:13617; *Mingshi,* 126:3745, 247:6411, and so forth. In *Songshi,* 334:10733, dogmeat is associated with beef.
17. Needham and Huang, *Fermentations and Food Sciences,* 57; see also Fiskesjö, "Rising from Blood-Stained Fields."
18. Sabban, "Un savoir-faire oublié"; Xie Chengxia, *Yang niu yang shi,* chap. 7; DuBois, "China's Dairy Century."

19. On bezoar in East Asian medical cultures, see Lomi, "Ox Bezoars."
20. On the crucial importance of equines, especially donkeys, in North China, see Shahar, "The Donkey."
21. Guo Shengbo, "Sichuan da shengchu yangzhi," 82–83, notes a difference in use in Sichuan during the Tang. According to him, the water buffalo was reserved for sacrificial use and taurine cattle for work in the fields, a difference complicated by a distinction in the use of species between Han and other ethnic groups. This observation appears atypical given what is known about the rest of China.
22. Cartier, "L'homme et l'animal," 192.
23. Needham and Bray, *Agriculture,* 141.
24. Cartier, "L'homme et l'animal," 182. Plowing with cattle has existed in Mesopotamia since the third millennium BCE.
25. Bodde, *Festivals,* 201–209, 223–241.
26. Morgan, *Tableau du bœuf de printemps.*
27. Cartier, "L'homme et l'animal," 179.
28. Ibid., 183.
29. Furubayashi Morihiro, "Sōdai no kōgyū," 84–88.
30. Ibid., 100–103.
31. Xie Chengxia, *Yang niu yang shi,* 53–55.
32. During the Tang, the court maintained herds of tens of thousands of cattle in addition to 100,000–300,000 sheep in present-day Shanxi and Shaanxi. See Wang Lihua, *Zhonggu Huabei yinshi wenhua,* 104–116.
33. Zeng Xiongsheng, "Pozu nongye de xingcheng," studies the development of cattle farming through technical vocabulary, from herds on pasture to animals isolated in enclosures and led by a tether.
34. Suga Yutaka, "Tojikomerareta hitsujitachi." This livestock farming is motivated by a taste for mutton and sacrifices to the ancestors.
35. Animals consumed by-products of cereal cultivation, such as hay, but humans also used these as fuel, which became increasingly scarce and expensive in China from the sixteenth century. This feed therefore represents a cost for the animal's owner. Cartier, "L'homme et l'animal," 194.
36. Vermeer, "Population and Ecology," 256–257.
37. However, there was trade in working cattle in both senses. See Wang Lihua, *Zhonggu Huabei yinshi wenhua,* 125–129, for the Tang; Serruys, *Sino-Mongol Relations,* 54–59, 97, for the Ming.
38. Qiu Shusen, *Huizu shi,* 640–642.
39. Ibid., 660–662; *Qingshilu, Jiaqing* 10–12-bingxu (January 26, 1806), 154:1121–1122. Peng Nian, "Beijing Huizu," 1, suggests that this trade was already important in the early Qing but decreased sharply from 1696 due to the limitations placed on trade between Mongols and non-Mongols.
40. This type of familiarity between a child and an animal is, I believe, more intimate than that between a breeder and cattle in the European countryside.
41. According to a poem from the nineteenth century, calves were sold in the second month: "Fangniu xing" 放牛行 by Chen Wenshu 陳文述 (1775–1845), *Qingshi duo,* 915. Nowadays, the calves are sold for slaughter.
42. Xie Chengxia, *Yang niu yang shi,* chap. 5.

43. Cartier, "L'homme et l'animal," 186; Furubayashi Morihiro, "Sōdai no kōgyū," 76. Li Bozhong, *Agricultural Development,* 43, thinks this practice was widespread during the Ming.
44. Cartier, "L'homme et l'animal," 188, cites statistics from the National Agricultural Research Bureau.
45. Figures and analyses in Sun Yinrui, "Niurou chengwei fushipin," 117–138; see also Cartier, "La marginalization des animaux," 10–11.
46. Cartier, " L'homme et l'animal," 187.
47. Hino Kaisaburō, "Sōdai no chingyū"; Hino Kaisaburō, "Sōdai no sogyū"; Hino Kaisaburō, "Sōdai no chōseigyū"; Xing Tie, "Songdai de gengniu chuzu," emphasizes the leasing of cattle as an important element of economic domination over landless peasants.
48. Hino Kaisaburō, "Sōdai no chōseigyū."
49. Furubayashi Morihiro, "Sōdai no kōgyū," 95; Shiba Yoshinobu, *Sōdai shōgyō shi kenkyū,* 233–237.
50. Sabban, "Un savoir-faire oublié," 48, cites a source from the seventeenth century.
51. Cartier, "L'homme et l'animal," 194–195.
52. Ibid., 195. The purchase prices of cattle given by Song texts (Furubayashi Morihiro, "Sōdai no kōgyū," 89–93), converted to current grain prices, were in this order of magnitude—between four hundred and one thousand liters of rice.
53. Xie Chengxia, *Yang niu yang shi,* 49. It should also be noted that some breeds of cattle that were explicitly raised only for meat and mentioned in sources from the middle of the first millennium disappear from later sources. Li Hu, *Han-Tang yinshi wenhua shi,* 26.
54. Sabban, "Un savoir-faire oublié," 48, 53–54.
55. A passage from *Pi ya,* 5:123–124, explains that there are different kinds of dogs—those for meat and those for companionship—and specifies that there is a similar difference between *cainiu* and *gengniu. Cainiu* thus designated the herds of animals raised for meat, common in the large estates of the Tang, which subsequently disappeared.
56. *Qing shilu, Jiaqing* 10–12-bingxu (January 26, 1806), 154:1121–1122.
57. It is always difficult to prove the nonexistence of a term. Still, it seems significant that I did not find any reference in the databases and indexes available for *cainiu* and only a few occurrences of *rouniu,* all of them ill-defined.
58. *Shenbao,* October 3, 1877. The journalist described *cainiu* in such a way that one wonders whether he might be talking about yaks, but it is much more likely that he was referring to livestock farming practiced by the Hui. See also *Shenbao,* September 28, 1877.
59. *Shenbao,* July 30, 1872, September 6, 1872, and September 19, 1873. These articles responding to each other illustrate the heated controversy around the ban. It is important to note here that the very idea of cattle raised for meat, expressed by the term *cainiu,* appears to have been new to the journalists, whether they approved of it or not.
60. Xie Chengxia, *Zhongguo yangma shi;* P. Smith, *Taxing Heaven's Storehouse,* 14–31. Unlike *mazheng,* the term *niuzheng* 牛政 does not appear in sources before the twentieth century.

61. Cartier, "L'homme et l'animal," 193.
62. *Tuntian* were often military colonies in which the settlers practiced agriculture in ordinary times and were mobilized in the event of a disturbance or war.
63. Furubayashi Morihiro, "Sōdai no kōgyū," 79–84, discusses the different quotas per region and per household for cattle distributions during the Song.
64. Many cases of temporary or long-term exemption from commercial taxes on cattle transactions were also meant to facilitate the movement of herds.
65. *Guanniu* rented out to the peasants should be distinguished from the imperial herds reserved for the needs of the court, even if the latter are also sometimes called *guanniu.*
66. Xie Chengxia, *Yang niu yang shi,* 55–58.
67. Will, *Bureaucracy and Famine,* 264.
68. Xie Chengxia, *Yang niu yang shi,* 63–64.
69. *Taiwan guanxi jishi,* 113, specifies that in nineteenth-century Taiwan, cattle that passed through state-controlled cattle markets were branded.
70. The Japanese colonial authorities in Taiwan established cattle registration after 1895, a policy continued by the nationalist regime after 1945.
71. For the Song, see, for example, "Shang Fu sicheng lun minjian libing liutiao," *Beixi daquan ji,* 47.4b–5a.
72. "Lun daoan" 論盜案 by Li Yu 李漁 (1611–1680), *Huangchao jingshi wenbian,* 94.4a. Sun Yinrui, "Niurou chengwei fushipin," 38–41, also discusses the prevalence of cattle theft in the nineteenth century based on the legal records of Taiwan.
73. *Sha* simply refers to killing, while *tu* and *zai* typically, though not necessarily, refer to butchery.
74. The term *si,* "private," referred to the infringement by an individual on a state monopoly and was considered akin to other offenses such as smuggling salt (*siyan* 私鹽) or distilling alcohol (*sishao* 私燒), with which *sizai* was also frequently associated.
75. *Huainan honglie jijie,* chap. 16, "Shuoshan xun" 說山訓, 541.
76. Xie Chengxia, *Yang niu yang shi,* 49, cites a document found in Juyan 居延.
77. *Jinshu,* 78:2064. Some of these references (now easily identifiable thanks to the online publication of the text of the dynastic histories by the Academia Sinica) were already provided by Sun Yinrui, "Niurou chengwei fushipin," 15–22; Xie Chengxia, *Yang niu yang shi,* 47–50, 62–63; Guo Jian, "Liangshan haohan," 108–110. Ancient Chinese scholars had already collected some data from dynastic histories to trace the history of the beef taboo. See *Yijue liao zaji, xia,* 60, and especially *Guisi cungao,* 9:267–269.
78. *Songshu,* 8:160; 26:755, decree motivated by a bovine epizootic.
79. *Nanshi,* 59:1460. A local official enforced the interdiction in a region where it was ignored.
80. *Weishu,* 7:141; 9:224.
81. *Songshu,* 6:121, during work in the fields; *Jiu Tangshu,* 18 *xia:*628. For three years, the prohibition even applied to sacrifices to heaven. Perhaps this was in a context of a temporary ban of sacrifices added to the permanent prohibition relating to slaughter in ordinary times.

82. *Tanglü shuyi,* article 203, pp. 262–263. This article also stipulates a steeper penalty if the killing resulted from premeditated theft (see also articles 279, 356) and the amount of reimbursement for the lost value if one injured a horse or a bovine belonging to someone else or if one injured or killed another animal. Accidental killing was not punished. Officials were worried about the lack of zeal put into the enforcement of the law. See "Qing jin tuniu zou" 請禁屠牛奏 (dated 848), *Quan Tang wen,* 968.2a–b.
83. Song: *Song xingtong,* 15:267–270; Ming: *Da Ming lü jijie fu li,* 16:1227–1237; Qing: *Da Qing huidian shili,* 777.2b–3b (1908 ed.). The penalties stipulated by the code were increased in 1727. See *Shizong Xian huangdi yu xing qiwu zouyi,* 5.3a–5b.
84. *Songshi,* 386:1867; *Qingyuan tiaofa shilei,* 79.21a–b; *Song huiyao jigao,* "Zhiguan 職官, 48," 31 (edict from 1112), "Xingfa 刑法, 2," 104 (edict from 1130). Other edicts preserved in the *Song huiyao jigao,* which are more precise, are quoted below. On the Song laws, see also Shio Takugo, "Sōdai gyūniku," 93–94, and Xing Tie, "Songdai de gengniu chuzu," 83.
85. *Jinshi,* 15:344.
86. *Yuanshi,* 5:89, 6:112, 8:167, 45:949, a prohibition pertaining specifically to soldiers; *Da Yuan shengzheng guochao dianzhang,* "Xingbu 刑部," "Jin zaisha 禁宰殺," n.p.
87. I will discuss the decisions of local Qing officials on this matter below.
88. *Jiu Tangshu,* 199 *shang:*5320.
89. Taira Masayuki, "Tabous et alimentation carnée," 173.
90. For example, *Zuoyi zizhen,* 47a. On these handbooks, see Will, *Handbooks and Anthologies.*
91. *Jiu Wudai shi,* 29:403 (in 923, during the Hou Tang), 31:428 (the following year), 34:467 (in 926), 38:529 (in 927), 41:560 (in 930), 81:1069 (in 940, during the Jin).
92. *Sanguo zhi,* 22:643. The official pardoned the culprit who had been sentenced for having sacrificed a bovine to pray for his father's recovery.
93. *Song huiyao jigao,* "Xingfa, 2," 4.
94. *Jinshu,* 78:2064.
95. *Nan Qi shu,* 27:510, and *Nanshi,* 16:467 (one official who is dismissed); *Liangshu,* 15:264 and *Nanshi,* 20:560 (one official who is dismissed); *Jiu Tangshu,* 58:2309 (a commoner, imprisoned); *Xin Tangshu,* 90:3765.
96. This procedure had already been proposed at the end of the Tang in 851. See "Qing yanjin tuniu zou 請嚴禁屠牛奏," *Quan Tang wen,* 968.6b–7a. A handbook for officials from the beginning of the twelfth century mentions the form to be filled out on this occasion. See *Zuoyi zizhen,* 16a. An anecdote from the eleventh century illustrates such a request. See "Taining niu meng 泰寧牛夢," *Yijian zhi,* Sanji 三己, 5, 1337. All references to the *Yijian zhi* are given with series number, chapter (*juan*) number, and page number at first occurrence and with only page number at following occurrences.
97. *Minggong shupan qingming ji,* 14:534–535, contains a case of a conviction and a proclamation of the prohibition; McKnight and Liu, *The Enlightened Judgments,* 475.
98. An anecdote from the thirteenth century describes the bribes that the beef butcher had to pay. See "Zhang Yi changzhai 張一償債," *Yijian zhi,* Ding 丁,

5, 575–576. By the twelfth century, the state had to prohibit the levying of a tax when the peasants came to the yamen to notify them of the death of a bovine. See *Qingyuan tiaofa shilei,* 79.5a–b. The Yuan law allowed the heads of isolated villages to issue the authorization. See *Da Yuan shengzheng guochao dianzhang,* "Xingbu," "Jin zaisha," n.p., "Daosi niu ma lizheng zhushou gaobao guo kaibo" 倒死牛馬里正主首告報過開剝 (a law from 1303).

99. Will, *Bureaucracy and Famine,* 55, 248–250.
100. Wang Jiange, "Nongye shengtai," 48.
101. A Qing-era handbook for officials even recounts the astonishing decision to allow peasants to borrow grain from public granaries for cattle feed in case of need. See *Jianyu xiansheng fu Yu tiaojiao,* 4.12a.
102. Will, *Bureaucracy and Famine,* 248.
103. The nationalist government passed a law to "protect plow cattle," but the aim was to protect the breed (by selection) and not to prohibit slaughter. See "Baohu gengniu guize 保護耕牛規則," *Zhonghua minguo fagui huibian,* 8:568–569. However, during a flood in 1931, the Nanking government prohibited the trade and slaughter of cattle and attempted to set up structures to accommodate cattle from affected peasant families. See *Zhonghua minguo fagui huibian,* 8:569–570.
104. *Liangshu,* 26:394; *Nanshi,* 60:1470.
105. *Quan Tang wen,* 27.15a; *Tang da zhaoling ji,* 109:565. See also Liu Shufen, "Niansan yueshi," 21.
106. Quote from *Mengzi,* "Liang Huiwang, shang 梁惠王上."
107. *Qing shilu,* Yongzheng 7–6-*bingshen* (July 18, 1729), 82:91–92.
108. An edict of 1143 authorizes this procedure even for state-owned *guanniu.* See *Song huiyao jigao,* "Shi huo 食貨, 63," 114. An anecdote from the Tang relates the case of a monk who approached various butchers to sell them the carcass of a bovine that had died naturally. See "Shanggong 上公," *Taiping guangji,* 134:960, quoting the *Yutang xianhua* 玉堂閒話.
109. "Taining niu meng," *Yijian zhi,* 1337.
110. For the Song, see *Song huiyao jigao,* "Shihuo, 63," 114, and Shio Takugo, "Sōdai gyūniku," 93–94. The decrees of the Yuan were more explicit. See *Da Yuan shengzheng guochao dianzhang,* "Xingbu," "Jin zaisha," n.p., "Zai lao bing si niu ma 宰老病死牛馬" (a law from 1276). This authorization could only be obtained between the tenth and the twelfth month when there was no work in the fields—at least in North China because then the Yuan did not control South China—and only for family consumption without the possibility of selling the meat. See also, in the same chapter, "Daosi niu ma lizheng zhushou gao bao guo kaibo" (a law from 1303). For the Qing, see *Da Qing huidian shili,* 777.3a *shang* (1908 ed.).
111. In a detailed memoir on the issue, a famed neo-Confucian scholar living in southern Fujian dwelled on the relationship between beef butchers and cattle thieves. See "Shang Fu sicheng lun minjian libing liutiao," *Beixi daquan ji,* 47.4b–5a.
112. A decree from 1110 detailed the prices and suggested that, indeed, an animal sold for meat could bring in four times the purchase price. See *Song huiyao jigao,* "Xingfa 2," 52.

113. *Jiu Wudai shi,* 38:521; *Wudai huiyao,* 9:119.
114. *Song huiyao jigao,* "Xingfa, 2," 52 (edict from 1110).
115. An edict from 1016, which enforced the prohibition against the theft and killing of cattle, followed a report by an official on the beef stalls lined up along the roads. See *Song huiyao jigao,* "Shihuo, 1," 18, and "Shihuo, 63," 165; also *Minggong shupan qingming ji,* 14:534.
116. *Song huiyao jigao,* "Xingfa, 2," 20 (edict from 1034).
117. Ibid., 12 (edict from 1014).
118. Ibid., 104 (edicts from 1031 and 1034). "Ji Wang shangshu shi 記王尚書事," *Jianghu changweng ji,* 22.18a, recounts the legal case of a man who was arrested for transporting beef. The skillful judge discovered a conspiracy between the man's wife and her lover to convict the cuckold husband.
119. *Da Ming lü jijie fu li,* 16:1236–1237. This is an additional article.
120. Before the creation of Western-style slaughterhouses from the end of the nineteenth century, butchers conducted the business of buying and slaughtering the animals whose meat they sold in their homes. Furubayashi Morihiro, "Sōdai no tosatsu," provides a detailed study of the organization of the meat trades during the Song.
121. "Changsheng niu 長生牛," *Yijian zhi,* Bing 丙, 5, 404, suggests that soldiers ignored slaughter bans. The anecdote is dated 1131. Similarly, *Songshi,* 67:1480.
122. *Songshi,* 262:9077.
123. A fourteenth-century poem describes a family's love for their ox ("they raised their ox the same way they raised a child") and their despair when soldiers take and eat it. See "Yangniu tan 養牛歎," *Chaweng shiji,* 4.35a–b.
124. Decrees from 923 and 927 reiterate the prohibition against slaughtering cattle and horses specifically for the military. See *Wudai huiyao,* 9:119. For the same in 1359, see *Yuanshi,* 45:949.
125. For example, the prohibition of the cult of Xiang Yu 項羽 and its cattle sacrifices in the seventh century. See *Liangshu,* 26:397, and *Nanshi,* 18:499, 506. It seems that the cult was considered heterodox in general and that the cattle sacrifices were an aggravating circumstance.
126. *Fengsu tongyi jiaozhu,* 9:401–403; *Hou Han shu,* 41:1397.
127. This law is mentioned in the *Fengsu tongyi* but not in the *Hou Hanshu.* An anecdote from the third century also describes the death sentence of a man who sacrificed a bovine to pray for healing for his father. See *Sanguo zhi,* 22:643.
128. Nakamura Jihei, "Shizanbyō no gyūsai," 6–10, has collected many examples dating from the Tang and Song.
129. *Taiping huanyu ji,* 102.9b–10a, citing *Niusu jiwen* 牛肅記聞; Nakamura Jihei, "Shizanbyō no gyūsai," 8.
130. "Bishan shen 壁山神," *Beimeng suoyan,* 420–421 (cited in *Taiping guangji,* 515:2497).
131. *Song huiyao jigao,* "Xingfa, 2," 52 (edict of 1110). This text must be taken into account because it was promulgated by the Daoist emperor Song Huizong, who led a religious and sacrificial reform policy. However, the interdiction against sacrificing cattle and horses to "demons" is repeated during the

Southern Song. See *Qingyuan tiaofa shilei,* 79.21b, and "Tuniu yu miao 屠牛于廟," *Minggong shupan qingming ji,* 14:534. *Jingde ji,* 2.8b, relates the case of a man convicted of sacrificing a bovine for a prayer for healing.

132. A similar case occurred again in 1310. A merciful magistrate pardoned people who had sacrificed cattle during a ritual to pray for rain during a drought. See *Yuanshi,* 170:3996.
133. The following is based on Nakamura Jihei, "Shizanbyō no gyūsai" and Hansen, *Changing Gods,* 148–152.
134. For this reason, Valerie Hansen included it in her study.
135. Nakamura Jihei, "Shizanbyō no gyūsai," 6.
136. *Songshi,* 302:10025.
137. Hansen, *Changing Gods,* 157–159, and Hymes, *Way and Byway,* 136–144.
138. "Shen zhusi qi jin shehui zhuang 申諸司乞禁社會狀," "Yi shen Shangshusheng qi jin benjun zaixing niuji shi 以申尚書省乞禁本軍再行牛祭事," *Huangshi richao,* 74.19a–28a and 28a–31a.
139. "Yi shen Shangshusheng," *Huangshi richao,* 74.19a–b.
140. Aubin, "Cheval céleste"; see also ter Haar, *Ritual and Mythology,* 157–158.
141. Ter Haar, *Ritual and Mythology,* 151–179; Tian Zhaoyuan, *Mengshi shi.*
142. *Xin Tangshu,* 126:4435.
143. *Songshu,* 45:1381.
144. The *Liji,* "Quli 曲禮," mentions the sacrifices of cattle by ordinary officers.
145. *Jiu Wudai shi,* 153:1912–1913; *Wudai huiyao,* 3:39–40; *Jinshi,* j. 31, "Lizhi 禮志, 4," "Zayi 雜儀," 765–769.
146. Regarding the debates during the Jin, *Jinshi,* 95:2110, describes the resistance of Confucian officials in the face of the imperial desire to suppress cattle sacrifices.
147. Including Song Changhong, *Zhongguo niu wenhua;* Li Lulu, *Chunniu bidi;* Zheng Tuyou, *Niu.*

## CHAPTER 3: THE REVELATION OF A NEW SIN

1. Xuancheng, which still bears this name, is located about a hundred kilometers west of Huzhou.
2. "Shiniu mengjie 食牛夢戒," *Yijian zhi,* Yi 乙, 1, 191–192.
3. The thirty-three anecdotes of this corpus are cited throughout the following pages. I also cite some of the many anecdotes that shed light on the relationship between humans and cattle but do not explicitly mention the taboo. They are therefore not included in the corpus. The dates of composition of the anecdotes (and not of the events they recount) are distributed as follows: two from the ninth century, twenty-one from the twelfth century, four from the thirteenth century, and six from the Song more generally. For this corpus, see Shio Takugo, "Sōdai gyūniku," who quotes nineteen anecdotes, and ter Haar, "Buddhist-Inspired Options," who quotes five.
4. "Jiang Jian shiniu 蔣堅食牛," *Yijian zhi,* Zhijia 支甲, 10, 788–790.
5. "Shiniu shi 食牛詩," *Yijian zhi,* Yi 乙, 13, 295.
6. "Haidao dazhu 海島大竹," *Yijian zhi,* Yi 乙, 13, 295–296.
7. Stephen Teiser, *The Scripture on the Ten Kings,* recommends using the word "purgatory" rather than "hell" to designate the Chinese afterlife where the

deceased are tried and condemned because they are places of passage where one is not locked up for eternity. This argument is valid and sound, but the fundamental role of punishment in the hereafter described in the sources I use (while purgatory is not used to punish in the Christian tradition) prompts me to keep the term "hell," which has been used traditionally.

8. "Jie shi niurou 戒食牛肉," *Huhai xinwen Yijian xuzhi,* 97–98.
9. "Zhao Shanyi mengjing 趙善弌夢警," *Yijian zhi,* Bu 補, 3, 1573.
10. "Shiniu bao 食牛報," *Qidong yeyu,* 14:264.
11. *Kuiche zhi,* 2:15 (untitled).
12. "Koubingtang seng 扣冰堂僧," *Yijian zhi,* Zhijia, 10, 794.
13. "Gu Daiwen 顧待問," *Yijian zhi,* Bu 4, 1579.
14. "Junming jianguan 浚明減官," *Fenmen gujin leishi,* 20.14b. The protagonist of the story was called Song Junming 宋浚明. The source of this story is given as *Jiesha lu* 戒殺錄, an otherwise unknown text.
15. "Niu shelita 牛舍利塔," *Yijian zhi,* Ding 丁, 16, 672–673.
16. *Wenjian jinlu,* 7b–8a (untitled).
17. *Mozhuang manlu,* 9.1b (untitled). The same story was repeated in other sources from the Song period.
18. "Huangyi furen 黃衣婦人," *Yijian zhi,* Zhiding 支丁, 2, 978.
19. "Wang San zainiu 汪三宰牛," *Yijian zhi,* Sanzhi Ren 三志壬, 10, 1546–1547. In "He Baijiu 何百九," *Yijian zhi,* Zhijing 支景, 3, 899, a cattle butcher, a notorious brigand who had been convicted previously, skinned an animal. A piece of the skin clung to his son and caused the offspring terrible pain. This was generally believed to be retribution for their criminal activity.
20. "Changsheng niu," *Yijian zhi,* 404.
21. "Jiang tuniu 江屠牛," *Yijian zhi,* Zhiyi 支乙, 8, 860. The subject of poisoned cattle was fairly common. A bovine fed with a substance that made it grow big and fat poisoned people who ate it after sacrificing it. The guilty cattle dealer was also found drowned. See "Huaixi niushang 淮西牛商," *Yijian zhi,* Zhiding 支丁, 5, 1008–1009.
22. "Ertu dingpeng 二屠鼎烹," *Yijian zhi,* Sanzhi xin 三志辛, 1, 1390–1391. Another anecdote recounted the case of a cattle broker who cruelly killed his animals and eventually died in the same way. See "Dong Baie 董白額," *Yijian zhi,* Jia 甲, 13, 112.
23. "Niutou wang," *Yijian zhi,* Sanzhixin 三志辛, 6, 1430–1431.
24. "Zhai Ji dezi 翟楫得子," *Yijian zhi,* Yi 乙, 17, 325.
25. "Niuwang gong mangfan 牛王宮囗飯," *Chunzhu jiwen,* 3:48.
26. *Youyang zazu,* anecdote 563, 135, translated in C. Reed, *Chinese Chronicles,* 46. The anecdote was included in the *Taiping guangji* in the chapter devoted to *yakṣa,* under the title "Qiu Ru 丘濡," 357:2826–2827.
27. Ji Yun was an intellectual of very high stature who directed the compilation of *Siku quanshu,* but he was nonetheless fond of fantastical anecdotes: see Chan, *The Discourse on Foxes and Ghosts.*
28. *Yuewei caotang biji,* 10:204–205. A recent comprehensive overview of this theme is found in Ren Zhaojie, "Bushi niurou."
29. Another version has "the meat of the *chou* 丑 animal." *Chou* is the cyclic sign associated with the ox in the twelve-animal cycle.

30. *Xuanshi zhi,* 37–38; the anecdote is included in the *Taiping guangji,* 356:2819–2820, "Zhu Xian nü 朱峴女."
31. "Tianmo sui 天魔祟," *Xu Yijian zhi,* 1:12.
32. "Zhongshu gui an 中書鬼案," *Nancun chuogeng lu,* 13:155–157.
33. These diseases, generally called by the generic terms *yi* 疫 or *wen* 瘟, are most often impossible to identify in our medical vocabulary. In pre–twentieth-century China, they included the bubonic plague, dysentery, and cholera, among others.
34. Katz, *Demon Hordes,* 39–75; Von Glahn, *Sinister Way,* chap. 4.
35. "Guan shumi 管樞密," *Yijian zhi,* Ding 丁, 2, 546.
36. *Wujun zhi,* 44:590, citing the *Tanxuan* 談選. This lost collection seems to date from the Song and is known via only a few quotations in the *Shuofu* 說郛, which do not include the present anecdote.
37. "Shiniu bao," *Qidong yeyu,* 14:264.
38. "Zhao Shanyi mengjing," *Yijian zhi,* 1573.
39. "Jie niurou 戒牛肉," *Suishi guangji,* 23:271.
40. *Jujia biyong shilei quanji,* Xinji 辛集, 75b. This text defended a double interdiction against cattle and horses and affirmed that other animals could be sacrificed and consumed.
41. See in particular Davis, *Society and the Supernatural,* chap. 4, which integrates and elaborates on previous work, and a full translation in French in Goossaert, *Vies des saints exorcistes.* The *sisheng* are Tianpeng 天蓬, Tianyou 天猷, Yisheng baode zhenjun, and Zhenwu 真武.
42. "Yisheng jing Liu Haichan 翊聖敬劉海蟾," *Chunzhu jiwen,* 3:40–41.
43. *Zhongxing xiaoji,* 33.9a–b.
44. "Shi niurou ruguan zhi jie 食牛肉入觀之戒," *Lushan Taiping xingguo gong Caifang zhenjun shishi,* 7.7b–8a.
45. Ferrières, *Histoire des peurs alimentaires,* 50.
46. Douglas, *Purity and Danger.*
47. Sawada Mizuho, "Chikurui shōsai tan," 231–236.
48. *Taiping guangji,* 434:3521–3522.
49. "Zhushi zi 朱氏子," *Taiping guangji,* 434:3522, excerpted from *Jishen lu* 稽神錄 by Xu Xuan 徐鉉 (916–991), "Buyi," 133. This anecdote was quoted in several Qing morality books.
50. *Taiping guangji,* 383:3053. The anecdote was excerpted from Liu Yiqing's 劉義慶 (403–444) *Youming lu* 幽明錄.
51. "Huangfu Xun 皇甫恂," *Taiping guangji,* 381:3033, excerpted from *Guangyi ji* 廣異記 by Dai Fu 戴孚 (second half of the seventh century). On this source, see Dudbridge, *Religious Experience and Lay Society.* The story of Huangfu Xun's visits to the underworld was developed in a much longer anecdote, which omitted the reference to beef. See "Huangfu Xun," *Taiping guangji,* 302:2393–2395, excerpted from *Tongyou ji* 通幽記.
52. *Leizhou fuzhi,* 3.14a.
53. "Zhao Shanyi mengjing," *Yijian zhi,* 1573.
54. *Wenjian jinlu,* 30a–b (untitled anecdote).
55. "Changsheng niu," *Yijian zhi,* 404.
56. "Taining niu meng," *Yijian zhi,* 1336.

57. "Zhao Zixian meng 趙子顯夢," *Yijian zhi,* Yi 乙, 1, 192–193.
58. "Jin tusha ji quan zhao 禁屠殺雞犬詔," *Quan Tang wen,* 26.1a.
59. *Song xingtong,* 15:269–270; *Qingyuan tiaofa shilei,* 79.21b, 22a.
60. It should be noted, however, that not all legal texts treated cattle as a mere subcategory of useful animals. For example, the text of a ruling by Hu Ying 胡穎 (*zi* Shibi 石壁, *jinshi* 1232) justified the penal prohibition by saying, "As their merit toward humans is immense, they cannot be treated in the same way as other animals." See *Minggong shupan qingming ji,* 14:534.
61. "Taining niu meng," *Yijian zhi,* 1573.
62. This did not prevent the same authors from writing texts in other genres dealing with the discourse of the taboo. The distinction to be made is not that between social classes (literati and others) but between literary genres.
63. *Er Cheng ji, Henan Cheng shi yishu* 河南程氏遺書, 21 *shang*:269.
64. *Peiwei zhai ji,* 17.16a–17a.
65. Wang Xu, "Bu shi tailao shuo 不食太牢說," *Quan Yuan wen,* vol. 19, 503.
66. Poem by Wu Ge 吳革 (*hao* Shuzhai 恕齋, fl. 1263–1270) cited in *Suiyin manlu,* 1:6.
67. Poem by Dai Fugu 戴復古 (Song period) quoted by *Yinshi shenyan,* 5.
68. Poem by Lu Fangchun 盧方春 (*zi* Liunan 柳南, *jinshi* 1238) cited in *Suiyin manlu,* 1:6.
69. *Qinzhai ji,* 8.10a. The poet searched for meat for his sick wife and (like Daoists) concluded that only dried venison would do.
70. "He He Siju jie shiniu 和何斯舉戒食牛," *Yunxi ji,* 11.6b–7a; poem by Wu Ge quoted in *Suiyin manlu,* 1:6.
71. He Menggui, "Zan Wang Ailian yu shiniu 贊汪愛蓮諭食牛," *Quan Yuan wen,* vol. 8, 180.
72. *Quan Yuan sanqu,* 319–322. See also the gloss and commentary by Tanaka Kenji, *Gafu sankyoku,* 251–268, and the translation by Idema, *Spiegel van de klassieke Chinese poëzie,* 586–590.
73. Idema, "Guanyin's Acolytes," 216; Idema, "The Ultimate *Sanqu* Song." Another case, analyzed by Idema, is the tale of Zhongshan wolf 中山狼 in which the central theme was also the injustice and ingratitude of humans toward animals. Tanaka Kenji, *Gafu sankyoku,* 267, also mentions poems in which a horse (*[Xinjiao jiujuan ben] Yangchun baixue,* 185–186) and a sheep (*Quan Yuan sanqu,* 519–520) complained about the way humans treated them. The horse was slaughtered by a butcher, but there was no element of supernatural vengeance, unlike in the ballad of the bovine.
74. "Tan niu 歎牛," *Liu Yuxi ji jianzheng,* 6:158–160.
75. Spring, *Animal Allegories,* 82–94, which besides the text by Liu Yuxi also analyzes the "Rhapsody about Cattle" (*Niu fu* 牛賦) by Liu Zongyuan 柳宗元 (774–819), in *Quan Tang wen,* 569.3b–4a. Liu Zongyuan also lamented the fate of bovines, which he equated with that of a rejected minister.
76. The Ming law, however, encouraged households to which cattle from imperial herds were entrusted to bury them when they died. See Xie Chengxia, *Yang niu yang shi,* 54.
77. One of these anecdotes, however, mentioned the case of a dead bovine punished by heaven for having eaten the shoots of cereals in a field. A debate

broke out among the villagers between those who wanted to throw it into the river and those who wanted to eat it. See "Yongningzhuang niu 永寧莊牛," *Yijian zhi,* Ding 丁, 6, 586. In another case, meat was thrown into the river. See "Huangyi furen," *Yijian zhi,* 978.

78. Ter Haar, "Buddhist-Inspired Options," 134.
79. *Yanshi jiaxun jijie,* chap. 16, "Guixin pian 歸心篇," 369.
80. Gjertson, *Miraculous Retribution,* 248–250.
81. "Changsheng niu," *Yijian zhi,* 404; "Huangyi furen," *Yijian zhi,* 978; "Taining niu meng," *Yijian zhi,* 1336; "Zhao Shanyi mengjing," *Yijian zhi,* 1573.
82. "Huangchi niu 黃池牛," *Yijian zhi,* Zhiwu 支戊, 4, 1080–1081.
83. "Tanyuan Tang tu 檀源唐屠," *Yijian zhi,* Bu 補, 3, 1575–1576.
84. "Meng du yishu 夢讀異書," *Yijian zhi,* Yi 乙, 1, 193–194.
85. I am grateful to Barbara Ambros for pointing this out to me. This discourse was very influential in Tokugawa Japan. See Ambros, *Refraining from Killing and Releasing Life.*
86. For an obvious example, see "Huang shiweng 黃十翁," *Yijian zhi,* Bing 丙, 8, 432–433. Ter Haar, "Buddhist-Inspired Options," 134, estimates that half of the anecdotes on vegetarianism have an explicitly Buddhist context.
87. The Buddhist tradition, as Stephen Teiser shows in *The Scripture on the Ten Kings,* contributed important elements to the Chinese conception of the bureaucracy of hell, but the very notion of the bureaucracy of hell was not Buddhist.
88. Spirit-writing, *jiangbi* 降筆 or *fuluan* 扶鸞 (and later *fuji* 扶乩), is organized by a worship group devoted to a deity. In group meetings, after purification of the members and invitation of the deity, one of the members acting as a medium goes into a trance and is possessed by the deity. The medium then writes on a prop (paper, ash, sand, or even in the air) characters that are then copied by a scribe and checked by the other members of the group before being collected and possibly published. On the history of this practice, see Kleeman, *A God's Own Tale,* 8–16; Jordan and Overmyer, *Flying Phoenix;* and Goossaert, *Making the Gods Speak.*
89. *Zitong dijun huashu,* 4.30b–32a. On this book, see Kleeman, *A God's Own Tale,* particularly p. 77 for the dating of 1316 of the fragment cited here.
90. "Jinjue niurou 禁絕牛肉," *Sanji zhiming quanti,* 34b–35a.
91. Anderson, *The Food of China,* 66, 82; Freeman, "Sung," 154 (consumption by the rich only), 164 (the author notes in particular that during the Song, beef seemed to disappear from recipes and banquet menus); Shiba Yoshinobu, *Sōdai shōgyō shi kenkyū,* 233–237; Mote, "Yüan and Ming," 201.
92. It is possible that there were many anecdotes about beef because the taboo was an important subject and not because consumption was widespread. Moreover, didactic anecdotes naturally tended to claim that there were many sinners.
93. In particular, "Niuwang gong mangfan," *Chunzhu jiwen,* 48, and "Shiniu bao," *Qidong yeyu,* 264.
94. "Zheng xingpo 鄭行婆," *Yijian zhi,* Zhiding 支丁, 3, 990.
95. Durand-Dastès, "Prodiges ambigus," particularly 321–322 concerning *Yijian zhi.*
96. The primary studies of religious history based on *Yijian zhi* are Hansen, *Changing Gods,* Boltz, "Not by the Seal of Office Alone," Davis, *Society and the Supernatural,* and ter Haar, "Buddhist-Inspired Options."

97. Ang, "Le culte de Lü Dongbin."
98. On Hong Mai's reliability, see Inglis, *Hong Mai's* Record of the Listener.
99. "Shiniu bao," *Qidong yeyu,* 264.
100. "Tuniu zhi bao 屠牛之報," *Huadang ge congtan,* 6:156–159.
101. Simoons, *Eat Not This Flesh,* 64–101 on pork and 135–143 on beef.
102. Wang Lihua, *Zhonggu Huabei yinshi wenhua,* 104–116.
103. Freeman, "Sung," 154.
104. Holm, *Killing a Buffalo,* 205–215.
105. Nakamura Jihei, "Shizanbyō no gyūsai," 8–9; Su Shi 蘇軾 (1036–1101), "Shu Liu Zihou niu fu hou 書柳子厚牛賦後," *Su Dongpo quanji,* 561–562, lamented the habit of the people in Hainan who sacrificed cattle when they were sick, and he asked a friend who was a monk to try to convert the natives.
106. See Ebrey and Gregory, *Religion and Society;* Davis, *Society and the Supernatural;* Hansen, *Changing Gods;* and Von Glahn, *Sinister Way,* chap. 5.
107. Shahar, *Chinese Animal Gods,* will undoubtedly provide more evidence and insights.
108. In the contemporary period, however, Niuwang's birthday is an opportunity in some places to sing or recite texts related to the taboo. See Zheng Tuyou, *Niu wenhua yu rensheng,* 55.
109. In ancient texts, generally written *yan* 鴈.
110. *Shangqing Lingbao dafa,* 8.8b–9a. This text prohibited Daoists from consuming the *sanyan,* the six domestic animals, and especially the pig and the dog, as well as all fetuses and eggs. This left dairy products, deer, ducks, and fish, but the text specified that these animal-based foods are only recommended when the priest's state of health justified it. The *sanyan* as a taboo of purity seems to have originated within the Daoist clergy, but they were also later observed in the context of a purification preceding some rites practiced by the laity. See *Wubian, qianji,* 4.92a–b; *Zunsheng bajian,* 449 (the *Siku quanshu* edition has an additional occurrence, 17.4a); *Chishui xuanzhu,* 10.74b. An anecdote, probably from the Song period, related the retribution visited upon a man who was a member of a family that observed the Daoist "three revulsions" but had accepted prohibited meat. See *Da Ming Renxiao huanghou quanshan shu,* 12.11a–b.
111. *Suiyin manlu,* 1:6.
112. The name Xuanwu was common until 1017, when it was changed to Zhenwu to observe an imperial taboo on the *xuan* character. Since the fourteenth century, the god has been frequently referred to as Xuantian shangdi 玄天上帝.
113. On Zhenwu and Wudang shan, see Chao Shin-yi, *Daoist Ritual;* De Bruyn, *Le Wudang shan;* and Little, *Taoism and the Arts of China,* 291–311.
114. The snake or eel and the turtle have been emblematic animals of the north and Zhenwu since antiquity.
115. *Yuanshi tianzun shuo Beifang Zhenwu miaojing* 元始天尊說北方眞武妙經, *Daojia jinshilüe,* 306–308; Chao Shin-yi, *Daoist Ritual,* 40–41.
116. *Wujun zhi,* 44:590.
117. The meaning of this sentence is far from clear. This is undoubtedly an allusion to the places where dog and beefeaters are punished, respectively. Indeed, a text revealed by Wenchang mentioned above cited Mount Tailao as a prison

for beefeaters. The "true forms" are symbolic diagrams of holy places, especially mountains, which serve as talismans. See Schipper, "The True Form."

118. Yuqing is the name of the celestial realm presided over by Yuanshi tianzun 元始天尊, the first of the Three Pures of the Daoist trinity.

119. *(Zengding) Jingxin lu,* 107a; *Tongshan lu,* 8.3a–b, 44a–b; *Niujie huichao,* 1b–2a, in which the text is titled *Xuandi zhen* 玄帝箴. Possibly the earliest quote of this text I have seen is in a commentary on the Jade Emperor scripture compiled ca. 1585, mostly composed of spirit-written contents: *Huangjing jizhu,* 6.22a.

120. *Xuantian shangdi chuixun,* unpaginated, second and fifth sheet. See also *(Zengding) Jingxin lu,* 108a–110b, and *Shengjing huizuan,* 1.29a–31a. Editions dated 1444 and 1457 of this text can be found in the British Library; Zhou Shaoliang, "Qisheng shilu shuji," 165, mentions an edition from 1596 in the National Library of China. I owe this information to the late Judith Boltz to whom I am deeply grateful. Text translated in French in Goossaert, *Livres de morale,* 53–67.

121. The interdictions against turtles and eels are obviously linked to the two emblematic animals of Zhenwu, the turtle and the snake. From the Song, we see anecdotes relating to the interdiction against eels appearing in an explicitly Daoist context. See, for example, "Shashan huiwu 殺鱔悔悟," *Huhai xinwen Yijian xuzhi,* 98, and "Shashan quming 殺鱔取命," *Huhai xinwen Yijian xuzhi,* 99.

122. *Taishang shuo Xuantian dasheng zhenwu benzhuan shenzhou miaojing,* 3.17a. However, most of the interdictions observed during the rituals devoted to Zhenwu in the texts of the Song or Yuan period were not specific and prohibited meat in general. See, for example, *Daomen kefan daquan ji,* 63.6a.

123. The canonical hagiography of these two figures mentioned the suppression of local cults practicing the sacrifice of cattle and pigs but did not contain elements relating to the taboo. See *Yisheng baode zhuan,* 2.4a; see also 1.2a for the rejection of meat offerings in general.

124. *Diqi shangjiang Wen taibao zhuan,* 1b; see also 2b. On this text, see Katz, *Demon Hordes,* 77–88.

125. The taboos against beef and the "three revulsions" are well known among the Daoist priests of Taiwan and southern China as well as in the various ethnic groups of the south where Daoism plays a vital role. See Qing Xitai, *Zhongguo daojiao shi,* 264, 269 and passim.

126. Goossaert, "Divine Codes."

127. *Daofa huiyuan,* 252.12b–13a.

128. *Guiguzi tiansui lingwen,* 1.8b.

129. *Daofa huiyuan,* 74.15a.

130. For example, "Shiniu bao," *Qidong yeyu,* 264; "Koubingtang seng," *Yijian zhi,* 794.

131. "Jiesha," *Leshan lu,* 4b–5a (*Shuofu sanzhong,* 6:3415–3416).

132. Cattle fighting persisted until the twentieth century in Jinhua 金華 (Zhejiang). The defeated animal, if seriously injured, was eaten by the community. See Eberhard, *Local Cultures,* 185; Xie Chengxia, *Yang niu yang*

*shi,* 88–90; and "Wuzhou douniu su 婺州鬥牛俗," *Yongxian zhai biji,* 5:103–104, for a nineteenth-century description.

133. *(Jiatai) Kuaiji zhi,* 6.23b. See also Mao Gengru, *Tiao Wuchang,* 18, which cites sources from the Ming and Qing periods showing that the sacrifice of cattle and dogs was still practiced, as well as the interdiction against pork, which was called "Cishan's fast," *Cishanzhai* 祠山齋.
134. "Cishan shenxian 祠山神顯," *Huhai xinwen Yijian xuzhi,* 215–216.
135. This ritual called *dianyan* 奠雁 is attested in the *Yili* 儀禮; Ebrey, *Confucianism and Family Rituals,* 58–59. It is still common today.
136. Taira Masayuki, "Tabous et alimentation carnée," 171–175; see also Nakazawa Katsuaki, *Nikushoku no shakaishi,* 162–173, and Yoshida Tadashi, *Gyūniku to Nihonjin.*
137. "Tuniu gaiye 屠牛改業," *Huhai xinwen Yijian xuzhi,* 96. Doolittle, *Social Life of the Chinese,* 190, translates a very similar anecdote without giving a source.
138. "Niuhun bian gui 牛魂變鬼," *Kuaiyuan,* 13:696.
139. "Quan sha niu ge 勸殺牛歌," *Shuijing lu,* 16a–b (this text dates no later than the sixteenth century). For a popular ballad in Hokkien, see Sun Yinrui, "Niurou chengwei fushipin," 49.
140. Regarding dogs, we should mention two anecdotes very similar to the one concerning cattle, which immediately precedes them. See "Jieshi quanrou 戒食犬肉," *Huhai xinwen Yijian xuzhi,* 98.
141. De Groot, "Miséricorde envers les animaux," 479–480 (the same text was published in *Le code du Mâhayâna,* 118–120).

## CHAPTER 4: THE BEEF TABOO AND LATE IMPERIAL CHINESE ETHICS

1. Zhang Erqi 張爾岐, "Guang jiesha niu wen 廣戒殺牛文," *Huangchao jingshi wenbian,* 69.2a–b.
2. The main works are Sakai Tadao, *Zōho Chūgoku zensho;* Brokaw, *Ledgers;* Yau Chi-on, *Quanhua jinzhen* and *Shan yu ren tong;* Goossaert, *Livres de morale.*
3. On the history of spirit-writing, see Goossaert, *Making the Gods Speak.*
4. There were earlier Sacred Edicts during the Ming, but this term usually refers to the sixteen maxims proclaimed by Emperor Kangxi in 1670 and the commentary (*Shengyu guangxun* 聖諭廣訓) by Emperor Yongzheng composed in 1724. This commentary was supposed to be recited in public (*xuanjiang* 宣講) in all villages on the first and fifteenth days of the month. There was a profusion of texts commenting on and adapting *Shengyu guangxun* to simple oral moral instruction. See Mair, "Language and Ideology."
5. On the dating of *Jueshi zhenjing,* see Sakai Tadao, *Zōho Chūgoku zensho,* 2:184–185.
6. Yau Chi-on, *Quanhua jinzhen,* 8.
7. On faithful anticlericalism, see Goossaert and Zuber, "Introduction." Denunciations of the immorality of the clergy are found in most morality books; a particularly ardent case is *Jueshi zhenzong,* edited in 1862 and published in 1875.

8. Clart, "Confucius and the Mediums," speaks more cautiously of "popular Confucianism" only in the case of groups producing and distributing morality books and explicitly claiming a Confucian identity (*ru* 儒). However, such groups did not appear until the late nineteenth century.
9. The debate on the "Confucian" or, conversely, the "consensual" nature of morality books is summarized by Bell, "A Precious Raft," 161–163.
10. This section draws on Goossaert, "Animals and Eschatology."
11. This text is part of a larger set of moral tracts, *Xunshiwen* 訓世文 (Tracts to exhort the world), revealed at an academy in Yuejun 越郡—that is, modern-day Shaoxing, Zhejiang. It does not feature in the first edition (1743) of the *Lüzu quanshu* 全書 (Lüzu canon) but was added as *juan* 25 of the 1774 enlarged Lüzu Canon. It was also included (as part of the *Lüdi wenji* 呂帝文集) in the *Daozang jiyao* 道藏輯要 (1806).
12. Kalpa (*jie* 劫) originally means a cosmic era and can refer particularly to the cataclysmic changes between two such eras. In late imperial Chinese, it referred most often to the idea of an imminent apocalypse.
13. Lai Chi-tim, *Daozang jiyao tiyao.*
14. *Taiwei xianjun gonggu oge* (twelfth century), discussed above, classified animals into useful (those that work for humans) or useless and lesser animals (mostly insects). The *gonggu oge* tradition gradually developed ever more complex systems for attributing moral value to animals. See in particular the early-Qing *Huizuan gonggu oge* 彙纂功過格 (Comprehensive compilation of ledgers of merits and demerits), whose *juan* 8 is entirely devoted to counting merits and demerits in relation to animals.
15. "Ciyi chiyu wen" 慈邑敕諭文, *Guandi quanshu,* 23:522–526. On the Taiping war context for revelations about saving lives, see Goossaert, *Making the Gods Speak,* chap. 8.
16. *Yuding jinke jiyao,* 535.
17. *Yuding jinke jiyao,* 541–543.
18. *Yuding jinke jiyao,* 542.
19. See the various reprint collections documented in the CRTA (Chinese Religious Texts Authority) database, https://crta.info/wiki/Main_Page.
20. *Taishang ganying pian,* 17.7a (7a–9b for commentary).
21. Including *Taishang ganying pian jizhu,* 4la–b; *(Ciguan fenxie ben) Taishang ganying pian yinjing qianzhu,* 72a–73a; *Taishang ganying pian zhu, xia,* 1 lb–13a; *Taishang ganying pian jizhuan,* 2.54a–56a.
22. *Taiwei xianjun gongguo ge,* 2b, gives more merit points to those who save animals that work for humans (horses and cattle) than to other animals but otherwise reproduces the discourse on animal life in general.
23. Sakai Tadao, *Zōho Chūgoku zensho,* 1:509–544; Hu Jiechen, "Wenchang dijun yinzhi wen qiyuan xinyan."
24. The cult of the *Tract on Hidden Rewards* is richly documented in *Records of the Red Cinnamon Palace.* An anecdote reports a man's successes in civil exams despite his lack of literary talent, even though his only daily intellectual activity was to purify himself and recite the *Tract on Hidden Rewards.* See "Feng *Yinzhi wen* 奉陰騭文," *Chishang caotang biji,* 1.21b–22b.
25. Sakai Tadao, *Zōho Chūgoku zensho,* 1:528.

26. An early example, *Gongguo ge zuanyao* 功過格纂要, included in *Dangui ji,* provides for fifty merit points for observing the beef and dogmeat taboo over one's lifetime (as much as helping a poor or threatened orphan), ten points for convincing others to observe this taboo, for saving animal lives except in the event of a ritual banquet, for saving an animal serving humans (cattle, horse, and dog; only five points for other animals), and for revering written characters and cereals. Many other later ledgers have similar content. Note also Xiong Hongbei's 熊弘備 famous *Bu feiqian gongde li* 不費錢功德例, which lists meritorious acts, classified by social groups (scholars, merchants, clergy, etc.), that can be accomplished without spending money. In the general category of acts everyone can practice, we find "not eating the meat of plow cattle and dogs." *Bufeiqian gongde li, Xunsu yigui* 訓俗遺規, 50b, *Wuzhong yigui.*
27. Chard, "Rituals and Scriptures," 40; *Jingzao quanshu,* "biji 避忌," 11b, "qianyin 籤引," 5a. *Xinchu xianchuan liyuan baojuan,* 48a–50a, mentions the role of Zaojun in the retribution inflicted on beef and dog eaters.
28. I have edited the table of contents and a selection of the source texts presented in this section (notably the whole *Niujie huichao*) in Goossaert, "Ming Qing yilai shanshu zhong de niujie wenxian jianjie."
29. *Qianqing tang shumu,* 16.17a. Curiously, these two works are classified as Buddhist books. *Niujin ji* is also mentioned in *Dansheng tang cangshu mu,* 9.19b. An early eighteenth-century text quotes an anecdote excerpted from *Jieniu huibian* 戒牛彙編 (which is not found in the extant version of *Jieniu huichao*). It is impossible to determine whether this is an alternative title for one of these two texts or another text altogether. "Jinniu zengshou 禁牛增壽," *Wanshan xianzi ji* 萬善先資集, j. 1, *Anshi quanshu,* n.p.
30. *(Chongzhen) Zhaoqing fuzhi,* j. 41.
31. *Guang'ai lu,* 43b–44a. This passage is also cited in "Guang'ai lu," *Chishang caotang biji,* 2.62a.
32. My warmest thanks go to Jérôme Bourgon, who obtained a copy of this work for me. This work may be identical to Ding Mingdeng's *Jieniu shu,* but I believe that this is unlikely.
33. "*Niujie huichao* xu 牛戒彙鈔序," *Zheng zhongcheng gongyilou ji,* j. 1.
34. "Shu *Niujie huichao* houba 書牛戒彙鈔後跋," *Jin Wentong gong ji,* 10.7a–8a.
35. *Tongshan lu,* 8.1a–3a. The introduction also states that the material in *Niujie huichao* was included in another work, *Haosheng lu* 好生錄, of which I have not found any trace.
36. *Guisi cungao,* 9:268–269. *Niujie xuchao* in three *juan* is mentioned in several official sources (*Huangchao wenxian tongkao,* 227.23b; *Huangchao tongzhi,* 101.14b; *[Qinding] Siku quanshu zongmu,* 133:1753), but it seems to have disappeared.
37. "Shanshi huasu shu 善世化俗疏," *Jianji tang wenji,* 1.28b–31b. This source names a book titled *Jiesha huichao,* but it must be a mistake or copying error for *Niujie huichao.*
38. *Dangui ji,* 3.5b; *Lizhi cuoyao,* 62. In these two sources, this text is attributed to the emperor, without allusion to Wei Yijie, and titled *Jieniu wen* 戒牛文.
39. *Qing shilu,* Shunzhi 11-5-*jiawu* (June 19, 1654), 83:653.
40. "Chongqin *Niujie huichao* xu 重鋟牛戒彙鈔序," *Gushan Weilin chanshi huanshanlu,* 4.665b–666a.

41. *Chenzhonglu,* 88a–92a; this is followed by a similar section on the taboo against dog meat, "Jiequan huichao 戒犬彙抄."
42. Hu Jiechen, "Xu Qian xiaokao."
43. Notably *Tongshan lu,* j. 8, and *Liangyan suoji,* "Jiesha fangsheng," 45a–55b. The following are two cases in which texts on cattle are mixed in with texts on nonkilling: *Haosheng jiujie bian* and *Qingshi duo* (a poetry collection that has sections on moral themes), chapters "Jiesha 戒殺" and "Aiwu 愛物," 906–921.
44. *Shuijing lu,* 16a–b. It is unusual for the title to omit the negative after *quan* 勸, "exhort" (not to kill), but this implied negative is the obvious meaning. The poem is found in *Zunsheng bajian,* 2:80, and later in *Liangyan suoji,* 52b–53a. The version in *Zunsheng bajian* (an anthology of longevity techniques published in 1591) features some variations and another quote from Zhenwu's revelation "Instructions on the Taboo against Cattle and Dogs." It is difficult to determine whether one is the source of the other.
45. *Huizuan gongguo ge jian zhushi,* 8.1a–20b. On this work, see Brokaw, *Ledgers,* 157–171.
46. This coherence is far from perfect. This is not only because of the different theoretical foundations of refraining from killing and the taboo. It can also be caused by sloppy editing: for instance, a point concerning meritorious animals (cattle, horses, and dogs) is illustrated by an anecdote about a man who tries to save a sheep. See *Huizuan gongguo ge jian zhushi,* 8.3b–4a.
47. The story of Li Yi 李鎰, *Dangui ji,* 3.8a, and the story of Bao Rubin 包如賓, *Yinzhi wen zhuzheng,* 22a. In *Taishang ganying pian zhu, xia,* 12b–13a, the commentator concludes a long elaboration by writing, "Do not kill [animals], and above all do not eat beef."
48. "Wu qing zaisha 勿輕宰殺," *Jueshi zhengzong,* 7.4b–5a. See also "Guansheng dijun xianying jieshi wen 關聖帝君顯應戒士文," *Dangui ji* (discontinuous pagination), which was revealed in 1775.
49. *Yinzhi wen tuzheng,* 81b (according to which the term was used in Tianjin); *Xinchu xianchuan liyuan baojuan,* 49b; "Niu bao'en 牛報恩," *Chishang caotang biji,* 6.15b–16b; "Feng quan jie shi niuquan wen 奉勸戒食牛犬文," *Shenbao,* July 22, 1872. This specific definition of the term *banzhai* must be distinguished from that common in Buddhism, which designates the midday meal. Another expression for abstaining from beef is "a fast for peace," *ping'an zhai* 平安齋. Liu Zhaoyuan, *Haizhou minsu zhi,* 110.
50. *Jiujie jingchan* 救劫經懺, in *Guandi quanshu,* 33.37b–38b.
51. *Lü Chunyang zushi quanshi jie shi niuquan* 呂純陽祖師勸世戒食牛犬, *Dangui ji* (discontinuous pagination).
52. "Zou sisisi Jie sha niu wen 鄒司四司戒殺牛文," *Jueshi zhengzong,* 9.29a–30b.
53. Goossaert, *Livres de morale,* 22–23.
54. In the earlier version of *Tract on Hidden Rewards,* the beef taboo was formulated differently but already paired with reverence for written characters.
55. Liang Qizi, *Shishan yu jiaohua,* 172–203; Fuma Susumu, *Chūgoku zenkai,* 651 and passim; Ye Xiaoqing, *The Dianshizhai Pictorial,* 213–217; Chau, "Script Fundamentalism."
56. *Laojun yibaibashi jie,* precept 112, *Yunji qiqian,* 39.5b, is the oldest known precept to revere characters.

57. "Dahua ge 大化歌," *Jueshi zhengzong,* 1.5b, but the parallel structure is a little less pronounced here than in *Tract on Hidden Rewards* and *True Scripture to Awaken Humanity,* and therefore the association is less striking. In *Taishang ganying pian,* the interdiction to eat only sacrificial meat was already associated with reverence for cereals.
58. On revering cereals, see Liu Zhiwan, *Chūgoku dōkyō no matsuri to shinkō,* 1:77–240, and Sakai Tadao, *Zōho Chūgoku zensho,* 2:164–168.
59. Bell, "A Precious Raft," 180, elaborates on how the abundance of commentaries on morality books stifles the sacredness of revelation. In this case, such an argument does not seem convincing since the commentaries cite other revelations.
60. *Dangui ji* (discontinuous pagination).
61. There are at least a dozen, most of which are listed below.
62. *Renpu leiji, xia,* 72a–73b. The author nevertheless is careful to quote Zhenwu's text while saying, "formerly it was said that," rather than naming the divinity. On Liu Zongzhou's strictly Confucian position in morality books, see Brokaw, *Ledgers,* 121–138.
63. Allusion to *Mengzi,* "Liang Huiwang, shang 梁惠王上." On this rite, see Rom, "Beat the Drums." This ancient rite of consecration no longer corresponded to actual practice when the song was composed.
64. *Fuyou shangdi Chunyang Lüzu tianshi shiji,* 3.19b–20a. Other versions (with some variations) in *Tongshan lu,* 8.3b–4a; *Liangyan suoji,* 54a–b; *Yinzhi wen xiangzhu,* 3.51a–52a; and *Guandi quanshu,* 17.17b–18a.
65. *Liji jijie,* "Wangzhi 王制," 354.
66. *Mengzi,* "Liang Huiwang, shang."
67. For example, the anecdote of Jiang Jian in *Jueshi zhenjing zhuzheng,* 17.16b, was excerpted from "Jiang Jian shiniu," *Yijian zhi,* 788–790 (discussed in chapter 3). The anecdote of the short poem sent by divine emissaries (*Dangui ji,* 3.8b) very closely resembles "Shiniu shi," *Yijian zhi,* 295 (discussed in chapter 3). The story of Ma Shize 馬世澤 (*Dangui ji,* 3.9a) was excerpted from "Zhushizi," *Jishen lu,* 133.
68. On the lore about the religious justification for examination success and failure, see Elman, *A Cultural History,* chap. 6.
69. For example, the story of Li Hua 李華, *Dangui ji,* 3.6a–b; the story of Li Tian 李田, *Dangui ji,* 3.6b; the story of Zhu Zhifan 朱之蕃, *Dangui ji,* 3.6b–7a; the story of Li Yi, *Dangui ji,* 3.8a; the story of Mr. Gu 顧, *Xichao renjian, shang,* 3.32b–33a. Henceforth, anecdotes without a title will be cited by the protagonist's name. Other texts often quote the same anecdotes, sometimes in abbreviated form or with slightly different wording, but I do not provide an exhaustive list. The author of one anecdote describes two bovines charging with their horns to force the chief examiner to pass a candidate who observes the taboo. See *Huizuan gongguo ge jian zhushi,* 8.3a–b. Elman, *A Cultural History,* 307n30, also cites a case of passing exams thanks to the winner's family not eating beef for three generations.
70. The story of Chen Xingyuan 陳星垣, *Xichao renjian, shang,* 3.32a; the story of Bao Rubin, *Yinzhi wen zhuzheng,* 22a (here, merit is linked to the act of having circulated texts urging people to observe the taboo); the story of Xiao Liangju 蕭良駒, *Jueshi zhenjing zhuzheng,* 16.56b; *Juguan rixing lu,* 5.50a–b.

71. A beefeater was about to be killed by an ox when he made a vow in his mind and was saved. *Chongming manlu,* 2.2a–b.
72. The story of Zhu Zhifan, *Dangui ji,* 3.6b–7a. On the importance of making a vow before the gods to strengthen the followers' determination to uphold the taboo, see *Huizuan gongguo ge jian zhushi,* 8.3a.
73. "Feng quanjie shi niuquan wen," *Shenbao,* July 22, 1872.
74. *Haosheng jiujie bian,* 5.3b.
75. The story of the yamen employee, *Dangui ji,* 3.7b–8a.
76. The story of Ma Shize, *Dangui ji,* 3.9a (the earlier version of this story in *Jishen lu,* 133, did not include this edifying conclusion).
77. The story of Jiang Zheng 姜徵, *Yinzhi wen xiangzhu,* 3.53a–b. In "Niujie," *Chishang caotang biji,* 3.55a–b, the protagonist is punished because his servants eat beef, but he can redeem himself by convincing 110 families to make a vow.
78. The story of Jing Shixiang 景世庠, *Jueshi zhenjing zhuzheng,* 17.16b–17a. This story dates from the Yuan since it is found in *Jujia biyong shilei quanji, guiji* 癸集, 59b–60a.
79. The anecdote dating from about 1586 is cited and analyzed by Smith, "Liberating Animals," 56, 66. In an anecdote taken from an unidentified collection and quoted in *(Tongzhi) Guangxin fuzhi,* 12.45b–46a, an official traveling on a boat was caught in a storm. He realized that the storm was caused by the spirits of vengeful cattle. He promised to enforce the interdiction against slaughter very strictly, and the storm subsided immediately.
80. "Quanjie shiniu zhiyuan shu 勸戒食牛志願書," *Gengniu lei,* 11a–b, in which the document sent to the god is signed by both the person vowing to abstain from beef and by a guarantor.
81. "Ganyinglu ceshi 感應錄冊式," *Niujie jilu,* 19a–b; also, with some modifications, in *Aiwu pian,* 36–38. See the edited text of the vow in Goossaert, "Ming Qing yilai shanshu zhong de niujie wenxian jianjie."
82. Wang Guang's 王光 story, *Dangui ji,* 3.9a–b.
83. "Niujie," *Chishang caotang biji,* 3.54a.
84. The story of Hu Duo 胡鐸, *Dangui ji,* 3.7a–b; the story of Yang Lizhai 楊立齋, *Dangui ji,* 3.8b (in this case, the City god executes the punishment); the story of the literati Jiang 姜學士, *Dangui ji,* 3.8a–b; the story of Wu Heng 吳恒, *Huizuan gongguo ge jian zhushi,* 8.17a; "Shaye xianxiao 殺業現消," "Shasheng ebao tuzai 殺生惡報一屠宰," *Fangsheng shasheng xianbao lu,* n.p. "Mingyou queji 冥游確記," *Chishang caotang biji,* 4.14a–17a, recounts a sick woman's journey into hell in detail. She visits the hells reserved for those who have killed animals. There, the first tribunal deals with beefeaters. Another long story of a cattle killer's journey to hell is found in "Ming duan zui an 冥斷罪案," *Kuangyuan zazhi,* 2.21b–23a.
85. The story of Li Hua, *Dangui ji,* 3.6a–b.
86. The story of Pan Qiniang 潘七娘, *Dangui ji,* 3.9a; the story of Mr. Wang 王, *Yinzhi wen zhuzheng,* 22a; the story of butcher Zhang 張, *Xichao renjian, xia,* 3.23a; "Tuniu ebao 屠牛惡報," *Kuaixue tang manlu,* 11a–b; "Fengshi zi tuniu bao 馮氏子屠牛報," *Kuaiyuan,* 7:619; *Yuewei caotang biji,* 10:204–205; the story of butcher Lu 陸, *Jueshi zhenjing zhuzheng,* 17.16b; "Mou tuniu 某屠

牛," *Zhiyi xubian,* 4.7a–8a; a Hui butcher is killed by an ox in 1596, *(Qinding) Xu Wenxian tongkao,* 227.13a–b; "Zainiu zhi bao 宰牛之報," *Guobao wenjian lu,* 23a–b; "Xiaoniu 孝牛," *Gusheng xubian,* 4.4b–5b; "Pi lian niubei 皮連牛背," *Kuangyuan zazhi,* 2.7b; "Niu shang wuren 牛傷五人," *Shenbao,* December 14, 1880; "Niu shang erming 牛傷二命," *Shenbao,* January 27, 1877; "Suyuan xinwen 蘇垣新聞," *Shenbao,* October 3, 1878; *Haosheng jiujie bian,* 5.6b–7a. "Shasheng ebao—tuzai," *Fangsheng shasheng xianbao lu,* summarizes several of these anecdotes and cites others.

87. "Wuxia suotan 吳下瑣談," *Shenbao,* November 1, 1877. A childless peasant had an old, sick bovine that he wanted to sell to a butcher, but the animal begged him, and he reconsidered. The bovine died of natural causes, and a child, who appeared to be the reincarnated bovine, was born to the peasant. The whole village then vowed to refrain from selling cattle to butchers.
88. The story of Zhao Yifeng 趙一鳳, *Jueshi zhenjing zhuzheng,* 17.17a–b.
89. "Tuniu zhi bao," *Huadang ge congtan,* 6:156–159. This anecdote cites several other cases of retribution inflicted on beef butchers.
90. Most poems of lamentation follow this tripartite structure, but in one notable case, a poem of lamentation incorporates many other themes in passing, such as the protection granted by the gods and success in civil exams promised to those who observe the taboo, the frequent failure to observe the prohibition against slaughter, the fact that bovines are reincarnated beefeaters, and so forth. "Gengniu qiming ge 耕牛乞命歌," *Yinzhi wen guangyi* 陰騭文廣義, in *Anshi quanshu,* n.p.
91. "Jieshi niurou wen 戒食牛肉文," *Guandi quanshu,* 23.40b–41b.
92. Yan Diaoyu's 嚴調御 "Tuniu tan 屠牛嘆," *Niujie huichao,* 5a–b; Zhixian's 智舷 "Gengniu bie zhu 耕牛別主," *Niujie huichao,* 5b–6a.
93. Shi Runzhang's 施閏章 (1619–1683) "Bei laoniu 悲老牛," *Qingshi duo,* 907; Duanmu Guohu's 端木國瑚 "Mainiu ci 賣牛詞," *Qingshi duo,* 914; Chen Guangning's 陳廣寧 "Jie shiniu ge 戒食牛歌," *Qingshi duo,* 916; Chen Laitai's 陳來泰 "Zhiniu xing 質牛行," *Qingshi duo,* 921. Ye Shijian's 葉士鑑 "Laoniu ge 老牛歌," *Qingshi duo,* 917, develops the same themes but does not make the bovine speak in the first person. In these poems, the themes of the bovine's revenge and retribution are almost absent, except for Shi Runzhang's "Bei laoniu," which elaborates on them.
94. An example in Hokkien in Sun Yinrui, "Niurou chengwei fushipin," 51.
95. *Dangui ji,* 3.5b–6a.
96. "Liu lao xianshi jie daniu wen 柳老仙師戒打牛文," *Jueshi zhengzong,* 9.31a–32b, revealed in 1855. The next text in this anthology warned those who mistreated dogs. See "Lüzu xianshi jie dagou wen 呂祖仙師戒打狗文," *Jueshi zhengzong,* 9.33a–34, revealed a few months before the previous one.
97. Chen Wenshu's "Fangniu xing," *Qingshi duo,* 915.
98. "Mainiu ge. Quan wu zaisha gengniu ye 賣牛歌.勸勿宰殺耕牛也," *Qingshi duo,* 466; Jiang Shiquan's 蔣士銓 "Mainiu tu ge 賣牛圖歌," *Qingshi duo,* 449. The pinnacle of this dark, realistic poetry was reached by Zhu Guchang's 朱穀昌 "Mainiu yao 賣牛謠," *Qingshi duo,* 460–461, and by "Mainiu xing 賣牛行," *Qingshi duo,* 462, both of which reminded the tearful peasant who sold his bovine that there were even worse cases: mothers who sold their children.

99. A morality book from the late seventeenth century considered the case of the peasant who was too poor to be able to afford to keep an old bovine: he should try to find a good person who would buy the animal rather than sell it to the butcher, and then the merit will be shared between the two. See *Huizuan gongguo ge jian zhushi,* 8.3b.
100. *Cui fujun ci lu,* 23b. Magistrate Cui, known to travel between the courts of this world and those of the hereafter, was the object of worship from the Tang onward. He was revered as an infallible judge and an exorcist in his hometown of Ci and other places. His cult was closely associated with those of Dizang and Eastern Peak. The Song, who had received divine help from Cui during the war against the Jin, established temples for him in Hangzhou, which remained active until the twentieth century. *Cui fujun ci lu* is a gazetteer of these Hangzhou temples.
101. "Zou sisisi Jiesha niu wen," *Jueshi zhengzong,* 9.29a–30b.
102. Untitled poem, *Liangyan suoji,* 53a–54a. "Treatise on the Love for Cattle" (*Ainiu shuo* 愛牛說) by Li Kai 李楷 (active in early Qing), which was cited in various texts, such as *Taishang ganying pian jizhuan,* 2.54b, also seems to have dealt with the theme of the horrors of butchering.
103. *Juguan rixing lu,* 5.52a–b, citing *Yanxing huizuan* 言行彙纂.
104. *Huainan honglie jijie,* chap. 13, "Fanlunxun 氾論訓," 460.
105. Elisseeff, "Les enterrements d'animaux," argues in favor of the thesis that the practice of animal burials declined after the end of antiquity.
106. Eliasberg, "Pratiques funéraires animales."
107. *Juguan rixing lu,* 5.50a–b.
108. "Niu bao'en," *Chishang caotang biji,* 6.15b–16b; likewise "Niu jiangshi 牛僵尸," *Zi buyu quanji,* 250. In "Niu bao," *Xinzheng lu,* 39a, a peasant promised his bovine to bury it when it died but ended up selling it to the butcher, who offered him a large sum. The bovine meted out cruel revenge. "Niu baochou 牛報仇," *Shenbao,* September 18, 1872, depicted an elderly and sick bovine unfit for work, which its owner promised to let live until its natural death. The owner changed his mind, sold it to the butcher, and then died after falling victim to the betrayed animal's vengeance.
109. Wen Qixiang's 聞啟祥 (fl. 1612) "Jie shaniu wen yin 戒殺牛文引," *Niujie huichao,* 3a–b.
110. According to the sources cited by Sun Yinrui, "Niurou chengwei fushipin," 57, most cattle in Taiwan were buried until the early twentieth century.
111. Xu Hualong, "Baishe zhuan yu yinshi wenhua," 272–273. The story of the White Serpent first appeared in the Tang, but the version in question dates from the Ming or Qing.
112. I am very grateful to Barbara Ambros for pointing out this interpretation; in Japan, sacrificial offerings of fish were also often discarded in waterways.
113. Shen Donglu's 沈東麓 "Jie shi quan shuo 戒食犬說," *Tongshan lu,* 8.44b–45a; "Beidou xingjun jie shi quanrou wen 北斗星君戒食犬肉文," *Guandi quanshu,* 17.18a–19a; and "Jie shi quanrou wen 戒食犬肉文," *Guandi quanshu,* 23.40b–41b. See also "Lüzu xianshi jie dagou wen," *Jueshi zhengzong,* 9.33a–34. *Huizuan gongguo ge jian zhushi* from the late seventeenth century accords great importance to dogs, with specific injunctions to bury them

(8.16b), not to beat them (8.19b), and so forth. Anecdotes concerning the taboo against dogs became quite numerous from the seventeenth century. The following list is not exhaustive: the story of Mr. Wang 王, *Yinzhi wen zhuzheng,* 22a; the story of Zhang Jingwen 張景文, *Yinzhi wen zhuzheng,* 22b; the story of Cai the Sixth 蔡六, *Xichao renjian, xia,* 3.23b–24a; "Wang jishi shiquanbao 王給事食犬報," *Kuaiyuan,* 7:618; "Qin shi zi shagou bao 欽氏子殺狗報," *Kuaiyuan,* 7:613. These stories highlight the dogs' vengeance by killing dog eaters or tearing up their corpses. Some anecdotes associate not observing the beef and dog taboos with the same punishments. See the stories of Jing Shixiang and Zhao Yifeng, *Jueshi zhenjing zhuzheng,* 17.16b–17b; "Quan bao 犬報," *Chishang caotang biji,* 6.68; five anecdotes in "Shasheng ebao tuzai," *Fangsheng shasheng xianbao lu,* n.p.

114. *Tongshan lu,* 8.3a. "Shu Beifang jin zao niuzhu hou 書北方禁造牛燭後," *Shenbao,* September 19, 1873, considered it unjust to elevate dogs to the same level as bovines.
115. Dog funerals were indeed practiced since antiquity. See Elisseeff, "Les enterrements d'animaux."
116. "Lifu shigou 李婦食狗," *Tixuan zhenren xianyi lu,* 11a–b (a collection of the miracles attributed to the Complete Transcendance patriarch Wang Chuyi 王處一, 1142–1217); "Liu Juhui jiaoshe 劉居晦醮設," *Yijian zhi,* Zhigui 支癸, 5, 1260 (on this anecdote, see Davis, *Society and the Supernatural,* 167–169).
117. "Jieshi quanrou," *Huhai xinwen Yijian xuzhi,* 98, discussed the taboo against dogs very explicitly and justified it by the notion that dogs were reincarnated humans, but the text also mentioned the Daoist rule; likewise, *Da Ming Renxiao huanghou quanshan shu,* 12.10a–b, 10b–11a.
118. Elisseeff, "L'étrange goût du chien"; Wang Lihua, *Zhonggu Huabei yinshi wenhua,* 115–116.
119. Anderson, *The Food of China,* 39, 179, 211; Sangji Zhaxi, *Xuquan tongling,* 237–246. While ignoring the Daoist taboo, both mention the Muslim interdiction against dogs to explain the virtual disappearance of dog consumption in North China from the Tang onward, which is very unconvincing. For a comparative approach to interdictions against dogs, see Simoons, *Eat Not This Flesh,* chap. 7, and White, *Myths of the Dog-Man.*
120. "Jie shiniu ming 戒食牛銘," *Tongshan lu,* 8.4b–5a, exalted the merit of dogs and horses but stated that bovines had even greater merit. *Guang'ai lu,* 46b–47a, lamented the slaughter of donkeys, recalled that epidemic diseases afflicted those who ate horses and cattle, and specified that in addition to cattle and dogs, it was also forbidden to eat donkeys and horses.
121. "Zou sisisi jie sha niu wen," *Jueshi zhengzong,* 9.29a–30b.
122. Feng Pei's 馮培 "Luo ma shi yao 騾馬市謠," *Qingshi duo,* 920, described the market for unfit horses in Beijing and lamented the fate of animals that had faithfully served humans before suffering this unworthy fate. Several other poems in this collection expressed deep pity for horses, mules, and donkeys. *Zhongyang yanjiuyuan Ming Qing dang'an,* A194–98 and A214–131, mentions two cases of horse butchers being arrested in Beijing in 1757 and 1772.

123. A tract on the interdiction on eels is included in a collection of eschatological spirit-written revelations composed during the Taiping war, which had many texts on animal lives: *Jiushengchuan,* 3.54b–55a.
124. Wang Wan's 汪琬 (1624–1691) "Shi shan luo shuo 食鱔蠃說," *Huangchao jingshi wenbian,* 69.2b; Wen Qixiang's (fl. 1612) "Jie shaniu wen yin," *Niujie huichao,* 3a–b, mentions a magistrate (a devotee of Zhenwu?) who prohibited fishing for eels and turtles.
125. For example, "Quan wu shi wa 勸勿食蛙," *Wanshan xianzi ji,* j. 2, *Anshi quanshu,* n.p. "Ji shi tianji 忌食田雞," *Liuhu,* 4:249–250, is an anecdote on the retribution for eating frogs that is very similar to the anecdotes concerning the beef taboo. Some magistrates prohibited killing frogs in the 1870s. See Fuma Susumu, *Chūgoku zenkai,* 657.
126. "Jiachu jiesha dan 家廚戒殺單," *Shenbao,* February 14, 1874. Similarly, *Xinchu xianchuan liyuan baojuan,* 48a–50a, specifies interdictions against cattle, frogs, crabs, turtles, and eels.
127. "Zou sisisi Jie sha niu wen," revealed in 1858, *Jueshi zhengzong,* 9.29a–30b, associates the sacrifice to heaven with this justification.
128. *Lü Chunyang zushi quanshijie shi niuquan, Dangui ji* (discontinuous pagination).
129. Alexander, "Virtues of the Vernacular," chap. 3.
130. *Xinchu xianchuan liyuan baojuan,* 48a–50a.
131. Alexander, *Teaching and Transformation*; Meyer-Fong, *What Remains,* chap. 2.
132. *Guang'ai lu,* 27a; Smith, "Liberating Animals," 61. I have not found the source in Chen Di's writings. Another anecdote used the same expression, *buxiao buren,* because eating beef amounted to insulting the ancestors who made their family observe this taboo. See *Haosheng jiujie bian,* 5.10b–12a.
133. *Guang'ai lu,* 29a–b.
134. *Xingshi yinyuan zhuan,* 2.
135. "Jin sizai gengniu bei 禁私宰耕牛碑" (1866), *Fengshan xian caifang ce,* 367–368.
136. Wen Qixiang's (fl. 1612) "Jie shaniu wen yin," *Niujie huichao,* 3a–b.
137. "Jiangsu ancha si yongjin Suzhou sizai gengniu bei 江蘇按察司永禁蘇州私宰耕牛碑" (1807), *Ming Qing yilai Suzhou shehui shi beike ji,* 574.
138. Yan Diaoyu's "Tuniu tan," *Niujie huichao,* 5a–b.
139. Holm, *Killing a Buffalo,* 205–215, also notes that among the Zhuang and various other ethnic groups in southern China, the water buffalo was the only animal that could be ritually assimilated or exchanged with a human.
140. On the consumption of beef in *Shuihu zhuan,* see Guo Jian, "Liangshan haohan"; Sun Yinrui, *Niurou chengwei fushipin,* 22–27; Liang Yan, "Beef, Fish, and Chestnut Cake"; Yue, "Beefy Outlaws."
141. Similarly, in Muslim literature, the consumption of horses is sometimes treated as close to cannibalism. See Benkheira, *Islâm et interdits alimentaires,* 99.
142. Chong, *Cannibalism in China,* mentions "learned cannibalism"; by contrast, Anderson, *The Food of China,* 82, denies the reality of such practices.
143. Zheng Yi, *Scarlet Memorial;* Sutton, "Consuming Counterrevolution."
144. Shahar, *Chinese Animal Gods;* Idema and Olof, *The Legend of Prince Golden Calf.*
145. Doolittle, *Social Life of the Chinese,* 188–191, cites and translates excerpts from several texts mentioned here, demonstrating their wide distribution.

146. Durand-Dastès, *La conversion de l'Orient.* I would like to thank Vincent Durand-Dastès for his help during my research on the beef taboo in Chinese novels.
147. *Xu Jinpingmei,* chap. 14, 129–132.
148. The story of Zhu Zhifan, *Dangui ji,* 3.6b–7a.
149. *Dongdu ji,* 676, 710–716, 793; Durand-Dastès, *La conversion de l'Orient.*
150. Li, a Beijing native, held various low-ranking administrative positions and is also known for his scholarly works. For an analysis of the novel's ideology, see Eberhard, "Ideas about Social Reforms," 419, which mentions the beef taboo, and Hsia, "The Scholar-Novelist."
151. *Jinghua yuan,* chap. 12, 74–75.
152. For an analysis of this play as a work of moral propaganda, see Guo Qitao, *Ritual Opera.*
153. On Yu Zhi, see in particular Yau Chi-on, *Quanhua jinzhen,* 99–110; Fuma Susumu, *Chūgoku zenkai,* 329–336, 345–362; and Alexander, "Virtues of the Vernacular," chap. 3; on his actions to protect animal life, see also Smith, "Liberating Animals," 67–68.
154. Yau Chi-on, *Quanhua jinzhen,* 108.
155. Huntington, "Singing Punishment and Redemption."
156. For another contemporaneous case of a play devoted to moral themes, in this case, the good conduct of officials, see Will, "La virtue administrative au théâtre."
157. For a German translation of this play, see Forke, *Elf chinesische Singspieltexte,* 375–390.
158. The reincarnation of a beef butcher as a bovine was frequently mentioned in other texts, such as *Liangyan suoji,* 53a–54a.
159. *Yinzhi wen xiangzhu,* 3.53a, 54a, 55a; *Yinzhi wen tushuo,* 22a, 23a; *Yinzhi wen tuzheng,* 81a.
160. "Guang jiesha niu wen," *Huangchao jingshi wenbian,* 69.2a.
161. Doolittle, *Social Life of the Chinese,* 188. A tract noted by Doolittle added an exhortation not to practice female infanticide.
162. De Groot, "Miséricorde envers les animaux," 481.
163. *Haosheng jiujie bian,* 5.10b–12a.
164. Doré, *Recherches sur les superstitions,* pt. 1, vol. 2, chap. 8, article 10, plate opposite p. 308; *Taiwan guanxi jishi,* 112; Li Lulu, *Chunniu bidi,* 273–276; Eberhard, *A Dictionary of Chinese Symbols,* cited by Ye Xiaoqing, *The Dianshizhai Pictorial,* 224n115.
165. Zhang Zuji, *Kejia jiu lisu,* 283–284. The version reproduced by Zhang Zuji is less influenced by Buddhism than figure 2 (which also mentions refraining from killing). Instead, Zhang's version emphasizes the impurity of beef and epidemic diseases afflicting those who eat it.
166. Zheng Tuyou, *Niu wenhua yu rensheng,* 55.
167. This quote may also be there to warn the reader not to discard the leaflet.
168. Poon, "'Husheng' yu 'Jintu.'"
169. For example, a memorandum used for children's education in the nineteenth century stated that families abstaining from eating beef, dogs, and frogs would be spared from epidemics. See "Mengguan tiaoyue 蒙館條約," *Deyi lu,* 10:635.

## CHAPTER 5: THE BEEF TABOO IN LATE IMPERIAL CHINESE SOCIETY

1. Doolittle was in China (in Fuzhou) from 1850 to 1864, where he was employed by the American Board of Commissioners for Foreign Missions.
2. Doolittle, *Social Life of the Chinese,* 186–191.
3. De Groot, "Miséricorde envers les animaux," 478, 481. See also *North China Herald,* August 16, 1873: "Domestic cattle are triply sacred. . . . The Chinese, indifferent as regard sheep and pigs, really consider the habitual killing of cows, wicked." And "All kinds of animal food enter into their diet except beef. The protection both of religion and custom has been thrown around horned cattle."
4. *Juguan rixing lu,* 5.46a.
5. "Zai jin zainiu 再禁宰牛," *Zongzhi Zhe Min wenxi,* 4.64a–65a, estimated that around seven thousand cattle were slaughtered annually in Hangzhou in the late Ming.
6. Guo Jian, "Liangshan haohan," 107–108.
7. *Suiyuan shidan,* 32, explained how to buy beef and provided a beef tongue recipe. The introduction specified that this was an unusual kind of meat for the southern Chinese, like mutton and venison. The unique and concise beef recipe is in stark contrast with an entire chapter on pork and several mutton recipes.
8. *Liweng mishu,* 166.
9. Several anthologies or encyclopedias such as *Zunsheng bajian* or *Jujia biyong shilei quanji* contain both morality texts on the taboo and practical indications on preparing beef.
10. Spence, "Ch'ing," 273–274.
11. "Fangniu xing," by Chen Wenshu, *Qingshi duo,* 915; *Taiwan guanxi jishi,* 110–111; *Xing'an huilan,* 12.5a, which uses both *juandian* and *tangguo.*
12. "Luo ma shi yao," by Feng Pei, *Qingshi duo,* 920; *Xing'an huilan,* 12.5a. Regarding sanctions against horse butchers, see *Zhongyang yanjiuyuan Ming Qing dang'an,* A194–98, A214–131 (dated 1757 and 1772).
13. See an illustration of violent cattle butchers in *Tuhua ribao,* 2842, published in 1909.
14. "Roucheng huozhong 肉成火種," "Shashen gebao—tuzai," *Fangsheng shasheng xianbao lu,* n.p.
15. "Niu tao ming 牛討命," *Shenbao,* October 1, 1872, recounted the story of a butcher who made a peasant believe that his bovine was seriously ill, bought it from him, and slaughtered it. He soon became the victim of a cruel death.
16. "Zainiu chengshi 宰牛成市," *Shenbao,* November 20, 1881, described a town, bordering several districts, that was inhabited by the owners of gambling houses and cattle butchers, who bought animals from peasants in financial distress.
17. "Fazhike 法制科," *Taopi gongdu,* 80a.
18. "Tanmeng langsi 貪萌浪死," "Shasheng ebao—tuzai," *Fangsheng shasheng xianbao lu,* n.p.
19. "Xiaoniu," *Gusheng xubian,* 4.4b–5b, dated 1684, contains the story of two peasants who bought a pregnant cow at the cattle market. When the castrated

calf became fit for work in the fields, they slaughtered the cow and sold the meat. The calf took revenge by goring one of the peasants.

20. *(Ciguan fenxie ben) Taishang ganying pian yinjing qianzhu,* 72a–b; *Taishang ganying pian jizhuan,* 2.54a.
21. Traditionally, Chinese butchers cooked the offal and low-quality pieces after slaughter but sold the premium cuts. See Furubayashi Morihiro, "Sōdai no tosatsu." An itinerant beef vendor was portrayed in a nineteenth-century painted album depicting small Chinese trades and intended for Western audiences: Huang Shijian and Sargent, *Shijing fengqing,* 279.
22. Golvers, *François de Rougemont,* 613, 624; Spence, "Ch'ing," 290 (data dating from 1675 and 1790, respectively).
23. "Duo zai gengniu 多宰耕牛," *Shenbao,* January 13, 1877. The price of beef dropped from 200 to 90 cash per pound (*jin*) during a great famine in North China. A bit later, at the height of the famine ("Henan jinshi 河南近事," *Shenbao,* November 26, 1877), it fell to 50 cash and became "the only cheap product."
24. *Taizong Wen huangdi shengxun,* 6.10a–11a.
25. *Qing shilu,* Shunzhi 11–5–*jiawu* (June 19, 1654), 83:653.
26. "Yuzhi *Niujie huichao* xu 御製牛戒彙鈔序," *Tongshan lu,* 8.1a–3a.
27. *Qing shilu,* Yongzheng 7–4–*xinsi* (May 4, 1729), 80:47–48; Yongzheng 7–6–*bingshen* (July 18, 1729), 82:91–92 (also *Shizong Xian huangdi shengxun,* 7.9a–10b); Jiaqing 10–12–*bingxu* (January 26, 1806), 154:1121–1122—this last edict mentions the *Tract on Hidden Rewards.* These three edicts were motivated by the issue of Hui beef butchery in Beijing, a topic to which we will return.
28. Mair, "Language and Ideology"; Takeuchi Fusaji, "Qingmo Sichuan." In most cases, the public recitation of the Sacred Edicts quickly became a mere formality without a real audience or even fell into oblivion. Still, some activists here and there tried to revive the practice at the end of the imperial era.
29. Sakai Tadao, *Zōho Chūgoku zensho,* 2:13–40.
30. I think that here, "Buddhist texts" (*fodian* 佛典) should be understood as religious texts in the broadest sense.
31. *Niujie huichao,* 1a.
32. Fan Shike's 樊世珂 "Wu zai gengniu 勿宰耕牛," *(Qianlong) Cangzhou zhi,* 15.74b–75a.
33. *Shizong Xian huangdi shangyu neige,* 66.18a–19a.
34. *Da Qing huidian shili,* 522.11a (1886 edition).
35. Spence, "Ch'ing," 283.
36. *Da Qing huidian shili,* 522.11a–b (1886 edition).
37. *Juguan rixing lu,* 5.4.8b; "Jie shaniu wen yin" by Wen Qixiang (fl. 1612), *Niujie huichao,* 3a–b, mentioned a magistrate who arrived at his new posting and noted that a tax in kind (horns, skin, and tendons) was levied on cattle slaughter (in fact, from the Song, horns, skin, and tendons were given to the yamen when permission to slaughter a sick or old bovine was granted). He banned this practice, which probably meant that he even prohibited the slaughter of unfit cattle, which many other magistrates authorized. A note written by a magistrate in 1890 (added to an eighteenth-century gazetteer)

recounted that he prohibited cattle slaughter that had been tolerated and taxed by his predecessor. *(Qianlong) Xu Yaozhou zhi,* 4.19b. *Taiwan tongshi,* 23:606, also mentioned a tax on beef butchers called *niuhu* 牛戶.

38. An eighteenth-century morality book enjoined magistrates not to content themselves with issuing prohibitions but to take concrete actions. "Jinwei lu—Jinyue bu 謹微錄–禁約部," *Wanshan xianzi ji,* j. 4, *Anshi quanshu,* n.p.
39. The story of Hu Duo, *Dangui ji,* 7a–b; "Dangsi 黨私," *Wanshan xianzi ji,* j. 1, *Anshi quanshu,* n.p.
40. The story of Xiao Liangju, *Jueshi zhenjing zhuzheng,* 16.56b. Two brothers convinced a magistrate to enforce the slaughter prohibition strictly, and all three subsequently had very successful careers.
41. "Niu qiujiu 牛求救," *Chishang caotang biji,* 8.22a–b (the bovine escaped slaughter, and the magistrate placed it in a monastery); "Chaofang niu 朝房牛," *Kuaixue tang manlu,* 15b; "Niu qiming 牛乞命," *Zi buyu quanji,* 24:439; *Juguan rixing lu,* 5.49a–50a (the bovine first takes refuge in the City god temple before going to the official). An anecdote from the Hongwu era, *(Yongzheng) Guangxi tongzhi,* 127.23b; *Niujie huichao,* 1b, and "Yiniu shuo 異牛說" by Liu Xixuan 劉錫玄 (*jinshi* 1607), *Niujie huichao,* 3b–5a.
42. A relatively reserved handbook for officials mentioned "the laws of retribution and the interdiction against defiling" but specified that this was only a secondary aspect of the interdiction against cattle slaughter. See "Jin zai gengniu," *Fuhui quanshu,* 31.15a–b.
43. *Juguan rixing lu,* 5.46b–51b. A magistrate himself recounted how he was able to arrest and convict cattle butchers with the supernatural help of the cattle victims' souls: "Niu quan ershi 牛犬二事," *Juzhai zaji,* 3a.
44. *Lizhi cuoyao,* 62.
45. "Yanna sizai gengniu xi 嚴拿私宰耕牛檄," *Peiyuan tang oucun gao,* 12.39a–40a. On Chen, see Rowe, *Saving the World.*
46. "Jiangsu ancha si yongjin Suzhou sizai gengniu bei," 1807, *Ming Qing yilai Suzhou shehui shi beike ji,* 574; "Jin sizai gengniu bei," 1866, *Fengshan xian caifang ce,* 367–368.
47. One example among dozens is "Jin sizai gengniu shi," *Shenbao,* October 17, 1879.
48. *Limeng pingzheng lu,* 2.85a–86b.
49. "Shenjin xiang tuniu xiangyue 申禁鄉屠牛鄉約," *Tianma shanfang yigao,* 6.10a–b, quotes a prefect giving a sermon in the teaching hall of the temple school of Confucius in 1540 that explained that beef was palatable for a moment but that this pleasure was poisonous since it attracted misfortunes, which were passed on to all the descendants. *Taiwan guanxi jishi,* 110–111, cites a magistrate's ruling without title or date—though it is potentially from the nineteenth century—which, in a style characteristic of Qing officials, mentioned the taboo while specifying that the issue of retribution was only an ancillary reason compared to the law and the moral duty to the working animal. A decision by the governor of Taiwan in 1885 to protect cattle goes so far as to quote anecdotes from *Youyang zazu* as well as Zhenwu's revelation "Instructions on the Taboo against Cattle and Dogs" ("the form [of cattle] corresponds in heaven to the constellation of the stars"). Text cited by Sun Yinrui, *Niurou chengwei fushipin,* 35–36.

50. "Jinzai gengniu 禁宰耕牛," *Huangzheng congshu, fulu,* 1.28a–b.
51. *Shizong Xian huangdi zhupi yuzhi,* 174–5.38a.
52. "Jin zainiu 禁宰牛," *Juguan guaguo lu,* 3.55a–b. The official ruling of a magistrate added that it was permissible to eat all meats, except for beef, and mentioned divine retributions. "Jin zai gengniu," *Zongzhi Zhe Min wenxi,* 2.38a–b, quotes *Tract on Hidden Rewards* and other morality books.
53. For example, "Jiangsu ancha si yongjin Suzhou sizai gengniu bei," 1807, *Ming Qing yilai Suzhou shehui shi beike ji,* 574.
54. According to *Taishang ganying pian jizhu,* 41b, magistrates issued prohibitions because they were motivated by taboos.
55. Some authors were convinced that peasants would never consent to the slaughter of a bovine and that beef butchery was only an issue related to theft. See *Pingping yan,* 4.48b–49b.
56. *Taiwan guanxi jishi,* 113.
57. *Juguan rixing lu,* 5.46a–b, 51b–52a; Chen Hongmou's argument in "Yanna sizai gengniu xi," *Peiyuan tang oucun gao,* 12.39a–40a, was similar.
58. However, the governor of Jiangxi established a system of denunciation and rewards. See "Liwan bisu 力挽敝俗," *Shenbao,* December 13, 1877. A similar system was already promoted by Chen Hongmou, "Yanna sizai gengniu xi," *Peiyuan tang oucun gao,* 12.39 a–40a. The author of an eighteenth-century morality book also believed that prohibitions were ineffective and that the only way to stop cattle butchering was to encourage customers to report butchers, destroy butcher shops, and pay informants with the goods confiscated from the butchers. Comment on the phrase "wu zai gengniu," *Yinzhi wen guangyi,* in *Anshi quanshu,* n.p.
59. For example, *Shizong Xian huangdi zhupi yuzhi,* 174–5.38a–b (memoir from 1727).
60. *Qing shilu,* Jiaqing 10–12–*bingxu* (January 26, 1806), 154:1121–1122.
61. "Jinzai gengniu," *Zongzhi Zhe Min wenxi,* 2.38a–b; "Zaijin zainiu," *Zongzhi Zhe Min wenxi,* 4.64a–65a; "Jie shaniu wen yin" by Wen Qixiang, *Niujie huichao,* 3a–b.
62. Reed, *Talons and Teeth.*
63. *Juguan rixing lu,* 5.5a–b; De Groot, "Miséricorde envers les animaux," 480; Doolittle, *Social Life of the Chinese,* 187–188, adds that yamen employees and officials received bribes from beef butchers. "Sihou fusheng 死後復生," *Wanshan xianzi ji,* j. 1, *Anshi quanshu,* n.p., coldly recommended giving yamen employees who denounce beef butchers a greater reward than the bribes offered by butchers.
64. For example, "Fu Liangjiang zhifu Ce gong wen xingge shiyi shu 覆兩江制府策公問興革事宜書" by Yuan Mei, *Huangchao jingshi wenbian,* 20.3a–5b.
65. *Zhongyang yanjiuyuan Ming Qing dang'an,* A135–102. I am grateful to Luca Gabbiani for providing me with this document.
66. "Kaibo biniu, fu zhouxian ji jiujin fenzhu zuoza yamen bingming, yingbian bude shanxing pibing 開剝斃牛赴州縣及就近分駐佐雜衙門稟明營弁不得擅行批稟," *Fujian shengli,* 853–855.
67. For example, the magistrate of Jiangdu (Jiangsu Province) promulgated a new interdiction and arrested four cattle butchers. See "Chengban tuhu 懲辦屠

戶," *Shenbao,* December 16, 1880; "Tuniu yijin," *Shenbao,* September 25, 1880. In that case, the magistrate also arrested a few cattle butchers but was far from being sure of having solved the problem.

68. "Yanjin sizai 嚴禁私宰," *Shenbao,* December 19, 1877, relates the fury of a governor who discovered an equine butcher shop in front of his yamen.
69. There is an interesting case, dating from 1763, in the archives of Baxian. The sharecropper of a temple slaughtered a bovine. He was denounced by the head of the community compact and a monk, was convicted by the magistrate, and lost his lease on the land he rented. See *Qingdai Baxian dang'an,* 170. See also Zhang Yafeng, "Nanbu dang'an," and Liu E, "Qingdai 'zaisha maniu' lü."
70. *Xing'an huilan,* 12.5a, 18.3a–4a; *Xing'an huilan xuzeng,* 6.4b–5a; *Xingbu bizhao jiajian cheng'an,* 5.16a–17a.
71. Sommer, *Sex, Law, and Society,* also shows that the official ideological discourse and related laws on sexual mores were widely known but ignored and that crimes such as adultery, prostitution, homosexuality, and so forth generally went unpunished unless the culprits were brought to court for some other reason.
72. The exception was a ruling promulgated in Hangzhou in 1878 prohibiting the consumption of beef, dogs, and frogs: "En ji qinshou 恩及禽獸," *Shenbao,* March 1, 1878. See also the case of a magistrate who exceeded the framework of the legal code and required burial for dead cattle in *Juguan rixing lu,* 5.48b.
73. Dean, "The Growth of Local Control."
74. "Shi jin tuniu xiangyue 誓禁屠牛鄉約," *Tianma shanfang yigao,* 6.8b–10a.
75. "Shenjin xiang tuniu xiangyue," "Shenjin tuniu xiaotie 申禁屠牛小帖," *Tianma shanfang yigao,* 6.10a–b, 10b–11a.
76. "Lüshi xiangyue 呂氏鄉約," *Deyi lu,* 14:686, 687, 690, prohibited the slaughter and consumption of beef, dogs, and frogs; Wang Yifu, "Min-Tai xiangyue," 135–136, cites a community compact regulation dating from 1716 that prohibited beef butchery.
77. Fei Chengkang et al., *Zhongguo jiafa zugui,* 312 (regulation dated 1884).
78. An 1889 entry cited by Sun Yinrui, "Niurou chengwei fushipin," 36.
79. Taiwanese sources cited in ibid., 36–37.
80. For example, "Jin sizai gengniu bei" (dated 1866), *Fengshan xian caifang ce,* 367–368, in which the magistrate reiterated the slaughter prohibition in response to a long petition from scholars and merchants who asked him to put an end to "the massacre of innocent cattle out of compassion."
81. Bell, "A Precious Raft," 182–183.
82. On the charitable associations, see Liang Qizi, *Shishan yu jiaohua,* and Fuma Susumu, *Chūgoku zenkai.*
83. "Guang jiesha niu wen," *Huangchao jingshi wenbian,* 69.2a.
84. "Tuniu zhi bao," *Huadang ge congtan,* 6:156–159.
85. "Jie shiniu yuanqi 戒食牛緣啟," *Niujie huichao,* 2a–b, also cited by the *Juguan rixing lu,* 5.53a–b. The text added that longevity was promised to anyone who persuaded people to stop eating beef.
86. "Mainiu fangsheng 買牛放生," *Chishang caotang biji,* 4.36a–37a. For another case in which the redemption money was collected from the spectators, see "Xindong ganniu 心動感牛," *Kuangyuan zazhi,* 1.20a–b.

87. The story of Chen Xingyuan, *Xichao renjian, shang,* 3.32a. The same theme of pledging clothes to redeem cattle is in "Niu bao'en," *Chishang caotang biji,* 6.15b–16b. The bovine rewarded its benefactor by saving him from brigands. The bovine was already dead, but its spirit possessed a dog that chased away the brigands. A very similar illustrated anecdote is in "Renxin huobao 仁心獲報," *Dianshizhai huabao,* vol. Wei, 61 (published in 1890).
88. "Haosha zhi bao 好殺之報," *Dianshizhai huabao,* vol. Ding, 84 (published in 1885).
89. The expression *husu* is a quotation from the *Mengzi,* "Liang Huiwang, shang."
90. "Niu neng xunxiao 牛能殉孝," *Shenbao,* February 8, 1877. Sun Yinrui, "Niurou chengwei fushi pin," 115n54, reports that many Taiwanese believe that Yama punishes those who witness the slaughter of a bovine and do not do everything they can to save it. Therefore, people cover their eyes and ears when they pass a slaughterhouse to pretend they are not witnesses.
91. "Buren husu 不忍觳觫," *Wu Youru huabao,* "Gujin tancong tu, shang 古今談叢圖上," 22.
92. *Haosheng jiujie bian,* 5.10b–12a.
93. For two examples of merchants, see "Fangniu shanju 放牛善舉," *Shenbao,* October 4, 1873; "Niu zhi qiujiu 牛知求救," *Shenbao,* October 30, 1877; for an example of a yamen employee, see "Huaqiao niu 花橋牛," *Kuaixue tang manlu,* 15a–b.
94. The practice is relatively common today in Thailand. Personal communication, Peter Skilling, November 1999.
95. For an episode in a novel in which the protagonist meets cattle on the road, see *Xingshi yinyuan zhuan,* 79:1122.
96. This account is found both in an anecdotal collection—*Chishang caotang biji,* 1.23b–24a—and in a commentary on a morality book—*Xichao renjian, shang,* 3.33a.
97. "Fangniu xing" by Chen Wenshu, *Qingshi duo,* 915. Chen was a famous poet from Hangzhou and an active member of Daoist spirit-writing circles. He mentioned that his father contributed financially to the association created by Dong.
98. "Zuniu deshu 租牛得贖," *Chishang caotang biji,* 1.23b–24a.
99. "Dianniu ge 典牛歌" by Jiang Shiquan, *Qingshi duo,* 27.
100. "She ju dangniu 設局當牛," *Shenbao,* December 28, 1876; "Duo zai gengniu," *Shenbao,* January 13, 1877 (here named Zhiniu ju 質牛局); "Dangniu shanzheng 當牛善政," *Shenbao,* August 17, 1876. This was not about a situation of famine but about an office that took in cattle as pledges during the winter. See also "Jiangsu banzai zhangcheng shu 江蘇辦災章程疏," *Huangchao jingshi wen xubian,* j. 45, n.p., for the description of a Dangniu ju in operation from 1823 to 1831. The Dangniu ju described in "Lun dangniu shanzheng 論當牛善政," *Shenbao,* September 19, 1882 (its regulations were published in *Shenbao,* September 8, 1882) was established by an official. The author also called for agricultural equipment to be pledged and did not allude to the taboo.
101. "Renmin aiwu 仁民愛物," *Wu Youru huabao,* "Gujin tancong tu, shang," 12.
102. "Jieshi niu wenbian bian 戒食牛文辨辨," *Shenbao,* September 6, 1872. This institution was reminiscent of the Hindu *goshala,* which take in old bovines.

103. "Jin zai gengniu 禁宰耕牛," *Shenbao,* December 7, 1876. See "Chajin sizai 查禁私宰," *Shenbao,* September 12, 1873, for another case of charitable associations playing a role in investigating, monitoring, and denouncing beef butchers to magistrates, consequently forcing the last to take action.
104. One example: Doolittle, *Social Life of the Chinese,* 181. *Juguan rixing lu,* 5.49a–50a, relates a case in which an official placed a bovine he saved in a monastery.
105. "Yiyao ju liyuan dan 醫藥局立願單," *Deyi lu,* 4:524.
106. "Xigu hui yiyue 惜穀會議約," *Deyi lu,* 12:667.
107. Christian missionaries and their converts also distributed Bibles or religious leaflets at the entrance to exam facilities. This is how the young Hong Xiuquan 洪秀全 (1814–1864) came into contact with Christian literature, which he subsequently used to establish the Taiping movement, which caused the bloodiest civil war in world history.
108. Doolittle, *Social Life of the Chinese,* 190.
109. De Groot, "Miséricorde envers les animaux," 480.
110. "Lun Shanghai anyuan siguan shi 論上海庵院寺觀事," *Shenbao,* October 31, 1877, stated that the scholars of Shanghai were all mobilized to protect cattle even though there was a much more severe and urgent social problem: wrongdoings by religious specialists. Of course, the "clerical problem" was a collective fantasy just as much as the bovine issue, if not more so. On *Shenbao*'s anticlerical editorials, see Goossaert, "Anatomie d'un discours anticlérical."
111. "Ji Shi zhenren she niu shi 記施真人舍牛事" by Zheng Fujiao 鄭敷教, *Yuanmiao guan zhi,* 9.9a–b.
112. Doolittle, *Social Life of the Chinese,* 191; De Groot, "Miséricorde envers les animaux," 479–480.
113. *Renpu leiji, xia,* 72a–73b.
114. *Yuewei caotang biji,* 10:204–205, in which Ji Yun professed his respect for the beef taboo and explained that epidemic diseases did not affect those who observed it.
115. For example, "Zai jin zainiu," *Zongzhi Zhe Min wenxi,* 4.64a–65a.
116. *Yinzhi wen yinmeng,* 13b.
117. In Taiwan during the Qing, and perhaps also in other provinces, Mazu was elevated to this rank and received *tailao* at the magistrate's annual sacrifice: *Taiwan tongshi,* 22:573. For a precise list of sacrificial victims for each official cult (without taking into account the changes that took place during each dynasty), see *Mingshi,* 47:1235 and *Qingshi gao,* 82:2495.
118. On the history of the worship of Confucius, see Wilson, "Ritualizing Confucius" and "Sacrifice and the Imperial Cult."
119. Wilson, "Sacrifice and the Imperial Cult," 256n18; *Mingshi,* 47:1235, 50:1301.
120. "Taiwan fuxue shengmiao jipin bei 臺灣府學聖廟祭品碑," *Dongming wen houji* 東溟文後集, 3, *Zhongfu tang xuanji,* 173–176.
121. "Tuniu yijin 屠牛宜禁," *Shenbao,* September 25, 1880. For another allusion to the sale of beef during sacrifices to Confucius, see "Jin sizai gengniu shi 禁私宰耕牛示," *Shenbao,* October 17, 1879.
122. *Tuhua ribao,* 3071; *Tuhua ribao,* 2768, related a dispute between the various officials responsible for the school over the sharing of beef, and *Tuhua ribao,* 2646, mentioned the selection of the sacrificial victim by the official.

123. Emperor Yongzheng criticized several officials for talking enthusiastically about sacrificial cattle for Confucius during a ritual. *Shizong Xian huangdi zhupi yuzhi,* 48.14a, 53.22a, both in 1729.
124. The *Rulin waishi,* chap. 2, 25, recounts the case of a scholar who has to interrupt his vegetarian practice to eat the sacrificial meat of Confucius (the novelist does not specify which meat) offered by the superior of the school. The scholar's aunt urges him to eat the problematic gift because, according to her, Confucius will dispatch calamities his way if he does not.
125. "Niujie 牛戒," *Chishang caotang biji,* 3.54b–55a.
126. My definition of Confucian fundamentalism largely overlaps with that of "purists" offered by Chow Kai-wing, *The Rise of Confucian Ritualism;* see also Goossaert, "1898."
127. In the broad sense, all sacrifice is Confucian since the sacrificial liturgy is Confucian. See in particular Li Fengmao, "Jieqing jidian."
128. It is very difficult to determine with precision which animals were sacrificed to ancestors in a given cultural area. The vast majority of Chinese and Western descriptions that specified the species of the animals mentioned pig and sheep, and exceptions were often of Cantonese origin.
129. Fang Ling, "Les médecins laïques."
130. *Haosheng jiujie bian,* 5.10b–12a; "Niujie," *Juzhai zaji,* 11a–12a.
131. "Guang'ai lu," *Chishang caotang biji,* 2.62a.
132. "Niujie," *Chishang caotang biji,* 3.54a–56a.
133. Some doctors also opposed vegetarianism. There are anecdotes about people who made a vow to abstain from meat but were urged by a doctor to eat it. For example, "Shasheng bao 殺生報," *Kuaixue tang manlu,* 10b–11a.
134. In his ledger of merits and demerits, which followed most other ledgers in this respect, Zhuhong assigned more merit to good deeds (e.g., saving lives or burials) benefiting animals that had rendered service to humans (cattle, horses, and dogs) than other animals. See *Zizhi lu,* "Shanmen—renci lei 善門仁慈類," "Guomen—bu renci lei 過門不仁慈類," n.p. He also included a specific entry for those who bought turtles, beef, horsemeat, or dogmeat. See *Zizhi lu,* "Guomen—za bushan lei 過門雜不善類," n.p.
135. *Fangsheng shasheng xianbao lu,* whose section titled "Shasheng ebao—tuzai" comprised thirty anecdotes of retribution for butchers, including seventeen beef butchers (and five dog butchers) and then devoted a section titled "Shasheng ebao—shiniu jieniu 殺生惡報食牛戒牛," which included four anecdotes, to the beef taboo.
136. *Jiesha sishiba wen,* 201a.
137. "Sihou fusheng" (telling the story of a yamen employee who was asked in the underworld to convince a thousand people to vow to uphold the taboo); "Jinniu zengshou," *Wanshan xianzi ji,* j. 1, *Anshi quanshu,* n.p.; "Quan shi niu quan zhe 勸食牛犬者," *Wanshan xianzi ji,* j. 2, *Anshi quanshu,* n.p.
138. One can compare with the situation in contemporary Sri Lanka, where Buddhist activists are involved in cattle protection but in ways distinct from Hindus: Stewart, "Cow Protection."
139. "Seng shaniu 僧殺牛," *Xuansi suotan,* 2b–3a.
140. "Shengshan dao 生善道," *Yongchuang xiaopin,* 31.8a.

141. Welch, *The Practice of Chinese Buddhism,* 317.
142. This is a working hypothesis, which needs to be verified by wider surveys. Among the Daoists I interviewed on this subject (notably in Shanghai and Taiwan), who were interviewed by others (I would like to thank John Lagerwey in particular for sharing this information in personal communication), or who are quoted in published ethnographic reports, those who strictly observe the beef taboo are all members of Qingwei Lingbao lineages, while those who do not observe it are all initiated into a vernacular tradition. Filmed by Patrice Fava, a great ritual in the Yuanhuang 元皇 tradition in west-central Hunan in honor of a local hero, Han Xin, ends with the sacrifice of a water buffalo. Fava, *La revanche de Han Xin.* I understand this exceptional sacrifice as related to this exorcistic ritual's local vernacular roots.
143. For an example of an itinerant Daoist figure promoting the beef taboo, see "Huizui mianju 悔罪免鋸," "Shasheng ebao—shiniu jieniu," *Fangsheng shasheng xianbao lu,* n.p. A man about to kill his cattle realized his crime and became a Daoist practitioner. He took his bovine with him in his life of itinerant asceticism; see "Xiaoniu quan 孝牛泉," *Yunnan difang zhi daojiao he minzu minjian zongjiao ziliao suobian,* 7.
144. *Chunzhu jiwen,* 3:40–41; *Lushan Taiping xingguo gong Caifang zhenjun shishi,* 7.7b–8a.
145. *Zhenwu baojuan,* 20b–23b. I am very grateful to Chao Shin-yi for drawing my attention to this text and providing me with a copy.
146. "Jie shiniu bao," *Guobao wenjian lu,* 14b–15a, included in "Shijie gui'ai 誓戒鬼哀," "Shasheng ebao—shiniu jieniu," *Fangsheng shasheng xianbao lu,* n.p.
147. *Ming gongshi,* 54. An interdiction against donkey meat, which strangely did not mention horsemeat, also applied to Longde dian. On the Qin'an dian, see Goossaert, *The Taoists of Peking;* Tao Jin, "Chengqi yinggan."
148. Wang Guangde and Yang Lizhi, *Wudang daojiao shilüe,* 270. Readers of Zhenwu's biography in the form of a novel (*Huitu beiyou ji zhuan,* 262) composed in the sixteenth century had to observe dietary restrictions, but beef was simply included in a much longer list of foods.
149. Personal communication from several residents of Bangkok, collected in 1999.
150. "Xiwu suyang 戲侮速殃," *Wanshan xianzi ji,* j. 2, *Anshi quanshu,* n.p.
151. *Taishang ganying pian zhu, xia,* 12a–b. *Wudu fasheng,* 28.123a–b and "Niurou seng ru daochang bao" 牛肉僧入道場報, *Kuaiyuan,* 7:609, recounted the case of a monk who had eaten beef and was punished by the gods protecting the sacred area during a ritual. Similarly, an anecdote set in the Song, quoted in *Gujin tushu jicheng,* "Shenyi dian 神異典," fascicle 509, 254:51a, recounted the case of a beefeater who attended a Daoist *jiao* offering ritual and was punished by the gods.
152. "Gui xian yeyin 鬼顯業因," *Wanshan xianzi ji,* j. 2, *Anshi quanshu,* n.p.
153. Lagerwey, "Popular Ritual Specialists," 449; Cheung, "Receiving Prayer Beads."
154. Biography of Li Jianzi 李賤子, *(Yongzheng) Guangxi tongzhi,* 87.25a.
155. Personal communication, Elisabeth Hsü, June 2000.
156. De Groot, "Miséricorde envers les animaux," 480, mentions that divine punishments were inflicted on those who wore leather soles or buttons made of bovine bone and that people took care not to leave such objects on a

deceased person who was placed in a coffin. Nowadays, priests and devotees remove shoes, belts, and all other leather objects before entering a consecrated area. See also Qing Xitai, *Zhongguo daojiao shi,* 264.

157. Particularly among the Hui. See Qiu Shusen, *Huizu shi,* 648.
158. Doolittle, *Social Life of the Chinese,* 187.
159. "Jin niuyou zhu wen 禁牛油燭文," *Xinzheng lu,* 5a–b.
160. "Beifang jin zao niuzhu 北方禁造牛燭," *Shenbao,* September 17, 1873. This article prompted a hostile response. See "Shu Beifang jin zao niuzhu hou," *Shenbao,* September 19, 1873.
161. For example, the biography of the general who reconquered Taiwan for the Qing empire at the end of the seventeenth century. See "Jinghai hou Shi Lang zhuan 靖海侯施琅傳" by Tao Yuanzao 陶元藻, *Huangchao jingshi wenbian,* 84.1b–2a.
162. Dikköter, *The Discourse of Race.*
163. The Chinese imperial state never attempted to impose its bovine policy on Tibetans and Mongols who were subject to indirect administration and special laws. Tibetans or Mongols traveling or living in Han country were likely frequent customers of beef butchers, but I have not seen a source explicitly mentioning them.
164. Gillette, *Between Mecca and Beijing,* chap. 4. The issue of pork has constituted the most frequent reason for conflicts between the Hui and Han Chinese. See Allès, "À propos de l'Islam."
165. The Hui practice slaughter according to Koranic law, which is contrary to Chinese practice. This was banned briefly during the Yuan, in 1280, but not in later dynasties.
166. Gillette, *Between Mecca and Beijing,* chap. 4, notes that half of the Hui in Xi'an City are employed in food trades even today.
167. *Yuewei caotang biji,* 4:63. For an anecdote about a Hui butcher killed in 1596 by a vengeful bovine, see *(Qinding) Xu Wenxian tongkao,* 227.13a–b, and *(Xinke) Ertan,* 13.8a–b. See also "Wang huizi 王回子," *Kuaixue tang manlu,* 7a–b.
168. *Qing shilu,* Yongzheng 7–4–*xinsi* (May 4, 1729), 80:47–48.
169. *Qing shilu,* Yongzheng 7–6–*bingshen* (July 18, 1729), 82:91–92 (also *Shizong Xian huangdi shengxun,* 7.9a–10b).
170. *Qing shilu,* Jiaqing 10–12–*bingxu* (January 26, 1806), 154:1121–1122.
171. "Sizai bijue 私宰弊绝," *Shenbao,* March 23, 1878. In a report to Emperor Yongzheng, dated 1727, on the prohibition against cattle slaughter, an official reported that he had established a surveillance system specifically for the Hui. See *Shizong Xian huangdi zhupi yuzhi,* 174–5.38a–b.
172. *Rulin waishi,* chap. 4, 63–65.
173. Allès, "À propos de l'Islam."
174. "Niujin 牛禁," *Yongchuang xiaopin,* 31.8b, and "Jin shaniu 禁殺牛," *Zaolin zazu,* "Heji 和集," 36b.
175. *Juyi lu,* 12.7a–b. Another official acknowledged an exception for the Hui, writing, "Except for the Hui who have dietary restrictions, the foods allowed [the Han] are very numerous, so why should one eat beef?" See "Jinzai gengniu," *Huangzheng congshu, fulu,* 1.28a–b.

176. Zhang Shaodan, "Cattle Slaughter Industry"; Brown, "A Mountain of Saints and Sages," 464–467.
177. Qiu Shusen, *Huizu shi,* 646. A poem by Ding Yaokang 丁耀亢 (1599–1671) described with horror entire herds of cattle killed by the butchers in Beijing, the "barbarians from the west." See *Ding Yaokang quanji,* 29. There were also comments on Hui cattle butchers in Chengdu in the late nineteenth century. Wang Di, "The Rhythm of the City," 52, 56.
178. Peng Nian, "Beijing Huizu," 31.
179. Qiu Shusen, *Huizu shi,* 660–662; *Qing shilu,* Jiaqing 10–12–*bingxu* (January 26, 1806), 154:1121–1122; Peng Nian, "Beijing Huizu," 31; Imahori Seiji, *Chūgoku hōken shakai,* 174–182. In an episode in a late Ming novel, a protagonist meets two Hui merchants who take a herd of cattle to Beijing to sell them to a *tangguo.* See *Xingshi yinyuan zhuan,* chap. 79, 1122–1123. The identity of the merchants is only revealed later in the story.
180. Niida Noboru, *Pekin kōshō girudo,* 6:1387–1401; Niida Noboru, *Chūgoku no shakai to girudo,* 250–253, 275–280.
181. Peng Nian, "Beijing Huizu," 32–34.
182. Gillette, *Between Mecca and Beijing,* chap. 4.
183. *Guisi cungao,* 9:269.
184. See in particular Lombard-Salmon, *Un exemple d'acculturation,* and Hostetler, *Qing Colonial Enterprise.*
185. "Chongxiu Qiongzhou fu Erxian ci ji 重修瓊州府二賢祠記," *Huailu tang ji,* 65.1b, and "Ming gu Qiongzhou fu zhifu jiazeng Zizheng dafu Libu shangshu jian Wenyuan ge daxueshi Xu gong shendao beiming 明故瓊州府知府加贈資政大夫禮部尚書兼文淵閣大學士徐公神道碑銘," *Chongbian Qiongtai gao,* 24.10b. Qing Xitai, *Zhongguo daojiao shi,* 274, quotes an ethnographic report claiming that Daoists abolished cattle sacrifices among the Li.
186. *Zhongguo xi'nan diqu lidai shike huibian,* 20:115, reproduces an almost illegible rubbing of an 1882 inscription titled *Yanjin tusi leshou binggu he kansha gengniu gaoshi bei* 嚴禁土司勒收兵穀和砍殺耕牛告示碑 erected by the governor of Guizhou.
187. "Fangmiao 坊苗" by Wei Yuan 魏源 (1794–1856), *Huangchao jingshi wenbian,* 88.1a–b. He Xiling 賀熙齡 (1788–1846), "Lüchen Hunan miaojiang qingxing shu 縷陳湖南苗疆情形疏," *Huangchao jingshi wen xubian* (Ge Shijun), 80.7b–9a, affirmed that the taboo was observed.
188. Wei Yuan's "Hunan ancha shi zeng xunfu Fu Nai zhuan 湖南按察使贈巡撫傅鼐傳," *Huangchao jingshi wenbian,* 88.10a–13a. Lombard-Salmon, *Un exemple d'acculturation,* 221–222, notes the policy of prohibiting traditional festivals and sacrifices in the name of reducing wastefulness, but the cattle sacrifice played a fundamental role in these prohibitions.
189. Linqing is best known for this autobiography, *Hongxue yinyuan tuji* 鴻雪因緣圖記, comprising 240 illustrated anecdotes. See Minford, "Tracks in the Snow." In "Immortals and Patriarchs," Liu Xun demonstrates the close connections of Linqing's lineage (the Wanyan 完顏) with Daoism.
190. Linqing held this important post from 1832 to 1833.
191. "Cuiping fangmu 翠屏放牛," *Hongxue yinyuan tuji,* vol. 2, n.p.
192. *Yiwen Quanshan jing yizhu,* 184–191.

193. Originally, the expression contemptuously designated a well-fed servant as well as the king's guards, especially those of the Tower of London. It is also sometimes used by those who are not British to designate the latter.
194. It was at the same time, in the middle of the nineteenth century, that the extensive cattle farming that developed in the United States and South America (Argentina, Uruguay), as well as refrigeration and canning techniques (by the large Chicago slaughterhouses and factories that make corned beef) sharply increased beef consumption throughout the West. On the impact of these developments on China, see DuBois, "Many Roads."
195. "Chajin sizai," *Shenbao,* September 12, 1873.
196. "Zaisha gengniu 宰殺耕牛," *Shenbao,* October 28, 1878, and "Niurou shizhen 牛肉施賑," *Shenbao,* November 12, 1878, described two cases of beef butchers arrested by the Chinese authorities and accused of having slaughtered water buffaloes instead of Western beef cattle, which apparently would have been permissible. They were given a light sentence. For a survey of the Western introduction of beef consumption in Shanghai, see Swislocki, "Imagining Irreconcilability," 1166, 1184.
197. "Niuzhi qiujiu," *Shenbao,* October 30, 1877, depicted a Christian beef butcher.
198. *North China Herald,* August 16, 1873. Chinese ran slaughterhouses, but for Western customers. "Lun niuwen 論牛瘟," *Shenbao,* September 12, 1872, mentioned a Western cattle farmer near Shanghai. Westerners have also established dairy farms near concessions. Some of the cattle bred for Westerners were imported from the West. See "Cha mai wenniu 查賣瘟牛," *Shenbao,* January 14, 1880.
199. "Buren husu 不忍觳觫," *Dianshizhai huabao,* Geng:73 (published in 1886). On the beef taboo represented in *Dianshizhai huabao,* see Ye Xiaoqing, *The Dianshizhai Pictorial,* 217–220.
200. "Husu kemin 觳觫可憫," *Dianshizhai huabao,* Bing:82 (published in 1885). In "Niu tao ming," *Shenbao,* October 1, 1872, the increase in beef slaughter in Shanghai, which was described as a calamity, was also attributed to Westerners. "Maniu qifeng 馬牛其風," *Dianshizhai huabao,* Shu:64 (published in 1895) described a bovine that was taken to a Western slaughterhouse and escaped to save its life.
201. *Huangchao jingshi wenbian,* 69.2a–b.
202. A similar argument was used to criticize the discourse on animal life. See, for example, "Chanfa ershi jiesha lun 闡發二氏戒殺論," *Shenbao,* August 20, 1873.
203. "Guang shuowangjin tuzai shuo," *Shenbao,* July 19, 1878.
204. "Shu Beifangjin zao niuzhu hou," *Shenbao,* September 19, 1873. A similar argument is found in "Lunjin zai gengniu 論禁宰耕牛," *Shenbao,* September 28, 1877.
205. "Jin zai gengniu," *Shenbao,* December 7, 1876.
206. *Songshi,* 333:10698; *Yuanshi,* 170:3996.
207. "Jiqi dai gengniu shuo 機器代耕牛說," *Huangchao jingshi wen tongbian,* j. 24, n.p.
208. For example, "Feng quan jie shi niuquan wen," *Shenbao,* July 22, 1872, was a passionate tract in favor of the taboo. It provoked a rebuttal, "Jieshi niu wen

bian 戒食牛文辨," *Shenbao,* July 30, 1872, which was in turn refuted by "Jie shi niu wenbian bian," *Shenbao,* September 6, 1872. Another call for the taboo was titled "Baoniu lun 保牛論," *Shenbao,* January 4, 1889. All *Shenbao* articles, editorials, letters, or short articles were anonymous if written by a journalist and signed with a pseudonym if authored by an external contributor. It is therefore impossible to analyze the discourse by author.

209. "Lun shiyu jinzhi sizai guanban buru shenban 論實欲禁止私宰官辦不如紳辦," *Shenbao,* October 22, 1877.

210. *Pingping yan,* 4.48b–49b. This discourse, as well as the participation of charitable associations in tracking down beef butchers, should be considered in the context of the local elites' increasingly important roles in the management of public affairs after the Taiping war.

211. "Guang shuowang jin tuzai shuo," *Shenbao,* July 19, 1878.

212. "Lun Ningbo jin sizai shi 論寧波禁私宰事," *Shenbao,* October 22, 1880. Likewise, *Tuhua ribao,* 2779, published in 1909, denounced beef butchery as essentially unhealthy from a hygienic perspective.

213. "Lun niuwen," *Shenbao,* September 12, 1872; "Cha mai wenniu," *Shenbao,* January 14, 1880.

214. "Lun jin zai gengniu," *Shenbao,* September 28, 1877. The author described how the cattle dealer arrived in the villages, sold the cattle deemed fit for a high price, and had to give up the others for a pathetic sum. In a sequel to his editorial, the author also designated *cainiu* from northeast China as a different species: see "Zai lun jin sha gengniu shi 再論禁殺耕牛事," *Shenbao,* October 3, 1877.

215. A report from 1729 mentioned armies purchasing Mongolian cattle and horses, which were kept in pasture, for the transport of provisions. These animals were called *cainiu* and *caima* 菜馬. See *Shizong Xian huangdi zhupi yuzhi,* 31 *xia,* 40a.

216. "Jiangsu ancha si yongjin Suzhou sizai gengniu bei," *Ming Qing yilai Suzhou shehui shi beike ji,* 574.

217. "Lun Ningbo jin sizai shi," *Shenbao,* October 22, 1880, nevertheless proposed lifting the slaughter prohibition. "Tuniu yijin," *Shenbao,* September 25, 1880, stated that in Suzhou, there were no *cainiu* but mentioned animals being culled. And *Qing shilu,* Jiaqing 10–12–*bingxu* (January 26, 1806), 154:1121–1122.

218. "Jieshi niu wenbian," *Shenbao,* July 30, 1872.

219. "Jieshi niu wenbian bian," *Shenbao,* September 6, 1872. Similarly, a mid-nineteenth-century intellectual criticized the hypocrisy and immorality of people in his native district who ate beef, claiming that it was from *cainiu* and not from *gengniu.* See *Dushu zashi,* 9:156.

220. "Shu Beifangjin zao niuzhu hou," *Shenbao,* September 19, 1873.

221. "Zai lunjin sha gengniu shi," *Shenbao,* October 3, 1877.

222. "Jin sizai," *Weixinbian,* "Jiwu 幾務," *xia,* 52b–53b. This text was reprinted in *Muling shu,* 22.32a–b.

223. For an overview of the rise of the beef trade from the late nineteenth century onward, see Poon Shuk-wah, "Huniu yu shaniu."

224. Yoshida Tadashi, *Gyūniku to Nihonjin,* 23.

225. On Li Boyuan 李伯元 (1867–1906), the author of *Wenming xiaoshi,* and social protest novels in general, see Wang, *Fin-de-siècle Splendor,* chap. 4. All Shanghai intellectuals of the 1870s to 1890s who pursued "Western studies" had not abandoned the taboo. See Ye Xiaoqing, *The Dianshizhai Pictorial,* 217—citing Wang Tao 王韜 (1828–1897)—and 224n119.
226. *Wenming xiaoshi,* chap. 18, 125.
227. "Lun Taixi de yinshi zhi dao 論泰西得飲食之道," *Shenbao,* June 19, 1890.
228. Goossaert, "1898"; Goossaert and Palmer, *The Religious Question in Modern China.*
229. Sun Yinrui, "Niurou chengwei fushipin," 49.
230. The Japanese colonial regime established a policy that protected *gengniu* and prohibited the slaughter of working animals below the age of nine but encouraged the slaughter of older or weak animals and promoted livestock farming for slaughter. The nationalist regime continued this policy after 1945.
231. Sun Yinrui, "Niurou chengwei fushipin," 60–67. According to a Chinese source written in 1918, "those who eat it are few." See *Taiwan tongshi,* 23:606.
232. *Zhongguo difangzhi minsu ziliao huibian, Dongbei juan,* 167, citing *Andong xianzhi* 安東縣志 from 1931.
233. Quantitative data collected in Beijing around 1930 show that consumption was low even though beef was much cheaper than pork and mutton. See Gamble, *How Chinese Families Live,* 99.
234. The district in eastern Hunan where Mao himself was from.
235. *Hunan nongmin yundong kaocha baogao* 湖南農民運動考察報告, *Mao Zedong xuanji,* 1:37.
236. Yang, *A Chinese Village,* 47. The author also stresses the consideration shown to dogs. See 49–50.
237. Sun Yinrui, "Niurou chengwei fushipin," 116–157. The annual per capita beef consumption increased from 300 g in 1960 to 2.5 kg in 1992.
238. Longworth, Brown, and Waldron, *Beef in China.*

## CONCLUSION

1. Simoons, *Eat Not This Flesh,* 119–121.
2. For Japanese criticisms of the Chinese as meat-eating others, see Krämer, "Not Befitting Our Divine Country." I am very grateful to Barbara Ambros for pointing this out to me.
3. On this process, see Goossaert and Palmer, *Religious Question.*
4. Ter Haar, "From Field to Text in the Study."
5. Anderson, *The Food of China,* 181.
6. Xie Chengxia, *Yang niu yang shi.*
7. Song Changhong, *Zhongguo niu wenhua.*
8. Ibid., 65–66; Ren Cheng, *Zhongguo minjian jinji,* 320–321, which also attributes the interdictions against horses and dogs to totemism. Totemism concerning the dog is attested in the case of certain ethnic groups in southern China, but this interdiction could not possibly have influenced that of the Han.
9. Ren Cheng, *Zhongguo minjian jinji,* 320–321.

10. For a critique of the notion of "custom" used by legal experts as much as by Chinese folklorists in the twentieth century, see the various contributions in Bourgon, "La coutume et la norme."
11. Li Lulu, *Chunniu bidi,* 273–276.
12. Taira Masayuki, "Tabous et alimentation carnée."
13. Ambros, *Bones of Contention,* 58–63; Arch, *Bringing Whales Ashore;* Holtzman, "On Whale"; Itoh, *Japanese Culture;* Kalland, "Japanese Perceptions," and *Unveiling the Whale;* Kalland and Moeran, *Japanese Whaling;* Kishigami, Hamaguchi, and Savelle, *Anthropological Studies of Whaling;* Morikawa, *Whaling in Japan.*
14. Ferrières, *Histoire des peurs alimentaires,* 23–24; De Miramon, "Tabous alimentaires," wonders about the possibility of using the notion of taboo for horses and other foods prohibited by some Christian texts of the Middle Ages.
15. Simoons, *Eat Not This Flesh,* 187–193.
16. Poplin, "Le cheval."
17. An article published in *Shenbao* in 1894 compared the Western interdiction against dogs with the beef taboo in China. See "Shu jiugou xinzhang 書救狗新章," *Shenbao,* April 13, 1894.
18. Foreword to Durand, *Sacrifice et labour.*
19. Flandrin and Montanari, *Histoire de l'alimentation,* 118–119; also Benkheira, *Islâm et interdits alimentaires,* 145, 181.
20. Durand, *Sacrifice et labour.*
21. Rarely eaten in antiquity, beef became a common food among peasants in the Middle Ages but remained despised by the elites, who adopted it only from the sixteenth century. At the same time, the consumption of beef (and meat in general) decreased in the countryside from the sixteenth century. With the possible exception of the British Isles, beef was less widely consumed than pork until the boom in cattle farming in the nineteenth century. See Cumming, "The Relationship between Meat Consumption and Power," and Thirs, *Food in Early Modern England.*
22. Fabre-Vassas, *The Singular Beast.*

# BIBLIOGRAPHY

## Primary Sources

Daozang 道藏 texts are listed with their number in Schipper, Kristofer. *Concordance du Tao-tsang*. Paris: Ecole française d'Extrême-Orient, 1975.

Buddhist canonical texts are followed by T., which precedes the number assigned to them in *Taishō shinshū daizōkyō* 大正新脩大藏經. 100 vols. Edited by Takakusu Junjirō 高楠順次郎, Watanabe Kaigyoku 渡辺海旭, et al. Tokyo: Taishō issaikyō kankōkai, 1924–1932.


*Aiwu pian* 愛物篇. Prefaced 1860. In *Fushou baozang* 福壽寶藏. Shanghai: Leshanshe, 1936.

*Anshi quanshu* 安士全書. Zhou Mengyan 周夢顏 (1656–1739). http://www.anshiquanshu.com/.

*Baopu zi neipian jiaoshi* 抱朴子内篇校釋. Ge Hong 葛洪 (283–343), Wang Ming 王明, ed. Beijing: Zhonghua shuju, 1985.

*Beimeng suoyan* 北夢瑣言. Sun Guangxian 孫光憲 (?–968). Beijing: Zhonghua shuju, 2002.

*Beishi* 北史. Beijing: Zhonghua shuju, 1974.

*Beixi daquan ji* 北溪大全集. Chen Chun 陳淳 (1159–1223). Siku quanshu edition.

*(Qianlong) Cangzhou zhi* (乾隆)滄州志. Zhuang Rirong 莊日榮 et al., comp. 1743. Taipei: Chengwen chubanshe, 1976.

*Chaweng shiji* 槎翁詩集. Liu Song 劉崧 (1321–1381). Siku quanshu edition.

*Chenzhonglu* 晨鍾錄. First edition in 1763. 1886 edition in *Sandong shiyi,* vol. 6.

*Chishang caotang biji* 池上草堂筆記. Liang Gongchen 梁恭辰 (1814–1887). 1843. Kaifeng: Yiwentang, 1873, Taipei: Guangwen shuju, 1970. This collection was also published under other titles, notably *Beidong yuan bilu* 北東園筆錄 and *Quanjie lu* 勸戒錄.

*Chishui xuanzhu* 赤水玄珠. Sun Yikui 孫一奎 (1538–1600). Siku quanshu edition.

*Chongbian Qiongtai gao* 重編瓊臺稿. Qiu Jun 丘濬 (1418–1495). Siku quanshu edition.

*Chongming manlu* 蟲鳴漫錄. Caihengzi 采蘅子. 1876. Biji xiaoshuo daguan 筆記小說大觀 edition.

*Chunzhu jiwen* 春渚紀聞. He Wei 何薳 (1077–1145). Beijing: Zhonghua shuju, 1983.

*Cui fujun ci lu* 崔府君祠錄. Zheng Lang 鄭烺 (zi Lixuan 荔軒). 1832. Wulin zhanggu congbian 武林掌故叢編 edition.

*Da Ming lü jijie fu li* 大明律集解附例. Wanli era edition. Taipei: Taiwan xuesheng shuju, 1970.

*Da Ming Renxiao huanghou quanshan shu* 大明仁孝皇后勸善書. 1407 edition, *Siku quanshu cunmu congshu* 四庫全書存目叢書, Zibu 子部, vol. 120.

*Da Qing huidian shili* 大清會典事例. Shanghai: Shangwu yinshuguan, 1908; Qing huidian guan, 1886.

*Da Yuan shengzheng guochao dianzhang* 大元聖政國朝典章. Yuan edition. Taipei: Guoli gugong bowuyuan, 1976.

*Dangui ji* 丹桂籍. 1711 edition at Bibliothèque nationale de France.

*Dansheng tang cangshu mu* 澹生堂藏書目. Qi Chengye 祁承㸁 (1565–1628). In *Mingdai shumu tiba congkan* 明代書目題跋叢刊. Beijing: Shumu wenxian chubanshe, 1994.

*Daodian lun* 道典論. Daozang 1130.

*Daofa huiyuan* 道法會元. Early fourteenth century. Daozang 1220.

*Daojia jinshilüe* 道家金石略. Chen Yuan 陳垣, comp., Chen Zhichao 陳智超 and Zeng Qingying 曾慶瑛, eds. Beijing: Wenwu chubanshe, 1988.

*Daomen kefan daquan ji* 道門科範大全集. Daozang 1225.

*(Chongkan) Daozang jiyao* 重刊道藏輯要. Jiang Yupu 蔣予蒲 (1755–1819), comp. 1906 Erxian an edition.

*Deyi lu* 得一錄. Yu Zhi 余治 (1809–1874). 1869. *Guanzhen shu jicheng*, vol. 8.

*Dianshizhai huabao* 點石齋畫報. 1884–1898. Guangzhou: Guangdong renmin chubanshe, 1983–1984.

*Ding Yaokang quanji* 丁耀亢全集. Ding Yaokang 丁耀亢 (1599–1671). Zhengzhou: Zhongzhou guji chubanshe, 1999.

*Diqi shangjiang Wen taibao zhuan* 地祇上將溫太保傳. 1274. Daozang 780.

*Dongdu ji* 東度記. Qingxi daoren 清溪道人. In *Mingdai xiaoshuo jikan* 明代小說輯刊. Chengdu: Bashu shushe, 1993, vol. 3.

*Dongxuan Lingbao Daoxue keyi* 洞玄靈寶道學科儀. Daozang 1126.

*Dongxuan Lingbao Qianzhen ke* 洞玄靈寶千真科. Daozang 1410.

*Dushu zashi* 讀書雜釋. Xu Zi 徐鼒 (1810–1862). Beijing: Zhonghua shuju, 1997.

*Er Cheng ji* 二程集. Beijing: Zhonghua shuju, 1981.

*(Xinke) Ertan* (新刻)耳談. Wang Tonggui 王同軌 (early seventeenth century). Ming edition, *Siku quanshu cunmu congshu* 四庫全書存目叢書, Zibu 子部, vol. 248.

*Fangsheng shasheng xianbao lu* 放生殺生現報錄. Jiang Shenxiu 江慎修. 1922, https://book.bfnn.org/books/0858.htm.

*Feng Zikai manhua quanji* 豐子愷漫畫全集. Beijing: Jinghua chubanshe, 1999.

*Fengshan xian caifang ce* 鳳山縣采訪冊. Lu Dejia 盧德嘉 et al., comp. In *Taiwan wenxian shiliao congkan*.

*Fengsu tongyi jiaozhu* 風俗通義校注. Ying Shao 應劭 (ca. 140–before 204), Wang Liqi 王利器, ed. Beijing: Zhonghua shuju, 1981.

*Fenmen gujin leishi* 分門古今類事. Song period. Siku quanshu edition.

*Fuhui quanshu* 福惠全書. Huang Liuhong 黃六鴻. 1699. *Guanzhen shu jicheng*, vol. 3.

*Fujian shengli* 福建省例. ca. 1873. In *Taiwan wenxian shiliao congkan*.

*Fuyou shangdi Chunyang Lüzu tianshi shiji* 孚佑上帝純陽呂祖天師詩集. (Chongkan) Daozang jiyao edition.

*Gengniu lei* 耕牛淚. Shanghai: Mingshan shuju, n.d. (Republican period).

*Guandi quanshu* 關帝全書. Huang Qishu 黃啟曙. In *Guandi wenxian huibian* 關帝文獻匯編. Beijing: Guoji wenhua chubanshe, 1995, vols. 5–7.

*Guang'ai lu* 廣愛錄. Meng Chaoran 孟超然 (1731–1797). 1815 edition at Beijing University Library.

*Guang Hongming ji* 廣弘明集. Daoxuan 道宣 (596–667). T. 2103, vol. 52.

*Guangrenpin* 廣仁品. Li Changke 李長科, comp. 1633 edition, *Siku quanshu cunmu congshu* 四庫全書存目叢書, Zibu 子部, vol. 150–151.

*(Yongzheng) Guangxi tongzhi* (雍正)廣西通志. Jin Hong 金鉷 et al., comp. 1733. Siku quanshu edition.

*(Tongzhi) Guangxin fuzhi* (同治)廣信府志. 1873. Taipei: Chengwen chubanshe, 1970.

*Guanzhen shu jicheng* 官箴書集成. Hefei: Huangshan shushe, 1997, 10 vols.

*Guiguzi tiansui lingwen* 鬼谷子天髓靈文. Daozang 867.

*Guisi cungao* 癸巳存稿. Yu Zhengxie 俞正燮 (1775–1840). Congshu jicheng 叢書集成 edition.

*Gujin tushu jicheng* 古今圖書集成. Yongzheng era original edition.

*Guobao wenjian lu* 果報聞見錄. Yang Shichuan 楊式傳. Shuoling 說鈴 edition, Kangxi era, *Siku quanshu cunmu congshu* 四庫全書存目叢書, Zibu 子部, vol. 250.

*Gushan Weilin chanshi huanshanlu* 鼓山為霖禪師還山錄. Weilin Daopei 為霖道霈 (1615–1702). 1688. *Zokuzokyō* 續藏經, vol. 72.

*Gusheng xubian* 觚賸續編. Niu Xiu 鈕琇. 1700. *Siku quanshu cunmu congshu* 四庫全書存目叢書, Zibu 子部, vol. 250.

*Hanshu* 漢書. Beijing: Zhonghua shuju, 1975.

*Haosheng jiujie bian* 好生救劫編. In *Youfu dushu tang congke* 有福讀書堂叢刻, Yangzhou, 1901.

*Hongxue yinyuan tuji* 鴻雪因緣圖記. Linqing 麟慶 (1791–1846). 1847. Beijing: Beijing guji chubanshe, 1984.

*Hou Han shu* 後漢書. Beijing: Zhonghua shuju, 1973.

*Huadang ge congtan* 花當閣叢談. Xu Fuzuo 徐復祚 (Ming period). Congshu jicheng 叢書集成 edition.

*Huailu tang ji* 懷麓堂集. Li Dongyang 李東陽 (1447–1516). Siku quanshu edition.

*Huainan honglie jijie* 淮南鴻烈集解. Feng Yi 馮逸 and Qiao Hua 喬華, eds. Beijing: Zhonghua shuju, 1989.

*Huangchao jingshi wen tongbian* 皇朝經世文統編. Shao Zhitang 邵之棠, comp. Online edition at Academia Sinica. https://hanchi.ihp.sinica.edu.tw/ihpc/.

*Huangchao jingshi wen xubian* 皇朝經世文續編. Ge Shijun 葛士濬, comp. 1888, 1897 Saoye shanfang edition.

*Huangchao jingshi wenbian* 皇朝經世文編. He Changling 賀長齡 (1785–1848), comp. 1826. Shanghai: Guangbaisong zhai, 1889.

*Huangchao tongzhi* 皇朝通志. 1767. Siku quanshu edition.

*Huangchao wenxian tongkao* 皇朝文獻通考. 1747. Siku quanshu edition.

*Huangjing jizhu* 皇經集註. Daozang 1440.

*Huangshi richao* 黃氏日抄. Huang Zhen 黃震 (1213–1280). Siku quanshu edition.

*Huangzheng congshu* 荒政叢書. Yu Sen 俞森. 1690. Siku quanshu edition.
*Huhai xinwen Yijian xuzhi* 湖海新聞夷堅續志. Anonymous. Yuan period. Beijing: Zhonghua shuju, 1986.
*Huitu beiyou ji zhuan* 繪圖北遊記傳. In *Huitu Dong Nan Xi Bei si youji* 繪圖東南西北四遊記. Taipei: Fenghuang chubanshe, 1974.
*Huizuan gongguo ge jian zhushi* 彙纂功過格兼注釋. Chen Xigu 陳錫嘏 (1634–1687). 1818 edition at Harvard-Yenching Library.
*Husu jiwen* 觳觫紀聞. Shanghai: Shijie fojiao jushilin, n.d. (Republican period).
*Jianghu changweng ji* 江湖長翁集. Chen Zao 陳造 (1133–1203). Siku quanshu edition.
*Jianji tang wenji* 兼濟堂文集. Wei Yijie 魏裔介 (1616–1686). Siku quanshu edition.
*Jianyu xiansheng fu Yu tiaojiao* 健餘先生撫豫條教. Yin Huiyi 尹會一. In *Guanzhen shu jicheng*, vol. 4.
*Jie shiniu cuyan* 戒食牛粗言. Jiang Taiyi 江太易. Shanghai: Hongda, 1927.
*Jiesha mijie bian* 戒殺弭劫編. Xu Qian 徐謙 (1776–1864). Shanghai: Daode shuju, 1936.
*Jiesha sishiba wen* 戒殺四十八問. Zhou Siren 周思仁 (Zhou Mengyan 周夢顏, 1656–1739). *Zokuzokyō* 續藏經, vol. 107.
*Jin Wentong gong ji* 金文通公集. Jin Zhijun 金之俊 (1593–1670). Xuxiu siku quanshu 續修四庫全書 edition.
*Jingde ji* 淨德集. Lü Tao 呂陶 (1031–1107). Siku quanshu edition.
*Jinghua yuan* 鏡花緣. Li Ruzhen 李汝珍 (ca. 1763–1830). ca. 1820. Beijing: Zuojia chubanshe, 1955.
*(Zengding) Jingxin lu* (增訂)敬信錄. 1749. 1831 edition in *Sandong shiyi*, vol. 5.
*Jingzao quanshu* 敬竈全書. 1868 Shanghai edition in *Sandong shiyi*, vol. 11.
*Jinshi* 金史. Beijing: Zhonghua shuju, 1975.
*Jinshu* 晉書. Beijing: Zhonghua shuju, 1974.
*Jishen lu* 稽神錄. Xu Xuan 徐鉉 (916–991). Beijing: Zhonghua shuju, 1996.
*Jiu Tangshu* 舊唐書. Beijing: Zhonghua shuju, 1975.
*Jiu Wudai shi* 舊五代史. Beijing: Zhonghua shuju, 1976.
*Jiushengchuan* 救生船. 1905 edition in *Ming Qing minjian zongjiao jingjuan wenxian xubian*, vol. 9.
*Jueshi zhengzong* 覺世正宗. 1862. 1875 edition in *Ming Qing minjian zongjiao jingjuan wenxian*, vol. 11.
*Jueshi zhenjing zhuzheng* 覺世真經註證. Huang Qishu 黃啟曙. 1858. In *Guandi quanshu*, j. 15–17.
*Juguan guaguo lu* 居官寡過錄. Liu Zhenqing 劉振清. Qingzhao tang congshu 青照堂叢書 edition, *Guanzhen shu jicheng*, vol. 5.
*Juguan rixing lu* 居官日省錄. Jueluo Wuertong'a 覺羅烏爾通阿. 1852. In *Guanzhen shu jicheng*, vol. 8.
*Jujia biyong shilei quanji* 居家必用事類全集. Yuan period. Korean edition at Beijing tushuguan.
*Juyi lu* 居易錄. Wang Shizhen 王士禛 (1634–1711). Siku quanshu edition.
*Juzhai zaji* 矩齋雜記. Shi Runzhang 施閏章 (1619–1683). *Siku quanshu cunmu congshu* 四庫全書存目叢書, Zibu 子部, vol. 249.
*(Jiatai) Kuaiji zhi* (嘉泰)會稽志. Shen Zuobin 沈作賓 (fl. 1201) et al., comp. 1201. In *Song Yuan fangzhi congkan* 宋元方志叢刊. Beijing: Zhonghua shuju, 1990, vol. 7.

*Kuaixue tang manlu* 快雪堂漫錄. Feng Mengzhen 馮夢禎 (1546–1605). *Siku quanshu cunmu congshu* 四庫全書存目叢書, Zibu 子部, vol. 247.

*Kuaiyuan* 獪園. Qian Xiyan 錢希言 (Ming period). 1613. Qing manuscript in *Siku quanshu cunmu congshu* 四庫全書存目叢書, Zibu 子部, vol. 247.

*Kuangyuan zazhi* 曠園雜志. Wu Chenyan 吳陳琰. Shuoling 說鈴 edition, Kangxi era, in *Siku quanshu cunmu congshu* 四庫全書存目叢書, Zibu 子部, vol. 250.

*Kuiche zhi* 睽車志. Guo Tuan 郭彖. ca. 1165. Congshu jicheng 叢書集成 edition.

*Laojun yinsong jiejing* 老君音誦誡經. Daozang 785.

*Laozi shuo fashi jinjie jing* 老子說法食禁誡經. Dunhuang manuscript, *Zangwai daoshu,* vol. 21.

(*Wanli*) *Leizhou fuzhi* (萬歷)雷州府志. 1614. Ouyang Bao 歐陽保 et al., comp. Beijing: Shumu wenxian chubanshe, n.d.

*Lequan ji* 樂全集. Zhang Fangping 張訪平 (1007–1091). Siku quanshu edition.

*Leshan lu* 樂善錄. Li Changling 李昌齡 (fl. 1233). *Shuofu sanzhong* 說郛三種, Tao Zongyi 陶宗儀 (fourteenth century), comp. Shanghai: Shanghai guji chubanshe, 1988, vol. 6.

*Liangshu* 梁書. Beijing: Zhonghua shuju, 1973.

*Liangyan suoji* 良言瑣記. 1879 edition at Sterling Memorial Library, Yale University.

*Liji jijie* 禮記集解. Sun Xidan 孫希旦 (1736–1784). Beijing: Zhonghua shuju, 1989.

*Limeng pingzheng lu* 蒞蒙平政錄. Chen Chaojun 陳朝君 (end of seventeenth century). *Guanzhen shu jicheng*, vol. 2.

*Liu Yuxi ji jianzheng* 劉禹錫集箋證. Qu Tuiyuan 瞿蛻園, ed. Shanghai: Shanghai guji chubanshe, 1989.

*Liuhu* 柳弧. Ding Rouke 丁柔克 (1840–?). Beijing: Zhonghua shuju, 2002.

*Liweng mishu* 笠翁秘書. Li Yu 李漁 (1611–1680), Zhao Wenqing 趙文卿, Jiang Lüxiu 蔣聿修, and Zhang Shoumei 章壽眉, comp. Chongqing: Chongqing chubanshe, 1997.

*Lizhi cuoyao* 勵治撮要. Zhang Jingtian 張經田. Qing period manuscript in *Guanzhen shu jicheng,* vol. 6.

*Longshu jingtu wen* 龍舒淨土文. Wang Rixiu 王日休. T. 1970.

*Lunyu jishi* 論語集釋. Cheng Shude 程樹德, comp. Beijing: Zhonghua shuju, 1990.

*Lushan Taiping xingguo gong Caifang zhenjun shishi* 廬山太平興國宮採訪真君事實. 1154. Daozang 1286.

*Mao Zedong xuanji* 毛澤東選集. Mao Zedong 毛澤東 (1893–1976). Beijing: Renmin chubanshe, 1969, vol. 1.

*Ming gongshi* 明宮史. Liu Ruoyu 劉若愚 (1541–?). Beijing: Beijing guji chubanshe, 1980.

*Ming Qing minjian zongjiao jingjuan wenxian* 明清民間宗教經卷文獻. Wang Chien-ch'uan 王見川 and Lin Wanchuan 林萬傳, comp. Taipei: Xinwenfeng, 1999, 12 vols.

*Ming Qing minjian zongjiao jingjuan wenxian xubian* 明清民間宗教經卷文獻續編. Wang Chien-ch'uan 王見川 et al., comp. Taipei: Xinwenfeng, 2006, 12 vols.

*Ming Qing yilai Suzhou shehui shi beike ji* 明清以來蘇州社會史碑刻集. Wang Guoping 王國平, Tang Lixing 唐力行 et al., comp. Suzhou: Suzhou daxue chubanshe, 1998.

*Minggong shupan qingming ji* 名公疏判清明集. 1261. Beijing: Zhonghua shuju, 1987.

*Mingshi* 明史. Beijing: Zhonghua shuju, 1974.
*Mozhuang manlu* 墨莊漫錄. Zhang Bangji 張邦基 (Song). Siku quanshu edition.
*Muling shu* 牧令書. Xu Dong 徐棟, comp. 1848. *Guanzhen shu jicheng*, vol. 7.
*Nan Qi shu* 南齊書. Beijing: Zhonghua shuju, 1974.
*Nancun chuogeng lu* 南村輟耕錄. Tao Zongyi 陶宗儀 (fourteenth century). Beijing: Zhonghua shuju, 1959.
*Nanshi* 南史. Beijing: Zhonghua shuju, 1975.
*Niujie biechao* 牛戒別鈔. Guo Huijun 郭慧濬. 1935. https://commons.wikimedia.org/wiki/File:SSID-13428040_%E7%89%9B%E6%88%92%E5%88%A5%E9%88%94.pdf.
*Niujie huichao* 牛戒彙鈔. In *Riqian chushe* 日乾初揲, late Ming edition at Naikaku bunko 內閣文庫.
*Niujie huichao* 牛戒彙鈔. Undated edition at Beijing University Library 北京大學圖書館.
*Niujie jilu* 牛戒輯錄. 1868. Beijing: Zhuanyunzhai 篆雲齋. https://openresearch-repository.anu.edu.au/handle/1885/206045.
*North China Herald and Supreme Court and Consular Gazette*. Shanghai, *North China Herald*, weekly, 1870–1941.
*Pangong mianzai baojuan* 潘公免災寶卷. 1858 edition in *Baojuan chuji* 寶卷初集, vol. 23. Taiyuan: Shanxi renmin chubanshe, 1997.
*Peiwei zhai ji* 佩韋齋集. Yu Delin 俞德鄰 (jinshi 1274). Siku quanshu edition.
*Peiyuan tang oucun gao* 培遠堂偶存稿. Chen Hongmou 陳宏謀 (1696–1771). Undated edition at Bibliothèque de l'Institut des Hautes Études Chinoises.
*Pi ya* 埤雅. Lu Dian 陸佃 (fl. 1070–1100). Congshu jicheng jianbian 叢書集成簡編 edition.
*Pingping yan* 平平言. Fang Dashi 方大湜. 1892. *Guanzhen shu jicheng*, vol. 7.
*Qianqing tang shumu* 千頃堂書目. Huang Yuji 黃虞稷 (1629–1691). Siku quanshu edition.
*Qidong yeyu* 齊東野語. Zhou Mi 周密 (1232–1298). Beijing: Zhonghua shuju, 1983.
*Qing shilu* 清實錄. Beijing: Zhonghua shuju, 1986–1987.
*Qingdai Baxian dang'an huibian, Qianlong juan* 清代巴縣檔案匯編乾隆卷. Sichuan dang'an guan 四川檔案館, comp. Beijing: Dang'an chubanshe, 1991.
*Qingshi duo* 清詩鐸. Zhang Yingchang 張應昌 (1790–1874), comp. 1869. Beijing: Zhonghua shuju, 1960.
*Qingshi gao* 清史稿. Beijing: Zhonghua shuju, 1977.
*Qingyuan tiaofa shilei* 慶元條法事類, ca. 1200. Beijing: Kaitong shushe, 1948.
*Qinzhai ji* 勤齋集. Xiao Ju 蕭□ (1241–1318). Siku quanshu edition.
*Quan Tang wen* 全唐文. Beijing: Zhonghua shuju, 1983.
*Quan Yuan sanqu* 全元散曲. Sui Shusen 隋樹森, comp. Beijing: Zhonghua shuju, 1964.
*Quan Yuan wen* 全元文. Li Xiusheng 李修生, comp. Nanjing: Jiangsu guji chubanshe, 1997–2002.
*Renpu leiji* 人譜類記. Liu Zongzhou 劉宗周 (1578–1645). Siku quanshu edition.
*Rongchun tang ji* 容春堂集. Shao Bao 邵寶 (1460–1527). Siku quanshu edition.
*Rulin waishi* 儒林外史. Wu Jingzi 吳敬梓 (eighteenth century). Shanghai: Shanghai guji chubanshe, 1984.
*Sandong shiyi* 三洞拾遺. Hefei: Huangshan shushe, 2005, 20 vols.

*Sandong zhunang* 三洞珠囊. Wang Xuanhe 王懸河 (fl. 672–683), comp. Daozang 1139.
*Sanguo zhi* 三國志. Beijing: Zhonghua shuju, 1973.
*Sanji zhiming quanti* 三極至命筌蹄. Daozang 275.
*Santian neijie jing* 三天內解經. Daozang 1205.
*Shangqing dongzhen zhihui guanshen dajie wen* 上清洞真智慧觀身大戒文. Daozang 1364.
*Shangqing Lingbao dafa* 上清靈寶大法. Ning Quanzhen 寧全真 (1101–1181). Daozang 1221.
*Shenbao* 申報. Shanghai: Shenbaoguan, daily, 1872–1949.
*Shengchao poxie ji* 聖朝破邪集. Xu Changzhi 徐昌治, comp. 1639. 1805 edition.
*Shengjing huizuan* 聖經彙纂. 1806 edition at Bibliothèque nationale de France.
*Shiji* 史記. Beijing: Zhonghua shuju, 1959.
*Shizong Xian huangdi shangyu neige* 世宗憲皇帝上諭內閣. Siku quanshu edition.
*Shizong Xian huangdi shengxun* 世宗憲皇帝聖訓. Siku quanshu edition.
*Shizong Xian huangdi yu xing qiwu zouyi* 世宗憲皇帝諭行旗務奏議. Siku quanshu edition.
*Shizong Xian huangdi zhupi yuzhi* 世宗憲皇帝硃批諭旨. Siku quanshu edition.
*Shuijing lu* 水鏡錄. Daozang 1479.
*Shuyi ji* 述異記. Dongxuan zhuren 東軒主人. Shuoling 說鈴 edition, Kangxi era, *Siku quanshu cunmu congshu* 四庫全書存目叢書, Zibu 子部, vol. 250.
*(Qinding) Siku quanshu zongmu* (欽定)四庫全書總目. Beijing: Zhonghua shuju, 1997.
*Song huiyao jigao* 宋會要輯稿. Xu Song 徐松 (1781–1848) et al., comp. Beijing: Zhonghua shuju, 1957.
*Song xingtong* 宋刑統 (original title *Chongxiang dingxing tong* 重詳定刑統). Dou Yi 竇儀 (914–996) et al., comp. 963. Beijing: Falü chubanshe, 1999.
*Songshi* 宋史. Beijing: Zhonghua shuju, 1977.
*Songshu* 宋書. Beijing: Zhonghua shuju, 1974.
*Su Dongpo quanji* 蘇東坡全集. Su Shi 蘇軾 (1036–1101). Beijing: Zhonghua shuju, 1986 (reprint of 1936 edition).
*Suishi guangji* 歲時廣記. Chen Yuanqing 陳元靚 (thirteenth century). Congshu jicheng 叢書集成 edition.
*Suiyin manlu* 隨隱漫錄. Chen Shichong 陳世崇 (1245–1308). Congshu jicheng 叢書集成 edition.
*Suiyuan shidan* 隨園食單. Yuan Mei 袁枚 (1716–1798). In *Yuan Mei quanji* 袁枚全集. Nanjing: Jiangsu guji chubanshe, 1997, vol. 5.
*Taiji zhenren shuo ershisi men jiejing* 太極真人說二十四門戒經. Daozang 183.
*Taiping guangji* 太平廣記. Li Fang 李昉 (925–996) et al., comp. 978. Beijing: Zhonghua shuju, 1961.
*Taiping huanyu ji* 太平寰宇記. Yue Shi 樂史 (930–1007). ca. 980. 1803 edition of the Nanchang Wan family.
*Taiping jing hejiao* 太平經合校. Wang Ming 王明, ed. Beijing: Zhonghua shuju, 1960.
*Taishang ganying pian* 太上感應篇. Li Changling 李昌齡, comp. Daozang 1167.
*Taishang ganying pian jizhu* 太上感應篇集註. 1706. (Chongkan) Daozang jiyao edition.

*Taishang ganying pian jizhuan* 太上感應篇集傳. Wang Yanqiao 王燕樵. 1899. *Zangwai daoshu*, vol. 27.

*(Ciguan fenxie ben) Taishang ganying pian yinjing qianzhu* (詞館分寫本)太上感應篇引經箋註. Hui Dong 惠棟 and Luo Dunyan 羅惇衍. 1749. *Zangwai daoshu*, vol. 12.

*Taishang ganying pian zhu* 太上感應篇註. Wang Yantang 王硯堂. 1899 ed., *Zangwai daoshu*, vol. 12.

*Taishang Lingbao wufu xu* 太上靈寶五符序. Daozang 388.

*Taishang shuo Xuantian dasheng zhenwu benzhuan shenzhou miaojing* 太上說玄天大聖真武本傳神咒妙經. Chen Zhong 陳伀, comp. Daozang 754.

*Taiwan guanxi jishi, zhongyi ben* 臺灣慣習記事中譯本. 1901. Taizhong: Faxin ren Jiang Qinglin, 1984.

*Taiwan tongshi* 臺灣通史. Lian Heng 連横. 1918. Taiwan wenxian shiliao congkan edition.

*Taiwan wenxian shiliao congkan* 臺灣文獻史料叢刊. Taipei: Taiwan datong shuju, 1984.

*Taiwei lingshu ziwen xianji zhenji shangjing* 太微靈書紫文仙忌真記上經. Daozang 179.

*Taiwei xianjun gongguo ge* 太微仙君功過格. 1171. Daozang 186.

*Taizong Wen huangdi shengxun* 太宗文皇帝聖訓. Siku quanshu edition.

*Tang da zhaoling ji* 唐大詔令集. Song Minqiu 宋敏求 (Song), comp. Shanghai: Shangwu yinshuguan, 1959.

*Tanglü shuyi* 唐律疏議. Changsun Wuji 長孫無忌 et al., comp. Beijing: Zhonghua shuju, 1983.

*Taopi gongdu* 陶甓公牘. Liu Ruji 劉汝驥. 1911. *Guanzhen shu jicheng*, vol. 10.

*Tianma shanfang yigao* 天馬山房遺稿. Zhu Zhe 朱浙 (1486–1552). Siku quanshu edition.

*Tixuan zhenren xianyi lu* 體玄真人顯異錄. Daozang 594.

*Tongshan lu* 同善錄. Xu Qilin 徐起霖. 1718. Incomplete undated edition at Sterling Memorial Library, Yale University.

*Tuhua ribao* 圖畫日報. 1909–1910. In *Qingmo minchu baokan tuhua jicheng xupian* 清末民初報刊圖畫集成續篇, 20 vols., Guojia tushuguan fenguan 國家圖書館分館, comp. Beijing: Quanguo tushuguan wenxian weisuo fuzhi zhongxin, 2003.

*Tuniu bao* 屠牛報. Yu Zhi 余治 (1809–1874). *Shuji tang jinyue chuji* 庶幾堂今樂初集, 1880.

*Weishu* 魏書. Beijing: Zhonghua shuju, 1974.

*Weixin bian* 未信編. Pan Biaocan 潘杓燦. 1684. *Guanzhen shu jicheng*, vol. 3.

*Wenjian jinlu* 聞見近錄. Wang Gong 王鞏 (1048–after 1104). Song edition. Reprinted Beijing: Zhonghua shuju, n.d.

*Wenming xiaoshi* 文明小史. Li Boyuan 李伯元 (Li Baojia 寶嘉, 1867–1906). In *Li Boyuan quanji* 李伯元全集. Nanjing: Jiangsu guji chubanshe, 1997, vol. 1.

*Wu Youru huabao* 吳友如畫寶. Shanghai: Biyuan, 1909.

*Wubian* 武編. Tang Shunzhi 唐順之 (1507–1560). Siku quanshu edition.

*Wudai huiyao* 五代會要. Wang Pu 王溥 (922–982), comp. Congshu jicheng 叢書集成 edition.

*Wudu fasheng* 吳都法乘. Zhou Yongnian 周永年 (1582–1674). 1936 manuscript, *Zhongguo fosi shizhi congkan* 中國佛寺史志叢刊, 3rd series. Taipei: Danqing tushu gongsi, 1985.

*Wujun zhi* 吳郡志. Fan Chengda 范成大 (1126–1193). Nanjing: Jiangsu guji chubanshe, 1986.

*Wushang neibi zhenzang jing* 無上內秘真藏經. Daozang 4.

*Wuzhong yigui* 五種遺規. Chen Hongmou 陳宏謀 (1696–1771), comp. Sibu beiyao 四部備要 edition.

*Xichao renjian* 熙朝人鑑 (commentaries to *Yinzhi wen* and *Jueshi zhenjing*). 1887 edition at Sterling Memorial Library, Yale University.

*Xin Tangshu* 新唐書. Beijing: Zhonghua shuju, 1975.

*Xinchu xianchuan liyuan baojuan* 新出仙傳立願寶卷. 1897 edition in *Ming Qing minjian zongjiao jingjuan wenxian,* vol. 11.

*Xing'an huilan* 刑案匯覽 and *Xing'an huilan xuzeng* 刑案匯覽續增. Shanghai: Hongwen shuju, 1893.

*Xingbu bizhao jiajian cheng'an* 刑部比照加減成案. 1834 edition.

*Xingshi yinyuan zhuan* 醒世姻緣傳. Xizhousheng 西周生. Shanghai: Shanghai guji chubanshe, 1981.

*Xinzheng lu* 信徵錄. Xu Qing 徐慶. Shuoling 說鈴 edition, Kangxi era, *Siku quanshu cunmu congshu* 四庫全書存目叢書, Zibu 子部, vol. 250.

*Xu Jinpingmei* 續金瓶梅. Ding Yaokang 丁耀亢 (1599–1671). In *Jinpingmei xushu sanzhong* 金瓶梅續書三種. Ji'nan: Qilu shushe, 1988.

*(Qinding) Xu Wenxian tongkao* (欽定)續文獻通考. Siku quanshu edition.

*(Qianlong) Xu Yaozhou zhi* (乾隆)續耀州志. Wang Hao 汪灝 et al., comp. 1762. Reprint, Taipei: Chengwen chubanshe, 1976.

*Xu Yijian zhi* 續夷堅志. Yuan Haowen 元好問 (1190–1257). Congshu jicheng 叢書集成 edition.

*Xuandu lüwen* 玄都律文. Daozang 188.

*Xuanshi zhi* 宣室志. Zhang Du 張讀 (834?–after 882). Beijing: Zhonghua shuju, 1983.

*Xuansi suotan* 懸笥瑣探. Liu Chang 劉昌. *Wuchao xiaoshuo daguan* 五朝小說大觀.

*Xuantian shangdi chuixun* 玄天上帝垂訓. Ming edition, *Zangwai daoshu,* vol. 22.

*Xunzi jijie* 荀子集解. Wang Xianqian 王先謙, comp. Beijing: Beijing daxue chubanshe, 1988.

*(Xinjiao jiujuan ben) Yangchun baixue* (新校九卷本)陽春白雪. Yang Chaoying 楊朝英 (Yuan). Beijing: Zhonghua shuju, 1957.

*Yanshi jiaxun jijie* 顏氏家訓集解. Yan Zhitui 顏之推 (531–after 590), Wang Liqi 王利器, ed. Shanghai: Shanghai guji chubanshe, 1986.

*Yaoxiu keyi jielü chao* 要修科儀戒律鈔. Daozang 463.

*Yijian zhi* 夷堅志. Hong Mai 洪邁 (1123–1202). Beijing: Zhonghua shuju, 1981.

*Yijue liao zaji* 猗覺寮雜記. Zhu Yi 朱翌 (1097–1167). Congshu jicheng 叢書集成 edition.

*Yinshi shenyan* 飲食紳言. Long Zunxu 龍遵敘 (Ming period). Congshu jicheng 叢書集成 edition.

*Yinzhi wen song* 陰騭文頌. Cao Chenting 曹震亭. *Zhaodai congshu* 昭代叢書, 1849.

*Yinzhi wen tushuo* 陰騭文圖說. Huang Zhengyuan 黃正元, ed. 1865, *Zangwai daoshu,* vol. 27.

*Yinzhi wen tushuo* 陰騭文圖說. Rong Zhu 榮柱. 1801. Original edition held in the collections of the Library of the Australian National University, http://hdl.handle.net/1885/112068.

*Yinzhi wen tuzheng* 陰騭文圖證. Xu Guangqing 許光清 (text) and Fei Danxu 費丹旭 (illustrations). 1878. *Zangwai daoshu,* vol. 27 and slightly different edition in *Ming Qing minjian zongjiao jingjuan wenxian,* vol. 10.

*Yinzhi wen xiangzhu* 陰騭文像註. Zhao Rusheng 趙如升. 1719. *Zangwai daoshu,* vol. 12.

*Yinzhi wen yinmeng* 陰騭文引蒙. Ding Sheng 丁生, in an untitled *congshu,* 1836, Bibliothèque de l'Institut des Hautes Études Chinoises.

*Yinzhi wen zhu* 陰騭文註. Zhu Gui 朱珪. (Chongkan) Daozang jiyao edition.

*Yinzhi wen zhuzheng* 陰騭文註證. In *Wendi quanshu* 文帝全書, 1876 edition at Sterling Memorial Library, Yale University.

*Yisheng baode zhuan* 翊聖保德傳. Wang Qinruo 王欽若 (962–1025). Daozang 1285.

*Yiwen Quanshan jing yizhu* 彝文勸善經譯注. Ma Xueliang 馬學良 et al., eds. Beijing: Zhongyang minzu xueyuan chubanshe, 1986.

*Yongchuang xiaopin* 湧幢小品. Zhu Guozhen 朱國禎 (jinshi 1589). Biji xiaoshuo daguan 筆記小說大觀 edition.

*Yongxian zhai biji* 庸閒齋筆記. Chen Qiyuan 陳其元 (1811–1881). Beijing: Zhonghua shuju, 1989.

*Yougong de niu dage* 有功的牛大哥. Lu Yiyan 陸衣言 and Jiang Jingfu 蔣鏡芙. Shanghai: Zhonghua shuju, 1923.

*Youyang zazu* 酉陽雜俎. Duan Chengshi 段成式 (?–863). Beijing: Zhonghua shuju, 1981.

*Yuanmiao guan zhi* 元妙觀志. Gu Yuan 顧沅. 1832 edition, *Zangwai daoshu,* vol. 20.

*Yuanshi* 元史. Beijing: Zhonghua shuju, 1976.

*Yuanshi tianzun shuo Beifang Zhenwu miaojing* 元始天尊說北方眞武妙經. Daozang 27.

*Yuding jinke jiyao* 玉定金科輯要. In *Sandong shiyi,* vol. 12.

*Yuewei caotang biji* 閱微草堂筆記. Ji Yun 紀昀 (1724–1805). Tianjin: Tianjin guji chubanshe, 1994.

*Yunji qiqian* 雲笈七籤. Daozang 1032.

*Yunnan difang zhi daojiao he minzu minjian zongjiao ziliao suobian* 雲南地方志道教和民族民間宗教資料瑣編. Yunnan sheng bianji zu 雲南省編輯組, comp. Kunming: Yunnan renmin chubanshe, 1986.

*Yunxi ji* 筠谿集. Li Mixun 李彌遜 (1089–1153). Siku quanshu edition.

*Zangwai daoshu* 藏外道書. Chengdu: Bashu shushe, 1992–1994, 36 vols.

*Zaolin zazu* 棗林雜俎. Tan Qian 談遷 (1594–1657). Biji xiaoshuo daguan 筆記小說大觀 edition.

*(Chongzhen) Zhaoqing fuzhi* 崇禎肇慶府志. Chen Xuankui 陳烜奎, comp. 1640 edition.

*Zheng zhongcheng gong yilou ji* 鄭中丞公益樓集. Zheng Eryang 鄭二陽 (fl. 1609–1646). Siku weishoushu jikan 四庫未收書輯刊 edition.

*Zhen'gao* 真誥. Tao Hongjing 陶弘景 (456–536). Daozang 1016.

*Zhenwu baojuan* 真武寶卷. Nanjing: Yide zhai shanshu fang, 1893.

*Zhiyi xubian* 志異續編. Qingchengzi 青城子. 1831. Shanghai: Shenbaoguan, 1877.

*Zhongfu tang xuanji* 中復堂選集. Yao Ying 姚瑩. 1867. Taiwan wenxian shiliao congkan.

*Zhongguo difangzhi minsu ziliao huibian* 中國地方志民俗資料匯編, Dongbei juan 東北卷, Huabei juan 華北卷. Ding Shiliang 丁世良 and Zhao Fang 趙放, eds. Beijing: Beijing tushuguan chubanshe, 1989.

*Zhongguo xi'nan diqu lidai shike huibian* 中國西南地區歷代石刻匯編. Tianjin: Tianjin guji chubanshe, 1998, 20 vols.

*Zhonghua minguo fagui huibian* 中華民國法規彙編. Shanghai: Shangwu yinshuguan, 1937.

*Zhongxing xiaoji* 中興小紀. Xiong Ke 熊克 (jinshi 1157). Siku quanshu edition.

*Zhongyang yanjiuyuan Lishi yuyan yanjiusuo xiancun Qingdai neige daku yuancang Ming Qing dang'an* 中央研究院歷史語言研究所現存清代內閣大庫原藏明清檔案. Taipei: Zhongyang yanjiuyuan, 1986.

*Zhuangzi jishi* 莊子集釋. Guo Qingfan 郭慶藩 (1844–1896), ed. Beijing: Zhonghua shuju, 1961.

*Zhuzi yulei* 朱子語類. Zhu Xi 朱熹 (1130–1200). Li Jingde 黎靖德, comp. 1270. Beijing: Zhonghua shuju, 1986.

*Zi buyu quanji* 子不語全集. Yuan Mei 袁枚 (1716–1798). Shijiazhuang: Hebei renmin chubanshe, 1997.

*Zitong dijun huashu* 梓潼帝君化書. Revealed between 1194 and 1316. Daozang 170.

*Zizhi lu* 自知錄. Zhuhong 袾宏 (1535–1615). In *Anshi quanshu*.

*Zongzhi Zhe Min wenxi* 總制浙閩文檄. Liu Zhaoqi 劉兆麒 (Ming). 1672. *Guanzhen shu jicheng,* vol. 8.

*Zunsheng bajian* 遵生八牋. Gao Lian 高濂 (fl. 1573). Edition by Wang Dachun 王大淳, based on first edition in 1591. Chengdu: Bashu shushe, 1992.

*Zuoyi zizhen* 作邑自箴. Li Yuanbi 李元弼 (fl. 1117). 1117. Sibu congkan 四部叢刊 edition.

## Secondary Sources

Alexander, Katherine Laura Bos. *Teaching and Transformation: Yu Zhi and Popular Confucian Literature in the Late Qing.* Ann Arbor: University of Michigan Press, forthcoming.

———. "Virtues of the Vernacular: Moral Reconstruction in Late Qing Jiangnan and the Revitalization of Baojuan." PhD diss., University of Chicago, 2016.

Allès, Élisabeth. "À propos de l'Islam en Chine: Provocations anti-religieuses et attitudes anticléricales du XIXe siècle à nos jours." *Extrême-Orient Extrême-Occident* 24 (2002): 64–75.

———. *Musulmans de Chine: Une anthropologie des Hui du Henan*. Paris: Éditions de l'École des Hautes Études en Sciences Sociales, 2000.

Ambros, Barbara. *Bones of Contention: Animals and Religion in Contemporary Japan*. Honolulu: University of Hawai'i Press, 2012.

———. *Refraining from Killing and Releasing Life: Animal Releases in Early Modern Japan*. Work in progress.

———. "Tracing the Influence of Ming-Qing Buddhism in Early Modern Japan: Yunqi Zhuhong's Tract on Refraining from Killing and on Releasing Life and Ritual Animal Releases." *Religions* 12 (2021): 889. https://doi.org/10.3390/rel12100889.

Anderson, Eugene N. *The Food of China*. New Haven: Yale University Press, 1988.

Ang, Isabelle. "Le culte de Lü Dongbin sous les Song du Sud." *Journal asiatique* 285, no. 2 (1997): 473–507.

Arch, Jacobina. *Bringing Whales Ashore: Oceans and the Environment of Early Modern Japan*. Seattle: University of Washington Press, 2018.

Aubin, Françoise. "Cheval céleste et bovin chtonien." In *Quand le crible était dans la paille: Hommage à Pertev Naili Boratav,* edited by Rémy Dor and Michèle Nicolas, 37–63. Paris: Maisonneuve et Larose, 1978.

Barstow, Geoffrey. *Food of Sinful Demons: Meat, Vegetarianism, and the Limits of Buddhism in Tibet*. New York: Columbia University Press, 2017.

Bell, Catherine. "'A Precious Raft to Save the World': The Interaction of Scriptural Traditions and Printing in a Chinese Morality Book." *Late Imperial China* 17, no. 1 (1996): 158–200.

Benkheira, Mohammed Hocine. *Islâm et interdits alimentaires: Juguler l'animalité*. Paris: PUF, 2000.

Bodde, Derk. *Festivals in Classical China: New Year and Other Annual Observances during the Han Dynasty 206 B.C.–A.D. 220*. Princeton: Princeton University Press, 1975.

Boileau, Gilles. "Some Ritual Elaborations on Cooking and Sacrifice in Late Zhou and Western Han Texts." *Early China* 23–24 (1998–1999): 89–123.

Bokenkamp, Stephen. "The Yao Boduo Stele as Evidence for 'Dao-Buddhism' of the Early Lingbao Scriptures." *Cahiers d'Extrême-Asie* 9 (1996–1997): 55–67.

Bokenkamp, Stephen, with Peter Nickerson. *Early Daoist Scriptures*. Berkeley: University of California Press, 1997.

Boltz, Judith Magee. "Not by the Seal of Office Alone: New Weapons in Battles with the Supernatural." In *Religion and Society in T'ang and Sung China,* edited by Patricia Buckley Ebrey and Peter N. Gregory, 241–305. Honolulu: University of Hawai'i Press, 1993.

Bourgon, Jérôme, ed. "La coutume et la norme en Chine et au Japon." Special issue, *Extrême-Orient Extrême-Occident* 23 (2001).

Brokaw, Cynthia J. *The Ledgers of Merit and Demerit: Social Change and Moral Order in Late Imperial China*. Princeton: Princeton University Press, 1991.

Brown, Tristan G. "A Mountain of Saints and Sages: Muslims in the Landscape of Popular Religion in Late Imperial China." *T'oung Pao* 105, no. 3–4 (2019): 437–491.

Broy, Nikolas. "Moral Integration or Social Segregation? Vegetarianism and Vegetarian Religious Communities in Chinese Religious Life." In *Concepts and Methods for the Study of Chinese Religions III,* edited by Paul R. Katz and Stefania Travagnin, 37–64. Berlin: De Gruyter, 2019.

Bujard, Marianne. *Le sacrifice au ciel dans la Chine ancienne: Théorie et pratique sous les Han occidentaux*. Paris: École Française d'Extrême-Orient, 2000.

Bumbacher, Stephan Peter. *The Fragments of the Daoxue zhuan*. Frankfurt: Peter Lang, 2000.

Campany, Robert Ford. *Strange Writings: Anomaly Accounts in Early Medieval China*. Albany: State University of New York Press, 1996.

———. *To Live as Long as Heaven and Earth: A Translation and Study of Ge Hong's Traditions of Divine Transcendents*. Berkeley: University of California Press, 2002.

Cartier, Michel. "La marginalisation des animaux en Chine." *Anthropozoologica* 18 (1993): 7–15.

———. "L'homme et l'animal dans l'agriculture chinoise ancienne et moderne." *Études rurales* 151–152 (1999): 179–197.

Chan, Leo Tak-hung. *The Discourse on Foxes and Ghosts: Ji Yun and the Eighteenth-Century Literati Storytelling.* Honolulu: University of Hawai'i Press, 1998.

Chang, K. C., ed. *Food in Chinese Culture: Anthropological and Historical Perspectives.* New Haven: Yale University Press, 1977.

Chao Shin-yi. *Daoist Ritual, State Religion, and Popular Practices: Zhenwu Worship from Song to Ming (960–1644).* London: Routledge, 2011.

Chard, Robert L. "Rituals and Scriptures of the Stove Cult." In *Ritual and Scripture in Chinese Popular Religion,* Chinese Popular Culture Project 3, edited by David Johnson, 3–54. Berkeley: Institute of East Asian Studies, 1995.

Chau, Adam Yuet. "Script Fundamentalism: The Practice of Cherishing Written Characters (Lettered Paper 惜字紙) in the Age of Literati Decline and Commercial Revolution." In *Chinese and European Perspectives on the Study of Chinese Popular Religion(s),* edited by Philip Clart, 129–167. Taipei: Boyang, 2012.

Chen Guofu 陳國符. *Daozang yuanliu kao* 道藏源流考. Beijing: Zhonghua shuju, 1985.

Cheung, Neky Tak-Ching. "'Receiving Prayer Beads': A Lay-Buddhist Ritual Performed by Menopausal Women in Ninghua, Western Fujian." In *Recovering Buddhism in Modern China,* edited by Jan Kiely and J. Brooks Jessup, 291–332. New York: Columbia University Press, 2016.

Chikusa Masaaki 竺沙雅章. "Kissai jima ni tsuite 喫菜事魔について." In *Chūgoku bukkyō shakaishi kenkyū* 中國佛教社會史研究, 199–227. Kyoto: Dōhōsha, 1982.

Chong, Key Ray. *Cannibalism in China.* Wakefield, NH: Longwood Academic, 1990.

Chow Kai-wing 周啟榮. *The Rise of Confucian Ritualism in Late Imperial China: Ethics, Classics, and Lineage Discourse.* Stanford: Stanford University Press, 1994.

Clart, Philip. "Confucius and the Mediums: Is There a 'Popular Confucianism?'" *T'oung Pao* 89, no. 1–3 (2003): 1–38.

Cook, Constance A. "Moonshine and Millet: Feasting and Purification Rituals in Ancient China." In *Of Tripod and Palate: Food, Politics and Religion in Traditional China,* edited by Roel Sterckx, 9–33. New York: Palgrave, 2005.

Cumming, Nicole Maceira. "The Relationship between Meat Consumption and Power in Late Medieval and Early Modern England." *Sloth* 5, no. 1 (2019). https://www.animalsandsociety.org/research/sloth/sloth-volume-5-no-1-winter-2019/the-relationship-between-meat-consumption-and-power-in-late-medieval-and-early-modern-england/.

Davis, Edward L. *Society and the Supernatural in Song China.* Honolulu: University of Hawai'i Press, 2001.

de Bruyn, Pierre-Henry. *Le Wudang shan: Histoire des récits fondateurs.* Paris: Les Indes Savantes, 2010.

De Miramon, Charles. "Tabous alimentaires entre Japon et Europe médiévale." In *Identités, marges, mediations: Regards croisés sur la société japonaise,* edited by

Jean-Pierre Berthon, Anne Bouchy, and Pierre F. Souyri, 183–197. Paris: École Française d'Extrême-Orient , 2001.

Dean, Kenneth. "The Growth of Local Control over Cultural and Environmental Resources in Ming and Qing Coastal Fujian." In *The People and the Dao: New Studies in Chinese Religions in Honour of Daniel L. Overmyer,* edited by Philip Clart and Paul Crowe, 219–247. Sankt Augustin: Monumenta Serica, 2009.

Détienne, Marcel, and Jean-Pierre Vernant, eds. *La cuisine du sacrifice en pays grec.* Paris: Gallimard, 1979.

Dikötter, Frank. *The Discourse of Race in Modern China*. London: Hurst, 1992.

Doolittle, Justus. *Social Life of the Chinese: With Some Account of Their Religious, Governmental, Educational, and Business Customs and Opinions, with Special but Not Exclusive Reference to Fuhchau.* 2 vols. New York: Harper, 1865.

Doré, Henri. *Recherches sur les superstitions en Chine.* Shanghai: Imprimerie de la Mission Catholique, 1911–1928.

Douglas, Mary. *Purity and Danger: An Analysis of Concepts of Pollution and Taboo.* New York: Praeger, 1966.

DuBois, Thomas David. "China's Dairy Century: Making, Drinking and Dreaming of Milk." In *Animals and Human Society in Asia: Historical, Cultural and Ethical Perspectives,* edited by Rotem Kowner, Guy Bar-Oz, Michal Biran, Meir Shahar, and Gideon Shelach-Lavi, 179–211. Cham: Springer, 2020.

———. "Counting the Carnivores: Who Ate Meat in Republican-Era China?" *Social Science History* 46, no. 4 (2022): 751–775.

———. "Many Roads from Pasture to Plate: A Commodity Chain Approach to China's Beef Trade, 1732–1931." *Journal of Global History* 14, no. 1 (2019): 22–43.

DuBois, Thomas David, and Alicia Gao. "Big Meat: The Rise and Impact of Mega-farming in China's Beef, Sheep and Dairy Industries." *Asia-Pacific Journal/ Japan Focus* 15, no. 1 (2017): 1–20.

Dudbridge, Glen. *Religious Experience and Lay Society in T'ang China: A Reading of Tai Fu's* Kuang-i Chi. Cambridge: Cambridge University Press, 1995.

Durand, Jean-Louis. *Sacrifice et labour en Grèce ancienne: Essai d'anthropologie religieuse.* Paris: La Découverte, Rome, École Française de Rome, 1986.

Durand-Dastès, Vincent. *La conversion de l'Orient: Une pérégrination didactique de Bodhidharma dans un roman chinois du XVIIe siècle.* Brussels: Institut Belge des Hautes Études Chinoises, 2008.

———. "Prodiges ambigus: Les récits non-canoniques sur le surnaturel entre histoire religieuse, histoire littéraire et anthropologie." *Revue bibliographique de Sinologie* 20 (2002): 317–343.

Eberhard, Wolfram. "Ideas about Social Reforms in the Novel *Ching-hua yuan*." In *Moral and Social Values of the Chinese: Collected Essays,* 413–421. Taipei: Chengwen chubanshe, 1971.

———. *The Local Cultures of South and East China.* Translated by Alide Eberhard. Leiden: Brill, 1968.

Ebrey, Patricia Buckley. *Chu Hsi's Family Rituals: A Twelfth-Century Chinese Manual for the Performance of Cappings, Weddings, Funerals, and Ancestral Rites.* Princeton: Princeton University Press, 1991.

———. *Confucianism and Family Rituals in Imperial China: A Social History of Writing about Rites*. Princeton: Princeton University Press, 1991.

———. "Cremation in Sung China." *American Historical Review* 95 (1990): 406–428.

Ebrey, Patricia Buckley, and Peter N. Gregory, eds. *Religion and Society in T'ang and Sung China*. Honolulu: University of Hawai'i Press, 1993.

Eichman, Jennifer. *A Late Sixteenth-Century Chinese Buddhist Fellowship*. Leiden: Brill, 2016.

Eliasberg, Danielle. "Pratiques funéraires animales en Chine ancienne et médiévale." *Journal asiatique* 280, no. 1–2 (1992): 115–144.

Elisseeff, Danielle. "Des animaux sous une chape de plomb." *Anthropozoologica* 18 (1993): 17–28.

———. "L'anthropozoologie: Un thème nouveau dans quelques revues chinoises." *Revue bibliographique de Sinologie* 16 (1998): 273–281.

———. "Les enterrements d'animaux en Chine ancienne: Le cas du chien de Confucius." In *La sépulture des animaux: Concepts, usages et pratiques à travers le temps et l'espace. Contributions à l'étude de l'animalité,* edited by Liliane Bodson, 77–93. Liège: Université de Liège, 2001.

———. "L'étrange goût du chien." In *Savourer, goûter,* edited by Flora Blanchon, 83–88. Paris: Presses de l'Université de Paris-Sorbonne, 1995.

Elman, Benjamin A. *A Cultural History of Civil Examinations in Late Imperial China*. Berkeley: University of California Press, 2000.

Engelhardt, Ute. "Dietetics in Tang China and the First Extant Works of *Materia dietetica*." In *Innovations in Chinese Medicine,* edited by Elisabeth Hsu, 173–191. Cambridge: Cambridge University Press, 2001.

Eskildsen, Stephen. *Asceticism in Early Taoist Religion*. New York: State University of New York Press, 1998.

Fabre-Vassas, Claudine. *The Singular Beast: Jews, Christians, and the Pig*. Translated by Carol Volk. New York: Columbia University Press, 1999.

Fang Ling. "Les médecins laïques contre l'exorcisme sous les Ming: La disparition de l'enseignement de la thérapeutique rituelle dans le cursus de l'Institut impérial de médecine." *Extrême-Orient Extrême-Occident* 24 (2002): 31–45.

Fava, Patrice. *La revanche de Han Xin, un mystère taoïste*. Paris: École Française d'Extrême-Orient/Centre National de la Recherche Scientifique, 2005. [DVD]

Fei Chengkang 費成康 et al., eds. *Zhongguo jiafa zugui* 中國家法族規. Shanghai: Shanghai shehui kexueyuan chubanshe, 1998.

Ferrières, Madeleine. *Histoire des peurs alimentaires: Du Moyen Âge à l'aube du XXe siècle*. Paris: Seuil, 2002.

Fiskesjö, Magnus. "Rising from Blood-Stained Fields: Royal Hunting and State Formation in Shang China." *Bulletin of the Museum of Far Eastern Antiquities* 73 (2001): 48–191.

Flandrin, Jean-Louis, and Massimo Montanari, eds. *Histoire de l'alimentation*. Paris: Fayard, 1996.

Forke, Alfred. *Elf chinesische Singspieltexte aus neuerer Zeit, nebst zwei Dramen in westlischer Manier*. Edited by Martin Gimm. Stuttgart: Steiner, 1993.

Forte, Antonino, and Jacques May. "Chōsai 長齋." In *Hōbōgirin*, 5:392–407. Paris: Maisonneuve, 1979.

Freeman, Michael. "Sung." In *Food in Chinese Culture: Anthropological and Historical Perspectives,* edited by K. C. Chang, 141–176. New Haven: Yale University Press, 1977.

Fuma Susumu 夫馬進. *Chūgoku zenkai zendōshi kenkyū* 中国善会善堂史研究. Kyoto: Dohosha shuppan, 1997.

Funayama, Tōru. "The *Fanwang jing* (Scripture of Brahma's Net) in the First Edition of the Korean Canon: A Preliminary Survey." *Zinbun* 45 (2015): 1–25.

Furubayashi Morihiro 古林森廣. "Sōdai no kōgyū ni tsuite 宋代の耕牛について." In *Chūgoku shakaishi no shosō* 中國社會史の諸相, edited by Yokoyama Suguru 横山英 and Teraji Jun 寺地遵, 74–109. Tokyo: Keisō shobō, 1988.

———. "Sōdai no tosatsu, shokunikugyō 宋代の屠殺,食肉業." In *Sōdai sangyō keizaishi kenkyū* 宋代産業經濟史研究, 140–165. Tokyo: Kokusho kankōkai, 1987.

Gamble, Sidney D. *How Chinese Families Live in Peiping.* New York: Funk and Wagnalls, 1933.

Gernet, Jacques. *Buddhism in Chinese Society: An Economic History from the Fifth to the Tenth Centuries.* Translated by Franciscus Verellen. New York: Columbia University Press, 1995.

———. "Ce qui distingue l'homme de l'animal." *Études chinoises* 18, no. 1–2 (1999): 15–30.

———. "Pitié pour les animaux." In *De Dunhuang au Japon: Études chinoises et bouddhiques offertes à Michel Soymié,* edited by Jean-Pierre Drège, 293–300. Geneva: Droz, 1996.

Getz, Daniel A., Jr. "T'ien-t'ai Pure Land Societies and the Creation of the Pure Land Patriarchate." In *Buddhism in the Sung,* edited by Peter N. Gregory and Daniel A. Getz Jr., 477–523. Honolulu: University of Hawai'i Press, 1999.

Gillette, Maris Boyd. *Between Mecca and Beijing. Modernization and Consumption among Urban Chinese Muslims.* Stanford: Stanford University Press, 2000.

Gjertson, Donald E. *Miraculous Retribution: A Study and Translation of T'ang Lin's* Ming-pao chi. Berkeley: Center for South and Southeast Asia Studies, University of California, 1989.

Goldfuss, Gabriele. *Vers un bouddhisme du XXe siècle: Yang Wenhui (1837–1911), réformateur laïque et imprimeur.* Paris: Collège de France, Institut des Hautes Études Chinoises, Mémoires de l'Institut des Hautes Études Chinoises, 2001.

Golvers, Noël. *François de Rougemont, S.J., Missionary in Ch'ang-shu (Chiang-nan): A Study of the Account Book (1674–1676) and the Elogium.* Leuven: Leuven University Press, 1999.

Goossaert, Vincent. "1898: The Beginning of the End for Chinese Religion?" *Journal of Asian Studies* 65, no. 2 (2006): 307–336.

———. "Anatomie d'un discours anticlérical: *Le Shenbao,* 1872–1878." *Extrême-Orient Extrême-Occident* 24 (2002): 113–131.

———. "Animals and Eschatology in the Nineteenth-Century Discourse." In *Animals through Chinese History: Earliest Times to 1911,* edited by Roel Sterckx, Martina Siebert, and Dagmar Schäfer, 181–198. Cambridge: Cambridge University Press, 2019.

———. "Divine Codes, Spirit-Writing, and the Ritual Foundations of Morality Books." *Asia Major* 33, no. 1 (2020): 1–31.

———. *Heavenly Masters: Two Thousand Years of the Daoist State*. Honolulu: University of Hawai'i Press, 2021.

———. "Late Imperial Chinese Piety Books." *Studies in Chinese Religions* 5, no. 1 (2019): 38–54.

———. "Les sens multiples du végétarisme en Chine." In *A croire et à manger: Religions et alimentation,* edited by Aïda Kanafani-Zahar, Séverine Mathieu, and Sophie Nizard, 65–93. Paris: L'Harmattan, 2007.

———. *Livres de morale révélés par les dieux*. Paris: Les Belles Lettres, 2012.

———. *Making the Gods Speak: The Ritual Production of Revelation in Chinese History*. Cambridge, MA: Harvard University Asia Center, 2022.

———. "Ming Qing yilai shanshu zhong de niujie wenxian jianjie 明清以來善書中的牛戒文獻簡介." *Shanshu, jingjuan yu wenxian* 善書、經卷與文獻 10 (2024): 47–90.

———. "The Beef Taboo and the Sacrificial Structure of Late Imperial Chinese Society." In *Of Tripod and Palate: Food, Politics and Religion in Traditional China,* edited by Roel Sterckx, 237–248. New York: Palgrave, 2005.

———. "The Invention of an Order: Collective Identity in Thirteenth-Century Quanzhen." *Journal of Chinese Religion* 29 (2001): 111–138.

———. *The Taoists of Peking, 1800–1949: A Social History of Urban Clerics*. Cambridge, MA: Harvard University Asia Center, 2007.

———. *Vies des saints exorcistes: Hagiographies taoïstes, 11ᵉ–16ᵉ siècles*. Paris: Les Belles Lettres, 2021.

Goossaert, Vincent, and David A. Palmer. *The Religious Question in Modern China*. Chicago: University of Chicago Press, 2011.

Goossaert, Vincent, and Valentine Zuber. "Introduction: La Chine a-t-elle connu l'anticléricalisme?" *Extrême-Orient Extrême-Occident* 24 (2002): 5–16.

Greene, Eric. "A Reassessment of the Early History of Vegetarianism in Chinese Buddhism." *Asia Major* 29, no. 1 (2016): 1–43.

Gregory, Peter N., and Daniel A. Getz Jr., eds. *Buddhism in the Sung*. Honolulu: University of Hawai'i Press, 1999.

de Groot, Jan J. M. *Le code du Mâhayâna en Chine: Son influence sur la vie monacale et sur le monde laïque*. Amsterdam: Johannes Müller, 1893.

———. "Miséricorde envers les animaux dans le bouddhisme chinois." *T'oung Pao* 3 (1892): 466–489.

———. *Sectarianism and Religious Persecution in China*. Amsterdam: Johannes Müller, 1903–1904.

Guo Fu 郭郛 and Cheng Qingtai 成慶泰. *Zhongguo gudai dongwuxue shi* 中國古代動物學史. Beijing: Kexue chubanshe, 1999.

Guo Jian 郭建. "Liangshan haohan chi shenme rou 梁山好漢吃什麼肉." In *Zhongguo fa wenhua manbi* 中國法文化漫筆, 107–112. Shanghai: Dongfang chuban zhongxin, 1999.

Guo Qitao. *Ritual Opera and Mercantile Lineage: The Confucian Transformation of Popular Culture in Late Imperial Huizhou*. Stanford: Stanford University Press, 2005.

Guo Shengbo 郭聲波. "Lishi shiqi Sichuan da shengchu yangzhi de dili chayi 歷史時期四川大牲畜養殖的地理差異." *Zhongguo nongshi* 中國農史, no. 2 (2001): 82–90.

ter Haar, Barend. "Buddhist-Inspired Options: Aspects of Lay Religious Life in the Lower Yangzi from 1100 until 1340." *T'oung Pao* 87, no. 1–3 (2001): 92–152.

———. "From Field to Text in the Study of Chinese Religion." In *Religion and Orientalism in Asian Studies,* edited by Kiri Paramore, 85–105. London: Bloomsbury, 2016.

———. *Practicing Scripture: A Lay Buddhist Movement in Late Imperial China*. Honolulu: University of Hawai'i Press, 2014.

———. *Ritual and Mythology of the Chinese Triads: Creating an Identity*. Leiden: Brill, 1998.

———. *The White Lotus Teachings in Chinese Religious History*. Leiden: Brill, 1992.

Halverson, John. "Animal Categories and Terms of Abuse." *Man,* n.s., 11, no. 4 (1976): 505–516.

Hansen, Valerie. *Changing Gods in Medieval China, 1127–1276*. Princeton: Princeton University Press, 1990.

Hao Chunwen. "She Association Manuscripts from Dunhuang and the Study of Medieval She Association." *Hualin International Journal of Buddhist Studies* 4, no. 1 (2021): 59–98.

Harris, Marvin. *Culture, People, Nature*. New York: Harper, 1993.

Heirman, Ann. "The Consumption of Garlic: Vinaya Rules." *Journal of Chinese Buddhist Studies* 34 (2021): 63–89.

Hino Kaisaburō 日野開三郎. "Sōdai no chingyū ni tsuite 宋代の賃牛に就いて." *Shien* 史淵 56 (1953): 85–116.

———. "Sōdai no chōseigyū 宋代の長生牛." *Tōyō gakuhō* 東洋學報 32, no. 3 (1950): 66–84.

———. "Sōdai no sogyū ni tsuite 宋代の租牛に就いて." *Shien* 史淵 58 (1953): 1–36.

Holm, David. *Killing a Buffalo for the Ancestors: A Zhuang Cosmological Text from Southwest China*. DeKalb: Center for Southeast Asian Studies, Northern Illinois University, 2003.

Holtzman, Jon. "On Whale: Conundrums of Culture and Cetaceans as Local Meat." *Ethnos* 82, no. 2 (2017): 277–297.

Hostetler, Laura. *Qing Colonial Enterprise: Ethnography and Cartography in Early Modern China*. Chicago: University of Chicago Press, 2001.

Hsia, C. T. "The Scholar-Novelist and Chinese Culture: A Reappraisal of *Ching-hua yuan*." In *Chinese Narrative: Critical and Theoretical Essays,* edited by Andrew Plaks, 266–305. Princeton: Princeton University Press, 1977.

Hu Jiechen 胡劼辰. "Xu Qian xiaokao: Fuji, jiangxue yu shanshu chuangzhi 徐謙 (1776–1864) 小考：扶乩、講學與善書創製." In *Fuluan wenhua yu minzhong zongjiao guoji xueshu yantaohui lunwenji* 扶鸞文化與民眾宗教國際學術研討會論文集, edited by Fan Chun-wu 范純武, 89–143. Taipei: Boyang, 2020.

———. "*Wenchang dijun yinzhi wen* qiyuan xinyan: Yi *Weishan yinzhi*, *Quanxing yinzhi wen* yiji *Zitong dijun jiujie baozhang* wei zhongxin 《文昌帝君陰隲文》起源新研 ： 以《為善陰隲》、《勸行陰隲文》以及《梓潼帝君救劫寶章》為中心." *Lishi, yishu yu Taiwan renwen luncong* 歷史、藝術與台灣人文論叢 11 (2017): 133–169.

Huang, Shih-shan Susan. *Picturing the True Form: Daoist Visual Culture in Traditional China*. Cambridge, MA: Harvard University Asia Center, 2012.

Huang Shijian 黃時鑒 and William Sargent. *Shijiu shiji Zhongguo shijing fengqing, sanbailiushi hang* 十九世紀中國市井風情，三百六十行 *Customs and Conditions of Chinese City Streets in 19th Century, 360 Professions in China.* Shanghai: Shanghai guji chubanshe, 1999.

Hulsewé, Anthony F. P. *Periodieke executie- en slacht-verboden in de T'ang tijd en hun oorsprong. Inaugural Lecture, June 4, 1948*. Leiden: Brill, 1948.

Huntington, Rania. "Singing Punishment and Redemption in the Taiping Civil War: Yu Zhi's Plays." *Frontiers of History in China* 13, no. 2 (2018): 211–226.

Hymes, Robert. *Way and Byway: Taoism, Local Religion, and Models of Divinity in Sung and Modern China*. Berkeley: University of California Press, 2002.

Idema, Wilt. "Guanyin's Acolytes." In *Linked Faiths: Essays on Chinese Religions and Traditional Culture in Honour of Kristofer Schipper,* edited by Jan A. M. de Meyer and Peter M. Engelfriet, 205–226. Leiden: Brill, 2000.

———. *Spiegel van de klassieke Chinese poëzie van het Boek der Oden tot de Qing-dynastie*. Amsterdam: Meulenhoff, 1991.

———. "The Ultimate Sanqu Song: Yao Shouzhong's 'The Complaint of the Ox' and Its Place in Tanaka Kenji's Scholarship on Sanqu." *Journal of Chinese Literature and Culture* 8, no. 1 (2021): 12–30.

Idema, Wilt, and Allard M. Olof. *The Legend of Prince Golden Calf in China and Korea*. Amherst, NY: Cambria Press, 2022.

Imahori Seiji 今堀誠二. *Chūgoku hōken shakai no kōzō* 中國封建社會の構造. Tokyo: Nihon gakujutsu shinkōkai, 1955.

Inglis, Alister David. *Hong Mai's* Record of the Listener *and Its Song Dynasty Context*. Albany: State University of New York Press, 2006.

Itoh, Mayumi. *The Japanese Culture of Mourning Whales: Whale Graves and Memorial Monuments in Japan*. Singapore: Palgrave Macmillan, 2018.

Jones, Charles Brewer. *Buddhism in Taiwan: Religion and the State, 1660–1990*. Honolulu: University of Hawai'i Press, 1999.

Jordan, David, and Daniel Overmyer. *The Flying Phoenix*. Princeton: Princeton University Press, 1986.

Kalland, Arne. "Japanese Perceptions of Whales and Dolphins." In *Wildlife in Asia: Cultural Perspectives,* edited by John Knight, 73–87. London: RoutledgeCurzon, 2004.

———. *Unveiling the Whale: Discourses on Whales and Whaling*. New York: Berghahn, 2012.

Kalland, Arne, and Brian Moeran. *Japanese Whaling: End of an Era?* London: Routledge, 2013.

Katz, Paul R. *Demon Hordes and Burning Boats: The Cult of Marshal Wen in Late Imperial Chekiang*. Albany: State University of New York Press, 1995.

Keesing, Roger M. "Tabou." In *Dictionnaire de l'ethnologie et de l'anthropologie,* edited by Pierre Bonte and Michel Izard, 695–697. Paris: PUF, 1991.

Kieschnick, John. "Buddhist Vegetarianism in China." In *Of Tripod and Palate: Food, Politics and Religion in Traditional China,* edited by Roel Sterckx, 186–212. New York: Palgrave, 2005.

———. *The Eminent Monk*. Honolulu: University of Hawai'i Press, 1997.

Kishigami, Nobuhiro, Hisashi Hamaguchi, and James M. Savelle, eds. *Anthropological Studies of Whaling.* Senri Ethnological Studies, no. 84. Osaka: National Museum of Ethnology, 2013.

Kleeman, Terry F. *A God's Own Tale: The* Book of Transformations *of Wenchang, the Divine Lord of Zitong.* Albany: State University of New York Press, 1994.

———. *Celestial Masters: History and Ritual in Early Daoist Communities.* Cambridge, MA: Harvard University Asia Center, 2016.

———. "Feasting without the Victuals: The Evolution of the Daoist Communal Kitchen." In *Of Tripod and Palate: Food, Politics and Religion in Traditional China,* edited by Roel Sterckx, 140–162. New York: Palgrave, 2005.

———. "Licentious Cults and Bloody Victuals: Sacrifice, Reciprocity, and Violence in Traditional China." *Asia Major,* 3rd ser., 7, no. 1 (1994): 185–211.

Kohn, Livia. "Daoist Monastic Discipline: Hygiene, Meals, and Etiquette." *T'oung Pao* 87, no. 1–3 (2001): 153–193.

———. "The Five Precepts of the Venerable Lord." *Monumenta Serica* 42 (1994): 171–215.

Korom, Frank J. "Holy Cow! The Apotheosis of Zebu, or Why the Cow Is Sacred in Hinduism." *Asian Folklore Studies* 59 (2000): 181–203.

Kowner, Rotem, Guy Bar-Oz, Michal Biran, Meir Shahar, and Gideon Shelach-Lavi, eds. *Animals and Human Society in Asia: Historical, Cultural and Ethical Perspectives.* Cham: Springer, 2020.

Krämer, Hans Martin. "'Not Befitting Our Divine Country': Eating Meat in Japanese Discourses of Self and Other from the Seventeenth Century to the Present." *Food and Foodways* 16, no. 1 (2008): 33–62.

Lagerwey, John. "Introduction: Special Issue on the Emergence of a Temple-centric Society." *Min-su chü-i* 民俗曲藝 205 (2019): 1–27.

———. "Popular Ritual Specialists in West Central Fujian." In *Shehui minzu yu wenhua zhanyan guoji yantao hui lunwen ji* 社會民族與文化展演國際研討會論文集, edited by Wang Qiugui 王秋桂, Zhuang Yingzhang 莊英章, and Chen Zhongmin 陳中民, 435–507. Taipei: Hanxue yanjiu zhongxin, 2001.

Lai Chi-tim 黎志添. "The Opposition of Celestial-Master Taoism to Popular Cults during the Six Dynasties." *Asia Major,* 3rd ser., 11, no. 1 (1998): 1–20.

———. 黎志添, ed. *Daozang jiyao tiyao* 道藏輯要提要. 3 vols. Hong Kong: Chinese University Press, 2021.

Lavoix, Valérie. "La contribution des laïcs au végétarisme: Croisades et polémiques en Chine du sud autour de l'an 500." In *Bouddhisme et lettrés dans la Chine médiévale,* edited by Catherine Despeux, 103–143. Paris-Louvain: Peeters, 2002.

Leach, Edmund R. "Anthropological Aspects of Language: Animal Categories and Verbal Abuse." In *New Directions in the Study of Language,* edited by Eric H. Lenneberg, 23–63. Cambridge, MA: MIT Press, 1964.

Lee, James Z., and Wang Feng. *One Quarter of Humanity: Malthusian Mythology and Chinese Realities, 1700–2000.* Cambridge, MA: Harvard University Press, 1999.

Leung, Angela Ki Che. "To Build or to Transform Vegetarian China: Two Republican Projects." In *Moral Foods: The Construction of Nutrition and Health in Modern Asia,* edited by Angela Ki Che Leung and Melissa L. Caldwell, 221–240. Honolulu: University of Hawai'i Press, 2019.

Lévi, Jean. "L'abstinence des céréales chez les taoïstes." *Études chinoises* 1 (1983): 3–47.

Li Bozhong. *Agricultural Development in Jiangnan, 1620–1850.* Basingstoke, UK: Macmillan, 1998.

Li Fengmao 李豐楙. "Jieqing jidian de gongwu yu Zhongguo yinshi wenhua, yige 'chang yu feichang' guan de jieqing yinshi 節慶祭典的供物與中國飲食文化，一個常與非常觀得節慶飲食." In *Disi jie Zhongguo yinshi wenhua xueshu yantao hui lunwen ji* 第四屆中國飲食文化學術研討會論文集, edited by Lin Qinghu 林慶弧, 331–358. Taipei: Zhongguo yinshi wenhua jijin hui, 1996.

Li Hu 黎虎, ed. *Han-Tang yinshi wenhua shi* 漢唐飲食文化史. Beijing: Beijing shifan daxue chubanshe, 1998.

Li Lulu 李露露. *Chunniu bidi* 春牛辟地. Beijing: Shehui kexue wenxian chubanshe, 1998.

Li Shiyu 李世瑜. "Tianjin Zaili jiao diaocha yanjiu 天津在理教調查研究." *Minjian zongjiao* 民間宗教 2 (1996): 169–210.

Liang Qizi (Angela Leung) 梁其姿. *Shishan yu jiaohua: Ming Qing de cishan zuzhi* 施善與教化. 明清的慈善組織. Zhangjiakou: Hebei jiaoyu chubanshe, 2001.

Liang Yan. "Beef, Fish, and Chestnut Cake: Food for Heroes in the Late Imperial Chinese Novel." *Journal of Chinese Literature and Culture* 5, no. 1 (2018): 119–147.

Lin Boqian 林伯謙. "Sushi yu Fofa xingchi 素食與佛法行持." In *Diwu jie Zhongguo yinshi wenhua xueshu yantao hui lunwen ji* 第五屆中國飲食文化學術研討會論文集, edited by Zhang Yuxin 張玉欣, 331–358. Taipei: Zhongguo yinshi wenhua jijin hui, 1998.

Little, Stephen, with Shawn Eichman. *Taoism and the Arts of China.* Chicago: Art Institute of Chicago, 2000.

Liu E 劉鄂. "Qingdai 'zaisha maniu' lü yanjiu 清代"宰殺馬牛"律研究." *Lishi dang'an* 曆史檔案, no. 3 (2015): 67–75.

Liu Shufen 劉淑芬. "Art, Ritual, and Society: Buddhist Practice in Rural China during the Northern Dynasties." *Asia Major,* 3rd ser., 8, no. 1 (1995): 19–49.

———. "Niansan yueshi. Zhonggu houqi de duantu yu zhaijie 年三月十.中古後期的斷屠與齋戒." *Dalu zazhi* 大陸雜誌 104, no. 1 (2002): 15–33; 104, no. 2 (2002): 64–78.

Liu Xun. "Immortals and Patriarchs: The Daoist World of a Manchu Official and His Family in Nineteenth Century China." *Asia Major,* 3rd ser., 17, no. 2 (2004): 161–218.

Liu Zhaoyuan 劉兆元. *Haizhou minsu zhi* 海州民俗志. Nanjing: Jiangsu wenyi chubanshe, 1991.

Liu Zhiwan 劉枝萬. *Chūgoku dōkyō no matsuri to shinkō* 中國道教の祭祀と信仰. Tokyo: Ōfūsha, 1983.

Lombard-Salmon, Claudine. *Un exemple d'acculturation chinoise: La province du Guizhou au XVIIIe siècle.* Paris: École Française d'Extrême-Orient, 1972.

Lomi, Benedetta. "Ox Bezoars and the Materiality of Heian-Period Therapeutics." *Japanese Journal of Religious Studies* 45, no. 2 (2018): 227–268.

Longworth, John W., Colin G. Brown, and Scott A. Waldron. *Beef in China: Agribusiness Opportunities and Challenges.* St. Lucia, Australia: University of Queensland Press, 2001.

Lu Huitzu. "Women's Ascetic Practices during the Song." *Asia Major* 15, no. 1 (2004): 73–108.

Lu Lianghao. "The Confluence of Karma and Hygiene: Vegetarianism with Renewed Meanings for Modern Chinese Buddhism." *Journal of Chinese Religions* 49, no. 1 (2021): 75–108.

Mair, Victor. "Language and Ideology in the Written Popularizations of the Sacred Edict." In *Popular Culture in Late Imperial China,* edited by David Johnson, Andrew J. Nathan, and Evelyn S. Rawski, 325–359. Berkeley: University of California Press, 1985.

Malamoud, Charles. *Cuire le monde: Rite et pensée dans l'Inde ancienne.* Paris: La Découverte, 1989.

Malek, Roman. "Ieiunium and Zhai: Foundations and Practice of Fasting and Abstinence in 17th–18th Century Chinese Catholicism." Paper presented at the International Conference "Court, Ritual Community, and the City: Chinese and Christian Rituality in Late Imperial Beijing," Leuven, June 17–19, 2004.

Mao Gengru 茆耕茹. *Xuhe liang'an de tiao Wuchang* 胥河兩岸的跳五猖. Taipei: Shi Hezheng jijinhui, 1995.

Martin, François. "Les 'quatre portes de la ville': Pratique bouddhique et jeu poétique sous les Six Dynasties." In *Bouddhisme et lettrés dans la Chine médiévale,* edited by Catherine Despeux, 67–102. Paris-Louvain: Peeters, 2002.

McKnight, Brian, and James T. C. Liu. *The Enlightened Judgments:* Ch'ing-ming Chi: *The Sung Dynasty Collection.* Albany: State University of New York Press, 1999.

Meyer-Fong, Tobie. *What Remains: Coming to Terms with Civil War in 19th Century China.* Stanford: Stanford University Press, 2013.

Minford, John. "Tracks in the Snow: Episodes from an Autobiographical Memoir by the Manchu Bannerman Lin-Ching (1791–1846) with Illustrations by Leading Contemporary Artists." Translated by Yang Tsung-han, edited by John Minford. *East Asian History* 6 (1993): 105–142.

Mollier, Christine. *Buddhism and Taoism Face to Face: Scripture, Ritual, and Iconographic Exchange in Medieval China.* Honolulu: University of Hawai'i Press, 2008.

———. "Les cuisines de Laozi et du Buddha." *Cahiers d'Extrême-Asie* 11 (1999–2000): 45–90.

———. *Une apocalypse taoïste du Ve siècle: Le livre des incantations divines des grottes abyssales.* Paris: Collège de France, Institut des Hautes Études Chinoises, Mémoires de l'Institut des Hautes Études Chinoises, 1990.

Morgan, Carole. *Le tableau du bœuf de printemps: Étude d'une page de l'almanach chinois.* Paris: Collège de France, Institut des Hautes Études Chinoises, Mémoires de l'Institut des Hautes Études Chinoises, 1980.

Morikawa, Jun. *Whaling in Japan: Power, Politics and Diplomacy.* New York: Columbia University Press, 2009.

Mote, Frederick W. "Yüan and Ming." In *Food in Chinese Culture: Anthropological and Historical Perspectives,* edited by K. C. Chang, 193–257. New Haven: Yale University Press, 1977.

Nakamura Jihei 中村治兵衛. "Sōdai Kōtokugun Shizanbyō no gyūsai ni tsuite. Sōdai shakai no ichijirei toshite 宋代廣徳軍祠山廟の牛祭について. 宋代社會の一事例として." *Shien* 史淵 109 (1972): 1–24.

Nakazawa Katsuaki 中澤克昭. *Nikushoku no shakaishi* 肉食の社会史. Tokyo: Yamakawa Shuppansha, 2018.

Needham, Joseph, and Francesca Bray. *Science and Civilisation in China: Vol. 6, Biology and Biological Technology; Pt. 2, Agriculture.* Cambridge: Cambridge University Press, 1984.

Needham, Joseph, and Huang Hsing-Tsung. *Science and Civilisation in China: Vol. 6, Biology and Biological Technology; Pt. 5, Fermentations and Food Sciences.* Cambridge: Cambridge University Press, 2000.

Needham, Joseph, and Robin D. S. Yates, with Krzysztof Gawlikowski, Edward McEwen, and Wang Ling. *Science and Civilisation in China: Vol. 5, Military Technology: Missiles and Sieges; Pt. 6, Chemistry and Chemical Technology.* Cambridge: Cambridge University Press, 1994.

Niida Noboru 仁井田陞. *Chūgoku no shakai to girudo* 中國の社會とギルド. Tokyo: Iwanami shoten, 1951.

———. *Pekin kōshō girudo shiryō shū* 北京工商ギルド資料集. 6 vols. Tokyo: Tōyō Bunka, 1975–1983.

Overmyer, Daniel L. "The White Cloud Sect in Sung and Yüan China." *Harvard Journal of Asiatic Studies* 42, no. 2 (1982): 615–642.

Pelliot, Paul. "Meou-tseu ou les doutes levés." *T'oung Pao* 19 (1920): 255–433.

Peng Nian 彭年. "Beijing Huizu de jingji shenghuo bianqian 北京回族的經濟生活變遷." *Huizu yanjiu* 回族研究, no. 3 (1993): 31–39.

Poon Shuk-wah 潘淑華. "Buddhist Activism and Animal Protection in Republican China." In *Concepts and Methods for the Study of Chinese Religions III,* edited by Paul R. Katz and Stefania Travagnin, 91–111. Berlin: De Gruyter, 2019.

———. "Huniu yu shaniu: Wanqing ji Minguo shiqi Zhongguo niurou jingji yinqi de zhengyi 護牛與殺牛：晚清及民國時期中國牛肉經濟引起的爭議." *Shijie lishi pinglun* 世界歷史評論, no. 3 (2021): 175–200.

———. "'Husheng' yu 'Jintu': 1930 niandai Shanghai de dongwu baohu yu Fojiao yundong「護生」與「禁屠」：1930 年代上海的動物保護與佛教運動." In *Gaibian Zhongguo zongjiao de wushinian, 1898–1948* 改變中國宗教的五十年, 1898–1948, edited by Kang Bao (Paul R. Katz) and Gao Wansang (Vincent Goossaert), 399–426. Nankang: Institute of Modern History, Academia Sinica, 2015.

Poplin, François. "Le cheval, viande honteuse." *Ethnozootechnie* 48 (1992): 23–34.

Qing Xitai 卿希泰, ed. *Zhongguo daojiao shi* 中國道教史. Vol. 4. Chengdu: Sichuan renmin chubanshe, 1995.

Qiu Shusen 邱樹森. *Zhongguo huizu shi* 中國回族史. 2 vols. Yinchuan: Ningxia renmin chubanshe, 1996.

Qu Ming'an 瞿明安. "Zhongguo gudai zongjiao jisi yinshi wenhua lüelun 中國古代宗教祭祀飲食文化略論." *Zhongguo shi yanjiu* 中國史研究, no. 3 (1998): 152–162.

Rawson, Jessica. "Western Zhou Archaeology." In *The Cambridge History of Ancient China,* edited by Michael Loewe and Edward L. Shaughnessy, 352–449. Cambridge: Cambridge University Press, 1999.

Reed, Bradly W. *Talons and Teeth: County Clerks and Runners in the Qing Dynasty.* Stanford: Stanford University Press, 2000.

Reed, Carrie E. *Chinese Chronicles of the Strange: The "Nuogao ji."* New York: Peter Lang, 2001.

Reinders, Eric. *Borrowed Gods and Foreign Bodies: Christian Missionaries Imagine Chinese Religion*. Berkeley: University of California Press, 2005.

Ren Cheng 任騁. *Zhongguo minjian jinji* 中國民間禁忌. Taipei: Hanxin wenhua chubanshe, 1993.

Ren Zhaojie 任兆傑. "Bushi niurou, jia wu yihuan. Zhongguo gudai 'Niujie' gushi yanjiu 不食牛肉，家無疫患. 中國古代牛戒故事研究." *Shilin* 史林, no. 5 (2019): 37–48.

Rols, Johan. "Les interdits de destruction de la faune et de la flore de l'Antiquité tardive au haut Moyen-Âge chinois." PhD diss., EPHE, PSL, 2021.

Rom, Avital Hedva. "Beat the Drums or Break Them: Bells and Drums as Communication Devices in Early Chinese Warfare." *Journal of Chinese Military History* 9 (2020): 125–167.

Rowe, William T. *Saving the World: Chen Hongmou and Elite Consciousness in Eighteenth-Century China*. Stanford: Stanford University Press, 2001.

Sabban, Françoise. "La viande en Chine: Imaginaire et usages culinaires." *Anthropozoologica* 18 (1993): 79–90.

———. "Un savoir-faire oublié: Le travail du lait en Chine ancienne." *Zinbun* 21 (1986): 31–65.

Sakai Tadao 酒井忠夫. *Zōho Chūgoku zensho no kenkyū* 增補中國善書の研究. Tokyo: Kokusho kankōkai, 1999.

Sangji Zhaxi 桑吉扎西. *Xuquan tongling* 戌犬通靈. Beijing: Shehui kexue wenxian chubanshe, 1998.

Sawada Mizuho 澤田瑞穗. "Chikurui shōsai tan 畜類償債譚." In *Bukkyō to Chūgoku bungaku* 佛教と中國文學, 229–258. Tokyo: Kokusho kankōkai, 1975.

Schipper, Kristofer. "Daoist Ecology: The Inner Transformation: A Study of the Precepts of the Early Daoist Ecclesia." In *Daoism and Ecology: Ways within a Cosmic Landscape,* edited by Norman J. Girardot, James Miller, and Liu Xiaogan, 79–93. Cambridge, MA: Center for the Study of World Religions, Harvard Divinity School, 2001.

———. "Le pacte de pureté du taoïsme." *Annuaire de l'École Pratique des Hautes Études, Section des Sciences Religieuses* 109 (2000–2001): 29–53.

———. "Taoist Ordination Ranks in the Tunhuang Manuscripts." In *Religion und Philosophie in Ostasien,* edited by Gert Naundorf, Karl-Heinz Pohl, and Hans-Hermann Schmidt, 127–148. Würzburg: Königshausen und Neumann, 1985.

———. "The True Form: Reflections on the Liturgical Basis of Taoist Art." *Sanjiao wenxian: Matériaux pour l'étude de la religion chinoise* 4 (2005): 91–113.

———. "Vernacular and Classical Ritual in Taoism." *Journal of Asian Studies* 45, no. 1 (1985): 21–51.

Schmithausen, Lambert. *Fleischverzehr und Vegetarismus im indischen Buddhismus: Bis ca. zur Mitte des ersten Jahrtausends n. Chr.* Bochum: Projektverlag, 2020.

Schumann, Matthias. "'For the Sake of Morality and Civilization': The Buddhist Animal Protection Movement in Republican China." *Twentieth-Century China* 46, no. 1 (2021): 22–40.

Serruys, Henry. *Sino-Mongol Relations during the Ming, III. Trade Relations: The Horse Fairs (1400–1600).* Brussels: Institut Belge des Hautes Études Chinoises, 1975.

Shahar, Meir. *Chinese Animal Gods: Draft Animals, Buddhism, and Rural Religion*. Work in progress.

———. "The Donkey in Late-Imperial and Modern North China." *Asia Major* 30, no. 2 (2017): 71–100.

Shiba Yoshinobu 斯波義信. *Sōdai shōgyō shi kenkyū* 宋代商業史研究. Tokyo: Kazama shobō, 1968.

Shio Takugo 塩卓悟. "Sōdai gyūniku shoku kō 宋代牛肉食考." *Chūgoku: Shakai to bunka* 中國. 社會と文化 16 (2001): 86–104.

Shryock, John. *The Temples of Anking and Their Cults: A Study of Modern Chinese Religion*. Paris: Paul Geuthner, 1931.

Simoons, Frederick J. *Eat Not This Flesh: Food Avoidances from Prehistory to the Present*. 2nd ed. Madison: University of Wisconsin Press, 1994.

Smith, Joanna Handlin. "Liberating Animals in Ming-Qing China: Buddhist Inspiration and Elite Imagination." *Journal of Asian Studies* 58, no. 1 (1999): 51–84.

———. *The Art of Doing Good: Charity in Late Ming China*. Berkeley: University of California Press, 2009.

Smith, Paul J. *Taxing Heaven's Storehouse: Horses, Bureaucrats, and the Destruction of the Sichuan Tea Industry, 1074–1224*. Cambridge, MA: Council on East Asian Studies, Harvard University, 1991.

Sogabe Shizuo 曾我部靜雄. "Godai Sō no gyūhizei 五代宋の牛皮税." In *Chūgoku shakai keizaishi no kenkyū* 中國社會經濟史の研究, 458–482. Tokyo: Yoshikawa kōbunkan, 1976.

Sommer, Matthew H. *Sex, Law, and Society in Late Imperial China*. Stanford: Stanford University Press, 2000.

Song Changhong 宋長宏. *Zhongguo niu wenhua* 中國牛文化. Beijing: Minzu chubanshe, 1997.

Soymié, Michel. "Les dix jours de jeûne du taoïsme." In *Yoshioka Yoshitoyo hakase kanri kinen dōkyō kenkyū ronshū* 吉岡義豐博士還暦紀念道教研究論集, 1–21. Tokyo: Kokusho kankōkai, 1977.

Spence, Jonathan. "Ch'ing." In *Food in Chinese Culture: Anthropological and Historical Perspectives,* edited by K. C. Chang, 259–294. New Haven: Yale University Press, 1977.

Spring, Madeline K. *Animal Allegories in T'ang China*. New Haven: American Oriental Society, 1993.

Stein, Rolf. "Conceptions relatives à la nourriture (Chine)." *Annuaire du Collège de France* (1973): 457–463.

———. "Les fêtes de cuisine du taoïsme religieux." *Annuaire du Collège de France* (1971): 431–440.

———. "Religious Taoism and Popular Religion from the Second to Seventh Centuries." In *Facets of Taoism,* edited by Anna Seidel and Holmes Welch, 53–81. New Haven: Yale University Press, 1979.

———. "Spéculations mystiques et thèmes relatifs aux 'cuisines' du taoïsme." *Annuaire du Collège de France* (1972): 489–499.

Sterckx, Roel. *The Animal and the Daemon in Early China*. Albany: State University of New York Press, 2002.

———, ed. *Of Tripod and Palate: Food, Politics and Religion in Traditional China*. New York: Palgrave, 2005.

Sterckx, Roel, Martina Siebert, and Dagmar Schäfer, eds. *Animals through Chinese History: Earliest Times to 1911*. Cambridge: Cambridge University Press, 2019.

Stevenson, Daniel B. "Protocols of Power: Tz'u-yün Tsun-shih (964–1032) and T'ien-t'ai Lay-Buddhist Ritual in the Sung." In *Buddhism in the Sung,* edited by Peter N. Gregory and Daniel A. Getz Jr., 340–408. Honolulu: University of Hawai'i Press, 1999.

Stewart, James. "Cow Protection in Sinhala Buddhist Sri Lanka." *Journal of the Oriental Society of Australia* 45 (2013): 19–48.

Strickmann, Michel. *Chinese Magical Medicine*. Edited by Bernard Faure. Stanford: Stanford University Press, 2002.

———. "Saintly Fools and Chinese Masters (Holy Fools)." *Asia Major,* 3rd ser., 7, no. 1 (1994): 35–57.

Suga Yutaka 菅豐. "Tojikomerareta hitsujitachi. Chūgoku Kōnan nōgyō shakai no hitsuji shiiku kara mita shōhin keizai no hatten 閉じこめられた羊たち.中國江南農業社會の羊飼育から見た商品經濟の發展." *Tōyō bunka kenkyūjo kiyō* 東洋文化研究所紀要 135 (1997): 95–139.

Sun Yinrui 孫寅瑞. "Niurou chengwei Taiwan hanren fushipin de lishi guancha 牛肉成為台灣漢人副食品的歷史觀察." MA thesis, Guoli zhongyang daxue, 2001.

Sutton, Donald S. "Consuming Counterrevolution: The Ritual and Culture of Cannibalism in Wuxuan, Guangxi (May–July, 1968)." *Comparative Studies in Society and History* 7, no. 1 (1995): 136–172.

Swislocki, Mark. "Imagining Irreconcilability: Cultural Differentiation through Human-Animal Relations in Late Qing Shanghai." *Positions: East Asia Cultures Critique* 20, no. 4 (2012): 1159–1189.

Taira Masayuki. "Tabous et alimentation carnée dans l'histoire du Japon." Translated by Pierre F. Souyri. In *Identités, marges, mediations: Regards croisés sur la société japonaise,* edited by Jean-Pierre Berthon, Anne Bouchy, and Pierre F. Souyri, 165–182. Paris: École Française d'Extrême-Orient, 2001.

Takeuchi Fusaji 武内房司. "Qingmo Sichuan de zongjiao yundong. Fuluan, xuanjiang xing zongjiao jieshe de dansheng 清末四川的宗教運動. 扶鸞宣講型宗教結社的誕生." In *Ming Qing yilai minjian zongjiao de tansuo. Jinian Dai Xuanzhi jiaoshou lunwen ji* 明清以來民間宗教的探索–紀念戴玄之教授論文集, edited by Wang Chien-ch'uan 王見川 and Jiang Zhushan 蔣竹山, 240–265. Taipei: Shangding wenhua chubanshe, 1996.

Tambiah, Stanley. "Animals Are Good to Think and Good to Prohibit." *Ethnology* 8, no. 4 (1969): 423–459.

Tanaka Kenji 田中謙二. *Gafu sankyoku* 樂府散曲. Tokyo: Chikuma shobō, 1983.

Tao Jin 陶金. "Chengqi yinggan: Qin'andian daochang 誠祈應感：欽安殿道場." *Zijincheng* 紫禁城 144 (2015): 102–183.

Teiser, Stephen F. *The Scripture on the Ten Kings and the Making of Purgatory in Medieval Chinese Buddhism*. Honolulu: University of Hawai'i Press, 1994.

Thirsk, Joan. *Food in Early Modern England: Phases, Fads, Fashions, 1500–1760*. New York: Continuum, 2007.

Thompson, Stuart E. "Death, Food, and Fertility." In *Death Ritual in Late Imperial and Modern China,* edited by James L. Watson and Evelyn S. Rawski, 71–108. Berkeley: University of California Press, 1988.

Tian Zhaoyuan 田兆元. *Mengshi shi* 盟誓史. Nanning: Guangxi minzu chubanshe, 2000.

Van der Toorn, Karel. "La pureté rituelle au Proche-Orient ancien." *Revue de l'histoire des religions* 206, no. 4 (1989): 339–356.

Vermeer, Eduard B. "Population and Ecology along the Frontier in Qing China." In *Sediments of Time: Environment and Society in Chinese History,* edited by Mark Elvin and Liu Ts'ui-jung, 235–279. Cambridge: Cambridge University Press, 1998.

Von Glahn, Richard. *The Sinister Way: The Divine and the Demonic in Chinese Religious Culture.* Berkeley: University of California Press, 2004.

Wang, David Der-wei. *Fin-de-Siècle Splendor: Repressed Modernities of Late Qing Fiction, 1849–1911.* Stanford: Stanford University Press, 1997.

Wang Di. "The Rhythm of the City: Everyday Chengdu in Nineteenth-Century Bamboo-Branch Poetry." *Late Imperial China* 24, no. 1 (2003): 33–78.

Wang Guangde 王光德 and Yang Lizhi 楊立志. *Wudang daojiao shilüe* 武當道教史略. Beijing: Huawen chubanshe, 1993.

Wang Jiange 王建革. "Jindai Huabei de nongye shengtai yu shehui bianqian 近代華北的農業生態與社會變遷." *Zhongguo nongshi* 中國農史, no. 1 (1999): 46–58.

Wang Lihua 王利華. *Zhonggu Huabei yinshi wenhua de bianqian* 中古華北飲食文化的變遷. Beijing: Zhongguo shehui kexue chubanshe, 2000.

Wang Yifu 汪毅夫. "Shilun Ming Qing shiqi de Min-Tai xiangyue 試論明清時期的閩台鄉約." *Zhongguo shi yanjiu* 中國史研究, no. 1 (2002): 131–144.

Wang-Toutain, Françoise. "Pas de boissons alcoolisées, pas de viande: Une particularité du bouddhisme chinois vue à travers les manuscrits de Dunhuang." *Cahiers d'Extrême-Asie* 11 (1999–2000): 91–128.

Welch, Holmes. *The Buddhist Revival in China.* Cambridge, MA: Harvard University Press, 1968.

———. *The Practice of Chinese Buddhism.* Cambridge, MA: Harvard University Press, 1967.

White, David Gordon. *Myths of the Dog-Man.* Chicago: University of Chicago Press, 1991.

Whitehead, Harriet. *Food Rules: Hunting, Sharing, and Tabooing Game in Papua New Guinea.* Ann Arbor: University of Michigan Press, 2000.

Will, Pierre-Étienne. *Bureaucracy and Famine in Eighteenth-Century China.* Translated by Elborg Forster. Stanford: Stanford University Press, 1990.

———. *Handbooks and Anthologies for Officials in Imperial China: A Descriptive and Critical Bibliography.* 2 vols. Leiden: Brill, 2020.

———. "La vertu administrative au théâtre: Huang Xieqing (1805–1864) et le miroir du fonctionnaire." *Études chinoises* 18, no. 1–2 (1999): 289–366.

Wilson, Thomas A. "Ritualizing Confucius/Kongzi: The Family and State Cults of the Sage of Culture in Imperial China." In *On Sacred Grounds: Culture, Society, Politics, and the Formation of the Cult of Confucius,* edited by Thomas A. Wilson, 43–94. Cambridge, MA: Harvard University Asia Center, 2002.

———. "Sacrifice and the Imperial Cult of Confucius." *History of Religions* 41 (2002): 251–287.

Wolf, Arthur P. "Gods, Ghosts, and Ancestors." In *Religion and Ritual in Chinese Society,* edited by Arthur P. Wolf, 131–182. Stanford: Stanford University Press, 1974.

Wu Shichi 吳詩池 and Huang Guirong 黃桂蓉. "Niunian manhua niu 牛年漫話牛." *Nongye kaogu* 農業考古, no. 1 (1997): 286–296.

Xie Chengxia 謝成俠. *Zhongguo yang niu yang shi (fu yang lu jianshi)* 中國養牛羊史 (附養鹿簡史). Beijing: Nongye chubanshe, 1985.

———. *Zhongguo yangma shi* 中國養馬史. Beijing: Kexue chubanshe, 1989.

Xing Tie 邢鐵. "Songdai de gengniu chuzu yu kehu diwei 宋代的耕牛出租與客戶地位." *Zhongguo shi yanjiu* 中國史研究, no. 3 (1985): 81–91.

Xu Dishan 許地山. *Fuji mixin de yanjiu* 扶乩迷信的研究. Changsha: Shangwu yinshuguan, 1941.

Xu Hualong 徐華龍. "Baishe zhuan yu yinshi wenhua 白蛇傳與飲食文化." In *Baishe zhuan lunwen ji* 白蛇傳論文集, compiled by Zhongguo minjian wenyi yanjiu hui Zhejiang fenhui 中國民間文藝研究會浙江分會, 267–281. Hangzhou: Zhejiang guji chubanshe, 1986.

Yang, Martin C. *A Chinese Village: Taitou, Shantung Province*. London: Kegan Paul, Trench, 1945.

Yau Chi-on (You Zi'an) 游子安. *Quanhua jinzhen. Qingdai shanshu yanjiu* 勸化金箴. 清代善書研究. Tianjin: Tianjin renmin chubanshe, 1999.

———. *Shan yu ren tong: Ming Qing yilai de cishan yu jiaohua* 善與人同: 明清以來的慈善與教化. Beijing: Zhonghua shuju, 2005.

Ye Xiaoqing. *The Dianshizhai Pictorial: Shanghai Urban Life, 1884–1898*. Ann Arbor: Center for Chinese Studies, University of Michigan, 2003.

Yoshida Tadashi 吉田忠. *Gyūniku to Nihonjin: Wagyū reisan* 牛肉と日本人:和牛禮讚. Tokyo: Nō-san-gyoson Bunka Kyōkai, 1992.

Yü Chün-fang. *The Renewal of Buddhism in China: Chu-Hung and the Late Ming Synthesis*. New York: Columbia University Press, 1981.

Yuan Jing 袁靖. "Zhongguo xinshiqi shidai jiachu qiyuan de wenti 中國新石期時代家畜起源的問題." *Wenwu* 文物, no. 5 (2001): 51–58.

Yue, Isaac. "Beefy Outlaws: Beef Consumption in Water Margin and Its Song-Yuan Antecedents." *Journal of Chinese Humanities* 7, no. 3 (2022): 342–365.

Zeng Xiongsheng 曾雄生. "Pozu nongye de xingcheng. Cong niu de fangmu fangshi kan Zhongguo nongqu xumuye de weisuo 破足農業的形成. 從牛的放牧方式看中國農區畜牧業的萎縮." *Zhongguo nongshi* 中國農史, no. 4 (1999): 35–44.

Zhang Shaodan. "Cattle Slaughter Industry in Qing China: State Ban, Muslim Dominance, and the Western Diet." *Frontiers of History in China* 16, no. 1 (2021): 4–38.

Zhang Yafeng 張雅岚. "Nanbu dang'an suojian Qingdai difang shehui dui zaisha gengniu de jinzhi 南部檔案所見清代地方社會對宰殺耕牛的禁止." *Sichuan dang'an* 四川檔案, no. 2 (2014): 44–45.

Zhang Zhongge 張仲葛. "Zhongguo gudai de niuzhong 中國古代的牛種." *Nongye kaogu* 農業考古, no. 1 (1997): 277–284.

Zhang Zuji 張祖基 et al. *Kejia jiu lisu* 客家舊禮俗. Taipei: Zhongwen tushu gongsi, 1986.

Zhao Kesheng 趙克生. "Tudiao zhi jin xingcheng de yuanyin ji yingxiang 屠釣之禁形成的原因及影響." *Zhongguo nongshi* 中國農史 20, no. 3 (2001): 3–7.

Zheng Tuyou 鄭土有. *Niu wenhua yu rensheng* 牛文化與人生. Shenyang: Liaoning guji chubanshe, 1996.

Zheng Yi. *Scarlet Memorial: Tales of Cannibalism in Modern China*. Edited and translated by T. P. Sym. London: Routledge, 1998.

*Zhongguo nongye nianjian 1991* 中國農業年鑒. Beijing: Nongye chubanshe, 1991.

Zhou Shaoliang 周紹良. "Xinkan Wudang zuben leibian quanxiang *Qisheng shilu* shuji 新刊武當足本類編全相啟聖實錄書記." *Wenxian* 文獻, no. 2 (1985): 161–174.

Zhu Yueli 朱越利, ed. *Dangdai Zhongguo zongjiao jinji* 當代中國宗教禁忌. Beijing: Minzu chubanshe, 2001.

# Index

## About the Author

Vincent Goossaert is professor of Daoism and Chinese religions at EPHE, PSL. His research deals with the social history of Chinese religion in late-imperial and modern times. He is coeditor of *T'oung Pao,* a leading journal in sinology, established in 1890. Recent publications include *Making the Gods Speak: The Ritual Production of Revelation in Chinese History, Heavenly Masters: Two Thousand Years of the Daoist State,* and *Vies des saints exorcistes: Hagiographies taoïstes, 11e–16e siècles.*

## About the Translator

Barbara R. Ambros is professor of East Asian religions in the Department of Religious Studies at the University of North Carolina at Chapel Hill. Her research on Japanese religions has focused on human-animal relationships, gender studies, and place and space. She is the former cochair of the Animals and Religion Unit of the American Academy of Religion. Her publications include *Le donne nell'ordine monastico buddhista: La cerimonia dedicata ad Ānanda come rito di affermazione, Women in Japanese Religions, Bones of Contention: Animals and Religion in Contemporary Japan,* and *Emplacing a Pilgrimage: The Early Modern Ōyama Cult and Regional Religion.*